THE GARLAND LIBRARY OF LATIN POETRY

selected by

Steele Commager
Columbia University

T. Lucreti Cari
DE RERUM NATURA
LIBRI SEX

Edited with notes
and a translation by
H.A.J. MUNRO

In three volumes
VOLUME I

GARLAND PUBLISHING, INC.

NEW YORK & LONDON
1978

The volumes in this series have been printed on acid-free, 250-year-life paper.

Library of Congress Cataloging in Publication Data

Lucretius Carus, Titus.
T. Lucreti Cari : de rerum natura libri sex.

(The Garland library of Latin poetry)
Reprint of the 1908 ed. which was reprinted from the 4th rev. ed. published in 1886 by G. Bell, London.
I. Munro, Hugh Andrew Johnstone, 1819-1885. II. Series.
PA6483.E5M8 1978 871'.01 77-70833
ISBN 0-8240-2957-7

Printed in the United States of America

T. LUCRETI CARI

DE RERUM NATURA

LIBRI SEX

VOLUME I

T. LUCRETI CARI
DE RERUM NATURA
LIBRI SEX

WITH NOTES AND A TRANSLATION

BY

H. A. J. MUNRO

FORMERLY FELLOW OF TRINITY COLLEGE CAMBRIDGE

FOURTH EDITION FINALLY REVISED

VOLUME I: TEXT

LONDON
GEORGE BELL AND SONS
CAMBRIDGE: DEIGHTON BELL AND CO.
1908

T. LUCRETI CARI
DE RERUM NATURA
LIBRI SEX

EDITED BY

H. A. J. MUNRO

FORMERLY FELLOW OF TRINITY COLLEGE CAMBRIDGE

FOURTH EDITION

LONDON
GEORGE BELL AND SONS
CAMBRIDGE: DEIGHTON BELL AND CO.
1908

First Edition, 1864. *Second Edition*, 1866. *Third Edition*, 1873.
Fourth Revised Edition, 1886. *Reprinted*, 1893.
1900, 1905, 1908

TO BENJAMIN HALL KENNEDY D.D.

REGIUS PROFESSOR OF GREEK IN CAMBRIDGE

AND LATE HEADMASTER OF SHREWSBURY SCHOOL

THESE VOLUMES ARE DEDICATED

BY HIS FORMER PUPIL THE EDITOR

My dear Dr Kennedy,

On the completion of a work which has cost both thought and labour I gladly dedicate it to you, to whom indirectly it owes so much. Many years have passed since the days when I was among your earliest pupils at Shrewsbury; but the memory of the benefits then received from your instructions is as fresh as ever. A succession of scholars year after year from that time to this will bear testimony to the advantages which they have derived from your zeal skill and varied knowledge; and over and above all from that something higher which gave to what was taught life and meaning and interest: denn es musz von Herzen gehen, was auf Herzen wirken will.

The present edition claims as you will see to do something both for the criticism and for the explanation of the poem. After the masterly work of Lachmann you will think perhaps that too much space has been allotted to the former; but that portion of the book is intended partly to give the reader in a condensed shape the results of his labours, partly to add to and correct them where circumstances or design rendered them incomplete. The scandalous negligence with which Havercamp and Wakefield executed what they professed to undertake has made their editions worse than useless, as the reader who trusts to them is only betrayed and led into error. What Lachmann performed is known to all who take an interest in such studies: from my first introduction readers will learn what opinion I entertain of his merits; they will also find that all which I have added to what he has done is with one insignificant exception derived from the original sources to which they refer. The manuscripts which I have cited were examined by myself; the editions and manuscript notes were open before me all the time I was at work. The large amount of critical material thus amassed I have endeavoured to put into as concise and compressed a form as possible; though much of this material needs perhaps to be recorded only once and might be greatly abridged if it has ever to appear again in a new shape.

The length of the explanatory notes calls I fancy for less excuse. This very year three centuries have elapsed since Lambinus published the first edition of his Lucretius; and from that day to this nothing new and systematical, nothing that displays pains and research has been done for the elucidation of our author. Transcendant as are the merits of that illustrious scholar, what was suited to 1564 can hardly satisfy the wants of 1864. No defence then is needed for the extent of this division of my commentary: if it were done over again, more would probably have to be added than taken away. It will not be so easy perhaps to excuse the translation. This however is really a part of the explanatory notes; and if it had been left undone, they must have been enlarged in many directions. Our author too unless I am mistaken will admit of being thus treated better than most; and the fashion of literal translations seems to be gaining ground in this country as well as in Germany and France.

To the advice and friendly assistance of my brother fellow Mr King, our highest authority in that branch of art, is due the likeness of the poet which appears on the titlepage. With K. O. Mueller, Emil Braun and other judges he is convinced that the original on a black agate represents our Lucretius. The style of art and the finely formed letters of the name point to the late republic. Almost unknown then in other respects, in this he has been more fortunate even than Virgil, whose so-called portraits are all I am told late conventional and unreal.

Sincerely yours

THE EDITOR.

TRINITY COLLEGE, OCTOBER 1864.

PREFACE TO THE THIRD EDITION

Although in outward shape this third edition exactly resembles the second, it will prove I trust in essential points to be more in advance of the second, than the second was of the first edition. Partly for other obvious reasons, and partly because the second impression was larger than the first and has now been exhausted for nearly a year, the interval given me for reflexion has been much longer; and as the author is now so familiar to me, I have been able to bring all my reading to bear upon the improvement of the text and the commentary. The critical notes are I believe improved in many important points, though their bulk of course has not been increased: compression was needed here rather than expansion. The explanatory notes however have been enlarged by the substance of at least fifty pages, chiefly through a somewhat closer printing. Nor does this at all represent the real amount of change, as many of the longer notes have been entirely rewritten and much that was superfluous or erroneous has been cut out. Many thousand fresh illustrations have been added.

For more precise conceptions on some points of the poet's philosophy, especially the motion of his atoms, I have been greatly indebted to the works of Professor Clerk Maxwell and Professor Tyndall, and to a thorough and excellent article in the 48th volume of the North British Review on 'the atomic theory of Lucretius': of Martha's brilliant work I have spoken elsewhere. For the general criticism of my author I owe much to the well-pondered remarks of Mr N. P. Howard, whose letter to me I have printed in the first number of the new Journal of Philology; and, especially in the third and fourth books, to the communications of my friend Professor J. E. B. Mayor, to whose notes I have appended his initials.

In the 25th and 26th volumes of the Philologus there is a long 'Jahresbericht' by Mr Fried. Polle on the Lucretius literature after Lachmann and Bernays; and some remarks of his occur in Jahn's Jahrbuecher. He hardly touches on the interpretation or philosophy of the poet nor have I been able to adopt any of his own conjectures which are not very numerous. The most valuable hint I have got from him is on v 312, though my own correction is very different from his. In several volumes of the same Philologus appear very prolix notes on the earlier books by Mr Susemihl and Mr Brieger. The former confines himself chiefly to rearranging paragraphs and to proposing numerous transpositions of verses, in neither I think with much success. Many of his new arrangements of paragraphs are I assert demonstrably wrong; and his violent transpositions would lead to the wildest confusion. Once however I have obeyed him in not making a new paragraph of IV 168—175: it was an accident that this was not done before, as my attention was absorbed in refuting Lachmann's errors there. Mr Brieger, who is the more combative of the two, indulges mainly in conjectural alterations of the text. Once or twice I have referred to Mr Holtze's 'Syntaxis Lucretianae lineamenta.'

On the whole my criticism is now I believe more conservative than it was. Again and again I have found that, seduced by the learning of Lachmann, I have followed him in changes which really corrupt the author. This must hold then in many other cases as well. If the text of Virgil rested, like that of Lucretius, on a single manuscript, how much there is in him we should refuse to accept as Latin! This 'must give us pause.' Yet I have not sinned I think in defending the indefensible. It is probable however that, if I should ever issue another edition, I should leave as manifestly corrupt some passages which defy anything like certain or even very specious correction.

My lamented friend Professor Conington published a lecture on the style of Lucretius and Catullus which has been reprinted among his Miscellaneous works. This lecture, written in a tone of the kindest courtesy, is for the most part a criticism of a single paragraph in the introduction to my explanatory notes; and, so far as Catullus is concerned, almost of a single sentence. This paragraph I have now omitted: justice could be done neither to him nor to myself within the limits that could be permitted here. If I should ever venture on any reply, some other place and opportunity must be found for it.

TRINITY COLLEGE, APRIL 1873.

PREFACE TO THE FOURTH EDITION.

THE present edition is divided into three volumes, the first containing the text and critical notes, the second the commentary and general index, the third the translation.

The text is practically the same as in the last edition: in one place only (I 442) a new reading is printed, and that was only omitted before through accident as was explained at the end of the index. There are a few additions, not more than half-a-dozen, to the critical notes; these have been inserted in square brackets. The translation too has undergone no change.

In the commentary there are few alterations but considerable additions amounting in all to more than twenty pages. These supplementary notes and illustrations have been taken from an interleaved copy of the last edition which was found among Mr Munro's books after his death in the spring of last year. Also on p. 333 of the commentary will be found some extracts from letters addressed by him to Professor Palmer of Trinity College, Dublin, discussing the reading of V 1010; Professor Palmer was kind enough to send me these letters. As the extracts deal with the criticism rather than the explanation of the passage, they should have been inserted in the first volume; but by an accident they were delayed until after that volume was printed. Nothing has been inserted from any other source whatever. Here too all that is new has been inclosed in square brackets. In the new examples the references have been verified. To the index large additions have been made by myself.

It remains to express my thanks to Dr Forbes, the relative and executor of Mr Munro, for the kindly feeling which led him to entrust me with the preparation of this edition, and also for the generous consideration he has shown throughout.

J. D. DUFF.

TRINITY COLLEGE, CAMBRIDGE,
FEB. 18, 1886.

LUCRETIUS.

NOTES I

ON THE FORMATION OF THE TEXT

If Lucretius had come down to us with a text as uninjured as that of Virgil and a few other ancient writers, he could scarcely have been reckoned among the most difficult Latin poets. Certainly he would have been more easy to explain than Virgil for instance or Horace; for he tells what he has to tell simply and directly, and among his poetical merits is not included that of leaving his reader to guess which of many possible meanings was the one he intended to convey. Fortune however has not dealt so kindly with him. Not that the great mass of his poem is not in a sound and satisfactory state: in this respect he is better off than many others; but owing to the way in which it has been handed down, his text has suffered in some portions irreparable loss. It is now universally admitted that every existing copy of the poem has come from one original, which has itself long disappeared.

Of existing manuscripts a fuller account will presently be given: let it suffice for the moment to say that the two which Lachmann has mainly followed and which every future editor must follow, are now in the library of Leyden. One is a folio written in the ninth century, the other a quarto certainly not later than the tenth. Large fragments of one, if not of two others, of the same age as the quarto and very closely resembling it are also still preserved, partly in Copenhagen, partly in Vienna. These manuscripts and at least one more must have lain for centuries in the monasteries of France or Germany, where they found at different periods several correctors, more or less competent. It is to be presumed then that they had some readers, though few if any traces of them are to be met with in the voluminous literature of the middle ages. In my previous editions I said that my friend Professor Mayor had given me a reference to Honorius of Autun in the bibliotheca maxima patrum XX p. 1001, who is there made to quote II 888 in this way, *Ex insensilibus me credas sensile gigni*, the context proving that he meant to say *ne*, not *me*; and asked whether this writer who flourished in the first half of the twelfth century had taken the line from the poem itself; or had borrowed it from Priscian inst. IV 27 who cites it with *nasci* instead of *gigni*, the editor of the bibliotheca having thought fit tacitly to substitute *gigni* from Lucretius. The latter is proved to be the fact by Mr Julius Jessen in the philologus, vol. 30 pp. 236—238: he quotes what follows from Barthius' very learned note on Stat. silv. II 7 76: 'nec vero cadentibus aut collapsis iam rebus Romanis auctoritatem suam amisit Lucretius noster, ut videre potes apud Magnentium Rhabanum praefatione Laudum Daedalarum Crucis, Gulielmum Hirsaugiensem in Institutionibus Philosophicis et Astrologicis, Honorium Augustodunensem in Historia Mundi, Ven. Bedam Libro de Metris'. Referring to the only printed edition of this work of William of Hirschau, who lived from 1026 to 1091, he shews that Honorius copied from him the passage in question, and that William cites it thus: 'Ex insensili credas sensile nasci', getting it clearly then from Priscian. Hrabanus Maurus and Beda seem just as little to have known Lucretius at first hand. [Hermes vol. 8 p. 332, it is said that in Brit. Mus. ms. 377 (13th century) of Daniel de Merlai's Philosophia, in p. 90 a, Lucretius is quoted.]

In Italy he was even more completely unknown. A catalogue which Muratori antiq. III p. 820 assigns to the tenth century, proves that the famous library of Bobbio contained at that time *librum Lucretii* I; but before the fifteenth no Italian poet or writer shews any knowledge of him whatever. In the year 1414 the celebrated Poggio Bracciolini went as apostolic secretary to the council of Constance and remained on this side the Alps in different countries, Switzerland Germany France and England, until 1420, with one short interval passed in Milan and Mantua. During these years he procured from various monasteries many most important Latin works hitherto totally unknown in Italy: see Mehus' preface to his life of Ambrosius Traversarius p. xxxiii foll. Among these was a manuscript of Lucretius, obtained apparently from some German monastery either by him or his companion Bartholomew of Montepulciano, about 1417 as his letters seem to indicate, and transmitted the same year to his intimate friend the Florentine Nicolò Niccoli, a most zealous scholar and patron of the revived classical studies. This manuscript, which Poggio wrongly supposed to be only a part of the poem, has itself disappeared, but was the parent of every copy written during the 15th century, that is to say of every one now extant with the exception of those specified above: it must have very closely resembled the Leyden folio. 'Et te, Lucreti, longo post tempore tandem Civibus et patriae reddit habere suae' says Landinus in his poem in praise of Poggio. Niccoli having such a treasure in his hands was in no hurry to part with it. We find Poggio writing to him in December 1429 to remind him that he had kept his Lucretius twelve years. A few days later it is 'you have had Lucretius now for fourteen years; I want to read him, but cannot get him; do you wish to keep him another ten years?' He had already tried in vain what coaxing could do: he promises him at one time to send the book back in fifteen days, at another time in one month, if he will only let him have it for so long; but feels sure his book will come to him at the Greek calends. Much as Niccoli loved Poggio, he loved still more to have the sole possession of a newly discovered Latin poet, and I doubt whether Poggio saw his Lucretius at all events before his return from Rome to Florence in 1434. Niccoli died in 1437 and left behind him a manuscript written by his own hand and now in the Laurentian library, the truest representative of Poggio's lost original, as is abundantly proved by the critical notes of the present edition. Between this date and that of the earliest printed editions a knowledge of the poem was diffused through Italy by many incorrect copies. Eight of these, including Niccoli's, are preserved in the Laurentian library, all of which I have examined, two with care, as being of no small importance for the text; six are in the Vatican, all seen by me as long ago as the autumn of 1849. Of the copies in England I have had in my hands at least seven; one of these belonging to our Cambridge library has been open before me the whole time I was writing my critical notes. Those manuscripts which have been of any importance in forming the text will be more fully spoken of, after the printed editions have been discussed.

The editio princeps, of which only three copies are known, was printed about 1473 by Ferandus of Brescia. It is the only one of the early editions which I do not possess; I have had to trust therefore to the very unskilful collation of Gerard at the end of the Glasgow edition of Wakefield. As it was printed from a manuscript a good deal corrected, but yet inferior to such amended copies as the Cambridge ms. for instance or that which I call Flor. 31, it is of little importance in the history of the text: of far less than the two next editions, since they by accident came to be the foundation of the vulgate. The former of these was published by Paulus Fridenperger at Verona in 1486 'die vigesimo octavo septembris calen. octobris'. It was printed from a ms. closely resembling the one written by Niccoli, as may be seen by the most cursory inspection of my critical notes. It is therefore very rude and inaccurate, but being less interpolated than the editio princeps or the majority of existing mss. it represents the archetype more faithfully than these do, though there is hardly a line without some monstrous blunder. The next edition was published in Venice 'per theodorum de ragazonibus de asula dictum bresanum' 4 september 1495. From some elegiac verses at the end one C. Lycinius would appear to be its editor, if editor he can be called; for it exactly reproduces for the most part the Verona edition even in the minutest points of its perverse punctuation. There are however throughout the poem not a few differences in the two editions, some of little, others of greater importance; for example IV 125—190 are wanting in the Verona, but not in the Venice. The reason why I dwell on this fact will appear presently.

In December 1500 Aldus published his first edition of our poem, the first systematic endeavour to make it intelligible throughout. The editor was Hieronymus Avancius of Verona, who dates his dedication 'Kalendis Martii. M.ID', old style I presume, and really therefore 1500: an interval of twenty-two months between the two dates would not be easy to understand. Avancius is known by other works also, especially the Aldine edition of Catullus. A slight inspection will shew that he took either the Verona or the Venice edition, upon which to form his text; a more careful examination will prove that it must have been the latter. My critical notes will furnish many other instances; let me here only mention that in III 994 he and Ven. have *torpedine* for *cuppedine*, while Ver. reads *turpidine*; 1011 he takes from Ven. its remarkable reading *egenus*, which Lachmann adopts and wrongly assigns to Marullus: Ver. follows the Leyden and all other known mss. in reading *egestas*; 1015 he and Ven. have the absurd reading *numela* for *luella*, where Ver. has the equally unmeaning *biela*. Ven. therefore is the 'ante impressus' spoken of by Aldus. Avancius' preface shews that for his day he was a good and well-read Latin scholar, and had studied Priscian Nonius and Macrobius for the illustration of his author. Aldus in his prefatory letter to Albertus Pius confirms this, and says that he knew Lucretius by heart, 'ut digitos unguesque suos'. Avancius in his preface asserts much the same; and the few critical remarks he there inserts shew that this was true at least to a certain extent. At the same time he admits with a seeming candour that owing to the immense difficulty of the work he has left much for others to do. Much indeed he has left undone; and it would have been a herculean task for one man fully to correct the desperately corrupt Venice edition, especially in those days when there were but few extraneous aids and the art of systematic criticism was still in its infancy, two generations having yet to elapse, before it reached its full growth in the hands of the illustrious school of French critics. What he has done however is very great and entitles him to high praise, if it is indeed his own. But this shall be considered presently. The next edition is that of the well-known scholar Ioannes Baptista Pius, published 1511 'kal. Maii' in his native Bologna. Lucretius' text is embedded in an enormous commentary which displays amid much cumbrous learning no slight acquaintance with the Latin poets, several of which he edited before and after his Lucretius. He thus describes what he has done: 'contulimus non sine aerumnis vigiliisque diutinis codicem veneti Hermolai: et Pomponi romani: codicemque non omnino malum: qui servatur Mantuae in bibliotheca quadam suburbana: qui fuit viri non indocti gentis clarissimae Strotiorum. non defuit Philippi

Beroaldi praeceptoris quondam mei: nunc collegae: impressus quidem: sed tamen perpense examinatus. Codri quoque grammatici Bononiensis: cuius copia mihi per Bartholomeum Blanchinum virum eloquii excultissimi facta est: Marullique poetae industria mira castigatum non defuit exemplar Severo Monaco Placentino graece latineque perdocto musarum athleta non gravatim offerente'. He makes no mention at all of the man to whom he was most indebted, Avancius: for his text is a reprint of the first Aldine, with however not a few changes of words or phrases, often for the better, often for the worse, either inserted in the text or proposed in the notes, and derived it may be presumed in many cases from one or other of the sources just mentioned. But strange to say when he makes a change in the text, the lemma of his note nearly always contains not this reading, but that of Avancius as if he had meant it to stand: thus I 9 he rightly reads *diffuso lumine*; but his lemma has *diffuso numine* with Avancius, which the latter however corrects at the end of his Catullus: and he adds 'sunt qui legunt *lumine*'. 15 for *capta* he wrongly inserts in the text *quodque*; but his lemma has *capta*, and his note rightly explains the construction and makes no mention of *quodque*. 34 his text properly has *Reiicit*, his lemma *Refficit* after Avancius; 35 his text wrongly gives *suspirans*, the lemma *suspiciens*; and so throughout the poem. This very singular circumstance I explain in this way: he was living at Rome when his edition was printed and seems to have sent the text and commentary separately; for the bookseller prints at the end a long page of errors with this notice prefixed, 'Hieronymus Platonicus Bononiensis bibliopola ad lectorem. contuli Pii exemplar cum edito Lucretio: labeculasque pauculas notavi cet.' Pius' edition was reprinted by Ascensius in 1514 with not a few changes in the text, some of them taken from the notes.

The next edition must be ever memorable in the history of Lucretius, that published by Philip Giunta 'anno salutis. M.D.XII. mense martio'. Whether this means 1513 new style I cannot tell; but I know that he dates a Gellius and a Romualdi vita as published in January 1513, 'Leone pont. max. christianam R.P. moderante' and 'Leonis X anno primo'. Now Leo X only became pope in March of that year; so that here he must be speaking of 1514; and in Florence at all events this mode of dating seems to have been in common use. The editor was Petrus Candidus who, great and important as the corrections are which he has introduced, has yet used a copy of the first Aldine upon which to make them, though he has never mentioned the name of Avancius. It seems to have been the practice of those times to take at least whatever was printed without acknowledgment: thus Giunta regularly made booty of Aldus, Aldus of Giunta in turn. What is said in the present case is grounded on a close inspection of the two volumes. Candidus, where he does not designedly leave him, follows Avancius in the minutest points of spelling and punctuation. The latter for instance says in his preface that he writes 'veteres imitatus *repertumst, itemst, necessest*' and the like: Candidus in his preface that 'in tam culto, tam nitido, tam undecunque castigato poeta' he will not admit archaisms like *volgum, volnera*; or *nullast, haudquaquamst* and the like. And so in his text while rejecting Avancius' *patefactast, volnere,* etc., he keeps his *frugiferenteis, rapaceis* and a thousand such forms which have no authority in their favour, while those which he discards have much. Lachmann always so hard upon Avancius says 'huius ineptissimam scribendi rationem Eichstadius studiose imitatus est', but has not a word of blame for Candidus.

But whence has the latter got his many and brilliant corrections? for few or none appear to come from himself. He says in his address to Thomas Sotherinus that what he did was to collate all the *vetusta exemplaria* that were in Florence and to expunge what was condemned by the obeli of Pontanus and Marullus, 'praestantissimorum aetate nostra vatum'. He refers of course to John Iovianus Pontanus and his friend and pupil Michael Marullus, after Politian two of the first scholars and Latin poets of the most flourishing period of Florentine learning, the latter half of the fifteenth century: 'Marullo ed il Pontan' have the honour to be mentioned together by Ariosto in the Orlando XXXVII 8. But Candidus goes on afterwards to speak only of Marullus 'cuius in hoc opere censuram potissimum secuti sumus'; and in a note at the end he says that in changing the order of verses here and in most other places he has followed the arrangement of Marullus. To Marullus therefore everything which is peculiar to the Juntine has usually been assigned, whether in the way of praise, or of blame as by Victorius and by Joseph Scaliger who inherited among many other of his father's antipathies his dislike to Marullus. But Lachmann has gone much farther than this, and has given to him not only by oversight, as will be seen in notes 1, much that belongs to older authorities; but everything that first appeared in Avancius' edition as well, calling the latter 'fur improbus' and other opprobrious names. That he got much assistance from the labours of Marullus is certain; but by ascribing to the latter everything that is in the Juntine, in some respects more, in others less credit is given to him than he deserves. As I can throw some light on this interesting question, I will examine it at some length here and in various parts of notes 1.

The scholar, poet and soldier, Michael Tarchaniota Marullus Constantinopolitanus, as he calls himself in the editions of his poems printed during his life, appears from this title and his epitaph in San Domenico of Ancona, where he and so many of his ancestors are buried, as well as from the epithet Bizantius given to him by his friend Petrus Crinitus, to have been born in Constantinople. As he can hardly have passed middle life when he perished in the river Cecina near Volterra April the 10th 1500, he must have been a mere child when on the capture of his native city he was brought to Italy, probably to Ancona. He received his training however in Florence, and he found a Maecenas in Lorenzo de' Medici. Though he never printed anything on Lucretius, his manuscript emendations appear to have been well known during his life, and a copy of the poet to have been found on him at his death: 'ex miseranda illa in mediis Cecinae undis Latinarum musarum iactura cladeque insigni unus est Lucretius receptus' says Candidus in his preface; and his friend Petrus Crinitus in his de honesta disciplina xv 4, published in 1504, but mostly written it would seem before Marullus' death, after well refuting an alteration of his which shall presently be referred to, adds 'quae ab eius quoque sectatoribus recepta sunt pro verissimis'. This intense love of Lucretius he seems only to have conceived in the latter years of his life. Candidus, whose preface full of feeling shews that he greatly loved Marullus and deeply deplored his untimely end, strives to make the most of what he did: he says 'Lucretianae adeo veneris per omnem aetatem studiosus fuit, ut cet.' But this must be an exaggeration: the first edition of his poems, published without a date, but not later than 1490, containing only two books of epigrams, shews so far as I can see no trace of any acquaintance with Lucretius. Catullus is chiefly imitated even in the elegiacs, and next to him Tibullus and Horace. Six pages from the beginning there is a poor poem of eight lines 'de poetis Latnis' [sic], in which he says that Tibullus Maro Terence Horace Catullus, each in his kind, are the only good Latin poets: *Hos si quis inter caeteros ponet vates, Oneret quam honoret verius.* The Roman editions of 1490 and 1493 I have not access to; but in December 1497, two years and a few months before his death, he published at Florence a much enlarged edition. A third and fourth book of epigrams are added: in these too I find no trace of Lucretius. Then follow four books of hymni naturales. In these, especially such as are written in heroics, the strain is 'of a higher mood', and we meet with frequent imitations of Lucretius, even in the lyrics, as *Opibusque late pollens tuis* which recalls *Ipsa suis pollens opibus.* But in these heroics it is to be noticed that the rhythm is Virgilian, not in any respect Lucretian even where he closely follows the latter's language, as in the hymn to earth: *Ante repentino caeli quam territus haustu Vagiat aetheriam in lucem novus editus infans. Cum proiectus humi nudus iacet, indigus, exsors Auxilii, infirmusque pedum infirmusque palati.* Then imitating at once and contradicting Lucretius' *ut aecumst, Cui tantum in vita restet* cet. he goes on *Atque uno non tantum infelix, quod sua damna Non capit et quantum superat perferre laborum.* This the last poem published in his lifetime is full from beginning to end of Lucretian phraseology. In this edition too he inserts two new verses in the poem 'de poetis Latinis' spoken of above, *Natura magni versibus Lucretii Lepore musaeo illitis*, the best in the poem and recalling *musaeo contingens cuncta lepore*. Crinitus l.l. XXIII 7 quotes this poem and mentions a conversation he had with Marullus in which 'factum est iudicium nuper a nostro Marullo de poetis Latinis egregie perfectum et prudenter', and Ovid and other poets are blamed; and then it is added 'itaque legendi quidem sunt omnes inquit [Marullus]; sed hi maxime probandi pro suo quisque genere Tibullus Horatius Catullus et in comoedia Terentius. Vergilium vero et Lucretium *ediscendos asserebat*'. Let what has just been said be at once applied to a striking interpolation. After I 15 the Juntine first inserted the v. *Illecebrisque tuis omnis natura animantum*, which long kept its place in the common editions. Lachmann of course attributes it to Marullus, as do most editors. Lambinus says of it 'neque eum Naugerius neque Pontanus habuerunt. Marullus unus vir doctus ex auctoritate veteris cuiusdam codicis, quemadmodum mihi religiose asseveravit Donatus Ianottus, nobis eum restituit. amicus quidam meus ingenio et doctrina praestantissimus putat esse ab ipso Marullo factum cet.' What his authority is for that which he says of Pontanus I do not know, but Naugerius editor of the Aldine of 1515 properly omits the line, though he in general minutely copies the Juntine. Now this line is written by the hand of Angelo Politian in the margin of a manuscript which belonged to him and forms XXXV 29 of the Laurentian library. Politian died in September 1494, when Marullus could hardly yet have done much for Lucretius; and besides this as he had been long the deadly enemy of Politian, it is not likely the latter would have inserted in his manuscript one of his verses. I infer therefore that it is Politian's own; and as Candidus says in his preface that he collated all the 'vetusta exemplaria' in Florence, he could not have neglected this manuscript which was then in the famous conventual library of San Marco. I conclude therefore that Candidus' taking it from the margin of Politian's ms. is the right explanation of Ianottus' assertion that Marullus got it from an ancient codex. It is quite possible indeed that Marullus copied it himself from this ms. which passed to San Marco immediately after Politian's decease, and thus robbed him of his verse after death, as he is said to have robbed him of his bride during life. Naugerius has in his first page another variation from the Juntine, but that a perverse one: in I 7 he reads *Adventuque tuo* and joins it with what follows. This corruption I believe to proceed from Marullus; for his hymn to the sun contains a passage evidently imitated from Lucretius: *Cum primum tepidi sub tempora verna favoni Aura suum terris genitalem exuscitat auctum*: Adventuque dei *gemmantia prata colorat*: *At pecudum genus omne viget, genus omne virorum Perculsi teneras anni dulcedine mentes*. I can shew in other cases that Marullus corrupted Lucretius, where he has not been followed by Avancius or Candidus: VI 650—652 are quite correctly given by Avancius, and in his learned preface he says with reference to 652 *Nec tota pars* cet. '*totus* prima brevi, quia *quoti* redditivus est'. Crinitus l.l. xv 4 quotes 650 651 rightly, and adds 'qua in re grammaticorum nobis authoritas patrocinatur, quando et *centesimus* et *millesimus* probe dicitur: *partem multesimam* inquit Nonius nove positum est a Lucretio pro *minima*, ne quis forte paulo incautius atque audacius a veteribus decedat. quae a me vel ob eam rationem sunt adnotata, quoniam Marullus Bizantius aetate nostra, vir alioqui diligens, paulo improbius delere haec et alia pro ingenio subdere tentavit; quae ab eius quoque sectatoribus recepta sunt pro verissimis'. Candidus gives these two verses rightly and says in note at end of Junt. 'citatur Nonio locus': he has got this clearly from Crinitus, who in the same chapter correctly quotes and illustrates I 640 *Quamde gravis* cet. which the Italian mss. and editions had corrupted: this too Candidus took from him: for Marullus appears to have read *Quam gravior Graios inter* as does Pius in his notes, and Gryphius of Lyons. Again VI 332 Avancius rightly gives *per rara viarum*, Candidus perversely after Marullus *per operta*: see his note. But fifty instances like the last might be quoted. Candidus has also missed some of the best of Marullus' conjectures: see for instance notes 1 to I 1013 where I have got from the margin of one of the Florentine mss. perhaps the most brilliant example of his critical acumen. Then again unless I greatly err I have shewn in my notes that Gifanius in preparing his edition had before him a copy of the Venice ed. of 1495, lent to him by the zealous scholar Sambucus, as he testifies both in his preface to Sambucus and in his address to the reader. In the former he says 'exemplum Lucretii ad nos dedisti, non illum quidem calamo exaratum, sed ita vetustum et idoneum, ut vicem optimi manuscripti fuerit, siquidem in eo vidi omnium paene mendorum origines, quae magnam partem a Michaele Marullo, cuius immutationes in eo adscriptae erant omnes, primum parta, mox admiserunt Florentini cet.': in the address he speaks of the 'Sambuci liber quem ipsius Marulli manu adnotatum magno pretio vir ille praestantissimus paravit'. Why then Lachmann p. 6 should write 'neque enim facile Gifanio credere possum Marulli ipsius manu annotatum fuisse illud exemplar impressum quod se ab Iohanne Sambuco utendum accepisse scribit' I cannot comprehend. Gifanius was a dishonest plagiary, but at the same time a most astute man. Why should he tell a gratuitous falsehood which Sambucus would at once detect? He was writing only two generations after Marullus' death; and even if Sambucus gave his money for what was not the handwriting of Marullus, it was at least a genuine copy of his notes. But notes 1 furnish abundant proof of what I say: see for instance those to I 806 II 16 V 44 and especially III 994. It appears then that Avancius got from Marullus much which the Juntine does not record, and on the other hand, that Candidus took from Avancius without acknowledgment much that Lachmann and others assign to Marullus. Candidus, as I have said above, formed his text on a copy of the first Aldine: in doing this he must have had before him another edition with the ms. notes of Marullus, perhaps the very one which he tells us was found on him at his death. If now all that is common to the first Aldine and the Juntine comes from Marullus, as Lachmann maintains, surely Candidus must have been struck with this coincidence and would have recorded it against Avancius the editor of the great rival publisher. Yet Avancius did borrow largely, very largely from Marullus, especially in the case of interpolated verses made by the latter. How is this to be explained? Evidently even before his death Marullus' labours on Lucretius were known; and probably there were more copies than one of these, the one not always agreeing with the other. On this point compare notes 1 to I 551—627, where Candidus makes some perverse transpositions of verses, on the authority of Marullus he says in his note at the end; but the learned annotator of one of the Laurentian mss. states that some put 551—564 after 576, and adds 'verum Marullo parum referre videtur quomodo legatur'. This annotator and Avancius Pius Candidus Gifanius can hardly all have had the same copy: perhaps all were different. Avancius then may have had his notes in the very copy of Ven. on which he formed his text; and may have looked on them as public property which he might make use of without acknowledgment according to the practice of the time; for neither Pius nor Candidus acknowledges in his turn what he got from Avancius; nor does Naugerius the editor of Ald. 2 say a syllable of Candidus whose edition he copied with few variations.

But Lachmann to III 98 cites in proof of his charge that Avancius was a dishonest plagiary three interpolated verses which doubtless were composed by Marullus and are corruptly given in Ald. 1. In notes 1 to III 98 I have attempted to shew from Gifanius that Marullus perhaps wrote *putarit*, and that Avancius intended to read the same: Avancius was probably as good a Latin scholar as Marullus, if less versed in Lucretius. In the line inserted after IV 102 *multae* for *multas* may be an error of the printer or an oversight of Avancius. In that inserted after IV 532 there can be little doubt that he purposely wrote *suis*, imagining that *oris* was a plural. The correcting of texts was then in its infancy, and Avancius had so grievous a task before him in making sense out of the monstrously corrupted Venice edition, that much must in fairness be excused: we cannot tell what were the exact relations between him and Aldus and his printers. At the end of his Catullus published two years later he has taken occasion to give four pages of Lucretian criticism, in which he has proposed many excellent alterations of his former text, though I do not find that any editor before me has noticed these which are very important for his reputation: see notes 1 to II 422 and other passages. The inference then I draw from all this is that both Avancius and Marullus did much for Lucretius, Marullus doubtless more than Avancius; that much which is peculiar to the Juntine is not from Marullus, and much of what Marullus did is not in the Juntine. Between them they vastly improved a grievously corrupt text; and though they introduced many perversities, we ought in simple justice to take into consideration only what is good. In my notes for obvious reasons, when Ald. 1 and Junt. agree in a reading, I mention both; when a reading is peculiar to Ald. 1, I assign it to Avancius by name; when it first appears in Junt., I still say Junt., though it is always to be inferred that the best readings are most likely due to Marullus. By assigning to him all alike one would often be doing him less, sometimes more than justice.

[In my second edition however I was able to throw fresh light on the history and criticism of Lucretius' text by the undoubted corrections of Pontanus and Marullus, still existing among the books and manuscripts of Peter Victorius which have formed for centuries so valuable a portion of the Munich library. They were examined by me and copied out in the summer of 1865, my attention having been directed to them by a Goettingen program of Prof. Sauppe. The learned writer informs us that he had examined the Munich ms. of Lucretius and found it corrected throughout by some Italian scholar. Where Candidus the editor of the Juntine mentions in his note a reading of Marullus, this reading invariably appeared among these corrections. From this and other indications he concluded, and the conclusion seemed most reasonable, that these were the very corrections of Marullus which Candidus had used for his edition. He makes the probable suggestion that the long connexion of Victorius with the Giuntas would readily explain his possession of a manuscript which had belonged to that firm.

At Munich through the courtesy of the librarian I had the full use of the following important documents: 1. the manuscript just mentioned: 2. a copy of the Venice edition of 1495 with corrections by Pontanus in the handwriting of Victorius who describes them in the first page as 'emendationes ex Pontani codice testantis ipsum ingenio eas exprompsisse': 3. another copy of the same edition likewise corrected throughout by the hand of Victorius who says at the end 'contuli cum duobus codicibus, altero Ioviani Pontani, altero vero Marulli poetae Bizantii, impressis quidem, sed ab ipsis non incuriose, ut patet, emendatis, quos commodum accepi ab Andrea Cambano patritio Florentino M.D.XX. Idibus Martiis. Petrus Victorius'. What the printed edition was from which he copied these emendations of Marullus I do not know: very likely it was this Venice edition itself which must have had a large circulation and was the very edition containing Marullus' notes which

Gifanius made use of, as has been already told. Victorius says of *grando* in v 1192 '*glando* in Pont. libro': now since not only the Venice edition, but the Verona and first Aldine have *grando*, and also the Brescian as I learn from Earl Spencer's librarian, Pontanus must have used some printed edition now unknown. The pains which so eminent a scholar as Victorius has taken in copying out twice the emendations of Pontanus and once those of Marullus would prove the high estimation in which those two learned men must have been held when he was a young man of twenty. As he has also filled a copy of the Juntine with long parallel passages from the Greek, he must himself at one time have contemplated an elaborate edition of the poet and has to be added to the long list of scholars with whom this remained an unaccomplished design.

We have then an undoubted copy of what Pontanus himself asserted to be his own original emendations; and as they are accurately repeated by Victorius in his second copy, if we subtract these we have in what remains the undoubted corrections of Marullus. Now the latter with only a few variations, easily to be accounted for as being earlier thoughts or in other ways, all reappear among the alterations of the Munich ms. which are however much more numerous. When we consider all this, and remember that wherever Candidus in his notes mentions the name of Marullus, the reading which he assigns to him is found here; that he tells us in his preface his text is grounded mainly on the revisions of Pontanus and Marullus, the latter more especially; that, as the present edition will demonstrate, the numerous readings which first appear in the Juntine, good bad and indifferent, where not taken from what we now know to be those of Pontanus, nearly always agree with the corrections of this manuscript; and finally that Candidus not unfrequently gives a new reading peculiar to this of all manuscripts known to me, as in his note to v 826 where he mentions *pariendo* as a variation, we may fairly conclude that Candidus in preparing his text had the use of this corrected manuscript, and that the corrector was Marullus. It would be natural too to conclude that this is his own copy amended by his own hand; and for the most part I do not doubt that this is so. However they cannot all have been written at the same time, as the ink differs in different places; and as so many of the emendations agree with those of Pontanus, it seems not improbable that the ms. was in his possession before it came into the hands of Marullus. As the Italian handwritings of that age resemble each other so much, at least to our eyes, the writing of the pupil may not have differed much from that of the master. However that may be, we must conclude that the corrections common to both belong to Pontanus, as he was the elder and we saw above that he claims them for his own, and the scholar would naturally borrow from the master. The emendations too of Pontanus, valuable as many of them are, have the appearance of being earlier and more rudimentary than those of the other: he not unfrequently too sees that something is wanting and says 'fragmentum', where the latter supplies a whole verse with more or less success. The scholar therefore completed what the master commenced; and the emendation of Lucretius links their names together not less honourably than does the verse we quoted from Ariosto. Upon the whole this fresh information has greatly raised my estimate of both, especially of Marullus. His industry is at least as conspicuous as his sagacity: he has evidently carefully collated manuscripts and editions and gathered materials from all accessible sources. Throughout the poem the many verses omitted in the Munich manuscript are supplied with unfailing diligence. He evidently was acquainted with several of the existing Florentine manuscripts; among others that of Niccoli I believe, as well as that of his enemy Politian, and Flor. 31 whose readings Lachmann so strangely assigns to the notary Antonius Marii. Upon the whole he must be placed as an amender of Lucretius immediately after Lambinus and Lachmann, if not indeed in the same front rank, when we consider the circumstances of his age and the imperfection of his materials; and Pontanus perhaps may rank after him. Lambinus, as well as Avancius and Naugerius editor of the second Aldine, must have had access to some copy of Pontanus' corrections.

What I said of Marullus in my first edition with much more imperfect materials from which to draw conclusions, I find now confirmed in essential points. There were in circulation different copies of Marullus' emendations; Gifanius had access to one of these: see notes 1 to I 274 IV 1005, as well as II 16 125 465 III 994 V 201 1151 VI 25: what I inferred from his own poems is borne out by II 719 and 749 and some other passages: the assertion of Crinitus quoted above that Marullus had corrupted VI 651 652 is fully confirmed here: Marullus for the correct *multesima* most unskilfully proposes *multa extima*; and for *tota* reads *sit*: the latter Candidus adopts. In other cases his more mature judgment as seen in the Munich manuscript doubtless differed from his earlier notions. A man who studied Lucretius so long and earnestly cannot fail to have often changed his mind on further reflexion and with new sources of information. Candidus does not by any means follow Pontanus or Marullus in his orthography: that is formed as I proved in my first edition mainly on Avancius. In many cases they might have taught him better; to avoid for instance such embellishments as his *amneis, virenteis.* He rightly however avoids such barbarisms as the *hymbres* and *sylva* of Marullus. From *succus littus arctus* and the like, which the latter carefully introduces, we may infer that he and Pontanus had some share in bringing such corruptions into common use. The careful collation which I have given in this edition of the emendations of Pontanus and Marullus will prove their importance, and shew how rash and unfounded Lachmann's procedure is in assigning everything that is new in the Juntine to Marullus: even in the many instances where he and I are in agreement, it must be remembered that he speaks without authority, while I possess the testimony of Marullus himself.]

The Juntine closes the first great epoch of improvement in the text of Lucretius: the second Aldine edited by the well-known scholar Andrew Naugerius and dated 'mense ianuario M.D.XV.' is for the most part a mere reprint of it without however one word of acknowledgment according to the usage of the time. Yet the changes are not few, mostly for the better, not always: two instances are given above from the first page, the one a gross corruption, the other a right rejection of an interpolation. For the next fifty years Ald. 2 appears to have been the model edition. Gryphius of Lyons published several texts, three of which I have before me: they generally follow Naugerius, but not always, often recurring to Avancius. Those of 1534 and 1540 have many marginal readings, most of them taken from Avancius or the notes of Pius, a few from sources not known to me: see notes 1 to I 977 *officiatque*. Yet even these two editions do not always agree with each other.

Little advance however was made on the Juntine before Dionysius Lambinus. He dates his address to Charles IX 1 November 1563 and afterwards speaks of his first edition as published in that year; though the title-page of my copy has 1564. Lambinus was among the most illustrious of the great Latin scholars who studied and taught at Paris in the sixteenth century. His knowledge of Cicero and the older Latin writers as well as the Augustan poets has never been surpassed and rarely equalled. Whoever doubts that the nicest critical and grammatical questions can be expressed in Ciceronian Latin without effort or affectation, let him study the commentaries of Lambinus. Scaliger says of him 'Latine et Romane loquebatur optimeque scribebat': his ease and readiness are astonishing. He made use he tells us of five mss.: four of these appear to have been Italian mss. of the fifteenth century: the fifth, of which he used a collation by Turnebus, and which he calls the Bertinian, was the same as the Leyden quarto. In his preface and throughout the work he acknowledges his obligations to Turnebus and Auratus. His Lucretius is perhaps the greatest of his works: there was more to be done here, and therefore he has done more. He had moreover a peculiar admiration for this author, of whom in the preface to his third edition he says 'omnium poetarum Latinorum qui hodie exstant et qui ad nostram aetatem pervenerunt elegantissimus et purissimus, idemque gravissimus atque ornatissimus Lucretius est'. If his boast that he has restored the text in 800 places goes beyond the truth, though I am not sure that it does, yet the superiority of his over all preceding texts can scarcely be exaggerated; for the quickness of his intellect united with his exquisite knowledge of the language gave him great power in the field of conjecture, and for nearly three centuries his remained the standard text. Lachmann says he did much less than Marullus. But so far as there is truth in this, it is merely saying that the one lived before the other: nine tenths of what Marullus effected, Lambinus could have done currente calamo; but I doubt whether Marullus could have accomplished one tenth of what Lambinus succeeded in doing. Lachmann accuses him of strange levity and rashness. But it must be remembered that in a short life he got through an amazing amount of work in conformity with the wants of his age. He only gave two years and a half to his brilliant edition of the whole of Cicero: and probably did not spend many more months on his Lucretius than Lachmann spent years. Nor was it possible in that age even for a Lambinus to apprehend the true relation of the mss. of Lucretius to one another. His copious explanatory and illustrative commentary however calls for unqualified eulogy, and has remained down to the present day the great original storehouse, from which all have borrowed who have done anything of value for the elucidation of their author. Scaliger says 'Lambinus avoit fort peu de livres': if so he made good use of them, as his reading is as vast as it is accurate, and its results are given in a style of unsurpassed clearness and beauty. His notes observe the mean between too much and too little: he himself calls them brief, while his thankless countrymen, thinking however more perhaps of his Horace than his Lucretius, have made *lambin* and *lambiner* classical terms to express what is diffuse and tedious. A second and much smaller edition with only a few pages of notes, but with many variations from the first, was published in 1565.

Scarcely could this first edition have issued from the press, when the well-known scholar and jurisconsult Obertus Gifanius of Buren began with systematical and unprincipled cunning to pillage it and convert it to his own purposes. His Lucretius was printed by Plantin of Antwerp in 1566 as stated at the end, though of two copies before me the title-page of one has on it 1566, the other 1565, which is the date of his own address to Sambucus, and of the two privilegia at the end; for the March 1564 of the first must be old style, as it is later than the February 1565 of the second. He brought nothing new to his task, except the ms. notes of Marullus in the old Venice ed. fully spoken of above; for the emendations and readings of Antonius Goldingamus homo Anglus, which he speaks of in his preface, and the *veteres libri* and the like which occur throughout his book are mere blinds to conceal his thefts from Lambinus. The way in which he contrives at once to bestow empty praise on this scholar and yet to extenuate his merits and put him as a commentator of Lucretius on the same level with other learned men, Turnebus for instance, is a marvel of astuteness. In the preface to his third ed. Lambinus states the truth with great terseness: 'omnia fere quae in eo Lucretio recta sunt, mea sunt; quae tamen iste aut silentio praetermittit aut maligne laudat aut sibi impudenter arrogat'. Yet so great was the skill with which all this was done that he deceived many and was thought to be a rival worthy of Lambinus. Contrary to what many believe, the age loved brief notes; and his were brief, the other's copious. Even the great critic of that generation Joseph Scaliger, who well knew the character of the man and accused him of gross deceit towards himself, says 'Gifanius estoit docte, son Lucrèce est très-bon'. Lambinus however knew the truth, and his wrath was as signal as the provocation. In 1570 he brought out a third edition greatly improved and enlarged; much of the additional matter however consists in invectives against the aggressor. In a long preface of great power and beauty of style he states his wrongs. There and throughout his commentary the whole Latin language, rich in that department, is ransacked for terms of scorn and contumely. The same charges are repeated in a hundred different shapes with curious copiousness and variety of expression. Gifanius with consistent cunning attempted no public reply to all this. Many years afterwards, when Lambinus had long been dead, a new edition of the other's book was brought out at Leyden in 1595, in which many additions are made to the brief notes, but not a word is said of the charges brought against him by Lambinus. He was rewarded for his reticence, and for a century or more opinion was divided as to whether he or Lambinus did more for Lucretius. In private he corresponded with the cankered and unhappy Muretus: the two exchanged futile charges of dishonesty against the dead critic, who was far too genuine a scholar to be capable of being a plagiary. Lachmann so stern with Avancius has nothing to say of this much more flagitious case: 'qui quo iure' he observes 'aut Lambinum aut alios compilasse dictus esset non quaesivi'. Gifanius had no business whatever to edit a poet: he was without poetical taste and grossly ignorant of metre.

For a century after Lambinus nothing was done for Lucretius: the common editions followed either Lambinus or Gifanius. In 1658 the singular labours of Gassendi were given to the world. Deeply versed in the works of the fathers and the philosophy of all ages down to the latest discoveries of Descartes he devoted himself with the zeal of a disciple to the dogmas of Epicurus. The two first of his huge folios are given to this philosophy, and a large portion of thèm to the exposition of Lucretius. Much that is curious may be gathered from them, and I have perused them with attention; but to say the truth I have not found much to my purpose in them. The author was utterly devoid of the critical faculty, and all that is of value in him on this head is borrowed from Lambinus; as well as the most useful of his illustrations: his corrections of the text are almost without exception worthless. In the 17th century several distinguished scholars, Salmasius J. F. Gronovius Nic.

Heinsius Isaac Vossius, turned their attention to Lucretius; but their labours were only desultory. Of the ms. notes by the two last which are in my possession I will speak afterwards. In 1662 Tanaquillus Faber or Tanneguy Lefebvre published at Saumur a text of Lucretius followed by *emendationes* and *notulae.* He was a clever but vain man, who seemed to think such work rather beneath him; he takes care however to inform his readers that he spent but little time or pains on it, and had only Lambinus and Gifanius before him, though he owed nothing to either. The truth is that without Lambinus he could not have advanced a step: clever man that he is, he affords a good proof how much Latin scholarship had deteriorated in France during the century between him and Lambinus. Of Pareus, Nardius, Fayus nothing need be said.

Had Bentley in 1689 or 1690 succeeded in his efforts to obtain for the Bodleian Isaac Vossius' famous library, he might have anticipated what Lachmann did by a century and a half. As he was at that very time working hard at Lucretius, if he had once got into his hands the two mss. now at Leyden, he would at a glance have seen their importance and would scarcely have failed to complete the edition which he was then meditating. The great knowledge of Epicurus' system which he displayed two years later in his Boyle lectures and his zeal for the recently published Principia of Newton would have aided him in expounding the tenets of the poet. This however was not to be; but his marginal notes published in the Glasgow edition of Wakefield prove what he could have done, if he had gone on with his design. I cannot doubt that Lucretius would have suited him better than Horace, and offered a fairer field for the exercise of his critical divination.

In 1695 there came from the Oxford press a Lucretius edited not by Bentley, but by Thomas Creech Fellow of All Souls, a man of sound sense and good taste, but to judge from his book of somewhat arrogant and supercilious temper. The text is nearly always a reproduction of one or other of the editions of Lambinus: such criticism indeed he seems in his preface to look upon as unworthy of him. His notes are in most cases mere abridgements of those of Lambinus or copied from Faber, and his illustrations are usually borrowed from the former. All this he does as if it were a matter of course, not thinking it necessary either to avow or conceal his obligations. His *interpretatio* is his own: how far it is of assistance to a student must depend upon what he seeks for in it. His Lucretius however owing to the clearness and brevity of the notes has continued to be the popular one from that time to the present.

The worthy London bookseller Jacob Tonson published in 1712 a finely printed text with various readings at the end collected from many quarters with a great deal of trouble, some of value, most quite worthless. This I chiefly mention on account of what follows. In 1725 Sigebert Havercamp Professor at Leyden gave to the world his variorum edition in two large volumes. Though his reputation has never been great, my readers will hardly perhaps be prepared for what I am going to say. As Professor in Leyden he had the full use of the two Vossian mss. there, the main foundation of a genuine text: how did he use this advantage, which in profession he makes so much of? The chief feature of his edition is a vast and cumbrous apparatus of various readings, derived from about thirty-one sources professedly distinct. Of these thirty-one twenty-two are simply the various readings of the London edition just mentioned which Havercamp has taken and tumbled into his own without changing the notation. Most of these are of the most futile nature, taken from worthless editions which reprint or ignorantly depart from those of Giunta, Aldus, Lambinus or Gifanius, such as that of Pareus, Gryphius, Fayus, Nardius and the French translator the Baron de Coutures: the more worthless the authority, the more fully it seems to be given. There are also some collations of the mss. of Vossius and that in the Bodleian which it did the London bookseller credit to get together. The nine remaining authorities are these: a certain Basil edition of 1531, its marginal readings, a collation of the Verona edition of 1486, also jottings in its margin from three unknown mss., a second collation of the Bodleian, and lastly the two all-important Leyden mss. The two last are the only authorities he has collated himself. How has he performed this task? he has not noted one reading in three; the most important variations he usually omits; and the readings he gives are as often wrong as right. That which he has borrowed from others and thrown in a lump into his edition is for the most part as worthless as the scribblings of a schoolboy. So incredibly careless is he, that the Vossian collations which he borrows from Tonson are or should be those of his Leyden mss.: see note 1 to v 471 for a glaring instance of a false reading which he slavishly copies from Tonson and ascribes to his Leyden quarto. Nay more the Bm of the London edition and his own X are one and the same Bodleian ms. so that we have this ludicrous result, that the same ms. is cited twice over as two independent authorities. His various readings are therefore not only cumbrously inane, but are a snare and delusion, and have led astray those who like Wakefield have trusted to them. Thus in his hands the two unrivalled Leyden mss. have been worse than useless. What he does himself is always worse done than what he borrows from others, poor as that generally is: he has collated none of the old editions except the Verona, and that was done for him, and better done than he would have done it for himself. Nor are his explanatory notes much better: he has heaped together in a crude mass those of the chief editors; but except in the case of Virgil and Horace and one or two others of the best known poets, indexes to which are in everybody's hands, he has not even supplied the references to Lambinus' learned notes who from the circumstances of his age could not himself furnish them; nay in one case he has given Lambinus' own words as those of Cicero. In his two bulky volumes there is not one week's genuine work beyond what scissors and paste could do: seldom has performance fallen so far short of profession and opportunity.

There is nothing to detain us between Havercamp and Wakefield who in 1796 and 1797 gave his three volumes to the world, rivalling the other's in magnitude. Yet the work, such as it is, is his own, and is not a mere slothful compilation from others. Gilbert Wakefield possessed one quality which a critic can ill dispense with, that of despising any amount of authority which did not rest on some real foundation, and refusing to admit that, because a reading had appeared in edition after edition for centuries, it might by that alone claim recognition. He therefore set about a new revision which was to be based on manuscript authority alone; but neither his knowledge nor his industry nor his ability nor his taste sufficed for such a work. He professed to collate five English mss., among them our Cambridge one, and most of the old editions. This task he executed with incredible carelessness. As he had the full use of the Cambridge ms., one might have expected that his collation of it would be done with some care; but it is quite untrustworthy. From this as well as the evidence of his own notes and the nature of the case I infer that his other collations are not more to be depended upon. Had this labour been faithfully performed, it would still have been of little use, as he had no notion of the true relation of these late mss. to one another. He looked on each as an independent authority and thought he could not do wrong, if the words he put in his text were found in one or other of them. Then he had to take from Havercamp the readings of the Leyden mss., and therefore could gain no true insight into their character. As he had no knowledge of the language or philosophy of his author, he undertook to explain whatever words he put into his text in long turgid notes of unmeaning verbiage. His work was got through with a strange precipitancy: when engaged on the first part, he had never read the other parts of the poem; when he came to them, he had forgotten what went before. Morbidly vain and utterly unconscious of the immeasureable distance between Lambinus and himself, he assails the most brilliant and certain emendations of the unrivalled scholar in a hideous jargon and with a vehemence of abuse that would be too great even for his own errors. Thus by some fatality or other, by its falling into the hands of a Gifanius Havercamp Wakefield instead of those of a Salmasius Gronovius Heinsius Bentley, the criticism of Lucretius remained for centuries where it had been left by Lambinus, nay even retrograded. And yet Wakefield did display occasional flashes of native genius, and our notes will shew that not a few certain corrections are due to him; but from the first to the last of his 1200 quarto pages there is not a single explanation of the words or philosophy of his author for which a schoolboy would thank him: so incurably inaccurate and illogical was his mind. Yet owing to the boldness with which he asserted his pretensions he was thought even by scholars to have done something great for his author: he received complimentary letters from Heyne and Jacobs, 'hominibus modestis et ab omni iudicii subtilitate abhorrentibus'; and more than thirty years afterwards Forbiger in preparing his compilation for the use of the general public took him for his supreme authority. Even later than that so great a scholar as Ph. Wagner often appeals to him in his notes to Virgil. But though long in coming the avenger was to be.

Already in 1832 Madvig in a short academical program, afterwards republished among his opuscula, exposed the futility of Wakefield's criticism and gave some intimations of the right course to pursue. Stimulated by his example more than one scholar followed up the attack. The most important contribution of this kind was made by Jacob Bernays in an article printed in the Rhenish Museum of 1847. This able paper would have produced a greater effect than it did, if it had not been so soon superseded by Lachmann's more complete and systematical work. This illustrious scholar great in so many departments of philology, sacred, classical and Teutonic, seems to have looked upon Latin poetry as his peculiar province. Lucretius his greatest work was the main occupation of the last five years of his life, from the autumn of 1845 to November 1850. Fortunately he had the full use for many months of the two Leyden mss. His native sagacity, guided and sharpened by long and varied experience, saw at a glance their relations to each other and to the original from which they were derived, and made clear the arbitrary way in which the common texts had been constructed. His zeal warming as he advanced, one truth after another revealed itself to him, so that at length he obtained by successive steps a clear insight into the condition in which the poem left the hands of its author in the most essential points. Like many other great scholars he seems to have kept few or no common-place books. Resolved to master his subject he perused the grammarians and poets and nearly the whole of the older writers in order to illustrate Lucretius through them and them by Lucretius, and the Latin language by all. He had an almost unequalled power of grasping a subject in its widest extent and filling up the minutest details. One mark of a great original critic, which eminently belongs to Lachmann, is this: even when wrong, he puts into your hands the best weapons for refuting himself, and by going astray makes the right path easier for others to find. Another test is this, when his influence extends far beyond his immediate author. Now hardly any work of merit has appeared in Germany since Lachmann's Lucretius in any branch of Latin literature without bearing on every page the impress of his example. When he is better known in England, the same result will follow here. Though his Latin style is eminently clear lively and appropriate, yet from his aim never to throw away words, as well as from a mental peculiarity of his, that he only cared to be understood by those whom he thought worthy to understand him, he is often obscure and oracular on a first reading. Had his commentary been twice the length it is, it would have been easier to master. But when once fully apprehended his words are not soon forgotten. His love for merit of all kinds incites in him a zeal to do justice to all the old scholars who have done anything for his author; while his scorn and hatred of boastful ignorance and ignoble sloth compel him to denounce those whom he convicts of these offences. In one instance, that of Forbiger, this sternness passes into ferocity: most of his errors that scholar could hardly avoid in the circumstances in which he was placed.

Hermann warns us, when we disagree with Lachmann, to think twice lest we, not he, be in fault. His defects however must not be passed over. While the most essential part of his work, the collation of the two Leyden mss., has been performed with admirable skill and industry, he has not been so happy in the use of secondary evidence, that of the Italian mss. and the older editions. Much he has taken on trust on insufficient evidence, and much that he had before him he has not always accurately used. Some proofs of this have been given, more will be seen below. But a still more serious defect must be told: he meant his book to be a critical revision of the text, and left to others the task of explaining and illustrating the meaning. So far good: but as the text of an author in the condition of that of Lucretius cannot be always rightly constructed without a sufficient knowledge of his system and its literature, he has not unfrequently strangely blundered and grossly corrupted the poet's words: for examples of this see I 599—634 II 522—529 1010 foll. V 513—516. His consummate knowledge of the Latin language as well as of the manner of Lucretius in particular enables him often to amend his author with great success. As he wishes too to produce, where it is possible, an intelligible text, many of his corrections he must himself have looked upon as only provisional. Yet his greatest admirers must concede that he has not Madvig's 'curiosa felicitas' in emendation. He has however achieved a work which will be a landmark for scholars as long as the Latin language continues to be studied, a work, *perfidiae quod post nulla arguet aetas.*

Jacob Bernays in 1852 edited a text of Lucretius for the Teubner series. There can be little doubt that carried away by the strength of his admiration for Lachmann he has followed him too faithfully; yet he not unfrequently differs from him. Where he recalls the old reading he is generally right; where he deserts him for a conjecture of his own, he is often very successful. Had he prepared a more elaborate edition, as he appears to have once had thoughts of doing, there is no doubt that Lucretius would have owed him much. The impulse given by Lachmann to the study of our poet has called forth numerous papers either inserted in the German philological reviews or published by themselves. Some are of more, some of less importance: my notes will shew where I have been indebted to them. One English publication of eminent merit, as it criticises not the text of the poem, but its matter and poetical beauties, shall be mentioned elsewhere.

To return now to the manuscripts whose history was sketched above. Though I examined the two at Leyden for some days so long ago as the autumn of 1849, what will now be said of them is borrowed from Lachmann who had them in his hands for six months and during that time applied the whole force of his practised and penetrating intellect to unravelling all their difficulties and obscurities. Both, as already mentioned, belonged to the magnificent collection of Isaac Vossius. The older and better of the two is of the ninth century written in a clear and beautiful hand: I call it A. It has been corrected by two scribes at the time that the ms. was written, as Lachmann tells us. One of these is of great importance: in most essential points he agrees minutely with the ms. of Niccoli, the oldest of the Italian mss.; and doubtless therefore gives the reading of the archetype. It will be seen in notes 1 how often I make the united testimony of A and Niccoli to outweigh all the rest. The other Leyden ms. which I call B is of nearly equal importance: it is of quarto size closely written in double columns, apparently in the tenth century. It is probable that it and the ms. next to be mentioned were copied from some copy of the archetype, not like A from the archetype itself. Four portions of the poem are omitted in their place, but come together at the end in this order, II 757—806 V 928—979 I 734—785 II 253—304. Lachmann has demonstrated that these sections formed each an entire leaf of the lost archetype: 16 29 39 115 are the numbers of these leaves. It is manifest then that after A was copied, these leaves of the archetype had fallen out of their places and been put together without order at the end, before B, or the original of B, was copied from it. More will be said on this point presently. B has had several correctors, but all of the 15th century; one a very brilliant critic for his age, to whom are due many of the finest emendations in the poem, as will be seen in notes 1. This ms. was once in the great monastery of St Bertin near St Omer. Turnebus collated it in Paris and his collation as we saw was used with much effect by Lambinus: it afterwards came into the possession of Gerard John Vossius, Isaac's father. A large fragment of another ms. closely resembling B in everything double columns and all, except that it is said to be a small folio, not quarto in shape, is now at Copenhagen: it contains book I and II down to 456, omitting however the same sections as B, viz. I 734—785 and II 253—

304, and doubtless for the same reasons, because copied from the same ms. from which B was taken. It usually goes by the name of the Gottorpian fragment from the place where it once was. I have three collations of it, one published by Henrichsen in 1846, another in the handwriting of Nic. Heinsius, another in that of Isaac Vossius. Formerly it had a very high reputation: in truth it much resembles, but is more carelessly written than B, and is seldom of much use, except once or twice to confirm A against B. Strangely enough there are in the Vienna library fragments of a precisely similar ms. containing large portions of the later books, viz. II 642 to III 621 inclusive, omitting however in the proper place II 757—806 exactly as B does; then VI 743 to the end; then follow, precisely as in B, the four omitted portions given above, proving this to be copied from the ms. from which B was taken. Naturally enough these Vienna fragments were assumed to belong to one and the same ms. as the Gottorpian; but Dr Ed. Goebel, from whom I have borrowed this description of them, seems to prove in the Rhenish Mus. n. s. XII p. 449 foll. that the two portions now bound together are of different sizes and belonged to different mss. However that may be, the former part seems to be the same ms. as the Gottorpian, and the other if not the same, is precisely the same in internal character; and in either case is of the same, that is of very little value. Probably therefore a more accurate collation would hardly repay the labour.

All other mss. known to exist were, as has been already said, copied mediately or immediately from Poggio's lost ms. which must have resembled A almost as closely as the Gottorpian resembles B. The most important are among the eight preserved at Florence in the Laurentian library, numbered 25 26 27 28 29 30 31 32 of desk XXXV. 30 was written by Nicolò Niccoli himself, who had Poggio's ms. so long in his possession: this we are told in the learned Mehus' preface to his life of Traversarius p. L. As he studied so many of Niccoli's manuscript letters, he must have known his writing better than anybody else. There are many corrections in a much later hand, but Niccoli himself seems on the whole to have copied Poggio's ms. faithfully, and not to have made many changes. His ms. therefore, as will be seen in notes 1, is of great value in deciding between A and B. It is unfortunate that Lachmann could make no use of it: I collated it with some care in the summer of 1851: the old Verona and Venice editions have a text closely resembling Niccoli's. 31 is next in importance to 30, but of a widely different character, having a text much more corrected than Niccoli's or even Ver. and Ven. It is clearly written and in excellent preservation, and much resembles in general character the manuscript in our public library which I had open before me all the time I was composing notes 1, and which is as well preserved and as distinctly written as the other. It excels the Cambridge on the whole, though the latter has many good corrections not in the other. These two therefore I have used as good examples of corrected codices. From whom come the many excellent emendations contained in these mss. is quite unknown. Lachmann used a not very complete collation of Flor. 31, and to it he attributes the corrections which it has for the most part in common with the Cambridge and doubtless some other mss. Having been told too by H. Keil from whom he got the collation that it was written by Antonius Marii filius, he fills his commentary from one end to the other with the name of this worthy Florentine notary. I can only say that I compared it with ten or more voluminous mss. written in magnificent style and signed by this man between 1420 and 1451 all closely resembling each other; and neither in general appearance nor in the form of particular letters nor in their abbreviations have they any resemblance to the ms. of Lucretius. This scribe's name therefore I have excluded from my notes. Of the other Laurentian mss. 29 is to be noticed for the marginal annotations of Angelo Politian spoken of above and often referred to in notes 1: it twice over has this note 'liber conventus Sancti Marci de Florentia ordinis Praedicatorum habitus a publicis sectoribus pro libris quos sibi ab eodem conventu commodatos Angelus Politianus amisit seu qui in morte Angeli Politiani amissi sunt'. 32 has some learned marginal remarks on the first book from which I have derived some facts about Marullus. The six mss. of the Vatican I collated as long ago as the autumn of 1849, but not with much care or skill; yet it will be seen from notes 1 that they have been of considerable service to me: their marks are as follows, 3275 and 3276 Vatic. 640 Urbin. 1136 and 1954 Othobon. and 1706 Regin., at the bottom of the first page of which are the words 'Nicolai Heinsii'.

As further helps I have had Gifanius' ed. of 1595 with ms. notes by Nic. Heinsius which I bought from H. G. Bohn many years ago: it will be seen that I have derived from it some valuable emendations not in Heinsius' adversaria nor elsewhere so far as I know. It has also a complete collation of A all through, of B in the first four books, and of the Gottorpian fragment. It contains too a complete collation of the codex Modii, which Heinsius denotes by *s*: he says of it 'variantes lectiones excerptae sunt ex libello edito Paris. an. 1565 quem Fr. Modius cum ms. suo contulit, ut ipse testatur fine lib. I inquiens: *Collatus cum ms. meo* 26 *Junii* 1579 *Coloniae*': it was lent to Heinsius by Liraeus; Liraeus had it from Gruter, Gruter from Nansius, Nansius from Modius himself. Heinsius says 'codex Modii non est idem cum B Vossiano, nam pag. 8 [I 227] ubi ex Modiano notatum *ad lumina*, Vossianus *in*'. Heinsius speaks I presume of the small 2nd ed. of Lambinus, as the one which Modius used: it has like others *in lumina*: if then Modius' codex is B, either he or Heinsius has made a gross mistake. I have noticed several other instances, where *s* is made to differ from B; but in these cases Lambinus' 2nd ed. has the reading which Heinsius gives to *s*, so that

Heinsius may have here been misled by Modius' negligence. It would seem certainly that *s* and B are the same: if they are two, then their agreement is very extraordinary, much closer than that between B and the Gottorpian fragment.

I also possess a copy of Faber's Lucretius with a poor collation of A and B and the Gottorp. as well as many other notes and illustrations in the writing of Isaac Vossius. Havercamp had a copy of the same notes, but has employed them with his usual carelessness. Notes 1 will shew what important use I have made of them: they have enabled me to strip him of several of the most showy feathers with which he had decked himself either from negligence or worse. Spengel, Christ, Goebel and some others have in various journals and publications made much ado about a codex Victorianus as they call it, once belonging to P. Victorius, now in the Munich library, as if it were a rival, or nearly so, of A and B. From the readings cited I see clearly that it is a common Italian fifteenth century ms. neither better nor worse than twenty others, much resembling the Verona and Venice editions and of no importance whatever. [As the reader has been already told, I examined this manuscript myself at Munich during the summer of 1865 and can confidently affirm that what I said of it is the truth. It is much interpolated: its corrections are not so valuable as those of Flor. 31 or I think of our Cambridge manuscript. I have recorded some of its readings in my critical notes under the term 'Mon.', and have occasionally spoken of it as the codex Victorii. Strange that learned men should have taken so much trouble about its own readings and said not a word of the much more important emendations of Marullus which it contains. This is not the case with Prof. Sauppe in the program spoken of above; but I cannot help citing from its first page a few lines which I read with no slight surprise: 'unum addo, quod ab aliis nondum quod sciam animadversum coniecturam de victoriani codicis origine propositam valde confirmet. Post l. 3 enim v. 360 versus novem scripti sunt, quos delendos esse homo quidam doctissimus in margine monuit, qui versus 403—411 per errorem hic illatos esse vidisset. ratione autem subducta inter v. 360 et 403 versus bis vicenos senos interpositos esse invenimus, ut facile intelligamus in singulis archetypi paginis versus vicenos senos scriptos fuisse eiusque inter scribendum cum unum vellet scriptorem victoriani duo folia vertisse. in archetypo vero oblongi C. Lachmannus ostendit p. 3. 49. 233. aliis locis eandem versuum rationem fuisse'. Probably before this time the learned writer will have discovered that his arithmetic is at fault and that he has counted forty-two as fifty-two; and that his theory is thus entirely upset. But it is not for such a trifle as that, that I have quoted his words. Does he really mean to assert that this Munich is not like every other fifteenth century ms. a descendant of the one brought into Italy by Poggio? that the long lost archetype was preserved by some mysterious intervention for the special use of the copyist of this codex? Again I would ask whether he looks upon the laborious and sagacious calculations, by which Lachmann demonstrated the number of pages in the lost archetype and the number of verses in each page, as a mere plaything thus to be trifled with; and not rather as a key to unlock many secrets of criticism and not to be understood even without some slight effort of mind. I beg to tell him that the number of lines in the archetype between III 360 and 403 was not either 52 or 42, but 44; that is to say 42 verses of the poem + two headings: and that III 360 did not commence, nor III 402 terminate a leaf; but that III 360 was the fifth line of page 108 of the archetype, and III 402 was the fourth line from the bottom of page 109. Further study too will perhaps make him regret that he has put the unfortunate paragraphs between I 503 and 634 to a fresh torture, and permit him to see that in no part of the poem is the argument or text in a sounder state.—But even while revising the 2nd ed. for the press I found in a recent program by Th. Bergk, with the name of Ed. Heine on the title-page, a fresh attempt to magnify this much vexed Victorian codex: in p. XIV it is said that it 'solus iusto ordine exhibet libro IV locum antiquitus archetypi schedae paginis inversis perturbatum: nam post v. 298 *Atque ea continuo* sequuntur v. 323 *Servet. ...*347 *Ac resilire*, tum v. 299 *Splendida*...322 *Quae sita sunt*, denique v. 348 *Quod contra.* hoc igitur insigne est virtutis documentum, atque possit aliquis inde colligere librum Poggianum ex archetypo descriptum esse, antequam illae paginae inversae sunt' etc. Is it not strange that so definite an assertion should be printed, when in truth this manuscript has the verses in just the same inverted order, in which they are given by the Leyden and all other known mss.? Nay more the corrector (Marullus without doubt) arranges the disordered lines, whether after Politian or not, exactly as Candidus does in the Juntine, who beyond any question adopted his arrangement from this manuscript. And yet the main purpose of the program spoken of is to prove Marullus not to be the corrector of this Victorian codex, and to prove it from this very passage!] It will be seen that by the materials which I have collected and just described I have in many important cases got nearer than has been done before to the readings of Poggio's ms. which was a worthy rival of the Leyden two.

But Lachmann's long experience and disciplined acuteness have enabled him to go beyond existing mss. and to tell us much of the lost archetype, as I call it after him, of all existing mss. Notes 1 will shew that many difficulties are cleared up by this knowledge. This archetype then, though it is not certain that even A was immediately taken from it, was written in thin capitals, like the medicean of Virgil; the words were not separated, but in the middle of verses points were put at the end of clauses. Ancient mss. as a rule keep with singular care to the same number of lines in a page: ours had 26 lines in a page, excepting only those which concluded a book. But remember there was a heading or title at the beginning of each section; and each of these headings occupied a line. Lachmann brings many proofs of this being the number. When this ms. was copied, it was clearly much torn and mutilated. It was stated above that four portions, omitted in their place by B, come together at the end, and that these each formed a leaf of the archetype which had fallen out of its proper place. Each of these alone or with its headings consists of 52 lines. Then turn to note 1 on IV 299—347 (323—347 299—322) where this inversion is explained in the same way, by the accident that is of a loose leaf being turned the wrong way: see also note 1 to I 1068—1075 and 1094—1101, where the mutilation is accounted for in the same manner. Thus we obtain six certain landmarks in different parts of the poem. The archetype therefore consisted of 300 pages, or admitting, as seems to be an undoubted fact, that a whole leaf is lost between VI 839 and 840, of 302; of which the first was not written upon, as well as one for some reason or other somewhere between I 785, which ends one of the loose leaves at the end of B, and 1068 which, as shewn in note 1, begins a fresh leaf. Page 190 which followed the end of IV was left blank. I may also note that pp. 137 and 191 contained an index of the headings of IV and V respectively, while the headings of VI are crowded into the lower part of p. 249, the upper part of which contained the last 13 lines of the text of V: see Lach. p. 398: although the different titles come in their places in these books too, as well as in the first three which have no such index prefixed. Having made for myself a list of these pages after the rules stated in various places by Lachmann, I have found it of great use; as the ends of lines throughout the poem towards the bottom of the several right-hand pages had been specially exposed to mutilation in the damaged archetype. Verses also omitted in their proper places were apt in this as in other mss. to be put afterwards at the bottom of pages. Besides the injuries which it had received from accident or ill usage, our archetype must have been carelessly enough written, though A and B prove that it retained many valuable vestiges of great antiquity, especially in the spelling of words, and though there may have been few stages between it and the age of the author. There is one point, the nature of the hiatus after IV 126, as to which it is not easy to accept Lachmann's theory. That there is a hiatus there, is indisputable and the special questions connected with it are fully discussed in note 1 to that passage. As the accidental loss of a whole leaf would not suit his system of pages, he boldly declares that twenty-five verses and one heading have perished, that is one single page of our archetype. Now it is easy enough, as we have seen, to explain the accidental loss of a leaf, by which every subsequent copy must necessarily want the contents of that leaf: it is easy enough to conceive any one ms., A or B or Poggio's, passing over by mistake one whole page. But it is in the highest degree unlikely that different copies, A B and Poggio's, neither of which as Lachmann admits was copied from the other, should all pass over a single page of their original; or that this single page should be wholly illegible, while that which preceded and the reverse page of the same leaf should be entirely uninjured. It seems to me therefore much more natural to assume that our archetype or one of its predecessors accidentally omitted an uncertain number of verses; or rather that a whole leaf of the archetype had been lost, as after VI 839. Lachmann's system of pagination would then be set right in this way: only books IV and V have an *index capitum* prefixed filling one page; for that of VI as I have said is crammed into the lower part of the last page of V: before this index in V Lachmann has shewn that the archetype had one blank page. Assume now that one page was similarly left blank before the index of IV and all will be right: the pages of the archetype would then be raised to 304. The *index capitum* prefixed to VI I accidentally omitted to notice in former editions, as it had no bearing on the question of pages. The assumption here made which is commended by Mr Polle, but blamed by Mr Susemihl in philolog. XXIX p. 427 foll., I still think probable. The latter asks what conceivable reason there could have been for the two blank pages before V, except to begin the new book with a new leaf, as was done with all the rest. Why, I which had no index prefixed began on the second page of a leaf; so did III, which had no such index; so did VI whose index is crowded together in the manner spoken of. Other mss. such as the medicean of Virgil, seem to have no preference for beginning a book on a new leaf. Why the two pages were left for the index between IV and V I do not know, any more than why a page was left vacant somewhere between I 785 and 1068: it had something to do perhaps with calculations about the parchment required. I was going to say more, but forbear to enlarge on so fruitless a topic.

But we are able to advance even beyond the archetype: in many parts of the poem there are manifest undoubted interpolations, which must have been inserted by some reader who wished at one time to confirm what is said, at another to convict it of inconsistency and the like. Generally, not always, these passages are repetitions of genuine passages; sometimes they consist of several, sometimes of a single verse: I 44—49 and III 806—818 are good and incontrovertible examples. But enough is said of these throughout our notes. Lachmann however still unsatisfied has not paused even here, but has gone up to the very times of the poet. No careful reader will refuse to admit that he has proved not a few passages, some of them among the finest in the poem, to have been subsequent additions made by the author, which he did not live to embody properly with the rest of his work. Lachmann has gone too far;

and unless I err, I have shewn that not a few sections thus marked by him are properly connected with what precedes and follows. Yet it is certain that his theory applies to II 165—183, and more than one long paragraph of IV V and VI. It has been shewn sufficiently in the notes to these passages that the most important of them have a close connexion in matter and manner with each other. Like Lachmann, I have marked them off by [ ]. All through the poem many single verses and passages of some length are designedly repeated by the poet, some of them again and again. It is probable that he would have removed many of them, if he had lived to revise his work: the exordium of IV for instance could hardly have been left.

Some readers may be surprised at the number of verses which have been transposed in the poem; but they should remember that every ancient writing which depends finally on one ms. is in a similar plight. When a scribe omitted by accident a verse, in order not to spoil the look of his book, he wrote it at once after the next verse, if he immediately discovered his error; if not, he omitted it altogether, or added it in some other place, often at the bottom of a page; he would then affix an *a, b* to mark the right order; the next scribe would not notice or would purposely omit these and so on: see Bentl. to Hor. ars 46. Every one of these errors has been committed again and again by the copyists of our poem. Most of these transpositions are certain and were made long ago by Lambinus Marullus Avancius and others; many were first made by Lachmann. Some of these I have not followed: not a few I have first ventured on myself. But connected with this question I must draw attention to one point which seems of importance. You would expect as a rule single verses to be thus transposed; and this is the case in Lucretius' mss. as in those of other writers: sometimes too one or more verses are repeated after the misplaced verse, which ought to follow it in its proper place, as if to shew the reader whither it ought to be transferred: comp. IV 991 i.e. 999 of the mss. followed in them by 1000—1003, which are only the vss. which follow it in its right place repeated after it in its wrong place: see also V 570 (573) and what comes after. But besides such usual instances of transposition there are throughout the poem many small groups of verses, forming generally sentences complete in themselves, which have got quite out of their right place: comp. I 984—987 (998—1001), II 652—657 (655—659 680) and IV 1227 1228 (1225 1226), three passages first transposed by me; also II 1139—1142, 1168—1170, III 686—690, IV 50—52, V 174 175, 1127 1128. Now that a scribe should so often transpose several consecutive verses always forming an entire and independent sentence by mere casual carelessness, is to me in the highest degree improbable. Again most of these passages read to me like possible additions not necessary to the context, though they improve it. I believe them then to be marginal additions by the poet, inserted on the same principle as the longer sections discussed above: these too the first editor, faithfully preserving everything in his copy, but not caring always to find the right place for what the author left ambiguous, has inserted out of their order. Add to these v 437—442 which the context could dispense with: these vss. are found out of place in Macrobius as in our mss. This increases the probability that they were out of their proper order from the first, two apparently independent authorities Macrobius and our archetype quoting them in the same way. Perhaps these single vss. might be added to the list, IV 202, 205, VI 957, 1225, 1237, 1270 as they might all be dispensed with. Look too at IV 129—142, so strangely disordered in the mss.: 133—135 may be all marginal additions by the author afterwards wrongly placed by the editor. The ms. arrangement of IV 299—348 has been already accounted for. If all these passages are subtracted, there will then be left a not very unusual number of single verses transposed by the ordinary negligence of copyists. The numbers occasionally given on the left hand of the page denote of course the order of the lines in mss. which Lachmann follows in his edition: where spurious vss. of the mss. are omitted from the text, he still allows them to count. For obvious reasons I have followed him in this, as he will be the future standard of comparison, and there is great advantage in a uniform numbering of the verses.

Since many special questions of orthography are noticed as they occur in the notes, I should have thought it unnecessary to say more in this place than that in essential points I follow Lachmann, if it were not for the apparent unwillingness of scholars in this country to accept even the smallest change in what they look upon as the usual or conventional rules of spelling. The notion of any uniform conventional spelling is quite a chimera: I never find two English editors following any uniform system; nay the same editor will often differ in different parts of the same book. But whence comes this 'conventional' system, so far as it does exist? from the meritorious and considering their position most successful endeavours of the Italian scholars in the fifteenth century to get rid of the frightful mass of barbarisms which the four or five preceding centuries had accumulated. They sought indeed to introduce rigorous uniformity in cases where variety was the rule of the ancients; and though these cases embraced only a few general heads, they yet comprised a great multiplicity of particular instances, because involving the terminations of cases, the assimilation of prepositions in compound verbs and the like. But where there was only one right course, they generally chose it; yet from the utter confusion into which the use of the aspirate had fallen, their own language having entirely lost it in sound, but at this time retained it in spelling; from the almost complete identity both in sound and writing of *c* and *t* before *i*, and the like, they never could tell whether *humor* or *umor*, *humerus* or *umerus*, *spatium* or *spacium*, *species* or *speties* was correct; and consequently as a rule chose the wrong. Their general principles however were not accepted by the most thoughtful scholars in any age, so far at least as concerned the text of ancient authors, unless it be during a part of the present century; neither by an Avancius in the 15th nor by a Lambinus or Scaliger in the 16th nor by a Gronovius in the 17th nor by a Bentley in the 18th. Yet this system gradually established itself, because it came to be used by scholars in their own writings, some of the barbarisms being gradually eliminated; new ones however being introduced, such as *coelum coena moereo sylva caetera* for *caelum cena maereo silva cetera* in order to derive them preposterously from Greek words: Marullus, as we said above, writes *sylva* and *hymbres*.

Many attempts were made in various directions to change this state of things: the best and most systematic was that of Ph. Wagner in his orthographia Vergiliana published in 1841. With admirable industry he amassed all the evidence afforded by the medicean and, so far as it was accessible to him, of the other ancient mss. of Virgil. As these, like other old mss. are as a rule very tenacious of the true spelling in those cases where there is only one right method, he performed this part of his work with eminent success, and still remains one of the best authorities on the subject. In those other cases however referred to above, in which variety is the rule of the ancients and which include a great multitude of particular instances, he has chosen to abandon the safe ground of evidence and experience and has made Virgil write what he decided on a priori principles he must have written. This seems to me the reason why his system was not more generally followed. Still less satisfactory was Madvig's spelling in his de finibus published in 1839: it was utterly unlike that of the mss. and yet in many points it was not what Cicero used; in still more you could not be sure whether it was what he used or not. Here too Lachmann bringing into play his extraordinary 'power of asking the right question,' and joining with it a minute knowledge of the whole evidence upon the subject, saw at once what could be obtained and what could not, and shaped his course accordingly. The Leyden mss. of Lucretius, imperfect in many respects, are on the whole admirable in their orthography, at least equal to any of the mss. of Virgil, confirming them in what is true and confirmed by them in turn: in some nice points, such as the frequent retention of the enclitic *st*, they far surpass them. With their aid he was able to confirm those improvements in spelling which Wagner had so well established in opposition to the system in common use. But in regard to the other class of words in which the usage of the ancients varied in different ages or even in the same age, he did not dogmatically determine what his author wrote and thus close the door to all future change; but knowing that certainty was not here attainable, he carefully sifted the evidence offered by his mss.

and made the best approximation he could to what his author might have written, always taking the most ancient form for which his authorities supplied any testimony direct or indirect. Thus the question was not foreclosed; nor were we left to vague generalities, but a firm historical groundwork was gained upon which future improvements might be built, if better evidence hereafter offered itself. Lachmann then in this, as in so many other departments of philology, seems at once to have produced conviction in the minds of the majority of the most thoughtful scholars, in Germany I mean; for in our own country most seem to scout the question as unworthy of serious attention: a great mistake; for Latin orthography is a most interesting and valuable study to those who care to examine it, and touches in a thousand points the history grammar and pronunciation of the language. Let me give two examples of the effect at once produced by Lachmann. Otto Jahn in 1843 published his elaborate edition of Persius in which he adopted throughout the spelling then in common use, though he had so many excellent mss. to guide him to a better course: in 1851, the year after Lachmann's work came out, he published the text of his Juvenal and followed in it most minutely the principles of Lachmann; and fortunately he had a most excellent authority in the codex Pithoeanus; so that the spelling is probably not very far removed from the author's own. In the years just preceding Lachmann Halm published several orations of Cicero with elaborate critical Latin notes: and yet, though his spelling was somewhat better than that of Jahn's Persius, it is still essentially 'conventional' and arbitrary: in the years following Lachmann he published a series of school editions of Cicero's orations with brief German notes, and now in these the spelling was wholly modelled on the system pursued by Lachmann. The same system too he has carried out in those volumes of the elaborate edition of Cicero edited by him and Baiter, which came out after Lachmann's Lucretius. Stimulated by the examples of Madvig Ritschl and Lachmann the rising generation of German scholars has pursued the critical study of Latin with eminent success; and nearly all of them follow in orthography the guidance of Lachmann. This system then may fairly I think be now regarded as the true 'conventional' system; for surely the Lachmanns and Ritschls of the nineteenth century have a better right to dictate to us in the present day what shall be accepted as 'conventional' than the Poggios and Vallas of the fifteenth. Since my first edition came out, Madvig has published the last books of his text of Livy, of which there exists but a single and very ancient ms.: these he has edited in a form differing from that of the other books, and has now given his very weighty authority in favour of adhering to the spelling of the oldest mss., with some reservations which I do not understand. And now too in his new edition of the de finibus he has entirely abandoned the orthography of the other.

In following Lachmann then I am sure that I have authority on my side; I believe that I have reason as well. In those cases indeed to which I have already referred, where the universal testimony of inscriptions and of mss. beyond a certain age proves that there is only one right way and about which the best scholars are all now agreed, there cannot be any doubt what course should be taken: we must write *querella loquella luella sollers sollemnis sollicito Iuppiter littera quattuor stuppa lammina*; on the other hand *milia conecto conexus coniti conixus coniveo conubium belua baca sucus litus* and the like; *condicio solacium, setius artus* (adj.) *autumnus suboles*: in many of them an important principle is involved: obeying the almost unanimous testimony of our own and other good mss. we cannot but give *umerus umor* and the like: also *hiemps*. I have heard it asked what then is the genitive of *hiemps*: to which the best reply perhaps would be what is the perfect of *sumo* or supine of *emo*. The Latins wrote *hiemps*, as they wrote *emptum sumpsi sumptum* and a hundred such forms, because they disliked *m* and *s* or *t* to come together without the intervention of a *p* sound; and our mss. all attest this: *tempto* likewise is the only true form, which the Italians in the 15th century rejected for *tento*. Then mss. and inscriptions prove that *d* took an *n* before it, *tandem quendam eundem* and the like, with the exception of *circumdo* in which the mss. both of Lucr. and Virgil always retain the *m*: and generally, though not invariably, *m* on the other hand remained before *q*: *quemquam tamquam* and so on; though the new corpus inscrip. Lat. has I find *nunquam*; and so has Augustus in his res gestae, but *quotiescumque*. Then always *quicque quicquam quicquid* (indef.), but generally *quidquid* (relative), though *quicquid* is found in the lex Rubria and once in our AB: always *peremo interemo neglego intellego* etc. Above all we must scout such barbarisms as *coelum moestus sylva caetera nequicquam*. In these points Wagner is as good a guide as Lachmann; but in regard to the cases in which ancient usage varied shall we follow the former who deserts the mss. for preconceived general rules, or Lachmann who here also is content to obey the best evidence he can get? I have unhesitatingly come over to the views of the latter: 'hypotheses non fingo' should be the rule in this as in other matters. As said above, all these uncertain spellings fall under a very few general heads. One of these is the assimilation or non-assimilation of prepositions: *inpero* represents the etymology, *impero* the pronunciation of the word. From the most ancient period of which we have any record, centuries before Cicero or Lucretius, a compromise was made between these opposing interests: words in common use soon began to change the consonant, those in less common use retained it longer. In the first volume of the corpus inscrip. Lat., the most recent of which are as old as the age of Lucretius, most of them much older, *imperator* occurs 26 times, and is always spelt with *m*, proving that in a word, which must daily have been in everybody's mouth, etymology in remote times yielded as was natural to sound: *imperium* again occurs three, *inperium* six times, being doubtless in somewhat less common use. Now in Lucretius *imperium impero* or *imperito* occurs six times, and the mss. always spell with *m*, and so Lucretius spelt I have no doubt: indeed many of these common words the silver age I believe more frequently wrote with *n*, than did that of Cicero. Then Virgil uses *imperium* 40 times; and Ribbeck's capital mss. have *m* in every instance, except M which twice has *inp.*, though one of these two cases is at least doubtful: for Aen. VIII 381 Fogginius prints *imperiis*. Yet in defiance of all this evidence Wagner gives us *inperium*, surely without reason on any view of the case; for the foundation on which we must build is thus withdrawn from under our feet. To take another common instance, *commuto* occurs 9 times in the corpus inscrip. and always with *m*; 12 times in Lucretius and always with *m*. Other words are more uncertain: we find in the mss. *impius* and *inpius*, *immortalis* and *inmortalis*, *conligere* and *colligere*, *compleo* and *conpleo*; and so with other prepositions, *ab*, *ob*, *sub*, *ad*: all tending to prove that usage was in most words uncertain. Again we have *exsto*, and *exto*, *exsolvo*, *exulto expiro expecto* cet., *s* being generally omitted; and this agrees with Quintilian I 7 4 who implies that it was a learned affectation of some to write *exspecto* in order to distinguish *ex* and *specto* from *ex* and *pecto*; it agrees too with all other good evidence: the mss. of Virgil furnish precisely the same testimony as those of Lucretius; yet Wagner in all such cases writes *exs*: surely we should keep *ex* where the mss. keep it, *exs* where they have *exs*: and so with *supter* or *subter*, *suptilis* or *subtilis*, *ab-* or *ap-*, *ob-* or *op-*, *sub-* or *sup-*, *succ-* or *susc-*, and the like: *appareo* occurs ten times in Lucr. and is always spelt thus by our mss.: so *apparo*, *appello* (both 1 and 3 conj.); but *adpetitur* and always *adpono*, *adporto* or *atporto*, in which words the separate force of the preposition continued to be felt: in exact conformity with this the first volume of the corp. inscr. has twenty times *appareo* and also *apparitor*, proving that in the earliest times the prepos. had been assimilated in this common technical word: thus too in the 21 instances of *appareo* in Virgil all Ribbeck's mss. always have *app.* except M once, Aen. XI 605, misled by the usage of its age: comp. the suggestive remark of Servius to Aen. I 616 '*applicat*: secundum praesentem usum per *d* prima syllaba scribitur: secundum antiquam orthographiam ...per *p*': yet in defiance of all this Wagner makes Virgil always write *adpareo* and the like. We find *haud* and *haut*, and sometimes *aliut aliquit quicquit* and the like, sound and etymology carrying on an undecided battle in the mss. of Lucretius, as in inscriptions and elsewhere: *adque* is sometimes but rarely found, sound having here as might be expected gained the victory: Wagner cannot be right in always forcing *adque* on Virgil. Lucretius seems to have recognised only *sed*: he once has *elabsa*, and once *praescribta*: see notes 2 to VI 92: in such forms sound must have at an early period prevailed; and *b d g* gave way to *p t c* before *s* and *t*: *lapsus* for *labsus* is the same principle as *rex* (*recs*), *rexi* (*recsi*) written sometimes *recxi*, *rectum* from *rego*: to judge from the best mss. *labsus* and the like became again much more common in the silver age. Mommsen has recently published an admirable copy and exposition of the res gestae of Augustus from the Ancyra monument. Augustus was somewhat of a purist in spelling and cashiered an officer for using in a dispatch the vulgarism *isse* (not *ixe*) instead of *ipse*. His system quite bears out what has just been said: he always writes *imperium* and *imperator*; he has *immortalis*, but *inmissus*; *impensa*, while the heading of the work, not written by him, but perhaps by Tiberius, has *inpensa*: generally *conlega* and *conlegium*, but once *collegium* and *collaticius*; *exilium*, but *exstinguere*; on the other hand *sexsiens* as well as *sexiens*, proving that *x* and *xs* were identical: he writes *appellaverunt*; but *adque* the only time he uses the word.

Another question involving a multitude of details is the use of *-is* or *-es* in the accus. plur. of participles and adjectives and substantives whose gen. plur. ends in *ium*, as well as of some other classes, *doloris* or *dolores*, *maioris* or *maiores*: here too Wagner involves himself in inextricable perplexities by his eclectic system, when his mss. were admirable guides, had he chosen to follow them. The mss. of Lucretius are no less admirable and probably represent very fairly the author's own usage: they offer *-is* five times out of six; and *-es* is somewhat more common in substantives in very general use, as *ignes vires aures*. Inscriptions quite bear out our mss.; and the sole relic of Latin yet disinterred from Herculaneum contains this v. *Utraque sollemn*is *iterum revocaverat or*bes. Pertz recently printed in the Berlin transactions the few remaining leaves of a ms. of Virgil, which he assigns to the age of Augustus and which may really be of the second or third century: we there find the acc. plur. of adjectives and participles ending 18 times in *-is*, 3 times in *-es pares felices amantes*; of substantives we find *sonoris*, but 4 times *vires*, and *artes messes crates classes aves*, quite confirming the testimony of our A and B. Varro de ling. Lat. VIII 66 writes *item quod in patrico casu hoc genus dispariliter dicatur* civitatum parentum *et* civitatium parentium: *in accusandi hos* montes fontes *et hos* montis fontis; and in Lucr. II 587 we find *potestates*, V 1239 *potestatis*: then ib. 67 he says *quid potest similius esse quam* gens mens dens? *quom horum casus patricus et accusativus in multitudine sint disparilis*; *nam a primo fit* gentium *et* gentis, *utrobique ut sit* i; *ab secundo* mentium *et* mentes, *ut in priore solo sit* i; *ab tertio* dentum *et* dentes, *ut in neutro sit* i; well our mss. six times have the acc. *gentis*, never *gentes*; *dentes* four times, never *dentis*; *mentes* five times, once only, II 620, *mentis*. As for the nomin. plur. of such words, Varro l. l. 66 says *sine reprehensione vulgo alii* *dicunt in singulari hac* ovi *et* avi, *alii hac* ove *et* ave, *in multitudinis hae* puppis restis *et hae* puppes restes: the fragment of Virgil just cited has the nomin. plur. *putris* and *messis,* though we saw it had *messes* in the accus.: in accordance then with these high authorities the mss. of Lucr. not unfrequently retain this nomin. in *-is,* which it would be monstrous to extirpate: I have always therefore kept it. In precise conformity with Lucr. Augustus has in the accus. *agentis* and *labentes, finis* and *fines, consules* and once *consulis*: once too the nomin. *pluris.* On the other hand he always uses the accus. *gentes,* departing in this word from the rule of Varro and Lucr. We see from the corpus inscr. that *-eis -is -es* were all in use: it is probable that Lucr. occasionally employed the termination *-eis,* intermediate in sound between *-es* and *-is*; but, if so, his manuscripts have left few or no traces, and it would be most perverse to follow Avancius Wakefield and others in thrusting it into his verses in season and out of season: v 1280 B has *mortaleis,* perhaps from Lucr.: Augustus more than once has this *-eis* in the abl. plur., *quadrigeis, emeriteis*; and the inscription in his honour still existing on the arch of Rimini erected in 727, midway therefore in time between his res gestae and Lucr., has *celeberrimeis, vieis, redditeis.* A and B have however not a few indications expressed or implied of the ending *-ei*: see note 2 to III 97 *oculei*: these have of course been carefully preserved.

On another question, comprehending a multitude of particular instances, I have followed Lachmann and our mss. which here too are on the whole excellent guides: I speak of the vowel or consonant *u* followed by another *u.* The old Latins appear to have been unable to pronounce *uu*; and therefore the ancient *o* long kept its place after *u*; or for *qu c* or *q* was used: *quom qum* or *cum,* never *quum*; *linquont linqunt* or *lincunt*; *sequontur, sequntur* or *secuntur*; *equos* (nom.) *equs* or *ecus*; *volgus divos divom aevom* and so on. They appear to have begun soonest to tolerate *uu* in terminations, when both were vowels, *suus tuus* and the like. Now the mss. of Lucretius have retained in very many instances *divom volnus volgo vivont* cet.; *equos* (nom.) and *ecus, ecum, aecum*; *relinquont relinqunt* or *relincunt* oftener than *relinquunt,* so *sequontur secuntur secutus locuntur locutus*; but with Lachmann I retain the *uu,* when the mss. offer it, in order not to get lost on a sea of conjectural uncertainty like Wagner and some others, who not only desert mss. but in many cases intrude a spelling older than the age of their author: thus Augustus has *rivus rivum annuum* (not once *-uo* or *-vo*); why not then Virgil, or at least Varius and Tucca? The mss. of Lucretius are also very pertinacious in retaining the genuine old forms *reicit eicit* or *eiĕcit* cet. and never offering *reiicit eiicit* and the like: *Grai Grais,* not *Graii Graiis.* But further details on the most interesting points of the ancient orthography will be found in various parts of my notes. Again in those many cases where the sound was intermediate between *u* and *i* and the spelling therefore uncertain, such as the penult of superlatives and certain other adjectives, and words like *lubet* or *libet*, *dissipat* or *dissupat*, *quadrupes* or *quadripes* and many others, I have of course submitted to the guidance of our mss. which only once for instance have *u* in the superl. and once *manufesta*, and twice offer *arbita*, not *arbuta*. Augustus, having learnt it probably in boyhood from the all-accomplished dictator, for whose apprehension nothing was either too little or too great and who, Gellius tells us, first introduced the *i* for *u* in superlatives, invariably writes *frequentissimus septimus vicensimus*, as well as *finitimus manibiae*: comp. what Suetonius says of his use of *sĭmus* for *sumus*, probably from a wish to be consistent. He would scarcely have thanked Varius and Tucca for bringing him the Aeneid embellished with Wagner's *maxumus, septumus* and the like, introduced so often in spite of his mss. [Both forms are found in the same sentence lex colon. Genetivae c. 66 (Ephem. Epigraph. vol. III p. 93) *optima lege optumo iure.*] I have likewise followed AB in the adoption of *e* or *o* in *vertere* or *vortere* and the like: *e* is naturally the more common, yet *vorti vorsum divorsi vortitur convortere vortex* are all found: also in reading *reddunda gignundis dicundum cernundi faciundum agundis* cet. or the more usual *agendum quaerendum* cet. Do I then claim in all these doubtful cases to reproduce the spelling of Lucretius or his first editor? Certainly not; but still in most of them Lucretius and his contemporaries undoubtedly allowed themselves much latitude; and I have not intentionally permitted anything to remain which might not have been found in one or other ms. before the death of Virgil. By adhering tenaciously to the mss. where not demonstrably wrong one gains a firm resting place from which to make further advances, if better evidence offer itself. However that may be, I cannot bring myself to accept the arbitrary and eclectic system of a Wagner, much less the hideous barbarisms of a Wakefield; nor on the other hand, after feasting on the generous cereals of a Lachmann and a Ritschl, can I stomach the 'conventional' husks and acorns of the Italians of the 15th century. At the same time it will be seen that my spelling differs less from this system, than does that of Wagner in his standard text of 1841, or even his subsequent modification of that text for common use which Prof. Conington has adopted in his Virgil.

Most of the abbreviations and marks used in the notes are sufficiently explained above: A and B denote the two Leyden mss., Gott. the Gottorpian fragment, Nicc. the Florentine ms. written by Nicolò Niccoli, Flor. 29, 31, 32 the mss. of the Laurentian library forming nos. 29, 31, 32 of desk XXXV; Camb. our Cambridge ms.; Vat. or Vatic. the Vatican mss.; and Urbin. Othob. or Reg. with the number attached identify more nearly the mss. contained in those several departments of the library: one Vat. 2 Vat. 3 Vat. mean one, two or three of the Vatican mss. where it was not worth while specifying them. In this new edition Mon. denotes the codex of Victorius in the Munich library. Brix. Ver. Ven. Ald. 1 Junt. Ald. 2 are the editions fully described above, where it is explained when and why the names Avancius, Candidus, Marullus, Naugerius are or are not used instead of that of one or other of these editions. The ms. notes of Heinsius and Vossius, which are often cited, indicate the notes by those scholars which are in my private possession and have been described above. Lamb. Wak. Lach. Bern. Bentl. need no explanation after what has been said; and in this edition Pont. and Mar. designate Pontanus and Marullus, whose readings I have got from the sources mentioned. The dots ... imply that one verse, * that more than one or an uncertain number are lost; such interpolations as it has been deemed advisable to retain in the text, are printed in small capitals; the letters syllables and words which are omitted in the mss. but can be restored with more or less certainty, are given in Italics. In quoting Ennius the last edition, that of Vahlen, has been used; for the fragments of the Roman scenic writers, except Ennius, that of Ribbeck: in citing Cicero the smaller sections are referred to as far the most convenient for reference: for Terence the several recent editions; for Plautus Ritschl and Fleckeisen in the plays they have published; in the others the old variorum ed. has been employed: in Pliny the sections of recent editions are cited, as the older divisions are intolerably awkward. Notes 1 have been made as short as is consistent with perspicuity: unless the contrary is expressly stated or implied, the word or words which appear first in the note are those of our text; thus '*genitabilis. genitalis* etc.' signifies that *genitabilis* is the right reading and is found in A and B and the other chief authorities, but *genitalis* is mentioned for the reasons given. Again '281 *quam* Lach. for *quem. quod* Junt.' means that Lachmann first gave the correct reading *quam* instead of *quem* which is the reading of A and B and other mss. as well as editions before the Juntine of 1512 which prints *quod*, the reading generally followed by the old editors. Of course if any one before Lachmann had read *quam*, he, not Lachmann, would have been cited for it. 'Ed.' means the present editor. Let it always be remembered that the corrupt reading, cited in a note, is that which appears in A and B, unless the contrary is expressly stated.

The passages which were first added to the second edition have been enclosed within [ ] in cases where ambiguity or awkwardness might be occasioned, if no distinction were made between the old and the new matter; but not otherwise.

T. LUCRETI CARI

DE RERUM NATURA

LIBER PRIMUS

Aeneadum genetrix, hominum divomque voluptas,
alma Venus, caeli subter labentia signa
quae mare navigerum, quae terras frugiferentis
concelebras, per te quoniam genus omne animantum
concipitur visitque exortum lumina solis:
te, dea, te fugiunt venti, te nubila caeli
adventumque tuum, tibi suavis daedala tellus
summittit flores, tibi rident aequora ponti
placatumque nitet diffuso lumine caelum.
nam simul ac species patefactast verna diei
et reserata viget genitabilis aura favoni,
aeriae primum volucres te, diva, tuumque
significant initum perculsae corda tua vi.
15 inde ferae pecudes persultant pabula laeta
14 et rapidos tranant amnis: ita capta lepore

11 *genitabilis*. *genitalis* has no authority, but it does not appear to be 'typographi Veronensis peccatum', as I found it in Vat. 1136 Othobon. 14 15: Niccoli followed by all the Flor. mss. Camb. etc. has these verses in the right order. 14 Wak. proposes *fere* which is indeed rather the ms. reading.

After 15 the v. *Illecebrisque tuis omnis natura animantum* is inserted in the Juntine and in most subsequent editions, not however by Naugerius in Aldine 2, as Lachmann incorrectly states. It has been generally assigned to Marullus, but as I found it in the margin of Flor. xxxv 29, for reasons given above p. 8 I attribute it to Angelo Politian. Victorius however inserts it among what profess to be solely Pontanus' conjectures; though he has not written it in the same style, nor apparently at the same time, as the rest: it is possible then that Pontanus or he may have got it from Politian's ms. Marullus in marg. Mon. for *capta* proposes

te sequitur cupide quo quamque inducere pergis.
denique per maria ac montis fluviosque rapacis
frondiferasque domos avium camposque virentis
omnibus incutiens blandum per pectora amorem
efficis ut cupide generatim saecla propagent.
quae quoniam rerum naturam sola gubernas
nec sine te quicquam dias in luminis oras
exoritur neque fit laetum neque amabile quicquam,
te sociam studeo scribendis versibus esse
quos ego de rerum natura pangere conor
Memmiadae nostro, quem tu, dea, tempore in omni
omnibus ornatum voluisti excellere rebus.
quo magis aeternum da dictis, diva, leporem.
effice ut interea fera moenera militiai
per maria ac terras omnis sopita quiescant.
nam tu sola potes tranquilla pace iuvare
mortalis, quoniam belli fera moenera Mavors
armipotens regit, in gremium qui saepe tuum se
reicit aeterno devictus vulnere amoris,
atque ita suspiciens tereti cervice reposta
pascit amore avidos inhians in te, dea, visus,
eque tuo pendet resupini spiritus ore.
hunc tu, diva, tuo recubantem corpore sancto
circumfusa super, suavis ex ore loquellas
funde petens placidam Romanis, incluta, pacem.
nam neque nos agere hoc patriai tempore iniquo

quodque: this Victorius in his copy of Marullus' corrections first wrote down, and afterwards erased, because I presume the line of the Juntine rendered it unnecessary: a strong indication that he got this v. from Junt. a copy of which now in the Munich library he has filled with elaborate notes of his own: his spelling too of *amneis* in his second copy of Ven. shews he took it from Junt.; as Pontanus and Marullus recognise only *-es* or *-is*. Again Lambinus who evidently had access to ms. notes of Pontanus as stated above, says distinctly in a passage already quoted in p. 8 'neque eum Naugerius neque Pontanus habuerunt': what he there says of Marullus is mere report. Nicc. and the Italians having changed in 16 *quamque* into *cunque* had rendered the sentence unintelligible without some addition. 16 *pergis* Nicc. A corr. etc. for *tergis*.

27 *ornatum* A corr. Priscian etc. for *oralatum*. 32 *fera moenera* Lamb. for *feram onera*. *moenia* scholiast of Statius. 33 *regit* Nicc. scholiast of Statius for *regium*. 34 *Reicit* B Gottorp. *Reficit* A Nicc. Camb. Pontanus etc. *devictus*. *devinctus* Pont. Lamb. and scholiast of Statius. 35 Nicc. rightly

possumus aequo animo nec Memmi clara propago
talibus in rebus communi desse saluti.

*

quod superest, vacuas auris animumque sagacem
semotum a curis adhibe veram ad rationem,
ne mea dona tibi studio disposta fideli,
intellecta prius quam sint, contempta relinquas.
nam tibi de summa caeli ratione deumque
disserere incipiam et rerum primordia pandam,
unde omnis natura creet res auctet alatque,
quove eadem rursum natura perempta resolvat,
quae nos materiem et genitalia corpora rebus
reddunda in ratione vocare et semina rerum
appellare suëmus et haec eadem usurpare
corpora prima, quod ex illis sunt omnia primis.
  Humana ante oculos foede cum vita iaceret
in terris oppressa gravi sub religione
quae caput a caeli regionibus ostendebat
horribili super aspectu mortalibus instans,
primum Graius homo mortalis tollere contra
est oculos ausus primusque obsistere contra,

gives *tereti* for *teriti*. 43 *desse* A corr. Nicc. for *id esse*. 44—49 = II 646—651. Is. Vossius in his ms. notes in my possession well observes that some one has inserted them here 'ut ostenderet Lucret. sibi adversari qui, cum Deos mortalia non curare affirmat [sic], Venerem tamen invocet'. Pont. Mar. Junt. omit them. Avancius in the text of Ald. 1 places them after 61 and has been followed by most editors before Lach.; but in his preface he well observes 'unum affirmare ausim *Omnis enim* cum quinque sequentibus ex prologo, cum abundent, demendos esse: hos aptius legas, cum de magna matre agit'. 50 *Quod superest, vacuas auris animumque sagacem*: so Bernays in Rhein. Mus. n. f. v p. 559 from the interpr. Verg. in Maii class. auct. t. VII p. 262. *Quod superest ut vacuas auris* AB. Nicc. followed by all the Flor. Camb. Mon. and most mss. and all the old editions omitted *ut* and added *mihi, Memmius, et te*. Lamb. *Memmiada*. At the end of Junt. is proposed *vacuas mihi quaeso Memmius aures Semotus curis*: Pont. gives *Quod superest quaeso vacuas mihi Memmius auris*. Lach. has rightly seen that our reading implies the loss of one or more verses in which the poet passed from Venus to Memmius: he suggests *animumque, age, Memmi*, which would complete the sentence in a way: so would *corque, inclute Memmi*, or the like. 66 *tollere*. *tendere* Lamb. ed. 3 Lach. from Nonius 'teste nostris antiquiore'. But where our mss. give, as here, a faultless reading, it seems uncritical to prefer that of such a careless writer as Nonius: older and better authorities than he is continually misquote: Seneca in 57 has *quoque* for *quove*, Gellius in 304 *aut* for *et*, 306 Nonius *candenti* for *dispansae in*, II 13 Lactantius *stultas* for *miseras*, 1001 *ful-*

quem neque fama deum nec fulmina nec minitanti
murmure compressit caelum, sed eo magis acrem
inritat animi virtutem, effringere ut arta
naturae primus portarum claustra cupiret.
ergo vivida vis animi pervicit, et extra
processit longe flammantia moenia mundi
atque omne immensum peragravit mente animoque,
unde refert nobis victor quid possit oriri,
quid nequeat, finita potestas denique cuique
quanam sit ratione atque alte terminus haerens.
quare religio pedibus subiecta vicissim
opteritur, nos exaequat victoria caelo.
  Illud in his rebus vereor, ne forte rearis
inpia te rationis inire elementa viamque
indugredi sceleris. quod contra saepius illa
religio peperit scelerosa atque impia facta.
Aulide quo pacto Triviai virginis aram
Iphianassai turparunt sanguine foede
ductores Danaum delecti, prima virorum.
cui simul infula virgineos circumdata comptus
ex utraque pari malarum parte profusast,
et maestum simul ante aras adstare parentem
sensit et hunc propter ferrum celare ministros
aspectuque suo lacrimas effundere civis,
muta metu terram genibus summissa petebat.
nec miserae prodesse in tali tempore quibat
quod patrio princeps donarat nomine regem;
nam sublata virum manibus tremibundaque ad aras
deductast, non ut sollemni more sacrorum
perfecto posset claro comitari Hymenaeo,
sed casta inceste nubendi tempore in ipso
hostia concideret mactatu maesta parentis,

gentia for *rellatum*. 68 *fama*. *fana* Bentl. and Lach. who says '*fama* non omnis necessario *magna* est': *fana* may be right: see v 75; but *fama deum* seems to me more emphatic and the *deum* to be equivalent to an epithet.

70 *effringere* Priscian and also I find Flor. 29 Vat. 1136 Othob. Mon. p. m. for *confringere*, rightly no doubt. *virtutem animi confringere* Nicc. 71 *cupiret* Prisc. A corr. for *cuperet*. 74 *omne* A corr. Flor. 28 and 32 for *omnem*.

77 *quanam* A corr. for *quantum*. 83 *atque*. *ac* B and Gott. 84 *Triviai* Prisc. for *Triviat*. 85 *Iphianassai* A corr. Avanc. for *Iphianassa*. *Iphianasseo*

exitus ut classi felix faustusque daretur.
tantum religio potuit suadere malorum.
  Tutemet a nobis iam quovis tempore vatum
terriloquis victus dictis desciscere quaeres.
quippe etenim quam multa tibi iam fingere possunt
somnia quae vitae rationes vertere possint
fortunasque tuas omnis turbare timore!
et merito; nam si certam finem esse viderent
aerumnarum homines, aliqua ratione valerent
religionibus atque minis obsistere vatum.
nunc ratio nulla est restandi, nulla facultas,
aeternas quoniam poenas in morte timendum*st.*
ignoratur enim quae sit natura animai,
nata sit an contra nascentibus insinuetur,
et simul intereat nobiscum morte dirempta
an tenebras Orci visat vastasque lacunas
an pecudes alias divinitus insinuet se,
Ennius ut noster cecinit qui primus amoeno
detulit ex Helicone perenni fronde coronam,
per gentis Italas hominum quae clara clueret;
etsi praeterea tamen esse Acherusia templa
Ennius aeternis exponit versibus edens,
quo neque permaneant animae neque corpora nostra,
sed quaedam simulacra modis pallentia miris;
unde sibi exortam semper florentis Homeri
commemorat speciem lacrimas effundere salsas
coepisse et rerum naturam expandere dictis.
quapropter bene cum superis de rebus habenda
nobis est ratio, solis lunaeque meatus
qua fiant ratione, et qua vi quaeque gerantur
in terris, tum cum primis ratione sagaci
unde anima atque animi constet natura videndum;
et quae res nobis, vigilantibus obvia, mentes

Nicc. all Flor. Camb. all Vat. etc. 104 *possunt* Mar. Junt. for *possum.* As A and the Italians have *iam*, B and Gott. *me*, I once thought the right reading might be *a me fingere possum*: see Cambridge Journal of philology I p. 42 and Lucr. III 271. 111 *timendumst* Orelli eclog. in notes, Lach. for *timendum.* 121 *edens. eidem* Lach. without cause. 122 *permaneant. permanent* Ang. Politian in marg. of Flor. 29, Ver. Ven. Ald. 1 Junt. etc. followed by all before Lach. *perveniant* Mar. 126 *Coepisse et* B corr. Flor. 31 for

terrificet morbo adfectis, somnoque sepultis,
cernere uti videamur eos audireque coram,
morte obita quorum tellus amplectitur ossa.
nec me animi fallit Graiorum obscura reperta
difficile inlustrare Latinis versibus esse,
multa novis verbis praesertim cum sit agendum
propter egestatem linguae et rerum novitatem;
sed tua me virtus tamen et sperata voluptas
suavis amicitiae quemvis sufferre laborem
suadet et inducit noctes vigilare serenas
quaerentem dictis quibus et quo carmine demum
clara tuae possim praepandere lumina menti,
res quibus occultas penitus convisere possis.
Hunc igitur terrorem animi tenebrasque necessest
non radii solis neque lucida tela diei
discutiant, sed naturae species ratioque.
principium cuius hinc nobis exordia sumet,
nullam rem e nilo gigni divinitus umquam.
quippe ita formido mortalis continet omnis,
quod multa in terris fieri caeloque tuentur
quorum operum causas nulla ratione videre
possunt ac fieri divino numine rentur.
156 quas ob res ubi viderimus nil posse creari
de nilo, tum quod sequimur iam rectius inde
perspiciemus, et unde queat res quaeque creari
155 et quo quaeque modo fiant opera sine divom.
159 Nam si de nilo fierent, ex omnibu' rebus
omne genus nasci posset, nil semine egeret.
e mare primum homines, e terra posset oriri
squamigerum genus et volucres erumpere caelo;
armenta atque aliae pecudes, genus omne ferarum,
incerto partu culta ac deserta tenerent.

Coepisset. 130 *tum* Flor. 25 and 31 Camb. p. m. Mar. for *tunc.* 141 *quemvis sufferre* Flor. 32 in margin, Heinsius in ms. notes, and Faber for *quemvis efferre.* [So perhaps Cic. epist. VIII 1 2 we should read *sermones suppressit*: *expressit* M.] Dion. Cat. distich. III 6 has *quemvis sufferre laborem,* perhaps taken from this. 155—158 Mar. Junt. and margin of Camb. have these vs. in right order, and *et* for *ut* in 157. Avancius *et*, and at end of his edition of Catull. 1502 has right order. *et* Pont. also.

161—164 are rightly thus punctuated by Lach. I find however from his proof sheets that until the final revision he had with Wak. put a stop after

nec fructus idem arboribus constare solerent,
sed mutarentur, ferre omnes omnia possent.
quippe, ubi non essent genitalia corpora cuique,
qui posset mater rebus consistere certa?
at nunc seminibus quia certis quaeque creantur,
inde enascitur atque oras in luminis exit,
materies ubi inest cuiusque et corpora prima;
atque hac re nequeunt ex omnibus omnia gigni,
quod certis in rebus inest secreta facultas.
praeterea cur vere rosam, frumenta calore,
vites autumno fundi suadente videmus,
si non, certa suo quia tempore semina rerum
cum confluxerunt, patefit quodcumque creatur,
dum tempestates adsunt et vivida tellus
tuto res teneras effert in luminis oras?
quod si de nilo fierent, subito exorerentur
incerto spatio atque alienis partibus anni,
quippe ubi nulla forent primordia quae genitali
concilio possent arceri tempore iniquo.
nec porro augendis rebus spatio foret usus
seminis ad coitum, si e nilo crescere possent;
nam fierent iuvenes subito ex infantibu' parvis
e terraque exorta repente arbusta salirent.
quorum nil fieri manifestum est, omnia quando
paulatim crescunt, ut par est, ...
. . . . semine certo
crescentesque genus servant; ut noscere possis
quicque sua de materia grandescere alique.
huc accedit uti sine certis imbribus anni
laetificos nequeat fetus submittere tellus
nec porro secreta cibo natura animantum
propagare genus possit vitamque tueri;

volucres and *armenta*, and none after *caelo*. Lamb. puts a colon after *pecudes* and alters *tenerent* to *teneret*. 168 *certa* A corr. Nicc. for *derta*. 176 *quia* Flor. 31 Camb. superscr. for *qui*. 175 *Vites*. *Uvas* Pont. 177 *creatur* A corr. Nicc. for *orcatu*. 185 *si e nilo*. *e nihilo si* Junt. Lamb. etc. not Mar.: so 291 *cum flumen*. *flumen cum* Lamb.; II 36 *si in plebeia*. *si plebeia in* Mon. Junt. and Lamb.: in all cases against mss. and the usage of Lucretius.

189 the homoeoteleuton has probably caused a v. of this kind to drop out: *tempore certo*, *Res quoniam crescunt omnes de s. c.* Lach. awkwardly *ut par est semine certo*

ut potius multis communia corpora rebus
multa putes esse, ut verbis elementa videmus,
quam sine principiis ullam rem existere posse.
denique cur homines tantos natura parare
non potuit, pedibus qui pontum per vada possent
transire et magnos manibus divellere montis
multaque vivendo vitalia vincere saecla,
si non, materies quia rebus reddita certast
gignundis e qua constat quid possit oriri?
nil igitur fieri de nilo posse fatendumst,
semine quando opus est rebus quo quaeque creatae
aeris in teneras possint proferrier auras.
postremo quoniam incultis praestare videmus
culta loca et manibus melioris reddere fetus,
esse videlicet in terris primordia rerum
quae nos fecundas vertentes vomere glebas
terraique solum subigentes cimus ad ortus.
quod si nulla forent, nostro sine quaeque labore
sponte sua multo fieri meliora videres.
  Huc accedit uti quicque in sua corpora rursum
dissoluat natura neque ad nilum interemat res.
nam siquid mortale *e* cunctis partibus esset,
ex oculis res quaeque repente erepta periret.
nulla vi foret usus enim quae partibus eius
discidium parere et nexus exsolvere posset.
quod nunc, aeterno quia constant semine quaeque,
donec vis obiit quae res diverberet ictu
aut intus penetret per inania dissoluatque,
nullius exitium patitur natura videri.
praeterea quaecumque vetustate amovet aetas,
si penitus peremit consumens materiem omnem,
unde animale genus generatim in lumina vitae
redducit Venus, aut redductum daedala tellus
unde alit atque auget generatim pabula praebens?
unde mare ingenuei fontes externaque longe

Crescere, resque genus. Crescendo Mar. Junt. Lamb. etc. 207 *possint* Pont. Ald. 1 Junt. for *possent*: a change which will often have to be made: mss. are more apt to put *possent* for *possint* than vice versa. 215 *quicque* Lamb. for *quicquid.* 217 *e* added by Nicc. 230 I follow the mss.: *mare,*

flumina suppeditant? unde aether sidera pascit?
omnia enim debet, mortali corpore quae sunt,
infinita aetas consumpse anteacta diesque.
quod si in eo spatio atque anteacta aetate fuere
e quibus haec rerum consistit summa refecta,
inmortali sunt natura praedita certe,
haut igitur possunt ad nilum quaeque reverti.
denique res omnis eadem vis causaque volgo
conficeret, nisi materies aeterna teneret,
inter se nexu minus aut magis indupedita;
tactus enim leti satis esset causa profecto,
quippe, ubi nulla forent aeterno corpore, quorum
contextum vis deberet dissolvere quaeque.
at nunc, inter se quia nexus principiorum
dissimiles constant aeternaque materies est,
incolumi remanent res corpore, dum satis acris
vis obeat pro textura cuiusque reperta.
haud igitur redit ad nilum res ulla, sed omnes
discidio redeunt in corpora materiai.
postremo pereunt imbres, ubi eos pater aether
in gremium matris terrai praecipitavit;
at nitidae surgunt fruges ramique virescunt
arboribus, crescunt ipsae fetuque gravantur;
hinc alitur porro nostrum genus atque ferarum,
hinc laetas urbes pueris florere videmus
frondiferasque novis avibus canere undique silvas;
hinc fessae pecudes pingui per pabula laeta
corpora deponunt et candens lacteus umor
uberibus manat distentis; hinc nova proles
artubus infirmis teneras lasciva per herbas
ludit lacte mero mentes perculsa novellas.
haud igitur penitus pereunt quaecumque videntur,
quando alid ex alio reficit natura nec ullam
rem gigni patitur nisi morte adiuta aliena.

ingenuei Lach. and Ed. in ed. 1. *externaque. extentaque* Lach. *longe. large* Bern. and Ed. in ed. 1. 240 *nexu* Mon. Junt. for *nexus*. Lamb. ed. 1 and 2 *nexas* (*nexus* ed. 1 is a misprint) and *indupedite;* ed. 3 *nexus...endopedita*. 257 *pingui* Iun. Philargyrius to Virg. geor. III 124 for *pinguis*, as Heyne there notices. 263 *alio* Nicc. for *allo*. 264 *adiuta* A corr. Nicc. for *adluta*.

Nunc age, res quoniam docui non posse creari
de nilo neque item genitas ad nil revocari,
nequa forte tamen coeptes diffidere dictis,
quod nequeunt oculis rerum primordia cerni,
accipe praeterea quae corpora tute necessest
confiteare esse in rebus nec posse videri.
principio venti vis verberat incita portus
ingentisque ruit navis et nubila differt,
interdum rapido percurrens turbine campos
arboribus magnis sternit montisque supremos
silvifragis vexat flabris: ita perfurit acri
cum fremitu saevitque minaci murmure ventus.
sunt igitur venti nimirum corpora caeca
quae mare, quae terras, quae denique nubila caeli
verrunt ac subito vexantia turbine raptant,
nec ratione fluunt alia stragemque propagant
et cum mollis aquae fertur natura repente
flumine abundanti, quam largis imbribus auget
montibus ex altis magnus decursus aquai
fragmina coniciens silvarum arbustaque tota,
nec validi possunt pontes venientis aquai
vim subitam tolerare: ita magno turbidus imbri
molibus incurrit validis cum viribus amnis:
dat sonitu magno stragem volvitque sub undis
grandia saxa: ruit qua quicquid fluctibus obstat.
sic igitur debent venti quoque flamina ferri,
quae veluti validum cum flumen procubuere
quamlibet in partem, trudunt res ante ruuntque
impetibus crebris, interdum vertice torto
corripiunt rapideque rotanti turbine portant.
quare etiam atque etiam sunt venti corpora caeca,

271 *portus* all Vat. Flor. 29 and 31 Flor. 30 corr. Camb. for *cortus*. *pontum* Mar. Politian in marg. of Flor. 29, Junt. and apparently Nicc. *cautes* Lach. which is very weak. 274 '*saevit, Marul.*' says Gifanius: and so Mar. corrects in Mon.; but Junt. has rightly *sternit*. 276 *ventus* Lach. for *pontus*. 282 *quam* Lach. for *quem*. *quod* Flor. 30 corr. Pont. Mar. Junt. 286 *turbidus* A corr. Nicc. for *turbibus*. 289 *quicquid* Ed. for *quidquid*: no further change is required: see notes 2: *ruitque ita quidquid* Lach. *ruitque aqua q*. Ed. formerly.

294 *rapide* Lach. for *rapidi* which Wak. absurdly retains. *rapidoque rotantia* Lamb. ed. 1 and 2 *rapidoque rotanti* ed. 3.

quandoquidem factis et moribus aemula magnis
amnibus inveniuntur, aperto corpore qui sunt.
tum porro varios rerum sentimus odores
nec tamen ad naris venientis cernimus umquam,
nec calidos aestus tuimur nec frigora quimus
usurpare oculis nec voces cernere suemus;
quae tamen omnia corporea constare necessest
natura, quoniam sensus inpellere possunt.
tangere enim et tangi, nisi corpus, nulla potest res.
denique fluctifrago suspensae in litore vestes
uvescunt, eaedem dispansae in sole serescunt.
at neque quo pacto persederit umor aquai
visumst nec rursum quo pacto fugerit aestu.
in parvas igitur partis dispergitur umor
quas oculi nulla possunt ratione videre.
quin etiam multis solis redeuntibus annis
anulus in digito subter tenuatur habendo,
stilicidi casus lapidem cavat, uncus aratri
ferreus occulte decrescit vomer in arvis,
strataque iam volgi pedibus detrita viarum
saxea conspicimus; tum portas propter aena
signa manus dextras ostendunt adtenuari
saepe salutantum tactu praeterque meantum.
haec igitur minui, cum sint detrita, videmus.
sed quae corpora decedant in tempore quoque,
invida praeclusit speciem natura videndi.
postremo quaecumque dies naturaque rebus
paulatim tribuit, moderatim crescere cogens,
nulla potest oculorum acies contenta tueri;
nec porro quaecumque aevo macieque senescunt,
nec, mare quae inpendent, vesco sale saxa peresa
quid quoque amittant in tempore cernere possis.
corporibus caecis igitur natura gerit res.
  Nec tamen undique corporea stipata tenentur
omnia natura; namque est in rebus inane.

304 *et*. *aut* Gellius v 15: but all mss. and Seneca Tertull. Nonius have *et*.

313: Isidor. Orig. xx 14 1 'Vomer ..de quo Lucretius *Uncus aratri Ferreus occulto decrescit vomer in arvis* Sumitque per detrimenta fulgorem' (not 'nitorem'). It is odd if the last words are Isidore's own: is a line of this kind lost, *Sumitque ipse suum per detrimenta nitorem?* 321 *speciem*. *spatium* Lach.: but see

quod tibi cognosse in multis erit utile rebus
nec sinet errantem dubitare et quaerere semper
de summa rerum et nostris diffidere dictis.
QUAPROPTER LOCUS EST INTACTUS INANE VACANSQUE
quod si non esset, nulla ratione moveri
res possent; namque officium quod corporis exstat,
officere atque obstare, id in omni tempore adesset
omnibus; haud igitur quicquam procedere posset,
principium quoniam cedendi nulla daret res.
at nunc per maria ac terras sublimaque caeli
multa modis multis varia ratione moveri
cernimus ante oculos, quae, si non esset inane,
non tam sollicito motu privata carerent
quam genita omnino nulla ratione fuissent,
undique materies quoniam stipata quiesset.
praeterea quamvis solidae res esse putentur,
hinc tamen esse licet raro cum corpore cernas.
in saxis ac speluncis permanat aquarum
liquidus umor et uberibus flent omnia guttis.
dissipat in corpus sese cibus omne animantum.
crescunt arbusta et fetus in tempore fundunt,
quod cibus in totas usque ab radicibus imis
per truncos ac per ramos diffunditur omnis.
inter saepta meant voces et clausa domorum
transvolitant, rigidum permanat frigus ad ossa,
quod nisi inania sint, qua possint corpora quaeque

notes 2: 'lege *videndo*' Bentl. 334 Bentl. says 'dele vers.'; and Lach. shews that sense and grammar prove him to be right. Spengel in the Muenchn. Gel. Anz. and others do not mend the matter by placing it after 345.

347 *licet* Nicc. for *liceret*. 349 *flent* Nicc. *fient* AB: 386 *fiat. flat* AB: 372 *alunt* AB: 449 *civent* AB: 580 *civeant* AB: this confusion of *l* and *i* is perpetual. In the small Roman capital, of the Medicean of Virgil for instance, in which some ancestor of our mss. must have been written, these letters are often undistinguishable. 356 *possint* Ed. for *possent*: by changing the punctuation of 357 I have made the sentence quite plain. Madvig emend. Livianae p. 302 n. '*possem possim, posset possit* perpetuo errore permutantur', and p. 550 '*possent.* scribendum *possint.* non aberratur fere, ut saepe dixi, nisi ubi una littera formae distant; *esset* pro *sit* scriptum non reperias'. See 207; and below 593 597 and 645, in all which places I have written *possint* for *possent*. Whether with Pont. Junt. Lamb. Lach. etc. you punctuate *Quod n. i. sint, q. possent c. q. Transire h. u. f. r. v.*, or with Gif. Creech Wak. etc. *Quod, n. i. s. q. p. c. q. Transire, h. u. f. r. v.*, in either case you get hardly grammar or sense: in 357 B and

transire? haud ulla fieri ratione videres.
denique cur alias aliis praestare videmus
pondere res rebus nilo maiore figura?
nam si tantundemst in lanae glomere quantum
corporis in plumbo est, tantundem pendere par est,
corporis officiumst quoniam premere omnia deorsum,
contra autem natura manet sine pondere inanis.
ergo quod magnumst aeque leviusque videtur,
nimirum plus esse sibi declarat inanis;
at contra gravius plus in se corporis esse
dedicat et multo vacui minus intus habere.
est igitur nimirum id quod ratione sagaci
quaerimus, admixtum rebus, quod inane vocamus.
Illud in his rebus ne te deducere vero
possit, quod quidam fingunt, praecurrere cogor.
cedere squamigeris latices nitentibus aiunt
et liquidas aperire vias, quia post loca pisces
linquant, quo possint cedentes confluere undae;
sic alias quoque res inter se posse moveri
et mutare locum, quamvis sint omnia plena.
scilicet id falsa totum ratione receptumst.
nam quo squamigeri poterunt procedere tandem,
ni spatium dederint latices? concedere porro
quo poterunt undae, cum pisces ire nequibunt?
aut igitur motu privandumst corpora quaeque
aut esse admixtum dicundumst rebus inane
unde initum primum capiat res quaeque movendi.
postremo duo de concursu corpora lata
si cita dissiliant, nempe aer omne necessest,
inter corpora quod fiat, possidat inane.
is porro quamvis circum celerantibus auris
confluat, haud poterit tamen uno tempore totum
compleri spatium; nam primum quemque necessest
occupet ille locum, deinde omnia possideantur.

Gott. for *fieri* have *valerent* which appears to come from ULLA twice written and FIEREI: yet Bernays in 356 reads *qua corpora quaeque valerent* for *qua possent c. q.* 366 *At* Flor. 30 corr. (cod. Nicc.) and Flor. 31 for *aut.* 367 *vacui minus* Pont. Junt. Lamb. etc. for *vacuim minus* B. and Gott. *vacuum* Wak. Lach. etc. retain with A, the Ital. and Camb. mss. 384 *concursu* Gott. p. m. Flor. 30 corr. 31, Pont. Mar. Junt. for *concurso.* 389 *quemque. quenque* Pont.

quod si forte aliquis, cum corpora dissiluere,
tum putat id fieri quia se condenseat aer,
errat; nam vacuum tum fit quod non fuit ante
et repletur item vacuum quod constitit ante,
nec tali ratione potest denserier aer,
nec, si iam posset, sine inani posset, opinor,
ipse in se trahere et partis conducere in unum.
  Quapropter, quamvis causando multa moreris,
esse in rebus inane tamen fateare necessest.
multaque praeterea tibi possum commemorando
argumenta fidem dictis conradere nostris.
verum animo satis haec vestigia parva sagaci
sunt per quae possis cognoscere cetera tute.
namque canes ut montivagae persaepe ferai
naribus inveniunt intectas fronde quietes,
cum semel institerunt vestigia certa viai,
sic alid ex alio per te tute ipse videre
talibus in rebus poteris caecasque latebras
insinuare omnis et verum protrahere inde.
quod si pigraris paulumve recesseris ab re,
hoc tibi de plano possum promittere, Memmi:
usque adeo largos haustus e fontibu' magnis
lingua meo suavis diti de pectore fundet,
ut verear ne tarda prius per membra senectus
serpat et in nobis vitai claustra resolvat,
quam tibi de quavis una re versibus omnis
argumentorum sit copia missa per auris.
  Sed nunc ut repetam coeptum pertexere dictis,
omnis ut est igitur per se natura duabus
constitit in rebus; nam corpora sunt et inane,
haec in quo sita sunt et qua diversa moventur.
corpus enim per se communis dedicat esse
sensus; cui nisi prima fides fundata valebit,
haut erit occultis de rebus quo referentes

Mar. Ald. 1 Junt. for *quisque*. 391 Creech supposes some vss. to be lost after this v. 395 *denserier* A corr. Flor. 31 for *condenserier*. 404 *ferai* Nicc. Flor. 31 Camb. etc. for *ferare*. *ferarum* A corr. 411 *de plano* Flor. 31 Mar. Junt. for *deptano*. 412 *magnis* A corr. Nicc. all the Ital. Camb. etc. for *magnes* of A p. m. *amnes* B and Gott. and also same A corr.; whence Bentl. and Bern. read *largis haustos e. f. amnis*, making 3 changes. *magneis* Heins. in ms.

confirmare animi quicquam ratione queamus.
tum porro locus ac spatium, quod inane vocamus,
si nullum foret, haut usquam sita corpora possent
esse neque omnino quoquam diversa meare;
id quod iam supera tibi paulo ostendimus ante.
praeterea nil est quod possis dicere ab omni
corpore seiunctum secretumque esse ab inani,
quod quasi tertia sit numero natura reperta.
nam quodcumque erit, esse aliquid debebit id ipsum;
435 cui si tactus erit quamvis levis exiguusque,
434 augmine vel grandi vel parvo denique, dum sit,
corporis augebit numerum summamque sequetur.
sin intactile erit, nulla de parte quod ullam
rem prohibere queat per se transire meantem,
scilicet hoc id erit, vacuum quod inane vocamus.
praeterea per se quodcumque erit, aut faciet quid
aut aliis fungi debebit agentibus ipsum
aut erit, ut possunt in eo res esse gerique.
at facere et fungi sine corpore nulla potest res
nec praebere locum porro nisi inane vacansque.
ergo praeter inane et corpora tertia per se
nulla potest rerum in numero natura relinqui,
nec quae sub sensus cadat ullo tempore nostros
nec ratione animi quam quisquam possit apisci.
  Nam quaecumque cluent, aut his coniuncta duabus
rebus ea invenies aut horum eventa videbis.
coniunctum est id quod nusquam sine permitiali
discidio potis est seiungi seque gregari,
pondus uti saxist, calor ignis, liquor aquai.
TACTUS CORPORIBUS CUNCTIS INTACTUS INANI

notes. 428 *quoquam. quaquam* Ven. Ald. 1 Lamb. etc.: but see notes 2. 435 434 rightly transposed by Lach.: centuries before him Flor. 32 in margin had this note, 'videtur proponere tantum de corpore, dicendo *Augmine vel* etc.; non enim conveniunt illa nisi corpori. cum tamen de inani quoque intellexisse appareat, ex illo *Sin intactile erit* etc. advertendum diligentius'. Then at bottom 'si legatur *Nam quodcumque...Cui si tactus...Augmine vel...Corporis*...patebit sermo'. 442 *possunt. possint* Flor. 31 Camb. etc. I now retain the ms. reading: see notes 2 to this v. and II 901 *ita ut debent.* 451 *nusquam. nunquam* Ver. Ven. and eds. before Lach. wrongly: comp. Aen. V 852 *clavumque...Nusquam amittebat*, and Conington there. *permitiali* AB rightly: see notes 2. *perniciali* vulg. and Lach. 453 *saxist* Lach. *saxi est* Wak. for *saxis*. 454 Lach. has proved to be spurious, as a nomin. *intactus*

servitium contra paupertas divitiaeque,
libertas bellum concordia, cetera quorum
adventu manet incolumis natura abituque,
haec soliti sumus, ut par est, eventa vocare.
tempus item per se non est, sed rebus ab ipsis
consequitur sensus, transactum quid sit in aevo,
tum quae res instet, quid porro deinde sequatur.
nec per se quemquam tempus sentire fatendumst
semotum ab rerum motu placidaque quiete.
denique Tyndaridem raptam belloque subactas
Troiiugenas gentis cum dicunt esse, videndumst
ne forte haec per se cogant nos esse fateri,
quando ea saecla hominum, quorum haec eventa fuerunt,
inrevocabilis abstulerit iam praeterita aetas;
namque aliut Teucris, aliut regionibus ipsis
eventum dici poterit quodcumque erit actum.
denique materies si rerum nulla fuisset
nec locus ac spatium, res in quo quaeque geruntur,
numquam Tyndaridis formae conflatus amore
ignis, Alexandri Phrygio sub pectore gliscens,
clara accendisset saevi certamina belli,
nec clam durateus Troiianis Pergama partu
inflammasset equos nocturno Graiiugenarum;
perspicere ut possis res gestas funditus omnis
non ita uti corpus per se constare neque esse,
nec ratione cluere eadem qua constet inane,
sed magis ut merito possis eventa vocare
corporis atque loci, res in quo quaeque gerantur.
   Corpora sunt porro partim primordia rerum,

cannot exist, and the datives are not consistent with the genitives of 453: Lamb. reads *saxis, calor, ignibu', liquor aquai*: but Lucr. never uses a dat. in *ai*. 455 *divitiae* A corr. Nicc. for *diviae*. 458 *eventa* the same for *evento*. 465 *Troiiugenas*, 476 *Troiianis*, 477 *Graiiugenarum* Lach. with A (477 *Graliug.* A): see Quintil. I 4 11 'sciat etiam Ciceroni placuisse, *aiio Maiiam*que geminata *i* scribere'; and Priscian inst. VII 19, who rightly says that in the oldest writings you find *eiius Pompeiius Vulteiius Gaiius* and the like: often so in extant inscriptions: see too Ribbeck prol. Verg. p. 138, Studemund Rhein. mus. XXI p. 588, and Corssen I p. 18. 467 *fuerunt* Gott. rightly for *fuerit* of AB. *fuere* Nicc. Flor. 31 Camb. etc. 469 *Teucris* Ed. for *terris*. *per sest* Lach. *saeclis* Bern. *rebus* Lamb. *terris* and *legionibus* Wak. 480 *cluere* B corr. Flor. 30 corr. Camb. for *luere*.

partim concilio quae constant principiorum.
sed quae sunt rerum primordia, nulla potest vis
stinguere; nam solido vincunt ea corpore demum.
etsi difficile esse videtur credere quicquam
in rebus solido reperiri corpore posse.
transit enim fulmen caeli per saepta domorum,
clamor ut ac voces; ferrum candescit in igni
dissiliuntque fero ferventia saxa vapore;
tum labefactatus rigor auri solvitur aestu;
tum glacies aeris flamma devicta liquescit;
permanat calor argentum penetraleque frigus,
quando utrumque manu retinentes pocula rite
sensimus infuso lympharum rore superne.
usque adeo in rebus solidi nil esse videtur.
sed quia vera tamen ratio naturaque rerum
cogit, ades, paucis dum versibus expediamus
esse ea quae solido atque aeterno corpore constent,
semina quae rerum primordiaque esse docemus,
unde omnis rerum nunc constet summa creata.
  Principio quoniam duplex natura duarum
dissimilis rerum longe constare repertast,
corporis atque loci, res in quo quaeque geruntur,
esse utramque sibi per se puramque necessest.
nam quacumque vacat spatium, quod inane vocamus,
corpus ea non est; qua porro cumque tenet se
corpus, ea vacuum nequaquam constat inane.
sunt igitur solida ac sine inani corpora prima.
praeterea quoniam genitis in rebus inanest,
materiem circum solidam constare necessest,
nec res ulla potest vera ratione probari
corpore inane suo celare atque intus habere,
si non, quod cohibet, solidum constare relinquas.
id porro nil esse potest nisi materiai

constet A Nicc. *constat* B Gott. 484 *quae* B corr. Camb. corr. for *qua*. 486 *Stinguere* AB. *Stringere* A corr. Nicc. and all later mss. and eds. before Lach.: but Flor. 30 has *Stinguere* in marg. 489 *fulmen* A corr. B corr. Nicc. corr. for *flumen*. Lach. strangely reads *caelum, p. s. domorum Cl. it*, as if the air, like a stone wall, were a good instance of a very solid thing: all mss. have *caeli* and *ut*. *ac* Avanc. first for *ad*. 491 *ferventia* Mar. Junt. and Lamb. ed. 1 for *fer-venti*. 492 *tum* Brix. Ver. Ven. for *cum*. 500 *constent* B corr. for *con-*

concilium, quod inane queat rerum cohibere.
materies igitur, solido quae corpore constat,
esse aeterna potest, cum cetera dissoluantur.
tum porró si nil esset quod inane vocaret,
omne foret solidum; nisi contra corpora certa
essent quae loca complerent quaecumque tenerent,
omne quod est, spatium vacuum constaret inane.
alternis igitur nimirum corpus inani
distinctum*st*, quoniam nec plenum naviter extat
nec porro vacuum. sunt ergo corpora certa
quae spatium pleno possint distinguere inane.
haec neque dissolui plagis extrinsecus icta
possunt nec porro penitus penetrata retexi
nec ratione queunt alia temptata labare;
id quod iam supra tibi paulo ostendimus ante.
nam neque conlidi sine inani posse videtur
quicquam nec frangi nec findi in bina secando
nec capere umorem neque item manabile frigus
nec penetralem ignem, quibus omnia conficiuntur.
et quo quaeque magis cohibet res intus inane,
tam magis his rebus penitus temptata labascit.
ergo si solida ac sine inani corpora prima
sunt ita uti docui, sint haec aeterna necessest.
praeterea nisi materies aeterna fuisset,
antehac ad nilum penitus res quaeque redissent
de niloque renata forent quaecumque videmus.
at quoniam supra docui nil posse creari
de nilo neque quod genitum est ad nil revocari,
esse inmortali primordia corpore debent,
dissolui quo quaeque supremo tempore possint,
materies ut subpeditet rebus reparandis.

stet. 504 *rerum longe.* 'leg. *longe rerum*' Bentl. 517 *inane queat rerum* seems quite right. *inane in rebu' queat* Lach. *tectum* Mar. Ald. 1 Junt. Lamb. ed. 1 and 2, *verum* Bern. for *rerum.* 520 *esset* A corr. Avanc. for *est. siquidem nil est* Nicc. *vocaret* is the old form: see notes 2. *vacaret* Lach. 525 *Distinctumst, quoniam* Lamb. most rightly for *Distinctum quoniam* which Lach. retains beginning the apodosis with *sunt ergo* in 526. Ald. 1 and Junt. seem to take *distinctum* for *distinctum est* and to understand the passage rightly. 527 *pleno* Mar. Ald. 1 and Junt. for *poena*, and *inane* for *inani.* 533 *findi* Flor. 31 Mon. Ver. Ven. for *fundi.* 542 *que renata* Lamb. for *quaeranta.*

sunt igitur solida primordia simplicitate
nec ratione queunt alia servata per aevom
ex infinito iam tempore res reparare.
  Denique si nullam finem natura parasset
frangendis rebus, iam corpora materiai
usque redacta forent aevo frangente priore,
ut nil ex illis a certo tempore posset
conceptum summum aetatis pervadere *ad auctum.*
nam quidvis citius dissolvi posse videmus
quam rursus refici; quapropter longa diei
infinita aetas anteacti temporis omnis
quod fregisset adhuc disturbans dissoluensque,
numquam relicuo reparari tempore posset.
at nunc nimirum frangendi reddita finis
certa manet, quoniam refici rem quamque *vi*demus
et finita simul generatim tempora rebus
stare, quibus possint aevi contingere florem.
huc accedit uti, solidissima materiai
corpora cum constant, possit tamen, omnia, reddi,

551—627: Junt. puts 577—583 after 627, and 551—564 after 583. At the end of his edition Candidus says 'Marulli nos hoc loco ordinem, atque item alibi in plerisque, ubi immutatum quid offenderis, secutos esse'; and so Marullus himself in the cod. Victor.: but he appears from Flor. 30 to have got the suggestion from Niccoli himself. The learned annotator of Flor. 32 says in the margin to 550 that some put 551—564 after 576, and adds 'verum Marullo parum referre videtur quomodo legatur', shewing again that there were different traditions about Marullus. Lamb. places only 577—583 after 627. All these transpositions are utterly wrong, though Candidus says of Marullus 'quem profecto, si ad amussim rem quanque examinabis, neutiquam (sic opinor) repudiaveris'. Sauppe, Christ and others likewise transpose in various ways these much-tortured vss.: the misapprehension of 599—634 is at the bottom of such causeless changes. 553 *forent* B corr. Nicc. for *fovent.* 555 *ad auctum* Ed. These words came at the end of page 23 of the archetype from which all mss. are derived, and therefore were at the outside margin and, as has happened in so many cases, were torn away by some accident. Some one then filled up the verse with *finis* which occurs three times at the end of a line in the next thirty verses. Lach. keeps *finis* and for *summum* reads *summa* which he thus awkwardly explains, '*summa*, hoc est universo vivendi actu, *aetatis pervadere fines*, per omne vitae spatium vadere'. *summum...florem* Mar. Junt. Lamb. ed. 1 and 2, Creech etc. which Lach. proves could only mean 'pass through' not 'arrive at the flower'. *summum...finem* Flor. 30 corr. Ver. Ven. Lamb. ed. 3, Wak. etc. This is doubly wrong, as *finis* in Lucretius is always feminine. 562 *quamque videmus* B corr. Nicc. for *quamque demus.* 566 *possit* Ed. for *possint*, a corruption which *constant* and *omnia* almost inevitably caused. [Sauppe I am

mollia quae fiunt, aer aqua terra vapores,
quo pacto fiant et qua vi quaeque gerantur,
admixtum quoniam semel est in rebus inane.
at contra si mollia sint primordia rerum,
unde queant validi silices ferrumque creari
non poterit ratio reddi; nam funditus omnis
principio fundamenti natura carebit.
sunt igitur solida pollentia simplicitate
quorum condenso magis omnia conciliatu
artari possunt validasque ostendere viris.

Porro si nullast frangendis reddita finis
corporibus, tamen ex aeterno tempore quaeque
nunc etiam superare necessest corpora rebus,
quae nondum clueant ullo temptata periclo.
at quoniam fragili natura praedita constant,
discrepat aeternum tempus potuisse manere
innumerabilibus plagis vexata per aevom.
denique iam quoniam generatim reddita finis
crescendi rebus constat vitamque tenendi,
et quid quaeque queant per foedera naturai,
quid porro nequeant, sancitum quandoquidem extat,
nec commutatur quicquam, quin omnia constant
usque adeo, variae volucres ut in ordine cunctae
ostendant maculas generalis corpore inesse,
inmutabili' materiae quoque corpus habere
debent nimirum. nam si primordia rerum
commutari aliqua possint ratione revicta,
incertum quoque iam constet quid possit oriri,
quid nequeat, finita potestas denique cuique
quanam sit ratione atque alte terminus haerens,

glad to see has fallen on the same conj. independently of me, as he makes no mention even of my ed. of 1860.] Lach. puts 568 after 585, where it is wholly out of place; Bentl. ejects it; Mar. and Junt. read *fiunt* and *geruntur*; and *fiant* in 567. Lamb. Creech etc. *cumque gerantur*: all corrupting the text and making Lucretius assert the absurd truism that all things which do become soft can become soft. 578 *quaeque. quaedam* Lamb. and Lach. 585 *crescendi* Ver. Ven. for *crescendis*. 588 *commutatur* B corr. Nicc. for *comitatur*. *constant. constent* Lach. 591 *inmutabili'* Lach. first for *inmutabiles*. *inmutabile* Flor. 31 Flor. 30 corr. vulgo absurdly. 593 and 597 *possint* Ed. for *possent*; which *constet* in 594 proves to be necessary: see 356 and note there: here too *possint* easily becomes *possent*, though *constet* does not pass into *constaret* so readily.

nec totiens possint generatim saecla referre
naturam mores victum motusque parentum.
Tum porro quoniam est extremum quodque cacumen

*

corporis illius quod nostri cernere sensus
iam nequeunt: id nimirum sine partibus extat
et minima constat natura nec fuit umquam
per se secretum neque posthac esse valebit,
alterius quoniamst ipsum pars, primaque et una
inde aliae atque aliae similes ex ordine partes
agmine condenso naturam corporis explent,
quae quoniam per se nequeunt constare, necessest
haerere unde queant nulla ratione revelli.
sunt igitur solida primordia simplicitate
quae minimis stipata cohaerent partibus arte,
non ex illarum conventu conciliata,
sed magis aeterna pollentia simplicitate,
unde neque avelli quicquam neque deminui iam
concedit natura reservans semina rebus.
praeterea nisi erit minimum, parvissima quaeque
corpora constabunt ex partibus infinitis,
quippe ubi dimidiae partis pars semper habebit
dimidiam partem nec res praefiniet ulla.
ergo rerum inter summam minimamque quid escit?
nil erit ut distet; nam quamvis funditus omnis
summa sit infinita, tamen, parvissima quae sunt,
ex infinitis constabunt partibus aeque.
quod quoniam ratio reclamat vera negatque

599—**634**: this passage which is difficult, but not corrupt, has been sadly mutilated by all editors from Lambinus to Lachmann and Bernays, who all in different ways force on Lucretius a succession of absurd and self-contradictory assertions. There seems after 599 to be a hiatus such as this *Corporibus, quod iam nobis minimum esse videtur, Debet item ratione pari minimum esse cacumen Corporis* cet.: besides this *illarum* for *illorum* in 611 is the sole change I have made, two or three slight and obvious errors of AB having been corrected in the later mss. or older editions: 599 for *quoniam* Lach. *quianam*, Bern. *quod iam*: 600 for *illius* Lach. and Bern. *ullius*. Lamb. *quoniam ext. quoiusque c. Cor. est aliquod*: 611 Lach. *ullorum* after Ald. 1 Junt. Lamb. etc.: 628 and 631 Lamb. followed by all subsequent editors perversely reads *ni* for *si*, *multis* for *nullis*. 608 *nulla* Flor. 31 Ver. Ven. etc. for *ulla*. *ut nequeant ulla* B corr. which may be right.

613 *iam* Flor. 31 Ver. Ven. etc. for *tam*. 626 *constent* Ald. Junt. for *con-*

credere posse animum, victus fateare necessest
esse ea quae nullis iam praedita partibus extent
et minima constent natura. quae quoniam sunt,
illa quoque esse tibi solida atque aeterna fatendum.
denique si minimas in partis cuncta resolvi
cogere consuesset rerum natura creatrix,
iam nil ex illis eadem reparare valeret
propterea quia, quae nullis sunt partibus aucta,
non possunt ea quae debet genitalis habere
materies, varios conexus pondera plagas
concursus motus, per quae res quaeque geruntur.
  Quapropter qui materiem rerum esse putarunt
ignem atque ex igni summam consistere solo,
magno opere a vera lapsi ratione videntur.
Heraclitus init quorum dux proelia primus,
clarus *ob* obscuram linguam magis inter inanis
quamde gravis inter Graios qui vera requirunt.
omnia enim stolidi magis admirantur amantque,
inversis quae sub verbis latitantia cernunt,
veraque constituunt quae belle tangere possunt
auris et lepido quae sunt fucata sonore.
  Nam cur tam variae res possint esse requiro,
ex uno si sunt igni puroque creatae;
nil prodesset enim calidum denserier ignem
nec rarefieri, si partes ignis eandem
naturam quam totus habet super ignis haberent.
acrior ardor enim conductis partibus esset,
languidior porro disiectis *dis*que supatis:
amplius hoc fieri nil est quod posse rearis
talibus in causis, nedum variantia rerum
tanta queat densis rarisque ex ignibus esse.
id quoque, si faciant admixtum rebus inane,
denseri poterunt ignes rarique relinqui.
sed quia multa sibi cernunt contraria nasci

stant. 634 *quae res* Mar. Junt. for *quas res.* 639 *ob* added by Festus.
645 *cur possint esse requiro,...si sunt* Ed. for *cur possent? requiro* etc.: comp. above 356 593 and 597. 646 *uno* B corr. Turnebus Lamb. ed. 3, Lach. for *uro.* *vero* A corr. Nicc. Flor. 31 Camb. Vat. Lamb. ed. 1 and 2, Creech. 649 *haberent* Nicc. for *haberet* A, *habere* B Gott. 651 *disiectis disque* A corr. Flor. 30 corr. for *disiectisque.* 657 *nasci* Ed. for *muse* A, *mu* B Gott. This word

et fugitant in rebus inane relinquere purum,
ardua dum metuunt, amittunt vera viai,
nec rursum cernunt exempto rebus inani
omnia denseri fierique ex omnibus unum
corpus, nil ab se quod possit mittere raptim;
aestifer ignis uti lumen iacit atque vaporem,
ut videas non e stipatis partibus esse.
quod si forte alia credunt ratione potesse
ignis in coetu stingui mutareque corpus,
scilicet ex nulla facere id si parte reparcent,
occidet ad nilum nimirum funditus ardor
omnis et *e* nilo fient quaecumque creantur.
nam quodcumque suis mutatum finibus exit,
continuo hoc mors est illius quod fuit ante.
proinde aliquit superare necesse est incolume ollis,
ne tibi res redeant ad nilum funditus omnes
de niloque renata vigescat copia rerum.
nunc igitur quoniam certissima corpora quaedam
sunt quae conservant naturam semper eandem,
quorum abitu aut aditu mutatoque ordine mutant
naturam res et convertunt corpora sese,
scire licet non esse haec ignea corpora rerum.
nil referret enim quaedam decedere abire,
atque alia adtribui, mutarique ordine quaedam,
si tamen ardoris naturam cuncta tenerent;

was the last in p. 27 of the archetype and therefore on the outside margin, and as in many other cases had become partly illegible. *mussant* Flor. 31 Camb. Pont. Lamb. ed. 2 and 3, etc. without sense. *multi* Mar. Junt. Lamb. ed. 1, etc. *inesse* Flor. 30 corr. Ver. Ven. Ald. 1 Candidus at end of Junt. *Memmi* Heins. in ms. notes. '*amusoe* i.e. *ἄμουσοι*' Is. Voss. in ms. notes. *adesse* Lach. *amussim* Bern. 'illud Lucretio Bernaysius restituens cedet hodie nisi fallor H. Munroni *nasci* emendanti' Ritschl opusc. II p. 272. 659 *vera viai* A corr. for *ver aula.* 660 *inani* Flor. 30 corr. Mar. Junt. for *inane.* 662 *raptim* Pont. Avanc. for *raptis.* 'quidam *raptim* agnoscunt. Marullus *natum*' Candidus at end of Junt. and so Flor. 30 corr. and Mar. in cod. Vict. 665 *alia* Lach. rightly for *mia. ulla* Mar. Ald. 1 Junt. etc. *una* Nicc. etc. 666 *coetu stingui* Pont. Turneb. Lamb. ed. 2 and 3, etc. for *coetus stingui. mutare* Mar. Junt. for *musare.* Ver. Ven. Mar. Ald. 1 Lamb. ed. 1 have absurdly *in coetus stringi massareque corpus*; and Flor. 31 Camb. *mussare.* 668 *funditus* B corr. for *funditur. ardor* A corr. Nicc. for *arbor.* 674 *vigescat* Heins. in notes and Lach. for *vivescat*: comp. 757. *virescat* Nicc. vulg. 680 *decedere* Lamb. Lach. etc. for *descendere. discedere* A corr. Mar. Junt. etc. 681 *alia* Mar. Lamb. most rightly for *alio*

ignis enim foret omnimodis quodcumque crearent.
verum, ut opinor, itast: sunt quaedam corpora quorum
concursus motus ordo positura figurae
efficiunt ignis, mutatoque ordine mutant
naturam neque sunt igni simulata neque ulli
praeterea rei quae corpora mittere possit
sensibus et nostros adiectu tangere tactus.
Dicere porro ignem res omnis esse neque ullam
rem veram in numero rerum constare nisi ignem,
quod facit hic idem, perdelirum esse videtur.
nam contra sensus ab sensibus ipse repugnat
et labefactat eos unde omnia credita pendent,
unde hic cognitus est ipsi quem nominat ignem;
credit enim sensus ignem cognoscere vere,
cetera non credit, quae nilo clara minus sunt.
quod mihi cum vanum tum delirum esse videtur;
quo referemus enim? quid nobis certius ipsis
sensibus esse potest, qui vera ac falsa notemus?
praeterea quare quisquam magis omnia tollat
et velit ardoris naturam linquere solam,
quam neget esse ignis, *quidvis* tamen esse relinquat?
aequa videtur enim dementia dicere utrumque.
Quapropter qui materiem rerum esse putarunt
ignem atque ex igni summam consistere posse,
et qui principium gignundis aera rebus
constituere, aut umorem quicumque putarunt
fingere res ipsum per se, terramve creare
omnia et in rerum naturas vertier omnis,
magno opere a vero longe derrasse videntur.
adde etiam qui conduplicant primordia rerum
aera iungentes igni terramque liquori,
et qui quattuor ex rebus posse omnia rentur
ex igni terra atque anima procrescere et imbri.
quorum Acragantinus cum primis Empedocles est,

which Lach. retains. Candidus at end of Junt. '*alio* pro *alii* positum. sunt qui *alia* legunt', i.e. Mar. 683 *crearent* Lamb. first for *crearet.* 690 *ignem* B corr. for *iq. nem.* 703 *quidvis* Lach. *summam* Nicc. and all before Lach. AB Gott. omit the word, which must be uncertain. 708 *putarunt* Nicc. B corr. for *putantur* B, A corr., *putant* A p. m. 710 *vertier* B corr. Nicc. for *verti.*

711 *longe derrasse* Vat. 3275, and unless I err 1136 Othob., for *longi derrasse* of

insula quem triquetris terrarum gessit in oris,
quam fluitans circum magnis anfractibus aequor
Ionium glaucis aspargit virus ab undis,
angustoque fretu rapidum mare dividit undis
Italiae terrarum oras a finibus eius.
hic est vasta Charybdis et hic Aetnaea minantur
murmura flammarum rursum se colligere iras,
faucibus eruptos iterum vis ut vomat ignis
ad caelumque ferat flammai fulgura rursum.
quae cum magna modis multis miranda videtur
gentibus humanis regio visendaque fertur,
rebus opima bonis, multa munita virum vi,
nil tamen hoc habuisse viro praeclarius in se
nec sanctum magis et mirum carumque videtur.
carmina quin etiam divini pectoris eius
vociferantur et exponunt praeclara reperta,
ut vix humana videatur stirpe creatus.
  Hic tamen et supra quos diximus inferiores
partibus egregie multis multoque minores,
quamquam multa bene ac divinitus invenientes
ex adyto tamquam cordis responsa dedere
sanctius et multo certa ratione magis quam
Pythia quae tripodi a Phoebi lauroque profatur,
principiis tamen in rerum fecere ruinas
et graviter magni magno cecidere ibi casu;
primum quod motus exempto rebus inani
constituunt, et res mollis rarasque relinquont,
aera solem ignem terras animalia frugis,

B Gott. A corr. *longi errasse* A p. m. *longeque errasse* Nicc. etc. 720 *undis*. *undans* Lach. *almae* Bern., without cause. Priscian I 35 confirms *undis*. 721 *Italiae* Nicc. for *Haeliae*. *Haeoliae* A corr. *Aeoliae* Heins. in ms. notes and Is. Vossius who says in ms. notes 'mss. habent *Haeoliae* vel *Aeoliae*. Puto olim sic dictam eam partem Italiae quam inhabitavit Jocastes Aeoli filius qui ad fretum Siculum habitabat: vid: Diodorum lib. 5. [ch. 8] G. V.' Thus Preiger and Lachmann's doubt is solved. Haverc. and Wak. also adopt this reading of Gerard father of Is. Vossius. 724 *vis ut vomat* Lamb. ed. 3 for *vis ut omniat*. *ut vis evomat* ed. 1 and 2 after Mar. Ald. 1 Junt. etc. 725 Heins. in ms. notes 'leg. *sursum*', to avoid the repetition of *rursum*. 737 *adyto* Nicc. for *adito*. 739 *profatur* A corr. Nicc. for *prosatur*. 741 *casu* A corr. Nicc. for *causa*.

744 *frugis* AB Flor. 31 etc. not Nicc.: so IV 577 and 992 *vocis* AB. *fruges* Lach. and l. l. *voces*: he says '[membranas] quamvis consentientes imitari ausus non

nec tamen admiscent in eorum corpus inane;
deinde quod omnino finem non esse secandis
corporibus faciunt neque pausam stare fragori
nec prorsum in rebus minimum consistere qui*cquam;*
cum videamus id extremum cuiusque cacumen
esse quod ad sensus nostros minimum esse videtur,
conicere ut possis ex hoc, quae cernere non quis
extremum quod habent, minimum consistere *in illis.*
huc accedit item, quoniam primordia rerum
mollia constituunt, quae nos nativa videmus
esse et mortali cum corpore funditus, utqui
debeat ad nilum iam rerum summa reverti
de niloque renata vigescere copia rerum;
quorum utrumque quid a vero iam distet habe*bis*.
deinde inimica modis multis sunt atque vene*no*
ipsa sibi inter se; quare aut congressa peribunt
aut ita diffugient ut tempestate coacta
fulmina diffugere atque imbris ventosque videmus.
  Denique quattuor ex rebus si cuncta creantur
atque in eas rursum res omnia dissoluuntur,
qui magis illa queunt rerum primordia dici
quam contra res illorum retroque putari?
alternis gignuntur enim mutantque colorem
et totam inter se naturam tempore ab omni.
sin ita forte putas ignis terraeque coire

sum hoc loco, ubi habent *frugis*, neque in IV 577 991 1000, ubi *vocis*; quamquam apud Nonium p. 149 16 e Varrone scriptum est *pacis*, et Manilii exemplaria in III 446 habent *lucis*'. But Varro de ling. Lat. IX 76 observes '*frugi* rectus est natura *frux*, at secundum consuetudinem dicimus ut *haec avis, haec ovis*, sic *haec frugis*'. I have no doubt then that the accus. plur. *frugis* and *vocis* come from Lucr. as well as *religionis* and the like; and that an abl. *frugi* was possible. Augustus in the monum. Ancyr. III 2 has *consulis* acc. plur. 747 *faciunt* Flor. 31 Camb. for *faciṗnt.* 748 *quicquam* Mar. Ald. 1 and Junt. for *qui. quire* Flor. 31 Camb. Vat. 1136 Othob. which may be right. 752 *in illis* I have added; and these must I think be the actual words of the poet: see Camb. Journ. of phil. I p. 29. *prorsum* Lach. who quite misunderstands the argument. *rebus* Nicc. and all before Lach. 755 *utqui* of mss. is quite right: see notes 2. Lach. reads 753 *utei* for *item*, and here *funditus usque.* 758 *habebis* A corr. Nicc. etc. for *habes. habebas* Lamb. vulg. wrongly. 759 *veneno* Wak. Lach. for *vene. venena* Flor. 31 Camb. vulgo: this l. ended p. 31 of the lost archetype; and therefore these four mutilated endings of verses were on the outer margin. 767 *Alternis* A corr. for *Aternis.* 769 = 762, repeated without mean-

corpus et aerias auras roremque liquoris,
nil in concilio naturam ut mutet eorum,
nulla tibi ex illis poterit res esse creata,
non animans, non exanimo cum corpore, ut arbos:
quippe suam quicque in coetu variantis acervi
naturam ostendet mixtusque videbitur aer
cum terra simul atque ardor cum rore manere.
at primordia gignundis in rebus oportet
naturam clandestinam caecamque adhibere,
emineat nequid quod contra pugnet et obstet
quominus esse queat proprie quodcumque creatur.
  Quin etiam repetunt a caelo atque ignibus eius
et primum faciunt ignem se vertere in auras
aeris, hinc imbrem gigni terramque creari
ex imbri retroque a terra cuncta reverti,
umorem primum, post aera, deinde calorem,
nec cessare haec inter se mutare, meare
a caelo ad terram, de terra ad sidera mundi.
quod facere haud ullo debent primordia pacto;
immutabile enim quiddam superare necessest,
ne res ad nilum redigantur funditus omnes.
nam quodcumque suis mutatum finibus exit,
continuo hoc mors est illius quod fuit ante.
quapropter quoniam quae paulo diximus ante
in commutatum veniunt, constare necessest
ex aliis ea, quae nequeant convertier usquam,
ne tibi res redeant ad nilum funditus omnes.
quin potius tali natura praedita quaedam
corpora constituas, ignem si forte crearint,
posse eadem demptis paucis paucisque tributis,

ing. 772 *ut* B corr. Flor. 31 Camb. for *et*. 774 *animans* Pont. Mar. Junt. for *animas*. 775 *quicque in coetu* Mar. Junt. for *quisque in coetum*.
776 *ostendet* Flor. 31 Avanc. for *ostendit*. 777 *atq. ardor cum rore* Lamb. acutely for *et quodam cum rore*. 778 *rebus oportet*. *rebu' necessest* Lach. Bern. without any necessity: if Ennius Accius Seneca Catullus, Virgil in his eclogues, Propertius Ovid and others can use the word, it is not too prosaic for Lucr. 780 *Emineat* Naugerius first for *demineat*. 781 *creatur* A corr. for *creatas*. 784 785 *hinc imbrem, ex imbri, a terra* Mar. Ald. 1 and Junt. for *hinc ignem, ex igni, in terram*: the change is peremptorily required: Catullus 62 7 *imbres* mss. for *ignes*. 789 *pacto* Mon. Ald. 1 Junt. for *facto*. 806 *ut*

ordine mutato et motu, facere aeris auras,
sic alias aliis rebus mutarier omnis?
'At manifesta palam res indicat' inquis 'in auras
aeris e terra res omnis crescere alique;
et nisi tempestas indulget tempore fausto
imbribus, ut tabe nimborum arbusta vacillent,
solque sua pro parte fovet tribuitque calorem,
crescere non possint fruges arbusta animantis'.
scilicet et nisi nos cibus aridus et tener umor
adiuvet, amisso iam corpore vita quoque omnis
omnibus e nervis atque ossibus exsoluatur;
adiutamur enim dubio procul atque alimur nos
certis ab rebus, certis aliae atque aliae res.
nimirum quia multa modis communia multis
multarum rerum in rebus primordia mixta
sunt, ideo variis variae res rebus aluntur.
atque eadem magni refert primordia saepe
cum quibus et quali positura contineantur
et quos inter se dent motus accipiantque;
namque eadem caelum mare terras flumina solem
constituunt, eadem fruges arbusta animantis,
verum aliis alioque modo commixta moventur.
quin etiam passim nostris in versibus ipsis
multa elementa vides multis communia verbis,
cum tamen inter se versus ac verba necessest
confiteare et re et sonitu distare sonanti.
tantum elementa queunt permutato ordine solo;
at rerum quae sunt primordia, plura adhibere
possunt unde queant variae res quaeque creari.
Nunc et Anaxagorae scrutemur homoeomerian

Prisc. for *et* of mss.: this change of a letter, as Bern. has seen, gives *imbribus* to the preceding sentence and completely restores the fine passage, which Lach. deplorably disfigures by transposing 806 and 807 and changing *arbusta* into *ambusta*, as if rain forsooth could like 'frost perform the effect of fire'. Lamb. and Gif. ed. 1 *et...vacillant*, the vulgate. Gif. ed. 2 keeps *et...vacillent* of mss. and says 'q. v. Marull. et vulg. *focillant*, q. v. *vacillant*, male'. Now Ald. 1 has *et tabes...focillant*. Ver. Ven. read *et tale...facillent*, whence comes *focillant*. Marullus in cod. Victor. makes no change. 814 *multa modis* Lamb. for *multimodis*. 824 *verbis* Flor. 31 Camb. Vat. Pont. Mar. etc. for *bellis*: see Lach. 830 *et*. *ut* Lach.: in five other places he changes *et*, and in two

quam Grai memorant nec nostra dicere lingua
concedit nobis patrii sermonis egestas,
sed tamen ipsam rem facilest exponere verbis.
principio, rerum quom dicit homoeomerian,
ossa videlicet e pauxillis atque minutis
ossibus hic et de pauxillis atque minutis
visceribus viscus gigni sanguenque creari
sanguinis inter se multis coeuntibu' guttis
ex aurique putat micis consistere posse
aurum et de terris terram concrescere parvis,
ignibus ex ignis, umorem umoribus esse,
cetera consimili fingit ratione putatque.
nec tamen esse ulla parte idem in rebus inane
concedit neque corporibus finem esse secandis.
quare in utraque mihi pariter ratione videtur
errare atque illi, supra quos diximus ante.
adde quod inbecilla nimis primordia fingit;
si primordia sunt, simili quae praedita constant
natura atque ipsae res sunt aequeque laborant
et pereunt neque ab exitio res ulla refrenat.
nam quid in oppressu valido durabit eorum,
ut mortem effugiat, leti sub dentibus ipsis?
ignis an umor an aura? quid horum? sanguen an ossa?

gives a far-fetched interpretation, because he says Lucr. could not use *et* for *etiam*. 834 *quom* Lach. for *quam*. Lamb. reads *Principium rerum quam* and joins it with what precedes: he is followed by all before Lach. and may be right. 'quid quod ita ne dixit quidem usquam Lucretius, sed *rerum principia* I 740 1047 II 789' says Lach. Yes, because his *primordia* are plural; but I 707 he writes *Et qui principium gignundis aera rebus Constituere* of those who have one first-beginning of things. 835 *e* Pont. Mar. Ald. 1 Junt. for *de*.

839 840 *aurique...aurum*: as he immediately enumerates the three other elements, Bentl. proposes *auraeque...auram*. 'quid hic aurum? oculos credo interpretum praestrinxit...Simplic. tamen [in Arist. phys. fol. 6 b] de Anaxag. πάντα τὰ ὁμοιομερῆ οἷον τὸ ὕδωρ ἢ πῦρ ἢ χρυσὸν etc.' This and other passages seem to defend the text: see notes 2: yet comp. 853. 841 *ignis, umorem*. *ignem, umorem ex* Lamb. and the plur. is awkward. 843 *ulla parte idem* Nicc. vulgo for *ulla idem parte*. *ulla idem ex parte* Lach. because Lucr. he says only omits the preposition when a genitive is added; but *in rebus* seems equivalent to one: comp. Juven. VI 437 *Adque alia parte in trutina suspendit Homerum*. 846 *illi supra quos* marg. Flor. 32 Ald. 1 Junt. for *illis uira quod* A, *quo* B Gott. *illis juxta quod* Camb. Vat. 1954 Othob. *viris iuxta quos* Flor. 31 *illis iuxta* Ang. Politian in marg. Flor. 29.

847 *inbecilla* Flor. 31 Camb. for *inbecilia*. 852 *effugiat* B corr. Flor. 31

nil, ut opinor, ubi ex aequo res funditus omnis
tam mortalis erit quam quae manifesta videmus
ex oculis nostris aliqua vi victa perire.
at neque reccidere ad nilum res posse neque autem
crescere de nilo testor res ante probatas.
praeterea quoniam cibus auget corpus alitque,
scire licet nobis venas et sanguen et ossa
. . . .
sive cibos omnis commixto corpore dicent
esse et habere in se nervorum corpora parva
ossaque et omnino venas partisque cruoris,
fiet uti cibus omnis, et aridus et liquor ipse,
ex alienigenis rebus constare putetur,
ossibus et nervis sanieque et sanguine mixto.
praeterea quaecumque e terra corpora crescunt
si sunt in terris, terram constare necessest
ex alienigenis, quae terris exoriuntur.
transfer item, totidem verbis utare licebit.
in lignis si flamma latet fumusque cinisque,
ex alienigenis consistant ligna necessest.
praeterea tellus quae corpora cumque alit, auget

*

ex alienigenis, quae lignis *his* oriuntur.

Pont. Mar. for *efficiat*. 853 *sanguen an ossa* marg. Flor. 32 Pont. Lamb. for *sanguis an os*. *sanguīs* was unknown to Lucr.: IV 1050 *sanguīs unde*; VI 1203 *sanguīs expletis*: see Lach. and add Sen. Med. 776 and Val. Flacc. III 234 *sanguīs*. Flor. 31 does not as Lach. says read *sanguis an, an os*. *sanguen os aurum* Lach., an awkward and improbable correction. 860: the verse lost here Lamb. thus supplies, *Et nervos alienigenis ex partibus esse*; which must be very like what Lucr. wrote. 861 *Sive* Flor. 31 Camb. for *Sine*. *corpore* Nicc. for *core*. 862 *Esse et* Nicc. for *Esset*. 866 *sanieque*. *venisque* Avanc. Lamb. Lach. wrongly: see notes 2: Avancius formed his text by correcting Ven. and it and Ver. have *sanisque*; hence *venis*. *mixto* Lach. after Mar. Ald. 1 Junt. Lamb. which have *misto*. *mixtim* Politian in marg. Flor. 29, which may be right. 873 here there is I believe a hiatus of two or more verses, which I formerly supplied thus, *Ex alienigenis quae tellure exoriuntur. Sic itidem quae ligna emittunt corpora, aluntur Ex* cet.: comp. especially 859—866 and notes 2. In 874 I have added *his* after *lignis*. I hardly understand Lach. who reads *quae alienigenis oriuntur*: see also Luc. Mueller de re metrica p. 284, who seems to prove that a monosyll. diphthong is never elided before a short vowel. Mar. Junt. followed by Gif. Creech omit both 873 and 874, Lamb. followed by Wak. only 873; which seems absurd: he reads in 874 *lignis*

Linquitur hic quaedam latitandi copia tenvis,
id quod Anaxagoras sibi sumit, ut omnibus omnis
res putet inmixtas rebus latitare, sed illud
apparere unum cuius sint plurima mixta
et magis in promptu primaque in fronte locata.
quod tamen a vera longe ratione repulsumst.
conveniebat enim fruges quoque saepe, minaci
robore cum saxi franguntur, mittere signum
sanguinis aut aliquid, nostro quae corpore aluntur.
885 consimili ratione herbis quoque saepe decebat,
884 cum lapidi in lapidem terimus, manare cruorem:
et latices dulcis guttas simili que sapore
mittere, lanigerae quali sunt ubere lactis,
scilicet et glebis terrarum saepe friatis
herbarum genera et fruges frondesque videri
dispertita in*ter* terram latitare minute,
postremo in lignis cinerem fumumque videri,
cum praefracta forent, ignisque latere minutos.
quorum nil fieri quoniam manifesta docet *res*,
scire licet non esse in rebus res ita mixtas,
verum semina multimodis inmixta latere
multarum rerum in rebus communia debent.
'At saepe in magnis fit montibus' inquis 'ut altis
arboribus vicina cacumina summa terantur
inter se, validis facere id cogentibus austris,
donec flammai fulserunt flore coorto'.
scilicet et non est lignis tamen insitus ignis,
verum semina sunt ardoris multa, terendo
quae cum confluxere, creant incendia silvis.

exoriuntur with Flor. 31 Camb. etc. 882 *cum saxi* Mar. Ald. 1 Junt. etc. for *cum in saxi*. 884 885 rightly transposed by N. P. Howard: see notes 2 for explanation of the whole passage in which much needless change has been made: 884 *in* om. Mar. Junt. etc. 'recte, ut puto, etsi cur addita sit [praep. *in*] non intellego' Lach. *terimus* Nicc. for *tenemus*. 885 *herbis*. *herbas* Mar. Ald. 1 Junt. Lach. vulgo. 886 *latices*. *laticis* Flor. 31 Camb. vulg. Lach. wrongly. 887 *quali* B, *qualis* A, *quales* A corr. Nicc. Flor. 31 Camb. *ubere*. *ubera* Lamb.: the exact reading is uncertain. 890 *inter terram* Lach. first for *in terram*: older editors have blundered strangely.

893 *res* added by Nicc. B corr. etc. 900 *flammai* Pont. Junt. for *flammae*: a simple correction, yet overlooked by many of the later editors: even Nauger. has here deserted Junt. and reads *fulserunt flammae fulgore*

quod si facta foret silvis abscondita flamma,
non possent ullum tempus celarier ignes,
conficerent volgo silvas, arbusta cremarent.
iamne vides igitur, paulo quod diximus ante,
permagni referre eadem primordia saepe
cum quibus et quali positura contineantur
et quos inter se dent motus accipiantque,
atque eadem paulo inter se mutata creare
ignes et lignum? quo pacto verba quoque ipsa
inter se paulo mutatis sunt elementis,
cum ligna atque ignes distincta voce notemus.
denique iam quaecumque in rebus cernis apertis
si fieri non posse putas, quin materiai
corpora consimili natura praedita fingas,
hac ratione tibi pereunt primordia rerum:
fiet uti risu tremulo concussa cachinnent
et lacrimis salsis umectent ora genasque.
  Nunc age quod superest cognosce et clarius audi.
nec me animi fallit quam sint obscura; sed acri
percussit thyrso laudis spes magna meum cor
et simul incussit suavem mi in pectus amorem
musarum, quo nunc instinctus mente vigenti
avia Pieridum peragro loca nullius ante
trita solo. iuvat integros accedere fontis
atque haurire, iuvatque novos decerpere flores
insignemque meo capiti petere inde coronam
unde prius nulli velarint tempora musae;
primum quod magnis doceo de rebus et artis
religionum animum nodis exsolvere pergo,
deinde quod obscura de re tam lucida pango
carmina, musaeo contingens cuncta lepore.
id quoque enim non ab nulla ratione videtur;
sed veluti pueris absinthia taetra medentes
cum dare conantur, prius oras pocula circum

after Nicc. etc. 909 *contineantur* Nauger. for *contingantur*, after Pont. apparently; for Victorius in his 2nd copy of Ven. seems to imply that *continuantur* of the first was his own error. 912 *et* B corr. Wak. for *e*. 918 *Hac* Nicc. B corr. for *Haec*. 919 *uti risu tremulo* Nicc. for *utiris ut aemulo*.

932 *animum*. *animos* Lamb. Creech after Lactantius inst. I 16. Pius says 'mo-

contingunt mellis dulci flavoque liquore,
ut puerorum aetas inprovida ludificetur
labrorum tenus, interea perpotet amarum
absinthi laticem deceptaque non capiatur,
sed potius tali pacto recreata valescat,
sic ego nunc, quoniam haec ratio plerumque videtur
tristior esse quibus non est tractata, retroque
volgus abhorret ab hac, volui tibi suaviloquenti
carmine Pierio rationem exponere nostram
et quasi musaeo dulci contingere melle,
si tibi forte animum tali ratione tenere
versibus in nostris possem, dum perspicis omnem
naturam rerum qua constet compta figura.
  Sed quoniam docui solidissima materiai
corpora perpetuo volitare invicta per aevom.
nunc age, summai quaedam sit finis eorum
necne sit, evolvamus; item quod inane repertumst
seu locus ac spatium, res in quo quaeque gerantur,
pervideamus utrum finitum funditus omne
constet an immensum pateat vasteque profundum.
  Omne quod est igitur nulla regione viarum
finitumst; namque extremum debebat habere.
extremum porro nullius posse videtur
esse, nisi ultra sit quod finiat; ut videatur
quo non longius haec sensus natura sequatur.
nunc extra summam quoniam nil esse fatendum,
non habet extremum, caret ergo fine modoque.
nec refert quibus adsistas regionibus eius;
usque adeo, quem quisque locum possedit, in omnis
tantundem partis infinitum omne relinquit.
praeterea si iam finitum constituatur
omne quod est spatium, siquis procurrat ad oras
ultimus extremas iaciatque volatile telum,
id validis utrum contortum viribus ire

dulatius *animos* leges'. But IV 7 *animum* Lamb. *animos* Creech. 942 *pacto* Heins. in ms. notes and Lach. rightly for *facto*. 954 *Necne sit* Pont. Lamb. for *nec sit*. 957 *vasteque* Nicc. corrupted into *adusque*; his followers *adusque* into *vel adusque*; or, as Mar. marg. Flor. 32 Ald. Junt., *patefiat ad usque*. 966 *omnis* Nicc. for *omnus*. 971 *Id validis* Lamb. first for *Invalidis*. Flor. 32 and Mar.

quo fuerit missum mavis longeque volare,
an prohibere aliquid censes obstareque posse?
alterutrum fatearis enim sumasque necessest.
quorum utrumque tibi effugium praecludit et omne
cogit ut exempta concedas fine patere.
nam sive est aliquit quod probeat officiatque
quominu' quo missum est veniat finique locet se,
sive foras fertur, non est a fine profectum.
hoc pacto sequar atque, oras ubicumque locaris
extremas, quaeram quid telo denique fiat.
fiet uti nusquam possit consistere finis
effugiumque fugae prolatet copia semper.
998 postremo ante oculos res rem finire videtur;
aer dissaepit collis atque aera montes,
terra mare et contra mare terras terminat omnis;
omne quidem vero nil est quod finiat extra.
984 Praeterea spatium summai totius omne
undique si inclusum certis consisteret oris
finitumque foret, iam copia materiai
undique ponderibus solidis confluxet ad imum
nec res ulla geri sub caeli tegmine posset
nec foret omnino caelum neque lumina solis.
990 quippe ubi materies omnis cumulata iaceret
ex infinito iam tempore subsidendo.
at nunc nimirum requies data principiorum
corporibus nullast, quia nil est funditus imum
quo quasi confluere et sedes ubi ponere possint.
995 semper in adsiduo motu res quaeque geruntur
partibus *e* cunctis infernaque suppeditantur

in margin explain *invalidis* as *valde validis*. 977 *officiat* Lamb. rightly and before him Gryphius of Lyons 1534 and 1540 for *efficiat*, after the constant usage of Lucr.: so Livy IV 31 5 Madvig after Faber reads *offecit* (mss. *effecit*) *quominus*. Lach. keeps *efficiat*. [But for *efficiat* see lex col. Genetivae II 4 7 *neve quis facito, quo minus ita aqua ducatur.*] 981 *fiat* Nicc. for *fiet*. 984—987 (998—1001) I have elsewhere proved should come in this place. 989 *inclusum* Nicc. for *inclusus*. 991 *confluxet* Flor. 31 first for *confluxit*. 997 *nullast* Politian in marg. Flor. 29 Ver. Ven. Heins. in ms. notes for *nullas*.

998 *possint* Ald. 1 Junt. for *possit*. 1000 *e* supplied by Mon. and Lach. is better than *in* of Mar. and older editors. *inferna* is quite right: see Camb. Journ. of phil. I p. 33. Lach. wrongly follows Mar. Ald. 1 Junt. Lamb. etc. in reading *aeternaque* and adds 'rei convenienter, quamvis secus videatur Wakefieldo et

ex infinito cita corpora materiai.
est igitur natura loci spatiumque profundi,
quod neque clara suo percurrere fulmina cursu
perpetuo possint aevi labentia tractu
nec prorsum facere ut restet minus ire meando:
usque adeo passim patet ingens copia rebus
finibus exemptis in cunctas undique partis.
  Ipsa modum porro sibi rerum summa parare
ne possit, natura tenet, quae corpus inani
et quod inane autem est finiri corpore cogit,
ut sic alternis infinita omnia reddat,
aut etiam alterutrum, nisi terminet alterum, eorum
simplice natura pateat tamen inmoderatum.

*

nec mare nec tellus neque caeli lucida templa
nec mortale genus nec divum corpora sancta
exiguum possent horai sistere tempus;
nam dispulsa suo de coetu materiai
copia ferretur magnum per inane soluta,
sive adeo potius numquam concreta creasset
ullam rem, quoniam cogi disiecta nequisset.
nam certe neque consilio primordia rerum
ordine se suo quaeque sagaci mente locarunt

Forbigero, qui quotiens philosophantur delirant': an insult quite out of place here. 1008 should commence a new paragraph. 1009 *inani* Mar. Ald. 1 Junt. for *inane*. 1013 Madvig opusc. pr. p. 313 rightly supposes some verses lost here; and long before him Marullus did the same, as I find from the margin of Flor. 32: 'credit Marullus deesse hic aliqua carmina, quae continerent transitum ab infinitate inanis ad infinitatem corporum; in his enim *Nec mare nec tellus*...procul dubio agit de infinitate corporum, cum supra [953] de utroque infinito se dicturum promiserit': so that Flor. 32 gives here the more mature, at least the better judgment of Marullus; since the cod. Victor. has the same perverse corrections which Junt. has. Lach. places the mark of hiatus after 1012, giving a most involved explanation of the passage: his arrangement moreover is scarcely grammatical, as *pateat* is thus answered in the apodosis by imperfects and pluperfects. Indeed the lacuna does not appear to me so great as it did either to Madvig or Lach.: the poet has not only shewn already that the *omne quod est*, but also 988 (984)—1007, that the *omne quod est spatium* is infinite: he now, 1008 foll., shews that matter is infinite. I formerly proposed roughly to supply what is wanting thus, *Sed spatium supra docui sine fine patere. Si finita igitur summa esset materiai, Nec mare cet.* 1023 the last four words are rightly supplied by Mar. and Junt. from v 421: the mss. here repeat the last three of 1022. Avancius blunders sadly, doubtless from not understanding

nec quos quaeque *darent motus pepigere profecto,*
sed quia multa modis multis mutata per omne
ex infinito vexantur percita plagis,
omne genus motus et coetus experiundo
tandem deveniunt in talis disposituras,
qualibus haec rerum consistit summa creata,
et multos etiam magnos servata per annos
ut semel in motus coniectast convenientis,
efficit ut largis avidum mare fluminis undis
integrent amnes et solis terra vapore
fota novet fetus summissaque gens animantum
floreat et vivant labentes aetheris ignes;
quod nullo facerent pacto nisi materiai
ex infinito suboriri copia posset,
unde amissa solent reparare in tempore quaeque.
nam veluti privata cibo natura animantum
diffluit amittens corpus, sic omnia debent
dissolui simul ac defecit suppeditare
materies aliqua ratione aversa viai.
nec plagae possunt extrinsecus undique summam
conservare omnem quaecumque est conciliata.
cudere enim crebro possunt partemque morari,
dum veniant aliae ac suppleri summa queatur.
interdum resilire tamen coguntur et una
principiis rerum spatium tempusque fugai
largiri, ut possint a coetu libera ferri.
quare etiam atque etiam suboriri multa necessest,
et tamen ut plagae quoque possint suppetere ipsae,
infinita opus est vis undique materiai.
  Illud in his rebus longe fuge credere, Memmi,
in medium summae, quod dicunt, omnia niti,
atque ideo mundi naturam stare sine ullis
ictibus externis neque quoquam posse resolvi

what he is taking from others. 1028 *rerum* Faber and Bentl. from v 194 most rightly for *rebus*. 1033 *summissaque* Pont. Mar. Junt. for *summaque*. 1034 *Floreat* Flor. 31 Camb. etc. for *floreant*. 1040 *Dissolui* Nicc. B corr. for *Dissoluit*. 1041 *viai* B corr. vulgo for *via*. *viaque* Lach.: but *ratione viaque* surely means 'by method and system': see Cic. de fin. I 29 *ut ratione et via procedat oratio*. 1047 *Principiis* Mar. Junt. for *principium*. 1061 *Et simili*. Lach. reads

summa atque ima, quod in medium sint omnia nixa:
ipsum si quicquam posse in se sistere credis:
et quae pondera sunt sub terris omnia sursum
nitier in terraque retro requiescere posta,
ut per aquas quae nunc rerum simulacra videmus.
et simili ratione animalia suppa vagari
contendunt neque posse e terris in loca caeli
reccidere inferiora magis quam corpora nostra
sponte sua possint in caeli templa volare;
illi cum videant solem, nos sidera noctis
cernere, et alternis nobiscum tempora caeli
dividere et noctes parilis agitare diebus.
sed vanus stolidis haec
amplexi quod habent perv
nam medium nil esse potest
infinita. neque omnino, si iam *medium sit*
possit ibi quicquam consistere
quam quavis alia longe ratione
omnis enim locus ac spatium quod in*ane vocamus*
per medium per non medium concedere *debet*
aeque ponderibus, motus quacumque feruntur.
nec quisquam locus est, quo corpora cum vener*unt*,
ponderis amissa vi possint stare *in* inani;

Adsimili and joins with it the preceding verse, putting a full stop at *posta.* I think him quite wrong: the simile is exactly the same as IV 418, where also Lach. makes unnecessary changes. 1068—1075: these 8 mutilated verses came at the beginning of p. 45 of the archetype; and the ends were therefore at the outer margin. B and Gott. omit them altogether, but append a cross and VIII. Nicc. gives them imperfect as in A. The later mss. Ald. 1, Junt. after Mar., Lamb. complete them in various ways. I formerly suggested in 1068 *error falsa probavit* or *error somnia finxit*: 1069 *perversa rem ratione*: 1070 *quando omnia constant*, or with Lach. *ubi summa profundist*: 1072 *eam magis ob rem*: 1073 *repelli.* 1073 Lach. reads *alio* for *alia*, and proposes *meare* at end, and *malle putari* in 1072: he declines to prophesy in 1068 and 1069. 1071 Mar. Junt. most truly *neque omnino si iam medium sit* for *denique omnino si iam.* 1074 the end is supplied by Mar. Ald. 1 and Junt. 1075 *debet* Wak., *oportet* older corr. 1076 *Aeque* Junt. for *aequis* which Wak. absurdly defends. 1078 *in* added by Mar. Ald. 1 Junt.

1082 *concilio* Mar. Junt. for *concilium*, the *m* coming from *medii*. *concilium...vectae* Lach. which seems less poetical. *vinctae* Bentl. 1085 1086 are transposed by Mar. and Junt. followed by all before Lach.: but Ussing, Tidsskr. for Philol. VI, has rightly seen that a v. is lost before 1085, which comparing VI 495 I would thus supply *Et quae de supero in terram mittuntur ut imbres.*

nec quod inane autem est ulli subsistere debet,
quin, sua quod natura petit, concedere pergat.
haud igitur possunt tali ratione teneri
res in concilio medii cuppedine victae.
  Praeterea quoniam non omnia corpora fingunt
in medium niti, sed terrarum, atque liquoris
. . . .
et quasi terreno quae corpore contineantur,
umorem ponti magnasque e montibus undas,
at contra tenuis exponunt aeris auras
et calidos simul a medio differrier ignis,
atque ideo totum circum tremere aethera signis
et solis flammam per caeli caerula pasci,
quod calor a medio fugiens se ibi conligat omnis,
nec prorsum arboribus summos frondescere ramos
posse, nisi a terris paulatim cuique cibatum
. . . .
. . . .
. . . .
. . . .
. . . .
. . . .
. . . .
. . . .

1091 *se ibi* Wak. for *sibi*. 1094—1101: A has faithfully left a blank space for these eight lost verses: they came at the beginning of p. 46 of the lost archetype; the eight mutilated lines above having headed the page on the other side of the leaf; Lach. therefore most justly concludes that this part of the leaf in the original of our mss. was by some accident torn away. Both the old ms. collations of A and B which I possess mention this lacuna: Heinsius says 'in A octo versuum hiatus erat relictus': the less careful Vossius, though the manuscript was his own, merely says 'vide ms. in quo hiatus post haec verba'. Think now of Havercamp, a Professor in the University where A and B then were, never noting this fact, but inserting the miserable makeshift verse of Mar. and Junt. *Terra det: at supra circum tegere omnia caelum*; stealing the critical note of the London bookseller's edition, and stating that this spurious verse was not in B, from which every reader must infer it was in A. I formerly made the following verses to shew the general sense of those which are lost: *Diffundat truncum ac ramos natura per omnis, Scilicet incerto diversi errore vagantes Argumenta sibi prorsum pugnantia fingunt. Quae tamen omnia sunt falsa ratione recepta. Nam quoniam docui spatium sine fine modoque Inmensumque patere in cunctas undique partis, Sic parili ratione necessest suppeditetur Infinita etiam vis undique materiai, Ne* cet. Pontanus saw that the passage was a fragment.

ne volucri ritu flammarum moenia mundi
diffugiant subito magnum per inane soluta
et ne cetera consimili ratione sequantur
neve ruant caeli penetralia templa superne
terraque se pedibus raptim subducat et omnis
inter permixtas rerum caelique ruinas
corpora solventes abeat per inane profundum,
temporis ut puncto nil extet reliquiarum
desertum praeter spatium et primordia caeca.
nam quacumque prius de parti corpora desse
constitues, haec rebus erit pars ianua leti,
hac se turba foras dabit omnis materiai.
  Haec sei pernosces, parva perductus opella
. . . .
namque alid ex alio clarescet nec tibi caeca
nox iter eripiet quin ultima naturai
pervideas: ita res accendent lumina rebus.

1105 *penetralia* Nicc. for *tonetralia*; rightly followed by all the old eds. before Lamb. who reads *tonitralia*: VI 865 *sonitus* all mss. for *penitus*: neither *tonetralia* nor *tonitralia* is Latin. 1108 *abeat* Ed. after Mar. Junt. for *abeant* wrongly adapted to the adjacent plural: comp. VI 286: *omnis* agrees with *terra*: comp. VI 605 sqq.: Lach. in 1106 reads *omnia*, as also II 719 without authority.
1114 *sei* Ed. after Nicc. Flor. 31 Camb. Mon. etc. for *sic*: a verse is here lost which I feel sure was of this kind, *Cetera iam poteris per te tute ipse videre*, with which the preceding words *parva perductus opella* must be joined: Lucr. says it is hard to master his principles, but when that is thoroughly done, then led on with little trouble you may learn the rest yourself: comp. especially 400—417, and see Camb. Journ. of phil. I p. 374. Lach. for *sic* reads *scio* and *perdoctus* for *perductus*, and then gets no satisfactory sense: Mar. and Junt. read *non* for *nec* in 1115: Lamb. *perfunctus* for *perdoctus*: Bern. *sis*, and *perdoctus* after Lach.

T. LUCRETI CARI

DE RERUM NATURA

LIBER SECUNDUS

Suave, mari magno turbantibus aequora ventis.
e terra magnum alterius spectare laborem;
non quia vexari quemquamst iucunda voluptas,
sed quibus ipse malis careas quia cernere suave est.
6 suave etiam belli certamina magna tueri
5 per campos instructa tua sine parte pericli.
sed nil dulcius est, bene quam munita tenere
edita doctrina sapientum templa serena,
despicere unde queas alios passimque videre
errare atque viam palantis quaerere vitae,
certare ingenio, contendere nobilitate,
noctes atque dies niti praestante labore
ad summas emergere opes rerumque potiri.
o miseras hominum mentes, o pectora caeca!
qualibus in tenebris vitae quantisque periclis
degitur hoc aevi quodcumquest! nonne videre
nil aliud sibi naturam latrare, nisi utqui
corpore seiunctus dolor absit, mente fruatur

5 and 6 rightly transposed by Avancius. 12 *praestante plabore* AB. *praestantes prae labore* Nicc. p. m. 16 *nonne videre* AB Gott. which Gif., followed tacitly by Lamb. ed. 3, has most properly retained. *videre est* was the common reading, which Lach. shews Lucr. could not have written. '*videtis* Marull.' says Gif.: and in cod. Victor. Marullus p. m. *videtis*; s. m. *videre est*, as Junt.: *videtis* Ald. 1, and this is mentioned as a var. lec. at end of Junt.: so also Lamb. ed. 1, but *videre est* ed. 2. 17—19 mss. are quite right: see notes 2: 17 *utqui*. *ut cui* Avanc. Lach. *ut quoi* Gif. 18 *mente*. *menti*'

iucundo sensu cura semota metuque?
ergo corpoream ad naturam pauca videmus
esse opus omnino, quae demant cumque dolorem.
delicias quoque uti multas substernere possint
gratius interdum, neque natura ipsa requirit,
si non aurea sunt iuvenum simulacra per aedes
lampadas igniferas manibus retinentia dextris,
lumina nocturnis epulis ut suppeditentur,
nec domus argento fulget auroque renidet
nec citharae reboant laqueata aurataque tecta,
cum tamen inter se prostrati in gramine molli
propter aquae rivum sub ramis arboris altae
non magnis opibus iucunde corpora curant,
praesertim cum tempestas adridet et anni
tempora conspergunt viridantis floribus herbas.
nec calidae citius decedunt corpore febres,
textilibus si in picturis ostroque rubenti
iacteris, quam si in plebeia veste cubandum est.
quapropter quoniam nil nostro in corpore gazae
proficiunt neque nobilitas nec gloria regni,
quod superest, animo quoque nil prodesse putandum;
si non forte tuas legiones per loca campi
fervere cum videas belli simulacra cientis,

Lach. without cause. 19 *semota.* *semotu'* Lamb. in notes, Gif. Bentl. Lach. for *semota.* 21 22 23 see notes 2 for the explanation of this passage which I have corrected by a better punctuation. 27 *fulget auroque.* *fulgenti* Lach. But comp. v 1049 *sciret animoque*, where Lachmann's *scirent* perverts the meaning. *fulgens, renidens* Macrob. sat. VI 2 Pont. Avanc. Junt. etc. *fulgens renidet* Mar. P. Crinitus de hon. disc. XVII 6. 28 *citharae.* *citharam* Macrob. sat. VI 2, *cithara* id. VI 4. *aurataque.* *ornataque* Lach. *arquataque* Bern. *tecta* Lach. for *templa*, and Macrob. sat. VI 4, but VI 2 *tempe*, which comes perhaps from the preceding passage of Virgil: yet the *templa* of the mss. of Lucr. may have a technical meaning. [But for *tecta* and *templa* confused see O. Hirschfeld untersuch. p. 149, and p. 187 n. 4.] 36 *Iacteris.* *Iactaris* Lamb. ed. 2 and 3. 41 *Fervere* Flor. 30 corr. Flor. 31 Camb. for *Fruere* A, *Eruere* B. 40—46: this passage I think I have arranged much better than Lach. or Bern.: 42 *et ecum vi* (*etecūvi*) Ed. for *epicuri*: comp. *tariter* of mss. for *pariter* in 43: 43 *Ornatasq. armis statuas pariterque* Ed. for *Ornatas armis itastuas* (*itasiuas* B Gott.) *tariterque*: then *Fervere cum videas classem lateque vagari*, which is not found in our mss. but is quoted by Nonius p. 503 from Lucretius lib. II, is clearly in its right place after 46, not 43, where Lach. and others have put it: I have also put a stop after *pavide* in 45. For *statuas* corrupted into *itastuas*

subsidiis magnis et ecum vi constabilitas,
ornatas*que* armis statuas pariterque animatas,
his tibi tum rebus timefactae religiones
effugiunt animo pavide; mortisque timores
tum vacuum pectus lincunt curaque solutum,
fervere cum videas classem lateque vagari
quod si ridicula haec ludibriaque esse videmus,
re veraque metus hominum curaeque sequaces
nec metuunt sonitus armorum nec fera tela
audacterque inter reges rerumque potentis
versantur neque fulgorem reverentur ab auro
nec clarum vestis splendorem purpureai,
quid dubitas quin omni' sit haec rationi' potestas?
omnis cum in tenebris praesertim vita laboret.
nam veluti pueri trepidant atque omnia caecis
in tenebris metuunt, sic nos in luce timemus
interdum, nilo quae sunt metuenda magis quam
quae pueri in tenebris pavitant finguntque futura.
hunc igitur terrorem animi tenebrasque necessest
non radii solis neque lucida tela diei
discutiant, sed naturae species ratioque.
  Nunc age, quo motu genitalia materiai
corpora res varias gignant genitasque resolvant

comp. Lach. to IV 283, and *istatuam* for *statuam* in Orelli inscript. 1120. Because Lucr. V 1227 has *Induperatorem classis super aequora verrit Cum validis pariter legionibus atque elephantis*, Lach. says 'apparet haec ita legenda esse, *Subsidiis magnisque elephantis constabilitas, Ornatas armis, validas, pariterque animatas*'. The *apparet* is anything but clear to me. Bern. reads *hastatis* for *epicuri*, *pariter* for *itastuas*. See Lach. on the way these two verses are written in AB: Nicc. omits them: later mss. Flor. 31 Camb. etc. treat them as a heading: the old eds. to Ald. 1 and Pius inclusive have them variously corrupted. Junt. first omits them in text with this note at end, '*Subsidiis magnis Epicuri constabilitas.* Marullus carmen hoc expungit. Nam illud, *ornatas armis statuas, stanteisque animatas*, procul dubio subditicium est': and in cod. Victor. Marullus does expunge them. All subsequent eds. before Lach. omitted them, except Gif. who mixes up a portion of them with a part of the line from Nonius in this fashion, *Fervere cum videas; classem lateque vagari, Ornatamque armis belli simulacra cientem.* Lamb. ed. 3 first gives the l. from Nonius in full. 46 *pectus* Lamb. for *tempus*: a necessary change. Aen. I 46 *tempore* Probus for *pectore.* 52 *purpureai* Nicc. for *purpura.* 53 Mar. Ald. 1 Junt. Lamb. *omne sit hoc rationis egestas*, perversely. 54 *laboret* Nicc. B corr. for *raboret.* 56 *sic*, as in III 88 VI 36. *ita* Senec. epist. 110, shewing what little

et qua vi facere id cogantur quaeque sit ollis
reddita mobilitas magnum per inane meandi,
expediam: tu te dictis praebere memento.
nam certe non inter se stipata cohaeret
materies, quoniam minui rem quamq*ue* videmus
et quasi longinquo fluere omnia cernimus aevo
ex oculisque vetustatem subducere nostris,
cum tamen incolumis videatur summa manere
propterea quia, quae decedunt corpora cuique,
unde abeunt minuunt, quo venere augmine donant,
illa senescere at haec contra florescere cogunt,
nec remorantur ibi. sic rerum summa novatur
semper, et inter se mortales mutua vivunt.
augescunt aliae gentes, aliae minuuntur,
inque brevi spatio mutantur saecla animantum
et quasi cursores vitai lampada tradunt.
  Si cessare putas rerum primordia posse
cessandoque novos rerum progignere motus,
avius a vera longe ratione vagaris.
nam quoniam per inane vagantur, cuncta necessest
aut gravitate sua ferri primordia rerum
aut ictu forte alterius. nam *cum* cita saepe
obvia conflixere, fit ut diversa repente
dissiliant; neque enim mirum, durissima quae sint
ponderibus solidis neque quicquam a tergo ibus obstet.
et quo iactari magis omnia materiai
corpora pervideas, reminiscere totius imum
nil esse in summa, neque habere ubi corpora prima
consistant, quoniam spatium sine fine modoquest
inmensumque patere in cunctas undique partis
pluribus ostendi et certa ratione probatumst.
quod quoniam constat, nimirum nulla quies est

reliance can be placed on such citations: comp. n. to I 66. 68 *quamque videmus* Nicc. B corr. for *quamquidemus.* 73 *augmine* B corr. Nicc. corr. for *agmine.* 84 *ferri* Nicc. B corr. for *terri.* 85 *nam cum* (*quom*) *cita* Wak. for *nam cita.* *cita superne* Nicc. *concita saepe* Flor. 31 Camb. 86 *conflixere* Lamb. in notes for *conflexere.* *confluxere* Nicc. etc. *cum flixere* Lamb. *ut* Avanc. for *uti.* *ita uti* Flor. 31 Camb. etc. 88 *tergo ibus* Is. Vossius in ms. notes (not Preiger) most rightly for *tergibus.* 95 *nulla* Nicc. for *multa.* *invita* Is.

reddita corporibus primis per inane profundum,
sed magis adsiduo varioque exercita motu
partim intervallis magnis confulta resultant,
pars etiam brevibus spatiis vexantur ab ictu.
et quaecumque magis condenso conciliatu
exiguis intervallis convecta resultant,
indupedita suis perplexis ipsa figuris,
haec validas saxi radices et fera ferri
corpora constituunt et cetera *de* genere horum
paucula quae porro magnum per inane vagantur.
cetera dissiliunt longe longeque recursant
in magnis intervallis: haec aera rarum
sufficiunt nobis et splendida lumina solis.
multaque praeterea magnum per inane vagantur,
conciliis rerum quae sunt reiecta nec usquam
consociare etiam motus potuere recepta.
cuius, uti memoro, rei simulacrum et imago
ante oculos semper nobis versatur et instat.
contemplator enim, cum solis lumina cumque
inserti fundunt radii per opaca domorum:
multa minuta modis multis per inane videbis
corpora misceri radiorum lumine in ipso
et velut aeterno certamine proelia pugnas
edere turmatim certantia nec dare pausam,
conciliis et discidiis exercita crebris;
conicere ut possis ex hoc, primordia rerum
quale sit in magno iactari semper inani.
dumtaxat rerum magnarum parva potest res
exemplare dare et vestigia notitiai.
hoc etiam magis haec animum te advertere par est
corpora quae in solis radiis turbare videntur,
quod tales turbae motus quoque materiai

Vossius in ms. notes. 98 *confulta* mss. and so Pont. Avanc. Pius Naugerius. *consulta* Ver. Ven. Gif. *conflicta* 2 Vat. Mar. Junt. Lamb. ed. 1 and 2, Wak. Creech. *contusa* Lamb. ed. 3. *conpulsa* Heins. in ms. notes.

99 *brevibus* Nicc. for *brevius.* 112 *memoro rei* Vat. 1706 Reg. ('olim Nicolai Heinsii') Pont. Avanc. vulg. for *memoror rei.* 118 *proelia pugnas*: so IV 1009. *proelia pugnasque* Camb. Nicc. corr. Mar. Junt. wrongly. 125 *magis haec.* 'Marull. contra v. l. scripserat, *huc*' Gif.: both Ald. 1 and Junt. have *mage ad*

significant clandestinos caecosque subesse.
multa videbis enim plagis ibi percita caecis
commutare viam retroque repulsa reverti
nunc huc nunc illuc in cunctas undique partis.
scilicet hic a principiis est omnibus error.
prima moventur enim per se primordia rerum;
inde ea quae parvo sunt corpora conciliatu
et quasi proxima sunt ad viris principiorum,
ictibus illorum caecis inpulsa cientur,
ipsaque proporro paulo maiora lacessunt.
sic a principiis ascendit motus et exit
paulatim nostros ad sensus, ut moveantur
illa quoque, in solis quae lumine cernere quimus
nec quibus id faciant plagis apparet aperte.
  Nunc quae mobilitas sit reddita materiai
corporibus, paucis licet hinc cognoscere, Memmi.
primum aurora novo cum spargit lumine terras
et variae volucres nemora avia pervolitantes
aera per tenerum liquidis loca vocibus opplent,
quam subito soleat sol ortus tempore tali
convestire sua perfundens omnia luce,
omnibus in promptu manifestumque esse videmus.
at vapor is quem sol mittit lumenque serenum
non per inane meat vacuum; quo tardius ire
cogitur, aerias quasi dum diverberet undas.
nec singillatim corpuscula quaeque vaporis
sed complexa meant inter se conque globata;
quapropter simul inter se *re*trahuntur et extra
officiuntur, uti cogantur tardius ire.
at quae sunt solida primordia simplicitate,
cum per inane meant vacuum nec res remoratur

hoc; but over *haec* in cod. Victor. was once written a word carefully erased, as some mark under *haec* has been, quite confirming Gif.: see above p. 9. 134 *conciliatu* Nicc. for *conciliata.* 137 *Ipsaque proporro* Turneb. advers. v 27 Lach. for *Ipsaque porro. Ipsaque quae* Camb. vulg. *Ictaque quae* Flor. 31. 152 *quasi dum diverberet. quod sol diverberat* Nicc. Flor. 31 Camb. vulg. Lamb. ed. 1. *quasi tum diverberet* Lamb. ed. 2, *quasi dum diverberat* ed. 3, as Pont. before, 'pessime' says Lach.: 'nam *dum* intellegendum est *donec*'. But in my opinion, though the subj. is quite right, Lamb. well defends the indic. which is also tenable. 155 *se retrahuntur* Priscian for *se trahuntur.* 158 *remoratur*

ulla foris atque ipsa, suis e partibus una,
unum in quem coepere locum conixa feruntur,
debent nimirum praecellere mobilitate
et multo citius ferri quam lumina solis
multiplexque loci spatium transcurrere eodem
tempore quo solis pervolgant fulgura caelum.

*

[nec persectari primordia singula quaeque
ut *vi*deant qua quicque geratur cum ratione.
  At quidam contra haec, ignari materiai,
naturam non posse deum sine numine credunt
tanto opere humanis rationibus admoderate
tempora mutare annorum frugesque creare,
et iam cetera, mortalis quae suadet adire
ipsaque deducit dux vitae dia voluptas
et res per Veneris blanditur saecla propagent,
ne genus occidat humanum. quorum omnia causa
constituisse deos cum fingunt, omnibu' rebus
magno opere a vera lapsi ratione videntur.
nam quamvis rerum ignorem primordia quae sint,
hoc tamen ex ipsis caeli rationibus ausim
confirmare aliisque ex rebus reddere multis,
nequaquam nobis divinitus esse creatam
naturam mundi: *tanta stat* praedita culpa.
quae tibi posterius, Memmi, faciemus aperta.

Pont. Mar. Ald. 1 Junt. for *remoravit.* 159 *ipsa, suis e partibus una, Unum* Ed. for *ipsa suis e partibus unum Unum*: the contrast with 153—156 shews this to be necessary: comp. also I 599 etc.: the repetition of *unum unum* has here no force whatever. 160 *conixa. conexa* mss. *connixa* Ver. Ven. followed by Nauger. and vulgo: it should be *conixa.*

165—183 Lach. has most justly marked off from the context, as interrupting the argument, though indisputably written by Lucretius: some verses too have clearly been lost before 165: as Pontanus has seen, who says 'fragmentum': Marullus supplied the unmeaning *Nam neque consilio debent tardata morari,* which became the vulgate. Bern. puts 167 before 165, and in 166 reads *persectati,* and supposes no lacuna. 166 *Ut videant* Nicc. for *Ut deant.* 168 *numine credunt* Ed. for *numine reddi,* and Pont. I now find: the *e* of *numine* has absorbed the *c,* and *redunt* in mss. much resembles *reddi. rentur* Mar. Junt. vulgo 'prorsus egregie' says Lach. Wak. absurdly defends *reddi.* 169 has been much tampered with in the vulg. eds. without any reason. 181 *tanta stat praedita* Lach., as in the repetition V 199, for *quamquam predita. quae tanta est praedita*

nunc id quod superest de motibus expediemus.]
Nunc locus est, ut opinor, in his illud quoque rebus
confirmare tibi, nullam rem posse sua vi
corpoream sursum ferri sursumque meare;
ne tibi dent in eo flammarum corpora fraudem.
sursus enim versus gignuntur et augmina sumunt
et sursum nitidae fruges arbustaque crescunt,
pondera, quantum in se est, cum deorsum cuncta ferantur.
nec cum subsiliunt ignes ad tecta domorum
et celeri flamma degustant tigna trabesque,
sponte sua facere id sine vi subigente putandum est.
quod genus e nostro quom missus corpore sanguis
emicat exultans alte spargitque cruorem.
nonne vides etiam quanta vi tigna trabesque
respuat umor aquae? nam quo magis ursimus alte
derecta et magna vi multi pressimus aegre,
tam cupide sursum revomit magis atque remittit,
plus ut parte foras emergant exiliantque.
nec tamen haec, quantum est in se, dubitamus, opinor,
quin vacuum per inane deorsum cuncta ferantur.
sic igitur debent flammae quoque posse per auras
aeris expressae sursum succedere, quamquam
pondera, quantum in sest, deorsum *de*ducere pugnent,
nocturnasque faces caeli sublime volantis
nonne vides longos flammarum ducere tractus
in quascumque dedit partis natura meatum?
non cadere in terram stellas et sidera cernis?
sol etiam *caeli* de vertice dissipat omnis

Pont. Junt. vulgo, which may be right. Wak. adopts the interpolation of Nicc. *quamquam haec sint praedita*, and gives a ludicrous explanation of it. 187 *fraudem. frudem* B: see VI 187. 193 *subigente* Lamb. Creech Lach. for *subiecta. subeunte* Bern. which is hardly so near the ms. reading: see Madvig emend. Liv. p. 210. 194 *Quod genus e nostro. Quod genus est* Lach. justly blamed by Madvig Lat. gram. ed. 3 p. IX for the way in which he deals with *quod genus* here and in other places. *quom* Nicc. *com* A Lach. *cum* B. 197 *ursimus. urgimus* A corr. Nicc. Camb. *alte* Flor. 31 for *altu*. 198 *Derecta. Deiecta* Lach. 199 *revomit* Pont. Nauger. for *removet*. 203 *debent flammae quoque* Ald. 1 Junt. for *q. d. fl.* 205 *in se est deorsum deducere* Mar. Ald. 1 Junt. for *inest deorsum ducere*. *in se est* Flor. 31 Camb. *quantum est in se deorsum ducere* one Vat. Pont. Lach. 209 *cadere in terram* Nicc. for *caderem in terra*. 210 *caeli* Bern. better than *summo*

ardorem in partis et lumine conserit arva;
in terras igitur quoque solis vergitur ardor.
transversosque volare per imbris fulmina cernis:
nunc hinc nunc illinc abrupti nubibus ignes
concursant; cadit in terras vis flammea volgo.
Illud in his quoque te rebus cognoscere avemus,
corpora cum deorsum rectum per inane feruntur
ponderibus propriis, *se* incerto tempore ferme
incertisque locis spatio depellere paulum,
tantum quod momen mutatum dicere possis.
quod nisi declinare solerent, omnia deorsum,
imbris uti guttae, caderent per inane profundum,
nec foret offensus natus nec plaga creata
principiis: ita nil umquam natura creasset.
Quod si forte aliquis credit graviora potesse
corpora, quo citius rectum per inane feruntur,
incidere ex supero levioribus atque ita plag*as*
gignere quae possint genitalis reddere motus,
avius a vera longe ratione recedit.
nam per aquas quaecumque cadunt atque aera rarum,
haec pro ponderibus casus celerare necessest
propterea quia corpus aquae naturaque tenvis
aeris haut possunt aeque rem quamque morari,
sed citius cedunt gravioribus exsuperata;
at contra nulli de nulla parte neque ullo
tempore inane potest vacuum subsistere rei,
quin, sua quod natura petit, concedere pergat;
omnia quapropter debent per inane quietum
aeque ponderibus non aequis concita ferri.
haud igitur poterunt levioribus incidere umquam
ex supero graviora neque ictus gignere per se

or *aetherio* of older editors: *caeli* I had myself restored from Cic. Arat. 297 *summo caeli de vertice tranans*. 214 *abrupti*. *abruptis* Macr. sat. VI 1 27.
218 *se* added by Ed. *ferme* Flor. 31 Camb. Mar. for *firme*. 219 mss. are quite right: see notes 2: *loci spatiis decellere* Lach. whom I before followed.
220 *momen*. *minimum* two Vat. and old eds. before Junt. 226 *feruntur*. *ferantur* Vict. 227 *plagas* B corr. and Lamb. for *plag*. *plagis* Nicc. followed by all before Lamb. 229 *Avius* Nicc. for *Aulus*. 233 *Aeris haud* Nicc. for *Haeraut* A, *Haeraud* B Gott. 234 *exsuperata* Mar. Junt. for *exsuperate*. *exsuperatae* Nicc. perhaps rightly. 240 *poterunt* Flor. 31 Camb. for *potue-*

qui varient motus per quos natura gerat res.
quare etiam atque etiam paulum inclinare necessest
corpora; nec plus quam minimum, ne fingere motus
obliquos videamur et id res vera refutet.
namque hoc in promptu manifestumque esse videmus,
pondera, quantum in *s*est, non posse obliqua meare,
ex supero cum praecipitant, quod cernere possis;
sed nil omnino *recta* regione viai
declinare quis est qui possit cernere sese?
  Denique si semper motus conectitur omnis
et vetere exoritur *semper* novus ordine certo
nec declinando faciunt primordia motus
principium quoddam quod fati foedera rumpat,
ex infinito ne causam causa sequatur,
libera per terras unde haec animantibus exstat
unde est haec, inquam, fatis avolsa *potestas*
per quam progredimur quo ducit quemque voluntas,
declinamus item motus nec tempore certo
nec regione loci certa, sed ubi ipsa tulit mens?
nam dubio procul his rebus sua cuique voluntas
principium dat et hinc motus per membra rigantur.
nonne vides etiam patefactis tempore puncto
carceribus non posse tamen prorumpere *e*quorum
vim cupidam tam de subito quam mens avet ipsa?
omnis enim totum per corpus materiai
copia conquiri debet, concita per artus
omnis ut studium mentis conixa sequatur;

runt. 241 *se* is found in all mss. 247 *se* before *est* added by Flor. 31 Camb. etc. 249 *recta* added by Nicc. whom all before Lach. rightly followed: it was absorbed by the similar letters in *regione*. *nulla regione* Lach. 250 *Declinare quis est qui possit cernere sese*: this reading of all mss. and editions I now keep: the constr. is not harsher than others in Lucr.: see notes 2. *de se* Ed. in small ed. for *sese*. *sensus* Bern. *praestet* Lach. for *possit*. 251 *motus* Flor. 31 Camb. for *motu*. 252 *semper* added after *exoritur* by Nicc. Flor. 31 Camb. all editors before Lach. *exacto* added by Lach. before *exoritur*: obviously not right, as the new motion does not first begin when the other ceases: the reason of the omission was the *semper* of 251. *novus atque ex ordine* Pont. 257 *potestas* Lach. for *voluptas*: a certain correction: comp. 286: Lamb. in vain transposes *voluptas* and *voluntas* of 258: Flor. 31 Camb. have *voluptas* in both places, but it can be right in neither. 264 *equorum* Brix. for *quorum*, not Nicc. Flor. 31 Camb. or Ver. Ven. 267 *conquiri* A corr. Gott. Nicc. vulg. for *conciri* of

ut videas initum motus a corde creari
ex animique voluntate id procedere primum,
inde dari porro per totum corpus et artus.
nec similest ut cum impulsi procedimus ictu
viribus alterius magnis magnoque coactu;
nam tum materiem totius corporis omnem
perspicuumst nobis invitis ire rapique,
donec eam refrenavit per membra voluntas.
iamne vides igitur, quamquam vis extera multos
pellat et invitos cogat procedere saepe
praecipitesque rapi, tamen esse in pectore no*stro*
quiddam quod contra pugnare obstareque possit?
cuius ad arbitrium quoque copia materiai
cogitur interdum flecti per membra per artus
et proiecta refrenatur retroque residit.
quare in seminibus quoque idem fateare necessest,
esse aliam praeter plagas et pondera causam
motibus, unde haec est nobis innata potestas,
de nilo quoniam fieri nil posse videmus.
pondus enim prohibet ne plagis omnia fiant
externa quasi vi; sed ne mens ipsa necessum
intestinum habeat cunctis in rebus agendis
et devicta quasi *hoc* cogatur ferre patique,
id facit exiguum clinamen principiorum
nec regione loci certa nec tempore certo.
  Nec stipata magis fuit umquam materiai
copia nec porro maioribus intervallis;
nam neque adaugescit quicquam neque deperit inde.
quapropter quo nunc in motu principiorum

A p. m. B which Lach. keeps: both must have been in the archetype. 268 *conixa* Gif. for *conexa*, as in 160. *conexa* is absurd, though in nearly all eds. before Lach. Lamb. says some mss. have *connixa*: but that I doubt. 275 *perspicuum nobisst* AB for *perspicuumst nobis*: see Lach. for the strange frequency with which *st* is thus transposed in AB. 277 *extera*. *extima* Pont. Mar. vulgo wrongly; prob. from the *extrema* of Nicc. 278 279 *Pellat...rapi* Avanc. rightly for *Pallat...rapit*. *Pellit...cogit...rapit* Junt. and vulg. before Wak. *Fallat* A corr. Nicc. Flor. 31 Camb. all Vat. *Pellat...cogat* Mar. *Fallit, cogit, rapit* Pont. 281 *copia* Flor. 31 Camb. for *cona*. 283 *residit* Flor. 31 for *residia*.
291 *quasi* Nicc. for *quaei*. *hoc* add. by Ed. *id* Lach. 294 *fuit umquam* Junt. not Mar. for *fultum quam*. Cic. ad Att. XIII 40 1 for the corrupt *hic autem ut fultum*

corpora sunt, in eodem ante acta aetate fuere
et post haec semper simili ratione ferentur,
et quae consuerint gigni gignentur eadem
condicione et erunt et crescent vique valebunt,
quantum cuique datum est per foedera naturai.
nec rerum summam commutare ulla potest vis;
nam neque, quo possit genus ullum materiai
effugere ex omni, quicquam est *extra*, neque in omne
unde coorta queat nova vis inrumpere et omnem
naturam rerum mutare et vertere motus.

Illud in his rebus non est mirabile, quare,
omnia cum rerum primordia sint in motu,
summa tamen summa videatur stare quiete,
praeterquam siquid proprio dat corpore motus.
omnis enim longe nostris ab sensibus infra
primorum natura iacet: quapropter, ubi ipsa
cernere iam nequeas, motus quoque surpere debent;
praesertim cum, quae possimus cernere, celent
saepe tamen motus spatio diducta locorum.
nam saepe in colli tondentes pabula laeta
lanigerae reptant pecudes quo quam*que* vocantes
invitant herbae gemmantes rore recenti,
et satiati agni ludunt blandeque coruscant;
omnia quae nobis longe confusa videntur
et velut in viridi candor consistere colli.
praeterea magnae legiones cum loca cursu
camporum complent belli simulacra cientes,
fulgor ibi ad caelum se tollit totaque circum
aere renidescit tellus supterque virum vi
excitur pedibus sonitus clamoreque montes

est read *hic autem, ut fuit tum, est.* 301 *vique valebunt. inque valebunt* Pont. Mar. Ald. 1 Junt. vulg. 'vix latine' says Lach. 305 *extra* added by Ed. after *quicquam est*, in which it was absorbed: the sentence requires this: comp. v 361 and I 963, and Camb. Journ. of phil. I p. 375. Lach. adds *seorsum* at end of verse. *neque rursus in omne* Mar. Ald. 1 Junt. vulg. 313 *ipsa* Gif. for *ipsum.* 314 *surpere* Pont. Junt. for *asurpere.* 322 *vel ut in* Lach. rightly for *veluti in* of all mss. and eds.: mss. seem to have a tendency to this blunder: 780 *uti in* for *ut in*; above v. 86 *fit uti* for *fit ut*; Virg. Aen. IV 402 *veluti ingentem* M a c, *velut* P γ b rightly; VI 708 *veluti in* FGM, *velut in* P etc. ap. Ribbeck: *uti* is never found before a vowel: see also 536 and Lach. there. 325 *ibi* Mar. Ald. 1 Junt. for *ubi.*

icti reiectant voces ad sidera mundi
et circumvolitant equites mediosque repente
tramittunt valido quatientes impete campos.
et tamen est quidam locus altis montibus *unde*
stare videntur et in campis consistere fulgor.
Nunc age iam deinceps cunctarum exordia rerum
qualia sint et quam longe distantia formis
percipe, multigenis quam sint variata figuris;
non quo multa parum simili sint praedita forma,
sed quia non volgo paria omnibus omnia constant.
nec mirum; nam cum sit eorum copia tanta
ut neque finis, uti docui, neque summa sit ulla,
debent nimirum non omnibus omnia prorsum
esse pari filo similique adfecta figura.
praeter eat genus humanum mutaeque natantes
squamigerum pecudes et laeta armenta feraeque
et variae volucres, laetantia quae loca aquarum
concelebrant circum ripas fontisque lacusque,
et quae pervolgant nemora avia pervolitantes;
quorum unum quidvis generatim sumere perge,
invenies tamen inter se differre figuris.
nec ratione alia proles cognoscere matrem
nec mater posset prolem; quod posse videmus
nec minus atque homines inter se nota cluere.
nam saepe ante deum vitulus delubra decora
turicremas propter mactatus concidit aras
sanguinis expirans calidum de pectore flumen;
at mater viridis saltus orbata peragrans
noscit humi pedibus vestigia pressa bisulcis,
omnia convisens oculis loca si queat usquam

330 *tramittunt* A, *transmittunt* B. 331 *unde* added by Nicc. 337 *constant* Nicc. Flor. 31 Camb. vulg. Lamb. for *constat*: 694 *constant* B Nicc. (?), Camb. vulg.: 724 *constent* AB vulg.: in all three places *constent* Lach.; but I believe the indic. to be right, and the subj. to have come from the adjacent verbs: see notes 2. 342 *Praeter eat* Ed. for *Praetere*. *Praeterea* Nonius p. 158. *Praestat rem* Ed. formerly. *Parturiunt* Lach. which I don't understand. *Praeterea* and 347 *Horum* for *Quorum* Junt. vulgo: not Mar. 343 *armenta* Bentl. and Tonson's edition for *arbusta*. 347 *quidvis* Lach. for *quodvis*, as IV 126. 356 *Noscit* Lach. for *Nonquit* A Flor. 31 Camb. etc. *Non quid* Nicc. *Oinquit* B, *Oinquid* Gott. *Linquit* B corr. Mar. Ald. 1 Junt. vulgo, without sense. *Novit* Brieger: but Lucr.

conspicere amissum fetum, completque querellis
frondiferum nemus absistens et crebra revisit
ad stabulum desiderio perfixa iuvenci,
nec tenerae salices atque herbae rore vigentes
fluminaque illa queunt summis labentia ripis
oblectare animum subitamque avertere curam,
nec vitulorum aliae species per pabula laeta
derivare queunt animum curaque levare:
usque adeo quiddam proprium notumque requirit.
praeterea teneri tremulis cum vocibus haedi
cornigeras norunt matres agnique petulci
balantum pecudes: ita, quod natura reposcit,
ad sua quisque fere decurrunt ubera lactis.
postremo quodvis frumentum non tamen omne
quique suo genere inter se simile esse videbis,
quin intercurrat quaedam distantia formis.
concharumque genus parili ratione videmus
pingere telluris gremium, qua mollibus undis
litoris incurvi bibulam pavit aequor harenam.
quare etiam atque etiam simili ratione necessest,
natura quoniam constant neque facta manu sunt
unius ad certam formam primordia rerum,
dissimili inter se quaedam volitare figura.
  Perfacile est tali ratione exsolvere nobis
quare fulmineus multo penetralior ignis
quam noster fuat e taedis terrestribus ortus;
dicere enim possis caelestem fulminis ignem
suptilem magis e parvis constare figuris

rather uses *nosco*. 359 *absistens* Ed. for *adsittens*. *adsidueis* Lach. which is very weak. *adsistens* B corr. Nicc. vulg. 361 *vigentes*. *virentes* Macrob. sat. vi 2. 362 *illa* AB Gott. *ulla* Macrob. l.l. 'B corr.' says Lach. A corr. as I and Heins. have noted, Camb. vulgo. 363 *subitam* I now keep: see notes 2. *sumptam* Ed. in 1st ed. *solitam* Lach.; but the care here is quite *insolita*. 365 *curaque*. *curamque* A corr. Nicc. 369 *Balantum* A Gott. Nicc. etc. *Balatum* B Flor. 31 Camb. etc. 371 *non tamen omne*. *non ita, Memmi* Bruno (Harburg 1872, p. 3): acutely; but see notes 2. 372 *quique* Lach. for *quidque*.
376 *pavit*. *lavit* Nonius Mar. Ald. 1 Junt. Lamb. in text, but in notes he prefers *pavit*. 381 *est tali* Lach. for *est animi*. *est parili* Bern. not so well: the *t* of *tali* was absorbed in *est*. *est iam animi* Lamb.; but *animi* is out of place.
383 *fuat* Faber and Bentl. for *fluat*: Livy xxv 12 6 mss. have *fluat* for *fuat*. 387

atque ideo transire foramina quae nequit ignis
noster hic e lignis ortus taedaque creatus.
praeterea lumen per cornum transit, at imber
respuitur. quare? nisi luminis illa minora
corpora sunt quam de quibus est liquor almus aquarum.
et quamvis subito per colum vina videmus
perfluere; at contra tardum cunctatur olivom,
aut quia nimirum maioribus est elementis
aut magis hamatis inter se perque plicatis,
atque ideo fit uti non tam diducta repente
inter se possint primordia singula quaeque
singula per cuiusque foramina permanare.

Huc accedit uti mellis lactisque liquores
iucundo sensu linguae tractentur in ore;
at contra taetra absinthi natura ferique
centauri foedo pertorquent ora sapore;
ut facile agnoscas e levibus atque rutundis
esse ea quae sensus iucunde tangere possunt,
at contra quae amara atque aspera cumque videntur,
haec magis hamatis inter se nexa teneri
propterea solere vias rescindere nostris
sensibus introituque suo perrumpere corpus.

Omnia postremo bona sensibus et mala tactu
dissimili inter se pugnant perfecta figura;
ne tu forte putes serrae stridentis acerbum
horrorem constare elementis levibus aeque
ac musaea mele, per chordas organici quae
mobilibus digitis expergefacta figurant;
neu simili penetrare putes primordia forma
in nares hominum, cum taetra cadavera torrent,
et cum scena croco Cilici perfusa recens est
araque Panchaeos exhalat propter odores;
neve bonos rerum simili constare colores
semine constituas, oculos qui pascere possunt,
et qui conpungunt aciem lacrimareque cogunt

ortus. *ortu* Lach.: comp. vi 909 *fit ortus*, and 1141. 390 *almus* B corr. Brix. Pont. *amnis* Mar. for *alimus*. 397 *cuiusque*. *coli usque* Bruno (Harburg 1872). 401 'oratio lenius decurret, si scribemus *pertorqueat*. sed potest ferri *pertorquent*' Lach. 403 *iucunde tangere* Nicc. for *iucundet tacere*. 413 *Mobilibus* Poli-

aut foeda specie di*ri* turpesque videntur.
omnis enim, sensus quae mulcet cumque, *figura*
haut sine principiali aliquo levore creatast;
at contra quaecumque molesta atque aspera constat,
non aliquo sine materiae squalore repertast.
sunt etiam quae iam nec levia iure putantur
esse neque omnino flexis mucronibus unca,
sed magis angellis paulum prostantibus, *utqui*
titillare magis sensus quam laedere possint;
faecula iam quo de genere est inulaeque sapores.
denique iam calidos ignis gelidamque pruinam
dissimili dentata modo conpungere sensus
corporis, indicio nobis est tactus uterque.
tactus enim, tactus, pro divum numina sancta,
corporis est sensus, vel cum res extera sese
insinuat, vel cum laedit quae in corpore natast
aut iuvat *e*grediens genitalis per Veneris res,
aut ex offensu cum turbant corpore in ipso
semina confundunt*que* inter se concita sensum;
ut si forte manu quamvis iam corporis ipse
tute tibi partem ferias atque experiare.
quapropter longe formas distare necessest
principiis, varios quae possint edere sensus.
  Denique quae nobis durata ac spissa videntur,
haec magis hamatis inter sese esse necessest
et quasi ramosis alte compacta teneri.

tian marg. Flor. 29 and Nauger. for *nobilibus*. 421 *diri turpesque* Lach. for *di turpesque*. *fedi turpesque*, *qui olidi t.*, *tetri t.*, *turpes olidique* have all been read. *caeli turpesque* Nicc. and oldest eds. 422 *figura* Lach. after Schneidewin Phil. III p. 538 for *videntur* which has come from 421 and supplanted the feminine substantive. *quae mulcet causa iuvatque* Junt. *quae mulcet cunque iuvatque* Avanc. without sense; but at end of his ed. of Catullus he bids us read *quae mulcet causa iuvatque*. *mulctat causa iuvatque* Mar. apparently; but the words are much erased.

423 *levore* Avanc. for *leviore*. 427 *unca*. *uncaque* mss. 428 *utqui* added by Ed. and N. P. Howard. *et quae* Flor. 31 Camb. vulgo. *quaeque* Lach. *unde* Bern. *quique*, i.e. *angelli*, Ed. formerly: the *que* at end of 427 comes from the lost *utqui*. Then 429 *possint* A Nicc. Flor. 31 Camb., and (as I learn from Lach. p. 298) cod. Sangallens. schol. in Iuvenalem; rightly, as the subj. is necessary. *possunt* B Gott. vulg. Lach. 430 *inulaeque* Lamb. first for *inviaeque*. *vinique* Nicc. 437 *egrediens* Flor. 31 Camb. etc. for *grediens*. 438 *aut*: Lach. seems to me wrong in changing this to *atque*. 439 *que* added by Mar. Junt. vulgo. 451 *e* Lach.

in quo iam genere in primis adamantina saxa
prima acie constant ictus contemnere sueta
et validi silices ac duri robora ferri
aeraque quae claustris restantia vociferantur.
illa quidem debent e levibus atque rutundis
esse magis, fluvido quae corpore liquida constant;
NAMQUE PAPAVERIS HAUSTUS ITEMST FACILIS QUOD AQUARUM
nec retinentur enim inter se glomeramina quaeque
et procursus item proclive volubilis exstat.
omnia postremo quae puncto tempore cernis
diffugere, ut fumum nebulas flammasque, necessest,
si minus omnibu' sunt e levibus atque rutundis,
at non esse tamen perplexis indupedita,
pungere uti possint corpus penetrareque *ve*sca
nec tamen haerere inter se; quodcumque videmus
sensibu' sedatum, facile ut cognoscere possis
non e perplexis sed acutis esse elementis.
sed quod amara vides eadem quae fluvida constant,
sudor uti maris est, minime mirabile habeto;
nam quod fluvidus est, e levibus atque rutundis
est, et *squalida multa creant* admixta doloris
corpora; nec tamen haec retineri hamata necessu*mst;*

for *ex*, as our mss. elsewhere have *e* before *l*. 452 *corpore* A corr. for *corpora.* 453 Lamb. justly ejects: it is quite out of place: does it refer to poppy seeds, or poppy juice? in the former case it is untrue, in the latter unmeaning: Lach. retains it, and for *quod* reads *quasi* after M. Haupt. 455 *procursus* Mar.? Junt. for *perculsus.* 456—463: a passage variously emended: the changes I have made are slight and I think not improbable. 458 *omnibu'* Lamb. after Muretus for *omnia*: comp. IV 82 where I read *Moenibu'* for *Moenia. omnino sint levibus* Pont. Junt. 460 *vesca* Ed. for *saxa*: with *penetrareque saxa* of mss. for *penetrareq. vesca* comp. VI 541 *summersosca* of mss. for *summersaq. saxa*; and VI 229 *sasca* mss. for *saxa. laxa* Ed. formerly. *sese* Lach. 462 *sedatum* of mss. I now keep: *sic latum* Ed. formerly: Lach. reads 461 *venenumst* for *videmus*, and 462 *sed rarum* for *sedatum*, making two changes. *Ventis esse datum* Bern. strangely for *Sensibus sedatum. Sentibus esse datum* Faber conjectures: but he thinks with Lamb. that 461—463 are spurious. 461 *quodcumque. quod quisque* Mar. Junt. vulg., wrongly joining this clause with the preceding. 465 *habeto* Ed. for *debet. habebis* Lach.: but he thinks *debet* may be right and a verse be lost, and this Bern. assumes. *est minime mirabile habendum* 3 Vat. Mon. Ald. 1 Junt. 'Marullus' says Gif. *cuiquam* Gif. 'Ita v. l.' i.e. Ver. Ven. he having the latter before him with Marullus' ms. emendations; among which Marullus had inserted the reading of his ms. Mon.: Brix. omits the word. 466 *fluvidus est. fluvidum est* Ver. Ven.

scilicet esse globosa tamen, cum squalida constent,
provolvi simul ut possint et laedere sensus.
et quo mixta putes magis aspera levibus esse
principiis, unde est Neptuni corpus acerbum,
est ratio secernendi; seorsumque videndi
umor dulcis, ubi per terras crebrius idem
percolatur, ut in foveam fluat ac mansuescat;
linquit enim supera taetri primordia viri,
aspera quo*m* magis in terris haerescere possint.
  Quod quoniam docui, pergam conectere rem quae
ex hoc apta fidem ducat, primordia rerum
finita variare figurarum ratione.
quod si non ita sit, rursum iam semina quaedam
esse infinito debebunt corporis auctu.
namque in eodem, una cuiusvis in brevitate
corporis inter se multum variare figurae
non possunt: fac enim minimis e partibus esse
corpora prima tribus, vel paulo pluribus auge;
nempe ubi eas partis unius corporis omnis,
summa atque ima locans, transmutans dextera laevis,
omnimodis expertus eris, quam quisque det ordo
formai speciem totius corporis eius,
quod superest, si forte voles variare figuras,
addendum partis alias erit, inde sequetur,

followed by all eds. before Lach. though the metre is thereby violated. 467 *Est e levibus atque rutundi admixta doloris Corpora* mss.: some of these words it is plain have come from 466 and supplanted the words of Lucr. *Est, et levibu' sunt aliunde* etc. Lach.: but he adds 'quamquam sic quoque mirationem faciunt illa *doloris Corpora*, quae sunt pungentia sensus et laedentia': quite true: Bern. reads *Est et squalida sunt illis* etc., and *squalida* indeed seems necessary: I have therefore written *Est, et squalida multa creant admixta doloris Corpora*: *doloris* being of course the accus. plur. 468 *necessumst* Lach. for *necessu.* 469 *constent* old eds. for *constet.* 471 *Et quo* Pont. Mar. Junt. for *Et quod.*

471—477: by a better punctuation and by doubling one letter I have rectified this passage; 473 I have placed a stop after *secernendi*, and removed that which all former editors have put after *videndi*, and 477 have written *quom magis* for *quo magis.* Lach. puts 476 before 474 and then leaves a most involved sentence. 474 *dulcis. dulcit* Gif. not Lamb.: Lamb. keeps *dulcis* ed. 1 and 2: he conjectures *acerbus* and reads *dulcet* ed. 3. 477 *possint. possunt* Mar. Junt. Lamb. vulgo. 483 *in eodem, una* Ed. for *in eadem una. eadem unius* Lach. 488 *transmutans* B corr. for *transmutas.* 497 *semina* A corr. for

adsimili ratione alias ut postulet ordo,
si tu forte voles etiam variare figuras.
ergo formarum novitatem corporis augmen
subsequitur. quare non est ut credere possis
esse infinitis distantia semina formis,
ne quaedam cogas inmani maximitate
esse, supra quod iam docui non posse probari.
iam tibi barbaricae vestes Meliboeaque fulgens
purpura Thessalico concharum tacta colore
. . . .
aurea pavonum ridenti imbuta lepore
saecla, novo rerum superata colore iacerent
et contemptus odor smyrnae mellisque sapores,
et cycnea mele Phoebeaque daedala chordis
carmina consimili ratione oppressa silerent;
namque aliis aliud praestantius exoreretur.
cedere item retro possent in deteriores
omnia sic partis, ut diximus in melioris;
namque aliis aliud retro quoque taetrius esset
naribus auribus atque oculis orisque sapori.
quae quoniam non sunt, *sed* rebus reddita certa
finis utrimque tenet summam, fateare necessest
materiem quoque finitis differre figuris.
denique ab ignibus ad gelidas iter usque pruinas
finitumst retroque pari ratione remensumst;
omnis enim calor ac frigus mediique tepores
interutrasque iacent explentes ordine summam.
ergo finita distant ratione creata,

femina. 499 *probari* Ald. 1 Junt. for *probare. esse probare* Mar. 501: I believe a verse is here lost of this nature *et quos ostendunt in solis luce colores. tacta* Lach. after Oudendorp Lucan x 491 for *tecta. tincta* Junt. vulg. 502 *ridenti* Fr. Medices for *rident* and 503 *novo* for *nova. Aurea, p. ridenti imitata* etc. Lach.: Lamb. and vulg. edd. *et* at end of 501. 503 *Saecla. Pepla* P. Burmann Wak. 504 *Et contemptus odor* Flor. 31 Camb. Brix. Ven. Mar. vulg. for *Et contemptus udor. Et contemptus suodor* Nicc. Ver.: hence I infer the ms. of Poggio had *$\overset{o}{\text{s}}$udor*. 512 *sed* added by Lach. 514 *finitis* Politian (?), Pont. Mar. Ald. 1 Junt. for *infinitis.* 515 *iter usque* Lach. for *hiemisque.* perhaps *hiemum usque.* 517 *Omnis* of mss. is right. *Extima* Ed. formerly. *Ambit* Lach. *Finis* Mar. Junt. *Finit* Lamb. vulgo. 518 *Interutrasque*: see notes 2. *Inter utrasque* mss. *Interutraque* Lach. here and in five other places, v 472 476 vi 362 1062, and iii 306 where I read *Inter utrosque*, and v 839 for *inter*

ancipi*ti* quoniam mucroni utrimque notantur,
hinc flammis illinc rigidis infesta pruinis.
  Quod quoniam docui, pergam conectere rem quae
ex hoc apta fidem ducat, primordia rerum,
inter se simili quae sunt perfecta figura,
infinita cluere. etenim distantia cum sit
formarum finita, necesse est quae similes sint
esse infinitas aut summam materiai
finitam constare, id quod non esse probavi
versibus ostendens corpuscula materiai
ex infinito summam rerum usque tenere,
undique protelo plagarum continuato.
nam quod rara vides magis esse animalia quaedam
fecundamque minus naturam cernis in illis,
at regione locoque alio terrisque remotis
multa licet genere esse in eo numerumque repleri;
sicut quadripedum cum primis esse videmus
in genere anguimanus elephantos, India quorum
milibus e multis vallo munitur eburno,
ut penitus nequeat penetrari: tanta ferarum
vis est, quarum nos perpauca exempla videmus.
sed tamen id quoque uti concedam, quamlubet esto
unica res quaedam nativo corpore sola,

utras. 521 *infesta* Lach. for *infessa*, and so Lamb. in notes, *insessa* in text after Mar. Junt. *infensa* Flor. 31 Vat. 1954 Othob. old eds.

522—568: this passage I have fully discussed in Camb. Journ. of phil. IV p. 143 etc. where I have shewn that Lach. is quite wrong in enclosing 522—528 in brackets, and beginning a new paragraph at 529, and there reading *Protinus* for *Versibus*: he gives us the alternative, which Bern. has adopted, of assuming one or more verses to have been lost before *Versibus*; and indeed all before him from Mar. Ald. 1 and Junt. downwards have inserted this line, *Quod quoniam docui, nunc suaviloquis age paucis.* Victorius in his copy of Marullus' notes has not this line; but, for *Versibus*, *Nunc vero*, Marullus' first thought, answering to Lachmann's *Protinus*. No stop is to be put at the end of 528, and 529 *ostendens* is to be read for *ostendam*; and then all difficulty vanishes. 533 *minus* Lamb. most rightly for *magis* which Wak. absurdly tries to explain. 535 *genere* Mar.? Junt. for *genera*. 536 *Sicut* Bentl. for *Sicuti*: III 816 mss. have the same error. Lachmann's note shews the strange tendency of mss. to read *sicuti* for *sicut*, as above *veluti* for *velut*: in the passage he quotes from Plautus mil. 727, it now appears from Ritschl that the Ambrosian palimpsest has rightly *sicut*: Cic. Arat. 131 on the other hand Orelli reads *Sicutĭ cum cœptant*: Cic. de senect. 14, though the latest editors read the verse of Ennius *Sic ut fortis equus*, 5 of their 6 mss. have *Sicuti*.

541 *lubet* B corr. Flor. 31 Camb. for *iubet*. 543 *nulla* added by Lach. *non*

cui similis toto terrarum *nulla* sit orbi;
infinita tamen nisi erit vis materiai
unde ea progigni possit concepta, creari
non poterit, neque, quod superest, procrescere alique.
quippe etenim sumam hoc quoque uti finita per omne
corpora iactari unius genitalia rei,
unde ubi qua vi et quo pacto congressa coibunt
materiae tanto in pelago turbaque aliena?
non, ut opinor, habent rationem conciliandi;
sed quasi naufragiis magnis multisque coortis
disiectare solet magnum mare transtra guberna
antemnas proram malos tonsasque natantis,
per terrarum omnis oras fluitantia aplustra
ut videantur et indicium mortalibus edant,
infidi maris insidias virisque dolumque
ut vitare velint, neve ullo tempore credant,
subdola cum ridet placidi pellacia ponti,
sic tibi si finita semel primordia quaedam
constitues, aevom debebunt sparsa per omnem
disiectare aestus diversi materiai,
numquam in concilium ut possint compulsa coire
nec remorari in concilio nec crescere adaucta;
quorum utrumque palam fieri manifesta docet res,
et res progigni et genitas procrescere posse.
esse igitur genere in quovis primordia rerum
infinita palam est unde omnia suppeditantur.
  Nec superare queunt motus itaque exitiales
perpetuo neque in aeternum sepelire salutem,
nec porro rerum genitales auctificique
motus perpetuo possunt servare creata.
sic aequo geritur certamine principiorum
ex infinito contractum tempore bellum:
nunc hic nunc illic superant vitalia rerum

sit in orbi B corr. *non sit in orbe* Nicc. Flor. 31 Camb. Mon. vulgo: perhaps rightly. 547 *sumam hoc quoque uti* Ed. for the meaningless *sumant oculi*: comp. 541. *si manticuler* Lach. strangely. Wak. tells us that Bentl. obelised the words; and it is strange that all editors before Wak., even Junt. and Lamb., left them unnoticed: Wak. conj. *sumant ollei.* 553 *guberna* Lamb. for *caverna. carinas* Nicc. 555 *aplustra* Politian Mar. Junt. for *plāustra* A, *plaustra* B Nicc. Camb. 560 *si finita* B corr. Ver. Ven. Mar. for *si infinita.*

et superantur item. miscetur funere vagor
quem pueri tollunt visentis luminis oras;
nec nox ulla diem neque noctem aurora secutast
quae non audierit mixtos vagitibus aegris
ploratus mortis comites et funeris atri.

Illud in his obsignatum quoque rebus habere
convenit et memori mandatum mentè tenere,
nil esse, in promptu quorum natura videtur,
quod genere ex uno consistat principiorum,
nec quicquam quod non permixto semine constet.
et quodcumque magis vis multas possidet in se
atque potestates, ita plurima principiorum
in sese genera ac varias docet esse figuras.
principio tellus habet in se corpora prima
unde mare inmensum volventes frigora fontes
adsidue renovent, habet ignes unde oriantur.
nam multis succensa locis ardent sola terrae,
eximiis vero furit ignibus impetus Aetnae.
tum porro nitidas fruges arbustaque laeta
gentibus humanis habet unde extollere possit,
unde etiam fluvios frondes et pabula laeta
montivago generi possit praebere ferarum.
quare magna deum mater materque ferarum
et nostri genetrix haec dicta est corporis una.

Hanc veteres Graium docti cecinere poetae
. . . .
sedibus in curru biiugos agitare leones,
aeris in spatio magnam pendere docentes
tellurem neque posse in terra sistere terram.
adiunxere feras, quia quamvis effera proles
officiis debet molliri victa parentum.

586 *quod cumque* Lach. for *quaecumque*: previous editors have gone much astray. 593 (and 607) *Eximiis* Avanc. for *Ex imis*. 'Sic v. l. o. ..Marull. ex Virg. lib. 5, *ex imis*, contra v. l.': the 'veteres libri omnes' are only the Ven. in which were Marullus' ms. notes: Ven. has *Eximis* which Gif. probably read *Eximiis*: Marullus perhaps referred to Aen. III 577 *fundoque exaestuat imo*, and divided the word: he makes no change in cod. Victor. 601: Lach. with reason supposes a verse to be lost here, which he thus supplies, *Magnifice divam ex ipsis penetralibu' vectam Sedibus*. Lamb. reads *Sublimem* for *Sedibus*. 605 *molliri* Nicc. Flor. 31 Camb. for *moliri*. 613 *orbem* Pont. Junt.

muralique caput summum cinxere corona,
eximiis munita locis quia sustinet urbes;
quo nunc insigni per magnas praedita terras
horrifice fertur divinae matris imago.
hanc variae gentes antiquo more sacrorum
Idaeam vocitant matrem Phrygiasque catervas
dant comites, quia primum ex illis finibus edunt
per terrarum orbem fruges coepisse creari.
gallos attribuunt, quia, numen qui violarint
matris et ingrati genitoribus inventi sint,
significare volunt indignos esse putandos,
vivam progeniem qui in oras luminis edant.
tympana tenta tonant palmis et cymbala circum
concava, raucisonoque minantur cornua cantu,
et Phrygio stimulat numero cava tibia mentis,
telaque praeportant violenti signa furoris,
ingratos animos atque impia pectora volgi
conterrere metu quae possint numini' divae.
ergo cum primum magnas invecta per urbis
munificat tacita mortalis muta salute,
aere atque argento sternunt iter omne viarum
largifica stipe ditantes ninguntque rosarum
floribus umbrantes matrem comitumque catervas.
hic armata manus, Curetas nomine Grai
quos memorant Phrygios, inter se forte *quod armis*
ludunt in numerumque exultant sanguinolenti
terrificas capitum quatientes numine cristas,

for *orbes*. 615 *Matris* Flor. 31 Camb. for *Matri*. *sint* Lamb. first for *sunt*: Lach. says nothing; but Ed. as well as Heins. ms. notes and Goebel Rh. Mus. n. f. xv p. 414 found *inventi sunt* in AB. *sint inventi* Lach.: I prefer the rhythm of the ms. order. 623 *metu...numini' divae* Lach. at the suggestion of an 'amicus quidam' of Haverc. for *metu...numine divae*. 626 *iter omne viarum* Turnebus Gif. Lamb. ed. 2 and 3, vulg. for *ite omnia virum*: a certain correction. *ite omnia mirum* Nicc. some Vat. and old eds. *iter, omnia circum* Flor. 31 Camb. some Vat. Pont. Mar. Junt. Lamb. ed. 1. 630 *quod armis* a certain correction of Lach.: the sentence requiring the conjunction *quod* or *quia*, the sense *armis*. *catervas* of mss. is a mere blunder of the scribe who has taken it from 628: a form of error common in our mss.: comp. 422 I 555 VI 15 etc. *catenas* of B is again a mere miswriting of *cateruas*, though it has deceived many. *choreas* Pont.

631 *sanguinolenti* Bentl. for *sanguine fleti*. *sanguine freti* Nicc. and old eds. *sanguine laeti* Pont. Junt. Lamb. 632 *numine*. *momine* Lach. whom I followed

Dictaeos referunt Curetas qui Iovis illum
vagitum in Creta quondam occultasse feruntur,
cum pueri circum puerum pernice chorea
armatei in numerum pulsarent aeribus aera,
ne Saturnus eum malis mandaret adeptus
aeternumque daret matri sub pectore volnus.
propterea magnam armati matrem comitantur,
aut quia significant divam praedicere ut armis
ac virtute velint patriam defendere terram
praesidioque parent decorique parentibus esse.
quae bene et eximie quamvis disposta ferantur,
longe sunt tamen a vera ratione repulsa.
omnis enim per se divom natura necessest
inmortali aevo summa cum pace fruatur
semota ab nostris rebus seiunctaque longe;
nam privata dolore omni, privata periclis,
ipsa suis pollens opibus, nil indiga nostri,
nec bene promeritis capitur neque tangitur ira.
655 hic siquis mare Neptunum Cereremque vocare
constituit fruges et Bacchi nomine abuti
mavolt quam laticis proprium proferre vocamen,
concedamus ut hic terrarum dictitet orbem
esse deum matrem, dum vera re tamen ipse
680 religione animum turpi contingere parcat.
652 terra quidem vero caret omni tempore sensu,
et quia multarum potitur primordia rerum,
multa modis multis effert in lumina solis.
660 Saepe itaque ex uno tondentes gramina campo
lanigerae pecudes et equorum duellica proles
buceriaeque greges eodem sub tegmine caeli

in my small ed.: but see Ph. Wagner in Philologus supplement I p. 400, Conington to Aen. II 123 and Lachmann's own note: comp. also IV 179. 636 *Armat et in numerum pernice chorea*: omitted by Pont. and Lamb. as manifestly made up out of 635 and 637. 653 *Constituit* Lach. for *Constituet*, as *mavolt* follows.

657 (680): this verse, which was the last of p. 73 of the archetype, has been transferred hither by Lach.: the scribe omitted it in its place and then wrote it at the bottom of the page. Pontanus acutely sees that both the vss. as given in mss. are fragmentary. *parcat* Lach. for *parato*. *parco* Flor. 31 Camb. etc.

658—660 (652—654) I have transferred hither: the *itaque* of 661 manifestly refers to them; so that if they are to keep their place, then (what comes to much the

ex unoque sitim sedantes flumine aquai
dissimili vivont specie retinentque parentum
naturam et mores generatim quaeque imitantur.
tanta est in quovis genere herbae materiai
dissimilis ratio, tanta est in flumine quoque.
hinc porro quamvis animantem ex omnibus unam
ossa cruor venae calor umor viscera nervi
constituunt; quae sunt porro distantia longe,
dissimili perfecta figura principiorum.
tum porro quaecumque igni flammata cremantur,
si nil praeterea, tamen haec in corpore condunt
unde ignem iacere et lumen summittere possint
scintillasque agere ac late differre favillam.
cetera consimili mentis ratione peragrans
invenies igitur multarum semina rerum
corpore celare et varias cohibere figuras.
denique multa vides quibus et color et sapor una
reddita sunt cum odore: in primis pleraque dona

. . . .

haec igitur variis debent constare figuris;
nidor enim penetrat qua fucus non it in artus,
fucus item sorsum, *sorsum* sapor insinuatur
sensibus; ut noscas primis differre figuris.
dissimiles igitur formae glomeramen in unum
conveniunt et res permixto semine constant.

same thing) 652—657 must be enclosed in brackets as a subsequent marginal addition of the poet's: see above, p. 29. 664 *sedantes* Nicc. B corr. for *sedentes*. Brieger puts this v. before 662. 665 *retinentque parentum* Flor. 31 Vat. 1136 Othob. 1954 Othob. s.m. Mar. Ald. 1 Junt. for *retinente parente*.

669 *quamvis...unam* Lamb. for *quamvis...una*. *quemvis...unā* Nicc. *quemvis... unum* Mar. Junt. 674 *condunt* Ed. for *traduntur*. *celant* Lach. *cludunt* Bern. 675 *ignem* Nicc. for *igne*. *ignes* B corr. 681 a v. is lost here such as *Quis accensa solent fumare altaria divom*: see notes 2: not a letter of the mss. is to be changed. *in privis pluraque dona* Lach. In consequence of 657 (680) having been misplaced the older editors have made strange confusion here. 683 684 *fucus...Fucus* Lach. most properly for *sucus...Sucus*: 'nam *fucus* color est'.

684 *sorsum* AB only once. '*seorsum et rerum* [Faber's text]. *et rerum* om. mss. vv. repetendum ut puto *τὸ sorsum* G.V.' ms. notes of Is. Vossius. Haverc. and through him Lach. misrepresent him: 'G.V.' is of course his father Gerard, whose reading therefore is the same as Lachmann's. 685 *primis* of mss. I now keep: see notes 2: *privis* Lach. after Vossius, Preiger, Haverc. who says 'egregie et hoc loco *privis* habet Marginalis noster': my ms. notes of Vossius are without

quin etiam passim nostris in versibus ipsis
multa elementa vides multis communia verbis,
cum tamen inter se versus ac verba necesse est
confiteare alia ex aliis constare elementis;
non quo multa parum communis littera currat
aut nulla inter se duo sint ex omnibus isdem,
sed quia non volgo paria omnibus omnia constant.
sic aliis in rebus item communia multa
multarum rerum cum sint primordia, verum
dissimili tamen inter se consistere summa
possunt; ut merito ex aliis constare feratur
humanum genus et fruges arbustaque laeta.
Nec tamen omnimodis conecti posse putandum est
omnia; nam volgo fieri portenta videres,
semiferas hominum species existere et altos
interdum ramos egigni corpore vivo,
multaque conecti terrestria membra marinis,
tum flammam taetro spirantis ore Chimaeras
pascere naturam per terras omniparentis.
quorum nil fieri manifestum est, omnia quando
seminibus certis certa genetrice creata
conservare genus crescentia posse videmus.
scilicet id certa fieri ratione necessust.
nam sua cuique cibis ex omnibus intus in artus
corpora discedunt conexaque convenientis
efficiunt motus; at contra aliena videmus
reicere in terras naturam, multaque caecis
corporibus fugiunt e corpore percita plagis,
quae neque conecti quoquam potuere neque intus
vitalis motus consentire atque imitari.
sed ne forte putes animalia sola teneri

it. 693 *isdem* Lamb. for *idem*: 'quod est sane simplicissimum, sed videtur abhorrere ab usu Lucretii' says Lach. who reads awkwardly *nulli* for *nulla*, and *idem*. But here and v 349 Lucr. unquestionably used *isdem*, as did his contemporaries. 694 *constant* Ed. with B Nicc. (?), Camb. Mon. Lamb. vulg. *constent* Lach. with A corr.: see 337. 696 for *rerum* 'f. verum G.V.' in Isaac's ms. notes: and before him Pont.; and so Lach.: yet *longe* of Flor. 31 Camb. Mar. may be right, as the scribe might well write *primordia rerum* mechanically from the mere fact of these words so often coming together. 716 *intus* Lach. for *inte*. *inter* B corr. Camb. *intra* Nicc.: *consentire* is here transitive.

legibus hisce, ea res ratio disterminat omnis.
nam veluti tota natura dissimiles sunt
inter se genitae res quaeque, ita quamque necessest
dissimili constare figura principiorum;
non quo multa parum simili sint praedita forma,
sed quia non volgo paria omnibus omnia constant.
semina cum porro distent, differre necessust
intervalla vias conexus pondera plagas
concursus motus, quae non animalia solum
corpora seiungunt, sed terras ac mare totum
secernunt caelumque a terris omne retentant.
Nunc age dicta meo dulci quaesita labore
percipe, ne forte haec albis ex alba rearis
principiis esse, ante oculos quae candida cernis,
aut ea quae nigrant nigro de semine nata;
nive alium quemvis quae sunt inbuta colorem,
propterea gerere hunc credas, quod materiai
corpora consimili sint eius tincta colore.
nullus enim color est omnino materiai
corporibus, neque par rebus neque denique dispar.
in quae corpora si nullus tibi forte videtur
posse animi iniectus fieri, procul avius erras.
nam cum caecigeni, solis qui lumina numquam
dispexere, tamen cognoscant corpora tactu,
ex ineunte aevo nullo coniuncta colore,
scire licet nostrae quoque menti corpora posse
vorti in notitiam nullo circumlita fuco.

in se Bern. which I don't understand. *inde* Brieger. 719 *Legibus his quaedam ratio disterminat omnis* mss. *omnia* Lach. after Junt. as in I 1106 without authority: *omnia* I doubt not comes from Marullus, as he uses it in the same way in his hymn to earth at the end of a passage partly quoted p. 7 in which Lucr. is closely imitated: see also reading of Junt. in 749; [the cod. Victor. proves my inference to be correct here and 749: Marullus cites Virgil's *quin protinus omnia Perlegerent oculis*]. *hisce eadem r. d. omne* Bern.: but *omne* is hardly thus used; therefore I read *hisce ea res r. d. omnis*: *quaedam* has no meaning. 721 *ita quanque* Junt. for *ita cumque.* 724 *constant* Ed. *constent* AB vulg. Lach.: see 337 and 694. 734 *colorem* Nicc. vulg. for *colore*: Lamb. and Lach. deny that *imbuta colorem* is Latin; but see notes 2. Lach. reads *Nive alium quemvis quo sunt inbuta colore*, cet.; but the nominative *quae* is absolutely required here. *induta* Lamb. for *inbuta.* 741 lumina Flor. 31 Camb. etc. for *numina.* 742 *Dispexere* Nicc. corr. Avanc. for *Despexere. Aspexere* Junt. Lamb. 743 Bentl.

denique nos ipsi caecis quaecumque tenebris
tangimus, haud ullo sentimus tincta colore.
quod quoniam vinco fieri, nunc esse docebo
. . . .
omnis enim color omnino mutatur in omnis;
quod facere haud ullo debent primordia pacto;
immutabile enim quiddam superare necessest,
ne res ad nilum redigantur funditus omnes.
nam quodcumque suis mutatum finibus exit,
continuo hoc mors est illius quod fuit ante.
proinde colore cave contingas semina rerum,
ne tibi res redeant ad nilum funditus omnes.
  Praeterea si nulla coloris principiis est
reddita natura et variis sunt praedita formis,
e quibus omne genus gignunt variantque colores
propterea, magni quod refert semina quaeque
cum quibus et quali positura contineantur
et quos inter se dent motus accipiantque,
perfacile extemplo rationem reddere possis
cur ea quae nigro fuerint paulo ante colore,
marmoreo fieri possint candore repente;
ut mare, cum magni commorunt aequora venti,
vertitur in canos candenti marmore fluctus;
dicere enim possis, nigrum quod saepe videmus,
materies ubi permixta est illius et ordo
principiis mutatus et addita demptaque quaedam,
continuo id fieri ut candens videatur et album.
quod si caeruleis constarent aequora ponti
seminibus, nullo possent albescere pacto;
nam quocumque modo perturbes caerula quae sint,
numquam in marmoreum possunt migrare colorem.
sin alio atque alio sunt semina tincta colore
quae maris efficiunt unum purumque nitorem,
ut saepe ex aliis formis variisque figuris

and Lach. place after 748: but see notes 2. 748 a v. is lost here. 749 *in omnis* Flor. 31 Camb. Nauger. for *et omnis*. *in omnia* Junt. after Marullus: see note to 719. 759 *omne genus* Lach. for *omnigenus*. *omnigenos* A corr. Nicc. Flor. 31 Camb. vulg. 760 *Propterea* Nicc. corr. Flor. 31 Camb. Mar. Junt. Lamb. ed. 1 for *Praeterea* which Wak. and, strange to say, Lamb. ed. 2 and 3 retain.

763 *extemplo* Brix. Lamb. for *exemplo*. 765 *possint* Lamb. for *possunt*.

efficitur quiddam quadratum unaque figura,
conveniebat, ut in quadrato cernimus esse
dissimiles formas, ita cernere in aequore ponti
aut alio in quovis uno puroque nitore
dissimiles longe inter se variosque colores.
praeterea nil officiunt obstantque figurae
dissimiles quo quadratum minus omne sit extra;
at varii rerum inpediunt prohibentque colores
quominus esse uno possit res tota nitore.
  Tum porro quae ducit et inlicit ut tribuamus
principiis rerum nonnumquam causa colores,
occidit, ex albis quoniam non alba creantur,
nec quae nigra cluent de nigris sed variis ex.
quippe etenim multo proclivius exorientur
candida de nullo quam nigro nata colore
aut alio quovis qui contra pugnet et obstet.
  Praeterea quoniam nequeunt sine luce colores
esse neque in lucem existunt primordia rerum,
scire licet quam sint nullo velata colore.
qualis enim caecis poterit color esse tenebris?
lumine quin ipso mutatur propterea quod
recta aut obliqua percussus luce refulget;
pluma columbarum quo pacto in sole videtur,
quae sita cervices circum collumque coronat;
namque alias fit uti claro sit rubra pyropo,
interdum quodam sensu fit uti videatur
inter curalium viridis miscere zmaragdos.
caudaque pavonis, larga cum luce repleta est,
consimili mutat ratione obversa colores;

779 *unaque figura* Nicc. for *unaque figuras.* *unaque figura est* Flor. 31 Camb. Mar. Junt. *unaeque figurae* Lamb. after Muretus; 'contra consuetudinem Lucretii' says Lach. 780 *ut in* Lach. for *uti in*: see 322. 781 *in aequore* Ver. Ven. Politian (?) Mar. Junt. for *in aequora.* 783 *colores* Nicc. for *calores.*

785 *extra* seems quite appropriate: Lach. reads *ex his.* 788 *ducit et inlicit ut tribuamus* Lamb. and Turneb. for *ducit et inlicitu tribuamus* (*et* om. A Nicc.). *ducit in licitum ut tribuamus* Camb. *ut illicitum hoc tribuamus* Mar. Junt.

790 *creantur* Nicc. for *creatur.* 791 *Nec quae* Flor. 31 Camb. for *Neque.* *variis ex* Wak. for *variis ea.* *variata* Pont. *variantur* Mar. Junt. *variant se* Ald. 1. 800 *refulget.* *refulgit* Lach. 802 *cervices.* *cervicemst* Brieger.

803 *rubra* Flor. 31 Camb. Mon. Ver. Ven. for *rubro.* 805 *curalium* Wak. for *caeruleum.* 'fo. *beryllum*' Bentl. 806 *larga cum luce* Nicc. B corr. for

qui quoniam quodam gignuntur luminis ictu,
scire licet, sine eo fieri non posse putandum est.
et quoniam plagae quoddam genus excipit in se
pupula, cum sentire colorem dicitur album,
atque aliud porro, nigrum cum et cetera sentit,
nec refert ea quae tangas quo forte colore
praedita sint, verum quali magis apta figura,
scire licet nil principiis opus esse colores,
sed variis formis variantes edere tactus.
  Praeterea quoniam non certis certa figuris
est natura coloris et omnia principiorum
formamenta queunt in quovis esse nitore,
cur ea quae constant ex illis non pariter sunt
omne genus perfusa coloribus in genere omni?
conveniebat enim corvos quoque saepe volantis
ex albis album pinnis iactare colorem,
et nigros fieri nigro de semine cycnos
aut alio quovis uno varioque colore.
  Quin etiam quanto in partes res quaeque minutas
distrahitur magis, hoc magis est ut cernere possis
evanescere paulatim stinguique colorem;
ut fit ubi in parvas partis discerpitur austrum:
purpura poeniceusque color clarissimu' multo,
filatim cum distractum est, dispergitur omnis;
noscere ut hinc possis prius omnem efflare colorem
particulas quam discedant ad semina rerum.
  Postremo quoniam non omnia corpora vocem
mittere concedis neque odorem, propterea fit
ut non omnibus adtribuas sonitus et odores.
sic oculis quoniam non omnia cernere quimus,
scire licet quaedam tam constare orba colore
quam sine odore ullo quaedam sonituque remota,

largo cum luce which may be right. 809 *Scire licet. Scilicet id* Lamb. *est* om. Nicc. 814 *sint* Ald. 1 Junt. not Mar. for *sunt.* 815 *opus esse colores* Lamb. after Nonius for *colore* of mss.: see Lach. 821 *Omne genus* Lach. for *Omnigenus*, as 759. *Omnigenis* Nicc. vulg. 829 *austrum. ostrum* Wak. conj. for *aurum*: but the right punctuation I owe to Goebel quaest. Lucr. crit. p. 14, though Ven. Ald. 1 and Junt. have a full stop after *aurum. aurea Purpura* and 831 *distracta* for *distractum* Lach. without judgment. *aurum* which previous editors retain has no sense. *usu* Bern. for *aurum.* 831 *dispergitur* Lach.

nec minus haec animum cognoscere posse sagacem
quam quae sunt aliis rebus privata notare.

Sed ne forte putes solo spoliata colore
corpora prima manere, etiam secreta teporis
sunt ac frigoris omnino calidique vaporis,
et sonitu sterila et suco ieiuna feruntur,
nec iaciunt ullum proprium de corpore odorem.
sicut amaracini blandum stactaeque liquorem
et nardi florem, nectar qui naribus halat,
cum facere instituas, cum primis quaerere par est,
quoad licet ac possis reperire, inolentis olivi
naturam, nullam quae mittat naribus auram,
quam minime ut possit mixtos in corpore odores
concoctosque suo contractans perdere viro,
propter eandem *rem* debent primordia rerum
non adhibere suum gignundis rebus odorem
nec sonitum, quoniam nil ab se mittere possunt,
nec simili ratione saporem denique quemquam
nec frigus neque item calidum tepidumque vaporem,
cetera; quae cum ita sunt tamen ut mortalia constent,
molli lenta, fragosa putri, cava corpore raro,
omnia sint a principiis seiuncta necessest,
inmortalia si volumus subiungere rebus
fundamenta quibus nitatur summa salutis;
ne tibi res redeant ad nilum funditus omnes.

Nunc ea quae sentire videmus cumque necessest
ex insensilibus tamen omnia confiteare
principiis constare. neque id manufesta refutant
nec contra pugnant, in promptu cognita quae sunt,
sed magis ipsa manu ducunt et credere cogunt
ex insensilibus, quod dico, animalia gigni.
quippe videre licet vivos existere vermes
stercore de taetro, putorem cum sibi nacta est

for *disperditur*. 841 *notare* Lach. for *notaque*. 845 *ieiuna* Flor. 31 Camb. etc. for *et una*. 846 *proprium*. *proprio* Lach. with Junt. not Mar.; but compare 855. *ullo* Pont. 850 *possis*. *potis es* Lamb. Lach.: see notes 2. 853 *contractans* Lach., and some mss. of Priscian VI 91 for *contractas*. *contractos* vulg. *servare* (*superare* Forbig.) *et perdere* Nonius p. 188.

854 *Propter eandem rem* Lach. most truly for *Propter eandem*. *Propterea tandem* Flor. 31 Camb. Mar., *Propterea demum* Lamb., absurdly. 860 *Molli*

intempestivis ex imbribus umida tellus;
praeterea cunctas itidem res vertere sese.
vertunt se fluvii frondes et pabula laeta
in pecudes, vertunt pecudes in corpora nostra
naturam, et nostro de corpore saepe ferarum
augescunt vires et corpora pennipotentum.
ergo omnes natura cibos in corpora viva
vertit et hinc sensus animantum procreat omnes,
non alia longe ratione adque arida ligna
explicat in flammas et *in* ignis omnia versat.
iamne vides igitur magni primordia rerum
referre in quali sint ordine quaeque locata
et commixta quibus dent motus accipiantque?

Tum porro quid id est, animum quod percutit, ipsum
quod movet et varios sensus expromere cogit,
ex insensilibus ne credas sensile gigni?
nimirum lapides et ligna et terra quod una
mixta tamen nequeunt vitalem reddere sensum.
illud in his igitur rebus meminisse decebit,
non ex omnibus omnino, quaecumque creant res,
sensile et extemplo me gigni dicere sensus,
sed magni referre ea primum quantula constent,
sensile quae faciunt, et qua sint praedita forma,
motibus ordinibus posituris denique quae sint.
quarum nil rerum in lignis glaebisque videmus;
et tamen haec, cum sunt quasi putrefacta per imbres,
vermiculos pariunt, quia corpora materiai
antiquis ex ordinibus permota nova re
conciliantur ita ut debent animalia gigni.
deinde ex sensilibus qui sensile posse creari
constituunt, porro ex aliis sentire suëti

Lamb. after Turnebus for *Mollia*. 875 *fluvii frondes* Lamb. for *fluvii in frondes*. 882 *in ignis* Flor. 31 Camb. Pont. Mar. etc. for *ignis*. 888 *gigni*. *nasci* Priscian IV 27: see above p. 1. 891 *rebus* Avanc. for *fedus*. *foedus* Wak. absurdly. 893 *Sensile* Nicc. for *Sensilia*. *et extemplo* Nauger. and a late corrector of the cod. Victor. who more than once agrees with, probably follows Naugerius, for *etemplo*. 903 a v. is lost here such as *Ipsi sensilibus, mortalia semina reddunt* (or *habebunt*): Christ I now find suggests a v. has dropped out. I do not alter a letter of the mss.: Lach. in 902 reads *ea* for ex, *seminibus* for *sensilibus*, and 903 *suëtis* with Lamb., and 904 *iam* for *cum*. *tum* Lamb.

. . . .
mollia cum faciunt. nam sensus iungitur omnis
visceribus nervis venis, quae cuique videmus
mollia mortali consistere corpore creta.
sed tamen esto iam posse haec aeterna manere:
nempe tamen debent aut sensum partis habere
aut simili totis animalibus esse putari.
at nequeant per se partes sentire necesse est;
namque alio sensus membrorum respicit omnis,
nec manus a nobis potis est secreta neque ulla
corporis omnino sensum pars sola tenere.
linquitur ut totis animantibus adsimulentur.
923 sic itidem quae sentimus sentire necessest,
915 vitali ut possint consentire undique sensu.
qui poterunt igitur rerum primordia dici
et leti vitare vias, animalia cum sint,
adque animalia *sint* mortalibus una eademque?
quod tamen ut possint, at coetu concilioque
920 nil facient praeter volgum turbamque animantum,
scilicet ut nequeant homines armenta feraeque
inter sese ullam rem gignere conveniundo.
924 quod si forte suum dimittunt corpore sensum
atque alium capiunt, quid opus fuit adtribui id quod
detrahitur? tum praeterea, quo fugimus ante,
quatenus in pullos animalis vertier ova
cernimus alituum vermisque effervere, terram
intempestivos quom putor cepit ob imbris,
scire licet gigni posse ex non sensibu' sensus.
  Quod si forte aliquis dicet dumtaxat oriri

905 *cuique* Ed. for *cumque*. *cuncta* Lach. 909 *simili* Lach. for *similis*. 910 *At* Mar. Junt. for *Aut*. 911 *alio* Lach. for *alios*, *respicit* for *respuit*. *Nam ratio* Bern. for *Namque alios*, retaining *respuit*. 915 (923) I follow Bern. in placing this verse here, rather than Lach. who makes it follow 916 (915).

919 *animalia sint* Lach. for *animalibus*: comp. 458 and IV 81: *sint* was added by Mar. and Junt. 920 *at coetu* Mon. Lach. for *ab eoretu*. *ab coetu* Junt. *concretu* Politian in marg. Flor. 29. 922 *nequeant*. *nequeunt* Gif. Bentl. Lach.: but the potential is in place. 926 *quo fugimus* Wak. for *quod fugimus* which Lach. in vain defends: the poet refers to 870 sqq., not to 886. *quod vicimus* Ed. in small ed. 928 *effervere, terram Intempestivos quom* (*cum*) *putor cepit* Mar. for *offervere t. Intempestivus quam p. cepit* A, *coepit* B. *effervere* Nicc.

posse a non sensu sensum mutabilitate,
aut aliquo tamquam partu quod proditus extet,
huic satis illud erit planum facere atque probare
non fieri partum nisi concilio ante coacto
nec quicquam commutari sine conciliatu.
principio nequeunt ullius corporis esse
sensus ante ipsam genitam naturam animantis,
nimirum quia materies disiecta tenetur
aere fluminibus terris terraque creatis,
nec congressa modo vitalis convenienti
contulit inter se motus, quibus omnituentes
accensi sensus animante in quaque cientur.
  Praeterea quamvis animantem grandior ictus,
quam patitur natura, repente adfligit et omnis
corporis atque animi pergit confundere sensus.
dissoluuntur enim positurae principiorum
et penitus motus vitales inpediuntur,
donec materies, omnis concussa per artus,
vitalis animae nodos a corpore solvit
dispersamque foras per caulas eiecit omnis.
nam quid praeterea facere ictum posse reamur
oblatum, nisi discutere ac dissolvere quaeque?
fit quoque uti soleant minus oblato acriter ictu
reliqüi motus vitalis vincere saepe,
vincere, et ingentis plagae sedare tumultus
inque suos quicquid rursus revocare meatus

coepit Junt. *putror* Lamb. 932 *Posse a non sensu* Wak. for *Posse ea non sensu*, rather better than *Posse ex* of Lamb. Lach. etc. *e* Pont. *sensum mutabilitate* Lamb. ed. 3 in note for *sensus mut.* Lach. keeps *sensus.* 933 *quod proditus extet* Ed. for *quod proditum extra. quod protinus extent* Lach. *quod proditur extra* Pont. Bern.; but the oratio obliqua requires the subjunctive. 936 *sine conciliatu. nisi conciliatum* Goebel. 938 *ipsam* Flor. 31 Camb. Pont. Mar. Ald. 1 Junt. for *lesam.* 940 *terraque creatis.* Wak. has properly retained this reading of all mss. *flammaque creatis* Mar. Ald. 1 Junt. vulg. before Wak. *aethraque creatis* Lach.: but I do not know what *aethra creata* are, unless they be the same as *terra creata*, the various products of the earth. 941 *convenienti* Lamb. for *convenientes* which Lach. retains: the termination of 942 has caused the mistake. 943 *animante in quaque cientur* Hugo Purmann in Jahn's Jahrb. f. Philol. 67 p. 673 for *animantem quamque tuentur. animantum concuterentur* Lach. 942 Bern. reads *omnicientes* and 943 keeps the ms. reading: *tuentur* is quite foreign to the sense of the passage; else Lucr. would not avoid using *omnituentes* and *tuentur* together. 951 *caulas* B corr. Flor. 31 for

et quasi iam leti dominantem in corpore motum
discutere ac paene amissos accendere sensus.
nam qua re potius leti iam limine ab ipso
ad vitam possit conlecta mente reverti,
quam quo decursum prope iam siet ire et abire?
  Praeterea quoniam dolor est ubi materiai
corpora vi quadam per viscera viva per artus
sollicitata suis trepidant in sedibus intus,
inque locum quando remigrant, fit blanda voluptas,
scire licet nullo primordia posse dolore
temptari nullamque voluptatem capere ex se;
quandoquidem non sunt ex ullis principiorum
corporibus, quorum motus novitate laborent
aut aliquem fructum capiant dulcedinis almae,
haut igitur debent esse ullo praedita sensu.
  Denique uti possint sentire animalia quaeque,
principiis si iam est sensus tribuendus eorum,
quid, genus humanum propritim de quibu' factumst?
scilicet et risu tremulo concussa cachinnant
et lacrimis spargunt rorantibus ora genasque
multaque de rerum mixtura dicere callent
et sibi proporro quae sint primordia quaerunt;
quandoquidem totis mortalibus adsimulata

cavias. *eiecit.* *eicit* Nicc. Flor. 31 Camb. 954 *oblato* old eds. for *oblata.*

961 *conlecta* Lamb. first for *coniecta* which Wak. absurdly retains. *possit* Lach. for *possint*: as the verb cannot refer to *sensus* or anything but *quamvis animantem* in 944. 963 *Praeterea.* *propterea* Lach. perversely: see notes 2: a new paragraph begins here. 975 *de quibu' factumst* Lamb. for *de quibus auctumst*, and 986 *non ex ridentibu' factus* for *non ex ridentibus auctus.* Nonius p. 511 has *de quibus actus.* Lamb. ed. 3 adds most truly 'Primum Latine dici non potest *auctus de re* aut *ex re aliqua*, sed *auctus re aliqua* [speaking of course of the atoms of which a thing is made: v 322 *quodcumque alias ex se res auget alitque*, and the like have nothing to do with the question]. nam *auctus* casum septimum sine praepositione postulat. deinde aliud est *auctus re aliqua*, aliud *factus de re* aut *ex re aliqua.* hoc qui nescit, fateatur se hospitem esse in lingua Latina': this he doubtless intended for Gifanius. Wak. more fearless than the angels keeps of course *auctum* and thus comments, 'editores *aptum* [most *factum*] ausi scilicet, libris omnibus religionem invocantibus contra profanos emendatores, dictionem Lucretio lubentissime frequentatam contextu emovere, et fetus proprios per audaciam odiosissimam atque perditissimam infercire. ὡς ἀργαλέον πρᾶγμ' ἐστίν, ὦ Ζεῦ καὶ θεοί'. Truly *delira haec furiosaque cernimus esse Et ridere potest non ex ridentibu' factus.* 976 AB have here *cacinnant*: and so perhaps Lucr.

ipsa quoque ex aliis debent constare elementis,
inde alia ex aliis, nusquam consistere ut ausis:
quippe sequar, quodcumque loqui ridereque dices
et sapere, ex aliis eadem haec facientibus ut sit.
quod si delira haec furiosaque cernimus esse
et ridere potest non ex ridentibu' factus
et sapere et doctis rationem reddere dictis
non ex seminibus sapientibus atque disertis,
qui minus esse queant ea quae sentire videmus
seminibus permixta carentibus undique sensu?
Denique caelesti sumus omnes semine oriundi;
omnibus ille idem pater est, unde alma liquentis
umoris guttas mater cum terra recepit,
feta parit nitidas fruges arbustaque laeta
et genus humanum, parit omnia saecla ferarum,
pabula cum praebet quibus omnes corpora pascunt
et dulcem ducunt vitam prolemque propagant;
quapropter merito maternum nomen adepta est.
cedit item retro, de terra quod fuit ante,
in terras, et quod missumst ex aetheris oris,
id rursum caeli rellatum templa receptant.
nec sic interemit mors res ut materiai
corpora conficiat, sed coetum dissupat ollis,
inde aliis aliud coniungit; et effit ut omnes
res ita convertant formas mutentque colores
et capiant sensus et puncto tempore reddant;
ut noscas referre eadem primordia rerum
cum quibus et quali positura contineantur
et quos inter se dent motus accipiantque,
neve putes aeterna penes residere potesse

wrote; but elsewhere they insert the *h*. 982 *alia* Ver. Ven. for *ali*.
985 *delira* Flor. 31 Camb. Brix. Mar. for *det ira*. 998 *adepta* B corr. Flor. 31 Camb. for *adempta*. 1000 *missumst* Lactantius, *missum est* Camb. etc. for *missus*. 1001 *rellatum*. *fulgentia* Lactant. inst. VII 12. 1002 *mors res, ut* Mar. Ald. 1 Junt. for *mors ut res*. 1004 *coniungit; et effit ut* Ed. for *coniungit et efficit*. *coniungitur et fit* Lach. who has a full stop at *ollis*. Mar. Ald. 1 Junt. vulg. have *ut* for *ita* in 1005: as no editor before Wak. would tolerate the omission of *ut*. 1007 *eadem* Avanc. for *earum*. 1010—1012 Lach. and Bern. with all previous editors have quite misunderstood this passage in which not a letter is to be changed: they take *quod* to be the conjunction; it is really the

corpora prima quod in summis fluitare videmus
rebus et interdum nasci subitoque perire.
quin etiam refert nostris in versibus ipsis
cum quibus et quali sint ordine quaeque locata.
si non omnia sunt, at multo maxima pars est
consimilis; verum positura discrepitant res.
sic ipsis in rebus item iam materiai
concursus motus ordo positura figurae
cum permutantur, mutari res quoque debent.
  Nunc animum nobis adhibe veram ad rationem.
nam tibi vementer nova res molitur ad auris
accedere et nova se species ostendere rerum.
sed neque tam facilis res ulla est quin ea primum
difficilis magis ad credendum constet, itemque
nil adeo magnum neque tam mirabile quicquam,
quod non paulatim minuant mirarier omnes.
suspicito caeli clarum purumque colorem,

relative: Lach. for *summis* unskilfully reads *cunctis*, and supposes 1013 to commence a new paragraph wholly unconnected with what precedes: he encloses in [ ] 1013—1104. The truth is 1013—1022 are closely united with what precedes if rightly understood. Mar. Junt. Lamb. ed. 1, vulg. have *parum* for *penes* in 1010. Lamb. ed. 3 has a long note shewing that his conception of the passage is no less confused than Lachmann's: the small word *quod* has given rise to these strange misapprehensions. 1015 1016 = I 820 821 with the exception of *Significant* for *Constituunt*: 1020 = 726 and V 438: Lach. has rightly seen that they are here quite out of place: in the first book they are properly said of the atoms, but here they interrupt the sense: 1020 the interpolator has transferred hither without taking the trouble of changing *vias* and *plagas* to *viae* and *plagae*, which was first done by Pont. and Mar. 1017 *sunt* Lach. for *sint*: he compares 458.

1023 *adhibe veram* B corr. Ver. Ven. Mar. for *adhibueram*. 1024 *vementer* Avanc. and Lach. rightly for *vehementes*: so *vemens* which occurs several times: in fact those were the only forms known to Lucr. and all writers of the best ages: see Lach. 1025 *Accĕdere* all mss. and old eds.: this old form I have retained here and V 609 where A has *Accedere*, Nicc. *Accendere*: see Vahlen's Varron. sat. Menipp. p. 95, and his Ennian. trag. rel. 114 and 281, where the best mss. of Ennius and Varro retain the same form *accĕdo*: it appears from Ribbeck that the mss. of Virgil preserve in many similar words *e* for *i*, but his judgment in adopting them seems often at fault: ap. Ribbeck trag. Lat. p. IX Fleckeisen gives examples from Plautus; Livy XXI 10 12 mss. have *accedere*: III 239 I retain *recĕpit* of mss. *peremo interemo neglego intellego* were the only forms admitted in the best ages, as the concurrent testimony of all good mss. proves. 1029 *minuant mirarier*. *mittant mirarier* Lach. which I adopted in the small ed. 1030 *Suspicito* Bern. for *Principio*. *Percipito* Lach. which can hardly be right: indeed *Principio* is so appropriate that I incline to think a verse is lost, such as this *Cuius, uti memoro, permulta exempla*

quaeque in se cohibet, palantia sidera passim,
lunamque et solis praeclara luce nitorem;
omnia quae nunc si primum mortalibus essent,
ex inproviso si nunc obiecta repente,
quid magis his rebus poterat mirabile dici
aut minus ante quod auderent fore credere gentes?
nil, ut opinor: ita haec species miranda fuisset.
quam tibi iam nemo, fessus satiate videndi,
suspicere in caeli dignatur lucida templa!
desine quapropter novitate exterritus ipsa
expuere ex animo rationem, sed magis acri
iudicio perpende et, si tibi vera videntur,
dede manus, aut, si falsum est, accingere contra.
quaerit enim rationem animus, cum summa loci sit
infinita foris haec extra moenia mundi,
quid sit ibi porro quo prospicere usque velit mens
atque animi iactus liber quo pervolet ipse.
  Principio nobis in cunctas undique partis
et latere ex utroque *supra* supterque per omne
nulla est finis; uti docui, res ipsaque per se
vociferatur, et elucet natura profundi.
nullo iam pacto veri simile esse putandumst,
undique cum vorsum spatium vacet infinitum
seminaque innumero numero summaque profunda
multimodis volitent aeterno percita motu,
hunc unum terrarum orbem caelumque creatum,
nil agere illa foris tot corpora materiai;
cum praesertim hic sit natura factus, ut ipsa
sponte sua forte offensando semina rerum,
multimodis temere incassum frustraque coacta,

videmus: *Principio*, 'chief of all'. Lamb. has *Principio quod non m. m. o. Paulatim, caeli* cet. on no authority, though he appeals to 'veteres libri'. 1031 *cohibet* Lach. for *cohibent*: he justly wonders no one before him saw this. *quemque ...cohibent* previous editors. 1033 *essent. extent* Orelli Lach. *adsint* Pont. Junt. Lamb. etc.: the imperfect seems necessary; I therefore in 1034 read *si nunc* for *si sint*: the *si* was written twice; hence the error. *essent...Ex inproviso visu subiecta* Bern. 1047 *iactus* Gronov. Bentl. for *tactus*. *iniectus* Mar. Junt. which gives the right sense. *libero quo pervolet ipse* B, *volet* A. *liber quo pervolet ire* Lamb. 1049 *supra supterque* Lach. rightly for *superque*. *superque infraque* Politian in marg. Flor. 29, *infraque superque* Mar. *subterque* Pont. *infra supraque* Ald. 1 Junt. Lamb. vulg. 1058 *ut* Ed. for *et*: Lach. inserts *ut* before *semina* in

tandem colarunt ea quae coniecta repente
magnarum rerum fierent exordia semper,
terrai maris et caeli generisque animantum.
quare etiam atque etiam talis fateare necesse est
esse alios alibi congressus materiai,
qualis hic est, avido complexu quem tenet aether.
  Praeterea cum materies est multa parata,
cum locus est praesto nec res nec causa moratur
ulla, geri debent nimirum et confieri res.
nunc et seminibus si tanta est copia quantam
enumerare aetas animantum non queat omnis,
vis*que* eadem *et* natura manet quae semina rerum
conicere in loca quae*que* queat simili ratione
atque huc sunt coniecta, necesse est confiteare
esse alios aliis terrarum in partibus orbis
et varias hominum gentis et saecla ferarum.
  Huc accedit ut in summa res nulla sit una,
unica quae gignatur et unica solaque crescat,
quin aliquoiu' siet saecli permultaque eodem
sint genere. in primis animalibus, inclute Memmi,
invenies sic montivagum genus esse ferarum,
sic hominum genitam prolem, sic denique mutas
squamigerum pecudes et corpora cuncta volantum.
quapropter caelum simili ratione fatendumst
terramque et solem lunam mare, cetera quae sunt,

1059. 1061 *colarunt* Nicc. 3 Vat. Mon. Junt. rightly: see notes 2. *colerunt* AB. *cooluerint* Lamb. *coluerunt* Lach. *coierunt* B corr. Flor. 31 Camb. one Vat. *coniecta* of all mss. seems to me quite right: comp. 1108. *convecta* Lach. which appears to be the right reading in the nearly identical passage v 429 where the mss. have *conventa*. Lach. objects to *coniecta* 'quasi Lucretius hic aliter quam in quinto dicere potuerit': but there he has also *conveniant*, here *colarunt*, there *saepe*, here *semper*; for Lach. vainly alters *saepe* to *semper*: he also says of *coniecta* 'sententiam non explet nisi addita loci significatione, ut paulo post *Conicere in loca quaeque*' cet.: but I 284 *Fragmina coniciens silvarum arbustaque tota*, we find it used absolutely. 1062 *exordia* Mar. Ald. 1 Junt. for *ex ordine*, as in the 5th book. 1070 *et*. *ex* Lach. but *et* is clearly right: *ex* makes the construction most awkward: then 1072 *Visque eadem et natura* Mar. Ald. 1 Junt. for *Vis eadem natura*. *Quis eadem natura* Lach. 1073 *quaeque queat simili* Flor. 31 Camb. for *quaeque atsimili*. 1079 *aliquoiu' siet* Gronov. for *aliquoiuis siet* B, *alioquoiuis* A: the older editors have gone widely astray. 1080 *inclute Memmi* Gronov. for *indice mente*. 1081 *Invenies* Pont. Mar. Ald. 1 Junt. for *Invenisse*. 1082 *genitam* Mar. Ald. 1 Junt. for *geminam*. 1089 *quod his*

non esse unica, sed numero magis innumerali;
quandoquidem vitae depactus terminus alte
tam manet haec et tam nativo corpore constant,
quam genus omne quod hic generatim*st* rebus abundans.
Quae bene cognita si teneas, natura videtur
libera continuo dominis privata superbis
ipsa sua per se sponte omnia dis agere expers.
nam pro sancta deum tranquilla pectora pace
quae placidum degunt aevom vitamque serenam,
quis regere immensi summam, quis habere profundi
indu manu validas potis est moderanter habenas,
quis pariter caelos omnis convertere et omnis
ignibus aetheriis terras suffire feracis,
omnibus inve locis esse omni tempore praesto,
nubibus ut tenebras faciat caelique serena
concutiat sonitu, tum fulmina mittat et aedis
saepe suas disturbet et *in* deserta recedens
saeviat exercens telum quod saepe nocentes
praeterit exanimatque indignos inque merentes?
Multaque post mundi tempus genitale diemque
primigenum maris et terrae solisque coortum
addita corpora sunt extrinsecus, addita circum
semina quae magnum iaculando contulit omne;
unde mare et terrae possent augescere et unde
appareret spatium caeli domus altaque tecta
tolleret a terris procul et consurgeret aer.
nam sua cuique locis ex omnibus omnia plagis
corpora distribuuntur et ad sua saecla recedunt.
umor ad umorem, terreno corpore terra
crescit et ignem ignes procudunt aetheraque *aether*,
donique ad extremam crescendi perfica finem

generatim rebus abundans mss. *est* Lach. for *his*. *hic...abundat* Bern. *hic generatimst rebus abundans* Ed. 1094 mss. giving *vltam* for *vitam* have caused Mar. Junt. Wak. etc. to err strangely: simple as it is, Avanc. first saw the truth. *vitam* Pont. before him. 1102 *in* added by Lactant. inst. III 17, Flor. 31 Ver. Ven. Mar. etc. 1110 *Appareret* Nicc. Camb. for *appariret*. Politian in marg. Flor. 29 says 'in vetusto *Appareret*': was this the ms. of Poggio? in 716 to *infra* he has in marg. 'P *inter*', with dots added: is P Poggio? AB there have *inte*. 1115 *aether* added by Flor. 31 Camb. Mar. *aëraque aër* Lach.: but see notes 2.

1116 *extremam...finem* Lach. rightly for *extremum...finem*, as this is the only place

omnia perduxit rerum natura creatrix;
ut fit ubi nilo iam plus est quod datur intra
vitalis venas quam quod fluit adque recedit.
omnibus hic aetas debet consistere rebus,
hic natura suis refrenat viribus auctum.
nam quaecumque vides hilar*o* grandescere adauctu
paulatimque gradus aetatis scandere adultae,
plura sibi adsumunt quam de se cor*por*a mittunt,
dum facile in venas cibus omnis inditur et dum
non ita sunt late dispessa ut multa remittant
et plus dispendi faciant quam vescitur aetas.
nam certe fluere adque recedere corpora rebus
multa manus dandum est; sed plura accedere debent,
donec alescendi summum tetigere cacumen.
inde minutatim vires et robur adultum
frangit et in partem peiorem liquitur aetas.
quippe etenim quanto est res amplior, augmine adempto,
et quo latior est, in cunctas undique partis
plura modo dispargit et ab se corpora mittit,
nec facile in venas cibus omnis diditur ei
nec satis est, proquam largos exaestuat aestus,
unde queat tantum suboriri ac subpeditare.
1146 omnia debet enim cibus integrare novando
et fulcire cibus, *cibus* omnia sustentare,
nequiquam, quoniam nec venae perpetiuntur
quod satis est neque quantum opus est natura ministrat.
1139 iure igitur pereunt, cum rarefacta fluendo

where the mss. make *finis* masc. *perfica* AB Nonius. *perfice* A corr. Nicc.

1120 *hic* Ed. for *his*, as in 1089. *his rebus* here has no more sense than there. 1122 *hilar...adauctu* AB. *hilari* Avanc. *hilaro* more rightly Lamb.

1124 *corpora* Nicc. B corr. for *cora*. 1126 *dispessa* Ed. for *dispersa*: comp. III 988 *dispessis membris*: *dispersa* has here no sense: a full-grown man is more *dispessus*, but not more *dispersus* than a child: *dispessa* is the same as the *res amplior et latior* of 1133. 1129 *debent* Flor. 31 Camb. for *debet*. 1131 *robur*. *robor* AB, perhaps rightly; but Quintilian says that 'summi auctores' write *robur*, *ebur*. 1135 *ab se* Lach. for *a se*, Lucr. as a rule using *ab* before *s*: but I have my doubts here: see Lach. to VI 925: Lucr. may have varied his usage.

1136 *diditur* Mar. Ald. Junt. for *deditur*. 1138 *queat* Mar. Junt. for *queant*.

1139—1142 (1146—1149): Goebel quaest. Lucr. crit. p. 33 has first seen that these verses are to come after 1138: the thing admits of no question; though it has escaped all the editors and Lach. 1140 *cibus* added by Is. Vossius in ms.

sunt et cum externis succumbunt omnia plagis,
quandoquidem grandi cibus aevo denique defit
nec tuditantia rem cessant extrinsecus ullam
corpora conficere et plagis infesta domare.
sic igitur magni quoque circum moenia mundi
1145 expugnata dabunt labem putris*que* ruinas.
iamque adeo fracta est aetas effetaque tellus
vix animalia parva creat quae cuncta creavit
saecla deditque ferarum ingentia corpora partu.
haud, ut opinor, enim mortalia saecla superne
aurea de caelo demisit funis in arva
nec mare nec fluctus plangentis saxa crearunt,
sed genuit tellus eadem quae nunc alit ex se.
praeterea nitidas fruges vinetaque laeta
sponte sua primum mortalibus ipsa creavit,
ipsa dedit dulcis fetus et pabula laeta;
quae nunc vix nostro grandescunt aucta labore,
conterimusque boves et viris agricolarum,
conficimus ferrum vix arvis suppeditati:
usque adeo parcunt fetus augentque labore.
iamque caput quassans grandis suspirat arator
crebrius, incassum manuum cecidisse labores,
et cum tempora temporibus praesentia confert
praeteritis, laudat fortunas saepe parentis
1170 et crepat, anticum genus ut pietate repletum
perfacile angustis tolerarit finibus aevom,
cum minor esset agri multo modus ante viritim.
1168 tristis item vetulae vitis sator atque *vietae*

notes: Faber omits the verse: Voss. inserts 'et fulcire cibus, cibus omnia sustentare'; and adds in marg. 'sic Ms. v.' 1149 *que* added by Nicc.

1150 *fracta* B corr. for *facta*. *aetas*. Heins. proposes in ms. notes *aetate*. *effeta* Nicc. for *effecta*. 1153 *opinor enim mortalia* Mar. Junt. for *opinore immortalia*. 1165 *manuum* Is. Voss. in ms. notes for *magnum*. 1166 Mon. and Junt. read *Et cum temporibus praesentia tempora*, and so Politian in marg. Flor. 29: it is to be noticed that here too Naugerius, as in I 15 and 16, does not follow Junt. but recurs to the true order of the words. 1168—1170 (1170—1172) Theod. Bergk in Jahn's Jahrb. vol. 67 p. 319 has rightly transferred to this place. 1171 mss. have at the end *fatigat*, taken from 1172 by a common blunder, for which Heins. in ms. notes reads *vietae*, comparing III 385 *viĕtam*: he suggests too *viĕtae* for *vetulae*, after Hor. epod. XII 7, and *senectae* for *fatigat*, used

temporis incusat momen caelumque fatigat
1173 nec tenet omnia paulatim tabescere et ire
ad capulum spatio aetatis defessa vetusto.

as in III 772. 1172 *momen* Pius in notes for *nomen*. *caelum* Wak. for *saeclum*. Pius, having of course *fatigat* in 1171, suggests ingeniously *saeclumque fatiscens*. Nicc. all Flor. Vat. Camb. old eds. omit this verse: I don't know whence Avanc. got it: Pius of course had it from him. 1174 '*Ad scopulum*. sic oblongus: quadratus *Ad copulum*, sed *s* littera ab ipso librario addita. de his Havercampus falsa refert: sed idem verissime et praeter morem suum ingeniose scribit *ire Ad capulum*' Lach.: Wak. also says of it, 'quae est Havercampi ingeniosissima ac dignissima pretii quantivis emendatio': but alas it is not Havercamp's, as may be seen from his own crit. note: it is due to Is. Vossius, who says in ms. notes 'ms. ut hic, al. ms. *scopulum*' and again '*copulum* v. lege *capulum* i.e. sepulturam': the two mss. are AB, then in his own library: Nicc. reads *scopulum* with A.

T. LUCRETI CARI

DE RERUM NATURA

LIBER TERTIUS

E tenebris tantis tam clarum extollere lumen
qui primus potuisti inlustrans commoda vitae,
te sequor, o Graiae gentis decus, inque tuis nunc
ficta pedum pono pressis vestigia signis,
non ita certandi cupidus quam propter amorem
quod te imitari aveo; quid enim contendat hirundo
cycnis, aut quidnam tremulis facere artubus haedi
consimile in cursu possint et fortis equi vis?
tu, pater, es rerum inventor, tu patria nobis
suppeditas praecepta, tuisque ex, inclute, chartis,
floriferis ut apes in saltibus omnia libant,
omnia nos itidem depascimur aurea dicta,
aurea, perpetua semper dignissima vita.
nam simul ac ratio tua coepit vociferari
naturam rerum, divina mente coorta,
diffugiunt animi terrores, moenia mundi
discedunt, totum video per inane geri res.
apparet divum numen sedesque quietae
quas neque concutiunt venti nec nubila nimbis
aspergunt neque nix acri concreta pruina
cana cadens violat semper*que* innubilus aether

1 *E* Mon. Brix. Ver. Ven. for *O* of A Vien. frag. om. B Nicc. *A* Flor. 31 Camb. 11 *libant* Avanc. Nauger. Gif. Lach. for *limant*. 'an magis *libant*' Mar. 15 *coorta* Orelli Lach. for *coortam*. 21 *semperque* Nicc. corr. Flor. 31 Camb. Vat. 1136 and 1954 Othob. Pont. Mar. Junt. Lamb. Lach. for *semper*. *semper sine nubibus* Ald. 1, because Ver., and Ven. on which Ald. 1 is

integit, et large diffuso lumine rident.
omnia suppeditat porro natura neque ulla
res animi pacem delibat tempore in ullo.
at contra nusquam apparent Acherusia templa
nec tellus obstat quin omnia dispiciantur,
sub pedibus quaecumque infra per inane geruntur.
his ibi me rebus quaedam divina voluptas
percipit adque horror, quod sic natura tua vi
tam manifesta patens ex omni parte retecta est.
Et quoniam docui, cunctarum exordia rerum
qualia sint et quam variis distantia formis
sponte sua volitent aeterno percita motu
quove modo possint res ex his quaeque creari,
hasce secundum res animi natura videtur
atque animae claranda meis iam versibus esse
et metus ille foras praeceps Acheruntis agendus,
funditus humanam qui vitam turbat ab imo
omnia suffundens mortis nigrore neque ullam
esse voluptatem liquidam puramque relinquit.
nam quod saepe homines morbos magis esse timendos
infamemque ferunt vitam quam Tartara leti
et se scire animae naturam sanguinis esse
46 aut etiam venti, si fert ita forte voluntas,
44 nec prosum quicquam nostrae rationis egere,
hinc• licet advertas animum magis omnia laudis
47 iactari causa quam quod res ipsa probetur.
extorres idem patria longeque fugati
conspectu ex hominum, foedati crimine turpi,
omnibus aerumnis adfecti denique vivunt,
et quocumque tamen miseri venere parentant
et nigras mactant pecudes et manibu' divis
inferias mittunt multoque in rebus acerbis
acrius advertunt animos ad religionem.
quo magis in dubiis hominem spectare periclis
convenit adversisque in rebus noscere qui sit;
nam verae voces tum demum pectore ab imo

founded, have *in nubibus* with 3 Vat. 22 *rident* Lach. for *ridet.* 28 *ibi* Pont. Gronov. Wak. for *ubi.* *tibi* Mar. Junt. 29 *sic natura* Avanc. for *signatura.* 33 *aeterno* Bentl. for *alterno.* 44 (46) first placed here by

eiciuntur *et* eripitur persona, manet res.
denique avarities et honorum caeca cupido
quae miseros homines cogunt transcendere fines
iuris et interdum socios scelerum atque ministros
noctes atque dies niti praestante labore
ad summas emergere opes, haec vulnera vitae
non minimam partem mortis formidine aluntur.
turpis enim ferme contemptus et acris egestas
semota ab dulci vita stabilique videntur
et quasi iam leti portas cunctarier ante;
unde homines dum se falso terrore coacti
effugisse volunt longe longeque remosse,
sanguine civili rem conflant divitiasque
conduplicant avidi, caedem caede accumulantes;
crudeles gaudent in tristi funere fratris
et consanguineum mensas odere timentque.
consimili ratione ab eodem saepe timore
macerat invidia. ante oculos illum esse potentem,
illum aspectari, claro qui incedit honore,
ipsi se in tenebris volvi caenoque queruntur.
intereunt partim statu*aru*m et nominis ergo.
et saepe usque adeo, mortis formidine, vitae
percipit humanos odium lucisque videndae,

Bentl. 58 *eiciuntur* Lamb. ed. 2 and 3, Gif. Lach. for *eliciuntur*: the two words being perpetually confounded, though *eliciuntur* is perhaps defensible here. Lach. is wrong however in saying that Lamb. 'tandem veritati concedens' adopted *eiciuntur* from Gif. without acknowledgment: in his first ed. he keeps *eliciuntur* in the text, but has the same note as in ed. 3: 'existimant quidam legendum *eiiciuntur*...et ita amicus meus putat legendum in oratione pro M. Caelio, *nonne ipsam domum metuet, nequam vocem eiiciat?* ubi vulgo legitur *eliciat*: cui propemodum nunc assentior, quamvis olim dissenserim' cet. Lamb. angry though he was, was too true a scholar to treat Gif. as Gif. treated him. Nor does what he here says of his friend Muretus call for the petty malignity with which the latter in his var. lect. II 17 speaks of him after his death. *manet res* Flor. 31 Camb. Pont. Mar. for *manare.* 65 *ferme. famae* Mar. Ald. 1 Junt. from *formae* of Brix. Ver. Ven. *fama et* Lamb. 66 *videntur* Lamb. for *videtur*, as *semota* is neut. plur. according to the usage of Lucr.: but it is with much doubt and hesitation and in deference only to two such scholars as Lamb. and Lach. that I refuse to allow to Lucr. the liberty which the purest writers seem to have claimed, of making the partic. and verb refer only to the last of two or more nominatives. 72 *fratris* Macrob. sat. VI 2 15, Junt. not Mar. for *fratres.* 78 *statuarum* Flor. 31 Camb. corr. Vat. 1954 Othob. Mar. Junt. for

ut sibi consciscant maerenti pectore letum
obliti fontem curarum hunc esse timorem,
. . . .
hunc vexare pudorem, hunc vincula amicitiai
rumpere et in summa pietatem evertere suadet;
nam iam saepe homines patriam carosque parentis
prodiderunt, vitare Acherusia templa petentes.
nam veluti pueri trepidant atque omnia caecis
in tenebris metuunt, sic nos in luce timemus
interdum, nilo quae sunt metuenda magis quam
quae pueri in tenebris pavitant finguntque futura.
hunc igitur terrorem animi tenebrasque necessest
non radii solis neque lucida tela diei
discutiant, sed naturae species ratioque.
Primum animum dico, mentem quam saepe vocamus,
in quo consilium vitae regimenque locatum est,
esse hominis partem nilo minus ac manus et pes
atque oculei partes animantis totius extant.
. . . .
sensum animi certa non esse in parte locatum,
verum habitum quendam vitalem corporis esse,
harmoniam Grai quam dicunt, quod faciat nos
vivere cum sensu, nulla cum in parte siet mens;
ut bona saepe valetudo cum dicitur esse
corporis, et non est tamen haec pars ulla valentis.
sic animi sensum non certa parte reponunt;

statum. 81 *consciscant* Nicc. for *coniciscant.* 82 I assume a v. to be lost here, such as *Qui miseros homines cogens scelus omne patrare* : see notes 2.

84 *suadet. fundo* Lamb. *fraude* Lach. *clade* Bern. 94 *quam* Charisius p. 187 (210) for *quem*: so Mon. Junt. Lamb. Lach. 'hoc ipsum dedit, ante quam Charisii liber innotuisset, Marullus; quod miror, cum ille tam subtiliter iudicare non soleat' says Lach.: but Marullus found it in his ms. out of which Candidus also got it. 95 *locatum* Mar. Ald. 1 Junt. for *vocatum.* 98 before this verse one or more have been lost: Ald. 1 thus supplies it, *Quamvis multa quidem sapientum turba putaret*: Mar. Junt. and eds. in general before Lach. give the same, but for *putaret* more correctly *putarunt*: Gif. has *putarit*, and this note, 'Ita v. q. l. [vetus quidam liber]. in al. *putaret.* al. *putarūt.*' It is not improbable the v. q. l. is the Ven. with Marullus' ms. notes: it is very possible too that *putaret* in Ald. 1 is a misprint for *putarit*: see what I say above p. 10 on the heavy charge brought against Avancius by Lach. here. [As Marullus therefore in cod. Victor. writes *putarunt*, *putarit* was probably an earlier suggestion: see n. to II 529: other instances will be noticed below.] 100 *faciat*

magno opere in quo mi diversi errare videntur.
saepe itaque, in promptu corpus quod cernitur, aegret,
cum tamen ex alia laetamur parte latenti;
et retro fit uti contra sit saepe vicissim,
cum miser ex animo laetatur corpore toto;
non alio pacto quam si, pes cum dolet aegri,
in nullo caput interea sit forte dolore.
praeterea molli cum somno dedita membra
effusumque iacet sine sensu corpus honustum,
est aliud tamen in nobis quod tempore in illo
multimodis agitatur et omnis accipit in se
laetitiae motus et curas cordis inanis.
nunc animam quoque ut in membris cognoscere possis
esse neque harmonia corpus sentire solere,
principio fit uti detracto corpore multo
saepe tamen nobis in membris vita moretur;
atque eadem rursum, cum corpora pauca caloris
diffugere forasque per os est editus aer,
deserit extemplo venas atque ossa relinquit;
noscere ut hinc possis non aequas omnia partis
corpora habere neque ex aequo fulcire salutem,
sed magis haec, venti quae sunt calidique vaporis
semina, curare in membris ut vita moretur.
est igitur calor ac ventus vitalis in ipso
corpore qui nobis moribundos deserit artus.
quapropter quoniam est animi natura reperta
atque animae quasi pars hominis, redde harmoniai
nomen, ad organicos alto delatum Heliconi;
sive aliunde ipsi porro traxere et in illam
transtulerunt, proprio quae tum res nomine egebat.

Nicc. B corr. for *taciat*. 106 *aegret* Lach. from 'grammaticus Vindobonensis Eichenfeldii' who quotes the verse on account of the word *aegret*. *aegrum* mss. *aegrit* Lamb. ed. 3. 108 *fit uti* Lamb. for *fit ubi*. 'Itali *fit uti*' says Lach. What Itali? not Nicc. nor Flor. 31 Camb. Ver. Ven. Pont. Mar. Ald. 1 Pius Junt. Ald. 2: all of which I have now before me except Nicc. and Flor. 31, and of these two I have a collation of my own. 118 *corpus senteire* Lach. from a conj. of Wak. for *corpus interire*. *harmoniam corpus retinere* Mar. Ald. 1 Junt. 132 is first rightly given by Is. Voss. in ms. notes, by simply reading *alto* for *altu* of AB. A corr. Nicc. and all late mss. read *ab organico* and *salto* or *saltu* or *sacro*: hence endless confusion. *ab organico saltu...Heliconis* in

quidquid *id* est; habeant: tu cetera percipe dicta.
Nunc animum atque animam dico coniuncta teneri
inter se atque unam naturam conficere ex se,
sed caput esse quasi et dominari in corpore toto
consilium quod nos animum mentemque vocamus.
idque situm media regione in pectoris haeret.
hic exultat enim pavor ac metus, haec loca circum
laetitiae mulcent; hic ergo mens animusquest.
cetera pars animae per totum dissita corpus
paret et ad numen mentis momenque movetur.
idque sibi solum per se sapit, *id* sibi gaudet,
cum neque res animam neque corpus commovet una.
et quasi, cum caput aut oculus temptante dolore
laeditur in nobis, non omni concruciamur
corpore, sic animus nonnumquam laeditur ipse
laetitiaque viget, cum cetera pars animai
per membra atque artus nulla novitate cietur.
verum ubi vementi magis est commota metu mens,
consentire animam totam per membra videmus
sudoresque ita palloremque existere toto
corpore et infringi linguam vocemque aboriri,
caligare oculos, sonere auris, succidere artus,
denique concidere ex animi terrore videmus
saepe homines; facile ut quivis hinc noscere possit
esse animam cum animo coniunctam, quae cum animi *vi*
percussast, exim corpus propellit et icit.
Haec eadem ratio naturam animi atque animai
corpoream docet esse; ubi enim propellere membra,
corripere ex somno corpus mutareque vultum
atque hominem totum regere ac versare videtur,
quorum nil fieri sine tactu posse videmus
nec tactum porro sine corpore, nonne fatendumst
corporea natura animum constare animamque?
praeterea pariter fungi cum corpore et una
consentire animum nobis in corpore cernis.

the old vulgate. 135 *id* added by Flor. 31 Camb. 145 *sapit, id sibi* Wak. for *sapit sibi*. *sapit et sibi* Nicc. vulg. 154 *ita palloremque* Nicc. Mar. etc. for *itaque pallorem*. *itaque et pallorem* Lamb. etc. 159 *animi vi* Ven. Mar. first for *animi*: Lach. is wrong: Flor. 31 reads *animai*. Ver. om. *vi*

si minus offendit vitam vis horrida teli
ossibus ac nervis disclusis intus adacta,
at tamen insequitur languor terraeque petitus
segnis, et in terra mentis qui gignitur aestus,
interdumque quasi exurgendi incerta voluntas.
ergo corpoream naturam animi esse necessest,
corporeis quoniam telis ictuque laborat.
  Is tibi nunc animus quali sit corpore et unde
constiterit pergam rationem reddere dictis.
principio esse aio persuptilem atque minutis
perquam corporibus factum constare. id ita esse
hinc licet advertas animum ut pernoscere possis:
nil adeo fieri celeri ratione videtur,
quam *sibi* mens fieri proponit et inchoat ipsa;
ocius ergo animus quam res se perciet ulla,
ante oculos quorum in promptu natura videtur.
at quod mobile tanto operest, constare rutundis
perquam seminibus debet perquamque minutis,
momine uti parvo possint inpulsa moveri.
namque movetur aqua et tantillo momine flutat
quippe volubilibus parvisque creata figuris,
at contra mellis constantior est natura
et pigri latices magis et cunctantior actus;
haeret enim inter se magis omnis materiai
copia, nimirum quia non tam levibus extat
corporibus neque tam suptilibus atque rutundis.
namque papaveris aura potest suspensa levisque
cogere ut ab summo tibi diffluat altus acervus;
at contra lapidum conlectum ipse euru' move*re*

with AB Nicc. *animi vis* Nonius Brix. 170 *offendit* B corr. for *offendis*. *teli* Mar. Junt. most truly for *leti*. 172 *terraeque petitus Segnis* Ed. for *t. p. Suavis*, because I can think of nothing better: *suavis* manifestly has no sense. *Suppus* Lach.: but why *suppus* rather than *pronus*? a man is generally wounded in front and then, as Lucr. says IV 1049, he falls forwards not backwards. *Saevus et* Bern. after a friend of Wak. Mr John Jones: but the copula *et* is never found in Lucr. out of its place, and a single example must not be introduced by conjecture. 183 *sibi* Wak. for *si*: V 1142 B has *si* for *sibi*.

198 *spicarumque* mss. Bern. has seen that in the letters MQUE the verb MOUERE lurks: in 236 mss. *multamqueri* for *multa moveri*: he reads *cauru' movere*: but whence comes the *spi*? I have therefore written *ipse euru' movere*. *spiritus acer* Lach.: but the sentence requires a verb. *spiclorum* and the like of

noenu potest. igitur parvissima corpora proquam
et levissima sunt, ita mobilitate fruuntur;
at contra quaecumque magis cum pondere magno
asperaque inveniuntur, eo stabilita magis sunt.
nunc igitur quoniam *est* animi natura reperta
mobilis egregie, perquam constare necessest
corporibus parvis et levibus atque rutundis.
quae tibi cognita res in multis, o bone, rebus
utilis invenietur et opportuna cluebit.
haec quoque res etiam naturam dedicat eius,
quam tenui constet textura quamque loco se
contineat parvo, si possit conglomerari,
quod simul atque hominem leti secura quies est
indepta atque animi natura animaeque recessit,
nil ibi libatum de toto corpore cernas
ad speciem, nil ad pondus: mors omnia praestat
vitalem praeter sensum calidumque vaporem.
ergo animam totam perparvis esse necessest
seminibus, nexam per venas viscera nervos;
quatenus, omnis ubi e toto iam corpore cessit,
extima membrorum circumcaesura tamen se
incolumem praestat nec defit ponderis hilum.
quod genus est Bacchi cum flos evanuit aut cum
spiritus unguenti suavis diffugit in auras
aut aliquo cum iam sucus de corpore cessit;
nil oculis tamen esse minor res ipsa videtur
propterea neque detractum de pondere quicquam,
nimirum quia multa minutaque semina sucos
efficiunt et odorem in toto corpore rerum.
quare etiam atque etiam mentis naturam animaeque
scire licet perquam pauxillis esse creatam
seminibus, quoniam fugiens nil ponderis aufert.
  Nec tamen haec simplex nobis natura putanda est.
tenvis enim quaedam moribundos deserit aura

older editors are absurd. *conlectum* Muretus for *coniectum* which Lamb. approves of in his notes and Lach. rightly adopts. 203 *est* added after *quoniam* by Pont. Mar. Ald. 1 Junt. It is added at the end of the verse by Flor. 31 Camb. 210 *si* for *se* Nicc. Mon. Ver. Ven. not Flor. 31 or Camb. 224 *Nil oculis*. 'leg. *nilo*' Heins. in ms. notes. 227 *rerum*. *rei* Lach., I now think

mixta vapore, vapor porro trahit aera secum.
nec calor est quisquam, cui non sit mixtus et aer;
rara quod eius enim constat natura, necessest
aeris inter eum primordia multa moveri.
iam triplex animi est igitur natura reperta;
nec tamen haec sat sunt ad sensum cuncta creandum,
nil horum quoniam recepit res posse creare
sensiferos motus *et homo* quae mente volutat.
quarta quoque his igitur quaedam natura necessest
adtribuatur; east omnino nominis expers;
qua neque mobilius quicquam neque tenvius exstat,
nec magis e parvis et levibus est elementis;
sensiferos motus quae didit prima per artus.
prima cietur enim, parvis perfecta figuris;
inde calor motus et venti caeca potestas
accipit, inde aer; inde omnia mobilitantur,
concutitur sanguis, tum viscera persentiscunt
omnia, postremis datur ossibus atque medullis
sive voluptas est sive est contrarius ardor.
nec temere huc dolor usque potest penetrare neque acre
permanare malum, quin omnia perturbentur

without reason. 232 *Tenuis* A corr. for *Tenus*. 234 *cui non sit mixtus et aer*. *cui mixtus non siet aer* Lach. who will not tolerate *et* for *etiam*.

236 *multa moveri* A corr. Nicc. and all before Lamb. for *multamqueri*: comp. 198. *multa cieri* Lamb. wrongly after Turnebus. 239 240 a most doubtful passage: 239 *res* Ed. after Bern. for *mens*, 240 it seems to me certain that *quaedam* has come here from the *quaedam* of 241, and as what the poet wrote must be uncertain, I have written *et homo quae* for *quaedam que*. Lach. 239 reads *quem* for *mens*, 240 *quaedam vis menti'*, just retaining the word he ought not and making a most awkward construction. Bern. strangely reads in 240 *quidam quod manticulatur*. Is. Voss. in ms. notes 'legendum videtur *qui dant quae mente volutes*'. 239 I retain *recĕpit* with AB: comp. n. to II 1025 *Accedere*: Virgil's and other old mss. retain many traces of this *e*, intermediate between the *a* of the simple verb and the later *i*. 244 *e parvis et levibus est elementis* Wak. in notes for *e p. et l. ex elem.* and justly: comp. VI 330: in his text he follows Camb. *est p. et l. ex el.* which may be right. *et p. et l. ex e.* Lach. *e parvis aut l. ex el.* Junt. Lamb. not Pont. or Mar. 249 is first rightly given by Pont. and Avanc. in notes at the end of his Catullus: AB have *Concutitur tum sanguis viscera persentisiunt*: Flor. 31 Camb. 3 Vat. give *persentiscunt*: this unrhythmical order of the first words appears in the Junt. and in the text even of Lamb. ed. 1; in ed. 2 and 3 and notes of 1 he reads *Tum quatitur sanguis, tum*: Nicc. misled by *persentisiunt* strangely gave *Concutitur tum sanguis per sentes viscera iunt*; and hence Ver. and Ven. *vint* for *iunt*; out of which Avanc. in Ald. 1 ingeniously devised

usque adeo *ut* vitae desit locus atque animai
diffugiant partes per caulas corporis omnis.
sed plerumque fit in summo quasi corpore finis
motibus: hanc ob rem vitam retinere valemus.
  Nunc ea quo pacto inter sese mixta quibusque
compta modis vigeant rationem reddere aventem
abstrahit invitum patrii sermonis egestas;
sed tamen, ut potero, summatim, attingere, tangam.
inter enim cursant primordia principiorum
motibus inter se, nil ut secernier unum
possit nec spatio fieri divisa potestas,
sed quasi multae vis unius corporis extant.
quod genus in quovis animantum viscere volgo
est odor et quidam color et sapor, et tamen ex his
omnibus est unum perfectum corporis augmen.
sic calor atque aer et venti caeca potestas
mixta creant unam naturam et mobilis illa
vis, initum motus ab se quae dividit ollis,
sensifer unde oritur primum per viscera motus.
nam penitus prorsum latet haec natura subestque
nec magis hac infra quicquam est in corpore nostro
atque anima est animae proporro totius ipsa.
quod genus in nostris membris et corpore toto
mixta latens animi vis est animaeque potestas,
corporibus quia de parvis paucisque creatast.
sic tibi nominis haec expers vis facta minutis
corporibus latet atque animae quasi totius ipsa
proporrost anima et dominatur corpore toto.
consimili ratione necessest ventus et aer
et calor inter se vigeant commixta per artus
adque aliis aliud subsit magis emineatque

Concutitur sanguis per venas, viscera vivunt Omnia, but he afterwards learnt better. 254 *ut* added by Lamb.

257 *retinere valemus* A corr. Nicc. all before Lach. most properly for *retinemus valemus*: he reads absurdly *retinemu' valentes*, as if we could not be in life without being in health: the origin of the corruption is obvious. 266 *viscere* B. *visere* A and clearly ms. of Poggio, as Nicc. and all late mss. and early editions so read, even Junt. but not Avanc.: 'alii viscere' Mar.: yet to Wak. *viscere* is 'sordidum et ineptum'! 267 *color* Lamb. conj. rightly for *calor*. *calor* vulgo Lach.

284 *aliis*. *alias* Brieger. 288 *etenim* Faber in emend. and Lach. for *etiam*:

ut quiddam fieri videatur ab omnibus unum,
ni calor ac ventus seorsum seorsumque potestas
aeris interemant sensum diductaque solvant.
est etenim calor ille animo, quem sumit, in ira
cum fervescit et ex oculis micat acribus ardor;
est et frigida multa comes formidinis aura
quae ciet horrorem membris et concitat artus;
est etiam quoque pacati status aeris ille,
pectore tranquillo fit qui voltuque sereno.
sed calidi plus est illis quibus acria corda
iracundaque mens facile effervescit in ira.
quo genere in primis vis est violenta leonum,
pectora qui fremitu rumpunt plerumque gementes
nec capere irarum fluctus in pectore possunt.
at ventosa magis cervorum frigida mens est
et gelidas citius per viscera concitat auras
quae tremulum faciunt membris existere motum.
at natura boum placido magis aere vivit,
nec nimis irai fax umquam subdita percit
fumida, suffundens caecae caliginis umbra,
nec gelidis torpet telis perfixa pavoris:
inter utrosque sitast, cervos saevosque leones.
sic hominum genus est. quamvis doctrina politos
constituat pariter quosdam, tamen illa relinquit
naturae cuiusque animi vestigia prima.
nec radicitus evelli mala posse putandumst,
quin proclivius hic iras decurrat ad acris,
ille metu citius paulo temptetur, at ille
tertius accipiat quaedam clementius aequo.
inque aliis rebus multis differre necessest

a necessary change. Lach. rightly follows Bentl. in joining *in ira* with *Cum fervescit*. 289 *acribus* Lamb. ed. 2 and 3 for *acrius*. 290 *et*. *ea* Lach. intolerant of *et* for *etiam*. 293 *fit qui*. *qui fit* Mar. Ald. 1 Junt. vulgo Lach.: but see notes 2. 298 is placed by Lach. before 296 without cause. 303 *nimis* Flor. 31 Camb. Vat. 1954 Othob. Mar. for *minus*. 304 *Fumida suffundens* Flor. 31 Camb. corr. for *Fumidas effundens*. *umbra* B. *umbram* A Nicc. Camb. which may be right: comp. Plaut. rud. 588 *Quasi vinis Graecis Neptunus nobis suffudit mare*. 305 *pavoris* Mar. Ald. 1 Junt. for *vaporis*. 306 *Inter utrosque sitast* Avanc. (*sita est* Mar. Junt.) for *Inter utrasque sitas*. *sitas* of mss. must be *sitast*: the scribe has then adapted *utrasque* to *sitas*. *Interutraque secus* Lach. *Interutraque secat* Bern. 309 *Naturae* Mar. Junt. for *Natura*. 317 *quot*. *quod*

naturas hominum varias moresque sequacis;
quorum ego nunc nequeo caecas exponere causas
nec reperire figurarum tot nomina quot sunt
principiis, unde haec oritur variantia rerum.
illud in his rebus videor firmare potesse,
usque adeo naturarum vestigia linqui
parvola quae nequeat ratio depellere nobis,
ut nil inpediat dignam dis degere vitam.
  Haec igitur natura tenetur corpore ab omni
ipsaque corporis est custos et causa salutis;
nam communibus inter se radicibus haerent
nec sine pernicie divelli posse videntur.
quod genus e thuris glaebis evellere odorem
haud facile est quin intereat natura quoque eius.
sic animi atque animae naturam corpore toto
extrahere haut facile est quin omnia dissoluantur.
inplexis ita principiis ab origine prima
inter se fiunt consorti praedita vita,
nec sibi quaeque sine alterius vi posse videtur
corporis atque animi seorsum sentire potestas,
sed communibus inter eas conflatur utrimque
motibus accensus nobis per viscera sensus.
praeterea corpus per se nec gignitur umquam
nec crescit neque post mortem durare videtur.
non enim, ut umor aquae dimittit saepe vaporem
qui datus est, neque ea causa convellitur ipse,
sed manet incolumis, non, inquam, sic animai
discidium possunt artus perferre relicti,
sed penitus pereunt convulsi conque putrescunt.
ex ineunte aevo sic corporis atque animai
mutua vitalis discunt contagia motus
maternis etiam membris alvoque reposta,
discidium *ut* nequeat fieri sine peste maloque;

AB, which Lucr. may have written: so *quod vis* AB in 1090: Augustus in his res gestae writes *aliquod*; as does B in VI 317: *capud* A or B repeatedly. 319 *videor* Faber for *video*. *firmare* Ver. Ven. for *formare*. 321 *nobis* Lach. for *noctis*. *dictis* Mar. Ald. 1 Junt. Lamb. ed. 1 and 2. *doctis* Lamb. ed. 3. 332 *fiunt consorti...vita* Mar. Junt. for *consorti fiunt...vitae*. 333 though sound, is much corrupted by Mar. Junt. Lamb. vulg. 335 *eas* Lach. for *eos*; as *eos* is contrary to the usage of Lucr. 346 *reposta* Avanc. for *reposto*. *reposti* Mar. Junt. without sense not

ut videas, quoniam coniunctast causa salutis,
coniunctam quoque naturam consistere eorum.
Quod superest, siquis corpus sentire refutat
atque animam credit permixtam corpore toto
suscipere hunc motum quem sensum nominitamus,
vel manifestas res contra verasque repugnat.
quid sit enim corpus sentire quis adferet umquam,
si non ipsa palam quod res dedit ac docuit nos?
at dimissa anima corpus caret undique sensu;
perdit enim quod non proprium fuit eius in aevo;
multaque praeterea perdit quam expellitur *ante.*
Dicere porro oculos nullam rem cernere posse,
sed per eos animum ut foribus spectare reclusis,
difficilest, contra cum sensus dicat eorum;
sensus enim trahit atque acies detrudit ad ipsas;
fulgida praesertim cum cernere saepe nequimus,
lumina luminibus quia nobis praepediuntur.
quod foribus non fit; neque enim, quia cernimus ipsi,
ostia suscipiunt ullum reclusa laborem.
praeterea si pro foribus sunt lumina nostra,
iam magis exemptis oculis debere videtur
cernere res animus sublatis postibus ipsis.
Illud in his rebus nequaquam sumere possis,
Democriti quod sancta viri sententia ponit,
corporis atque animi primordia singula privis
adposita alternis variare, ac nectere membra.
nam cum multo sunt animae elementa minora
quam quibus e corpus nobis et viscera constant,
tum numero quoque concedunt et rara per artus
dissita sunt dumtaxat; ut hoc promittere possis,

repostis. 347 *ut* added by Mar. Junt. 350 *refutat. renutat* Lamb. 358 *perdit quam expellitur ante* Ed. for *perditum expellitur aevo quam*: the v. is rejected by Creech in notes, and Bern. *Multaque. Nullaque* Lach. which seems scarcely to be Latin. Lamb. condemns 357 which Creech well defends. 361 *Difficilest. Desiperest* Lamb. ed. 2 and 3, Gif. Lach.: but see notes 2. *dicat* Lamb. for *ducat.* 362 Lamb. rejects. Lach. puts it after 363. 365 *quia* Lach. for *qua.* 372 *privis* Bentl. for *primis*: 389 *priva* is in the mss. 374 *animae elementa minora* AB Nicc.: this I have retained. *animai el. min.* Flor. 31 Camb. Mar. Ald. 1 Junt. vulgo; but the elision is not tolerable. *elementa minora animai* Lach. 375 *e* AB Lamb. ed. 3 Creech Lach. rightly. *et* A corr. B corr.

quantula prima queant nobis iniecta ciere
corpora sensiferos motus in corpore, tanta
intervalla tenere exordia prima animai.
nam neque pulveris interdum sentimus adhaesum
corpore nec membris incussam sidere cretam,
nec nebulam noctu neque aranei tenvia fila
obvia sentimus, quando obretimur euntes,
nec supera caput eiusdem cecidisse vietam
vestem nec plumas avium papposque volantis
qui nimia levitate cadunt plerumque gravatim,
nec repentis itum cuiusviscumque animantis
sentimus nec priva pedum vestigia quaeque,
corpore quae in nostro culices et cetera ponunt.
usque adeo prius est in nobis multa ciendum,
quam primordia sentiscant concussa animai
semina corporibus nostris inmixta per artus,
et quam in his intervallis tuditantia possint
concursare coire et dissultare vicissim.

Et magis est animus vitai claustra coercens
et dominantior ad vitam quam vis animai.
nam sine mente animoque nequit residere per artus
temporis exiguam partem pars ulla animai,
sed comes insequitur facile et discedit in auras
et gelidos artus in leti frigore linquit.
at manet in vita cui mens animusque remansit.
quamvis est circum caesis lacer undique membris
truncus, adempta anima circum membrisque remota
vivit et aetherias vitalis suscipit auras.
si non omnimodis, at magna parte animai
privatus, tamen in vita cunctatur et haeret;

Nicc. Flor. 31 Camb. all Vat. all eds. bef. Lamb. 3, Gif. Wak. 378 and 380 *prima. priva* Bentl. Lach. Ed. in ed. 1 : but see notes 2. 383 *aranei* Mar. Ald. 1 Junt. for *arani* : see Lach. 391 *ciendum* Avanc. for *ciendo.* 392 and 393 wrongly transposed by Mar. and in all editions including Lach. Bern. and Ed. formerly. 394 *Et quam in his intervallis* Lach. acutely for *Et quantis int. Et quam intervallis tantis* Mar. Ald. 1 Junt. vulg. *Et tantis intervallis* Wak. 400 *et discedit* Vat. 3276 Mar. Ald. 1 Junt. for *ediscedit.* 403 *circum* Flor. 31 Camb. corr. Mar. for *cretum.* 404 *remota* B corr. Lach. for *remot* B, *remotus* A, *remotis* vulg. 405 *aetherias. aerias* Lach.: without any just cause he alters this and many passages of Virgil and others on the assumption that *aetheriae*

ut, lacerato oculo circum si pupula mansit
incolumis, stat cernundi vivata potestas,
dummodo ne totum corrumpas luminis orbem
et circum caedas aciem solamque relinquas;
id quoque enim sine pernicie non fiet et orbei.
at si tantula pars oculi media illa peresa est,
occidit extemplo lumen tenebraeque secuntur,
incolumis quamvis aliquoi *sit* splendidus orbis.
hōc anima atque animus vincti sunt foedere semper.
Nunc age, nativos animantibus et mortalis
esse animos animasque levis ut noscere possis,
conquisita diu dulcique reperta labore
digna tua pergam disponere carmina cura.
tu fac utrumque uno sub iungas nomine eorum,
atque animam verbi causa cum dicere pergam,
mortalem esse docens, animum quoque dicere credas,
quatenus est unum inter se coniunctaque res est.
principio quoniam tenuem constare minutis
corporibus docui multoque minoribus esse
principiis factam quam liquidus umor aquai
aut nebula aut fumus:—nam longe mobilitate
praestat et a tenui causa magis icta movetur;
quippe ubi imaginibus fumi nebulaeque movetur:
quod genus in somnis sopiti ubi cernimus alte
exhalare vaporem altaria ferreque fumum;

cannot be joined with *aurae*. 411 *Et*. *Sed* Mon. Junt. Lamb. etc. wrongly. 412 and 415 are necessary to complete the comparison between the ball and pupil of the eye and the *anima* and *animus*: Lach. ejects them. 412 *et orbei* Ed. for *eorum*: see notes 2: Lamb. ruins the sense by reading *confiet* for *non fiet*. 415 *alioqui* is corrupt: I transpose a single letter and write *aliquoi*, adding *sit* which could easily fall out before *splendidus*. 420 *Digna tua...cura* Lach. for *Digna tua...vita*. *Perpetua...vita* Bern. with reference I presume to 13 *perpetua semper dignissima vita*: but surely *digna* or *dignissima* would be required: and see notes 2. *Digna tuo...vate* Creech: but *vates* to Lucr. had only a bad meaning. 421 *sub iungas nomine* Ed. for *subiungas nome* (*nomine* B corr.): this the context requires: see notes 2. *subiungas nomen* vulgo. *uni subiungas nomen* Lach. 428 I retain the ms. reading. Lach. writes *iam* for *nam*: but he thereby inverts the argument: comp. 203 sqq. Lucr. says 'the soul is seen to be marvellously nimble: therefore it is formed of very minute seeds': Lachmann's error is most manifest. 430 and 433 are ejected by Lach.: wrongly in my opinion. 430 *movetur* Mar. Junt. for *moventur*. 431 *Quod genus in somnis*. Here again Lach. reads *est* for *in*: comp. II 194. *alte Ex. vaporem* Lach. rightly for *alta Ex. vapore*. 432 *Exha-*

nam procul hinc dubio nobis simulacra genuntur:—
nunc igitur quoniam quassatis undique vasis
diffluere umorem et laticem discedere cernis
et nebula ac fumus quoniam discedit in auras,
crede animam quoque diffundi multoque perire
ocius et citius dissolvi *in* corpora prima,
cum semel ex hominis membris ablata recessit.
quippe etenim corpus, quod vas quasi constitit eius,
cum cohibere nequit conquassatum ex aliqua re
ac rarefactum detracto sanguine venis,
aere qui credas posse hanc cohiberier ullo?
corpore qui nostro rarus magis *is* cohibessit?
  Praeterea gigni pariter cum corpore et una
crescere sentimus pariterque senescere mentem.
nam velut infirmo pueri teneroque vagantur
corpore, sic animi sequitur sententia tenvis.
inde ubi robustis adolevit viribus aetas,
consilium quoque maius et auctior est animi vis.
post ubi iam validis quassatum est viribus aevi
corpus et obtusis ceciderunt viribus artus,
claudicat ingenium, delirat lingua, *labat* mens,
omnia deficiunt atque uno tempore desunt.
ergo dissolui quoque convenit omnem animai
naturam, ceu fumus, in altas aeris auras;
quandoquidem gigni pariter pariterque videmus
crescere et, *ut* docui, simul aevo fessa fatisci.

lare: *exalare*, v 463 *Exalantque*, vi 478 *alitus* AB, followed by Lach. who does not however omit the aspirate, where only A or B omit it, as ii 417 v 253 vi 811 and iv 864 vi 221. '*exala*: this form is better attested by ancient mss. than the common *exhalare*' Halm, Cic. phil. ii 30 ed. Mayor. This seems doubtful even in Cicero: his colleagues, Baiter Tusc. i 43 ii 22 and Jordan Verr. iii 28 retain *h*: of the capital mss. of Virgil only M seems ever to omit it. 433 *hinc* Bentl. for *haec*. *genuntur* Lamb. for *geruntur*. 438 *Ocius* Nicc. B corr. for *Opius*. *in* added by B corr. 441 *Cum*. *Quam* Mar. Junt. Wak. Lach. 444 *is cohibessit* Lach. for *incohibescit*. *am cohibessit* Lamb. Gif. *incohibessit* Wak. *usque liquescit* Bern. *in quo habitet sit* Ed. in small ed.: *in quo* might be looked on as one word and the elision thus defended; but see Luc. Mueller de re metr. p. 284 and notes 2 to i 1091. 450 *auctior* B corr. Nicc. corr. (?), Flor. 31 Camb. for *auctor*. 453 *lingua, labat mens* Lach. for *lingua mens*. *lingua madet mens* B corr. from 479. *linguaque mensque* Nicc. vulg. 456 *aeris* old eds. for *acris*. 458 *ut* added by B corr. *fatisci* Nicc. Flor. 31 Camb. Vat. Mon. Bentl. for *faetis*. *fatiscit* B

Huc accedit uti videamus, corpus ut ipsum
suscipere inmanis morbos durumque dolorem,
sic animum curas acris luctumque metumque;
quare participem leti quoque convenit esse.
quin etiam morbis in corporis avius errat
saepe animus; dementit enim deliraque fatur
interdumque gravi lethargo fertur in altum
aeternumque soporem oculis nutuque cadenti,
unde neque exaudit voces nec noscere voltus
illorum potis est, ad vitam qui revocantes
circumstant lacrimis rorantes ora genasque.
quare animum quoque dissolui fateare necessest,
quandoquidem penetrant in eum contagia morbi;
nam dolor ac morbus leti fabricator uterquest,
multorum exitio perdocti quod sumus ante.
denique quor, hominem cum vini vis penetravit
acris et in venas discessit diditus ardor,
consequitur gravitas membrorum, praepediuntur
crura vacillanti, tardescit lingua, madet mens,
nant oculi, clamor singultus iurgia gliscunt,
et iam cetera de genere hoc quaecumque secuntur,
cur ea sunt, nisi quod vemens violentia vini
conturbare animam consuevit corpore in ipso?
at quaecumque queunt conturbari inque pediri,
significant, paulo si durior insinuarit
causa, fore ut pereant aevo privata futuro.
quin etiam subito vi morbi saepe coactus
ante oculos aliquis nostros, ut fulminis ictu,
concidit et spumas agit, ingemit et tremit artus,
desipit, extentat nervos, torquetur, anhelat
inconstanter, et in iactando membra fatigat.
nimirum quia vis morbi distracta per artus

corr. Junt. Lamb. not Mar. 472 *dolor* Nicc. for *polor.* 474 475 *Et quoniam mentem sanari corpus ut aegrum Et pariter mentem sanari corpus inani*: an absurd interpolation: 474=510; for 475 Mar. Ald. 1 Junt. substitute 511. Lamb. first expelled both. 476 *quor.* *cōr* AB, which is the same thing: so II 194, IV 575 *com=quom* or *cum*: IV 116 *eorum* AB, *corum* Lach. i.e. *quorum*. *cŏr hominum* Nicc. Flor. 31 Camb. 5 Vat. old eds. before Mar. and Junt.: which Wak. absurdly keeps. 482 *Cur ea sunt* Nicc. for *curba sunt.* 492 *quia* Nicc. Flor. 31 Mar.

turbat, agens animam spumat, quasi in aequore salso
ventorum validis fervescunt viribus undae.
exprimitur porro gemitus, quia membra dolore
adficiuntur et omnino quod semina vocis
eiciuntur et ore foras glomerata feruntur
qua quasi consuerunt et sunt munita viai.
desipientia fit, quia vis animi atque animai
conturbatur et, ut docui, divisa seorsum
disiectatur eodem illo distracta veneno.
inde ubi iam morbi reflexit causa reditque
in latebras acer corrupti corporis umor,
tum quasi vaccillans primum consurgit et omnis
paulatim redit in sensus animamque receptat.
haec igitur tantis ubi morbis corpore in ipso
iactentur miserisque modis distracta laborent,
cur eadem credis sine corpore in aere aperto
cum validis ventis aetatem degere posse?
et quoniam mentem sanari, corpus ut aegrum,
cernimus et flecti medicina posse videmus,
id quoque praesagit mortalem vivere mentem.
addere enim partis aut ordine traiecere aecumst
aut aliquid prorsum de summa detrahere hilum,
commutare animum quicumque adoritur et infit
aut aliam quamvis naturam flectere quaerit,
at neque transferri sibi partis nec tribui vult
inmortale quod est quicquam neque defluere hilum.
nam quodcumque suis mutatum finibus exit,
continuo hoc mors est illius quod fuit ante.
ergo animus sive aegrescit, mortalia signa
mittit, uti docui, seu flectitur a medicina.
usque adeo falsae rationi vera videtur
res occurrere et effugium praecludere eunti
ancipitique refutatu convincere falsum.
Denique saepe hominem paulatim cernimus ire

old eds. for *qua*. 493 *spumat, quasi in* Lach. for *spumans in*, most acutely: former correctors and editors, even Lamb., had quite mistaken the meaning, and joined *agens animam* with *vis morbi*: their various readings are not worth mentioning: Wak. is unusually perverse. 497 *Eiciuntur* Lamb. for *Eliciuntur*: see 58 and IV 945. 523 *rationi* Mar. Ald. 1 Junt. for *rationis*. 525 *refutatu* Mar.

et membratim vitalem deperdere sensum;
in pedibus primum digitos livescere et unguis,
inde pedes et crura mori, post inde per artus
ire alios tractim gelidi vestigia leti.
scinditur itque animae hoc quoniam natura nec uno
tempore sincera existit, mortalis habendast.
quod si forte putas ipsam se posse per artus
introsum trahere et partis conducere in unum
atque ideo cunctis sensum deducere membris,
at locus ille tamen, quo copia tanta animai
cogitur, in sensu debet maiore videri;
qui quoniam nusquamst, nimirum ut diximus *ante*,
dilaniata foras dispargitur, interit ergo.
quin etiam si iam libeat concedere falsum
et dare posse animam glomerari in corpore eorum,
lumina qui lincunt moribundi particulatim,
mortalem tamen esse animam fateare necesse,
nec refert utrum pereat dispersa per auras
an contracta suis e partibus obbrutescat,
quando hominem totum magis ac magis undique sensus
deficit et vitae minus et minus undique restat.
  Et quoniam mens est hominis pars una, loco quae
fixa manet certo, velut aures atque oculi sunt
atque alii sensus qui vitam cumque gubernant,
et veluti manus atque oculus naresve seorsum
secreta ab nobis nequeunt sentire neque esse,
sed tamen in parvo licuntur tempore tabe,

Junt. for *refutatur*. 531 *Scinditur itque animae hoc* Ed. for *Scinditur atque animo haec*: comp. 526. *Sc. usque adeo haec* Lach. *Sc. aeque animae haec* Bern. *Sc. atqui animo haec* Mar. Junt. *Sc. atqui animae* Lamb. vulg. 535 *deducere* Camb. Ver. Ven. Mar. for *diducere*. 538 *ante* added by Nicc. 548 *loco quae* Lach. first for *locoque*. 551 *atque*. *aut* Lach.: but comp. v 965 *glandes atque arbita vel pira lecta*. 553 *Sed tamen in parvo linguntur tempore tali* mss. 'quidam doctus' says Lamb. who condemns the verse '*liquuntur*.' '*linguntur*. mss. puto legend.: *secta etenim parvo vincuntur tempore tabi*, nisi malis *liquuntur...tabi* pro *tabe*, ut *parti contagi* pro *parte contage* vet. passim' Is. Voss. in ms. notes. *Sed tamen* is of course quite right; I have written therefore with Creech in notes *Sed tamen in parvo licuntur tempore tabe* (Aen. III 28 P has *linguntur* for *licuntur* and Lucr. IV 1243 Ver. Ven. have *lignitur* for *liquitur*). *linquuntur* Flor. 31 vulg. *in parvo lincuntur tempore tabi* Lach. 'ita Vergil. *Alitibus linquere feris*, et Ovid. *leto poenaeque relictus*': but the moment the body is dead, *linquitur*

sic animus per se non quit sine corpore et ipso
esse homine, illius quasi quod vas *esse* videtur
sive aliud quid vis potius coniunctius ei
fingere, quandoquidem conexu corpus adhaeret.
  Denique corporis atque animi vivata potestas
inter se coniuncta valent vitaque fruuntur;
nec sine corpore enim vitalis edere motus
sola potest animi per se natura nec autem
cassum anima corpus durare et sensibus uti.
scilicet avolsus radicibus ut nequit ullam
dispicere ipse oculus rem seorsum corpore toto,
sic anima atque animus per se nil posse videtur.
nimirum quia *per* venas et viscera mixtim,
per nervos atque ossa, tenentur corpore ab omni
nec magnis intervallis primordia possunt
libera dissultare, ideo conclusa moventur
sensiferos motus quos extra corpus in auras
aeris haut possunt post mortem eiecta moveri
propterea quia non simili ratione tenentur.
corpus enim atque animans erit aer, si cohibere
sese anima atque in eo poterit concludere motus
quos ante in nervis et in ipso corpore agebat.
592 quin etiam finis dum vitae vertitur intra,
saepe aliqua tamen e causa labefacta videtur
ire anima ac toto solui de corpore *velle*
595 et quasi supremo languescere tempore voltus
molliaque exsangui *trunco* cadere omnia membra.

tabi, whether the *tabes* comes at once or years after; so that *tamen in parvo tempore* would have no meaning. 555 *homine* old eds. for *hominem*. *vas esse* Nicc. for *vasse*. 557 558 Lach. has no stop after *adhaeret*, and a comma after *Denique*: 558 begins a new paragraph; and I find from his proof-sheets that he altered the usual punctuation only in his final revise. 564 *ipse oculus* Flor. 31 Mar. (not Nicc. Camb. Brix. Ver. or Ven.) for *oculus ipse*. 566 *per* added by Nicc. *mixtim* Nicc. (not Flor. 31) Camb. Mon. Brix. Ver. Ven. for *mixti*. 571 *moveri* Lamb. for *movere*, 'inscitissime' says Wak.: see notes 2 to VI 595. 573 *animans erit* Lamb. for *animam serit*. 574 *eo* Faber for *eos*: a certain correction rightly admitted by Bentl. and Creech. Lach. strange to say has neglected it and received instead Wakefield's conjecture *In se animam* for *Sese anima*. 576—590 (592—606) Christ quaest. Lucr. p. 19 has acutely seen that these vss. are out of place: he puts them after 579 (594): I put them after 575: see notes 2. 578 *de corpore velle* Lach. acutely for *de corpore omnia membra* which has come from

quod genus est, animo male factum cum perhibe*tur*
aut animam liquisse; ubi iam trepidatur et omnes
extremum cupiunt vitae repraehendere vinclum.
conquassatur enim tum mens animaeque potestas
omnis et haec ipso cum corpore conlabefiunt;
ut gravior paulo possit dissolvere causa.
quid dubitas tandem quin extra prodita corpus
inbecilla foras in aperto, tegmine dempto,
non modo non omnem possit durare per aevom,
sed minimum quodvis nequeat consistere tempus?
quare etiam atque etiam resoluto corporis omni
tegmine et eiectis extra vitalibus auris
dissolui sensus animi fateare necessest
atque animam, quoniam coniunctast causa duobus.
  Denique cum corpus nequeat perferre animai
discidium quin in taetro tabescat odore,
quid dubitas quin ex imo penitusque coorta
emanarit uti fumus diffusa animae vis,
atque ideo tanta mutatum putre ruina
conciderit corpus, penitus quia mota loco sunt
fundamenta, foras anima emanante per artus
perque viarum omnis flexus, in corpore qui sunt,
atque foramina? multimodis ut noscere possis
dispertitam animae naturam exisse per artus
et prius esse sibi distractam corpore in ipso,
quam prolapsa foras enaret in aeris auras.
nec sibi enim quisquam moriens sentire videtur
ire foras animam incolumem de corpore toto
nec prius ad iugulum et supera succedere fauces,
verum deficere in certa regione locatam;
ut sensus alios in parti quemque sua scit
dissolui. quod si inmortalis nostra foret mens,
non tam se moriens dissolvi conquereretur,
sed magis ire foras vestemque relinquere, ut anguis.

580: Nicc. Mon. Brix. Ver. Ven. omit 579 and 580. 580 *trunco* added by Lach. *cadere omnia corpore membra* Flor. 31 Camb. Mar. vulg. 581 *perhibetur* B corr. for *peribet* B, *periberet* A Nicc. 591 *Quare* Nicc. B corr. for *Quae.* 597 *ex* Flor. 31 Camb. for *ea.* 598 *animae vis* Flor. 31 Camb. Ver. Ven. Mar. etc. for *anima eius.* 601 *foras anima emanante* Wak. for *foras manant animaeque. foras manante anima usque* Lach. After 614 Mar. Ald. 1 Junt. vulg. add

Denique cur animi numquam mens consiliumque
gignitur in capite aut pedibus manibusve, sed unis
sedibus et certis regionibus omnibus haeret,
si non certa loca ad nascendum reddita cuique
sunt, et ubi quicquid possit durare creatum,
*
atque ita multimodis partitis artubus esse,
membrorum ut numquam existat praeposterus ordo?
usque adeo sequitur res rem neque flamma creari
fluminibus solitast neque in igni gignier algor.
Praeterea si inmortalis natura animaist
et sentire potest secreta a corpore nostro,
quinque, ut opinor, eam faciundum est sensibus auctam;
nec ratione alia nosmet proponere nobis
possumus infernas animas Acherunte vagari.
pictores itaque et scriptorum saecla priora
sic animas intro duxerunt sensibus auctas.
at neque sorsum oculi neque nares nec manus ipsa
esse potest animae neque sorsum lingua, neque aures
auditu per se possunt sentire neque esse.
Et quoniam toto sentimus corpore inesse
vitalem sensum et totum esse animale videmus,
si subito medium celeri praeciderit ictu
vis aliqua ut sorsum partem secernat utramque,
dispertita procul dubio quoque vis animai
et discissa simul cum corpore dissicietur.
at quod scinditur et partis discedit in ullas,
scilicet aeternam sibi naturam abnuit esse.
falciferos memorant currus abscidere membra
saepe ita de subito permixta caede calentis,
ut tremere in terra videatur ab artubus id quod
decidit abscisum, cum mens tamen atque hominis vis
mobilitate mali non quit sentire dolorem;
et semel in pugnae studio quod dedita mens est,

Gauderet, praelonga senex aut cornua cervus. 617 *regionibus omnibus haeret. regionibu' pectoris h.* Lach. *hominis reg. haeret* Ed. formerly. After 619 some vss. are lost. 620 *partitis* Bern. for *pro totis. perfectis* Lach. 623 *solita neque insigni* AB. *in igni* Nicc. *solita est* Flor. 31 Camb. Pont. Mar. 624 *si immortalis* Nicc. for *si mortalis.* 628 *vagari* Lach. for *vacare. vagare* B corr. Lamb. vulg. perhaps rightly. 632 *animae* Pius conj. for *anima.* 633 *Auditu* Ed. for *Auditum. Haud igitur* Lach. who here begins a new sentence.

corpore reliqüo pugnam caedesque petessit,
nec tenet amissam laevam cum tegmine saepe
inter equos abstraxe rotas falcesque rapaces,
nec cecidisse alius dextram, cum scandit et instat.
inde alius conatur adempto surgere crure,
cum digitos agitat propter moribundus humi pes.
et caput abscisum calido viventeque trunco
servat humi voltum vitalem oculosque patentis,
donec reliquias animai reddidit omnes.
quin etiam tibi si, lingua vibrante, micanti
serpentis cauda e procero corpore, utrumque
. . . .
sit libitum in multas partis discidere ferro,
omnia iam sorsum cernes ancisa recenti
volnere tortari et terram conspargere tabo,
ipsam seque retro partem petere ore priorem,
volneris ardenti ut morsu premat icta dolorem.
omnibus esse igitur totas dicemus in illis
particulis animas? at ea ratione sequetur
unam animantem animas habuisse in corpore multas.
ergo divisast ea quae fuit una simul cum
corpore; quapropter mortale utrumque putandumst,
in multas quoniam partis disciditur aeque.
  Praeterea si inmortalis natura animai
constat et in corpus nascentibus insinuatur,
cur super anteactam aetatem meminisse nequimus
nec vestigia gestarum rerum ulla tenemus?
nam si tanto operest animi mutata potestas,
omnis ut actarum exciderit retinentia rerum,
non, ut opinor, id a leto iam longiter errat;
quapropter fateare necessest quae fuit ante

647 *semel* Lach. for *simul.* 650 *rotas* Nicc. for *rote.* 657 658 *micanti* and *cauda e* Ed. with Lach. for *minanti* and *caude.* 658 a v. is lost here such as *Et caudam et molem totius corporis omnem*: see VI 499: Lach. reads *serpentem* for *serpentis, utrimque* after Mar. Junt. for *utrumque*; and after all his construction is very forced. *l. v. minantis Serpentis caudam procero corpore, utrinque* Lamb. 662 *seque retro* Nicc. for *sequere retro.* 663 *dolorem* Lach. for *dolore.* 674 *tanto operest animi* Mar. for *tanto opere animist,* 680 *solitast animi* Mar. Ald. 1 for *solita animist*: see 623, II 275 and Lach. there. 676 *a leto* Lach., *longiter* Lamb. Lach. from Charisius and Nonius,

interiisse et quae nunc est nunc esse creatam.
Praeterea si iam perfecto corpore nobis
inferri solitast animi vivata potestas
tum cum gignimur et vitae cum limen inimus,
haud ita conveniebat uti cum corpore et una
cum membris videatur in ipso sanguine cresse,
sed velut in cavea per se sibi vivere solam.
CONVENIT UT SENSU CORPUS TAMEN AFFLUAT OMNE
690 quod fieri totum contra manifesta docet res;
namque ita conexa est per venas viscera nervos
ossaque, uti dentes quoque sensu participentur;
morbus ut indicat et gelidai stringor aquai
et lapis oppressus, subiit si e frugibus, asper.
686 quare etiam atque etiam neque originis esse putandumst
expertis animas nec leti lege solutas.
nam neque tanto opere adnecti potuisse putandumst
689 corporibus nostris extrinsecus insinuatas,
nec, tam contextae cum sint, exire videntur
incolumes posse et salvas exsolvere sese
omnibus e nervis atque ossibus articulisque.
quod si forte putas extrinsecus insinuatam
permanare animam nobis per membra solere,
tanto quique magis cum corpore fusa peribit.
quod permanat enim dissolvitur, interit ergo.
dispertitus enim per caulas corporis omnis
ut cibus, in membra atque artus cum diditur omnis,
disperit atque aliam naturam sufficit ex se,
sic anima atque animus quamvis integra recens *in*
corpus eunt, tamen in manando dissoluuntur,
dum quasi per caulas omnis diduntur in artus
particulae quibus haec animi natura creatur,
quae nunc in nostro dominatur corpore nata

for *ab l. longius.* 685 Lamb. has most properly rejected: it is clearly a sarcastic gloss. Lach. retains it and for *affluat* reads *arceat*: an unlikely conjecture. 686—690 (690—694): Lach. was the first to transpose these vss.; and strange it is he should have been the first. 689 *Morbus. Morsus* Lach. Bern. Ed. formerly. 690 *oppressus, subiit si e frugibus* Bern. for *oppressus subitis e frugibus. expressus, subiens e fr.* Lach. 702 *Dispertitus enim* Lach. for *dispertitur ergo. Dispertitur enim* Pont. Brix. Ald. 1 Lamb.

705 *quamvis integra recens in* Mar. Ald. 1 Junt. for *quamvis est integra re-*

ex illa quae tum periit partita per artus.
quapropter neque natali privata videtur
esse die natura animae nec funeris expers.
  Semina praeterea linquontur necne animai
corpore in exanimo? quod si lincuntur et insunt,
haut erit ut merito inmortalis possit haberi,
partibus amissis quoniam libata recessit.
sin ita sinceris membris ablata profugit
ut nullas partis in corpore liquerit ex se,
unde cadavera rancenti iam viscere vermes
expirant atque unde animantum copia tanta
exos et exanguis tumidos perfluctuat artus?
quod si forte animas extrinsecus insinuari
vermibus et privas in corpora posse venire
credis nec reputas cur milia multa animarum
conveniant unde una recesserit, hoc tamen est ut
quaerendum videatur et in discrimen agendum,
utrum tandem animae venentur semina quaeque
vermiculorum ipsaeque sibi fabricentur ubi sint,
an quasi corporibus perfectis insinuentur.
at neque cur faciant ipsae quareve laborent
dicere suppeditat. neque enim, sine corpore cum sunt,
sollicitae volitant morbis alguque fameque;
corpus enim magis his vitiis adfine laborat
et mala multa animus contage fungitur eius.
sed tamen his esto quamvis facere utile corpus,
cum subeant; at qua possint via nulla videtur.
haut igitur faciunt animae sibi corpora et artus.
nec tamen est utqui perfectis insinuentur
corporibus; neque enim poterunt suptiliter esse

cens. 710 *tum* Brix. Ver. Ven. rightly for *tunc*. *periit*. *peritat* Nicc. and later mss. and eds. before Pont. Junt. 718 *Ut* Ver. Ven. for *Et*. 723 *privas in* B corr. for *priva si*. 732 *alguque* Lamb. and mss. of Nonius for *algoque*. 733 *adfine* A p. m. (?) *atfine* B. *et fine* A corr. Nicc.: Gif. first restored *adfine* to text: the note in ed. 3 of Lamb. is amusing. Wak. returns to *et fine*. 734 *contage*. *contagibus* Lach. 736 *Cum subeant*. *Quod subeant* a friend of Faber's, both Faber and Bentl. approving. *Cui s*. Bern. *qua* Mar. Ald. 1 Junt. for *que*. 738 *utqui* Ed. for *ut quicum*: see notes 2 to I 755: *cum* was written over *qui* by some one who did not understand *qui*: *quidum* Bern. and Ed. in ed. 1. Lach. adopts from Lamb. *ut iam*, which he allows 'a

conexae neque consensus contagia fient.
Denique cur acris violentia triste leonum
seminium sequitur, volpes dolus, et fuga cervos,
A PATRIBUS DATUR ET A PATRIUS PAVOR INCITAT ARTUS
et iam cetera de genere hoc cur omnia membris
ex ineunte aevo generascunt ingenioque,
si non, certa suo quia semine seminioque
vis animi pariter crescit cum corpore toto?
quod si inmortalis foret et mutare soleret
corpora, permixtis animantes moribus essent,
effugeret canis Hyrcano de semine saepe
cornigeri incursum cervi tremeretque per auras
aeris accipiter fugiens veniente columba,
desiperent homines, saperent fera saecla ferarum.
illud enim falsa fertur ratione, quod aiunt
inmortalem animam mutato corpore flecti.
quod mutatur enim dissolvitur, interit ergo;
traiciuntur enim partes atque ordine migrant;
quare dissolui quoque debent posse per artus,
denique ut intereant una cum corpore cunctae.
sin animas hominum dicent in corpora semper
ire humana, tamen quaeram cur e sapienti
stulta queat fieri, nec prudens sit puer ullus
nec tam doctus equae pullus quam fortis equi vis.
scilicet in tenero tenerascere corpore mentem
confugient. quod si iam fit, fateare necessest
mortalem esse animam, quoniam mutata per artus
tanto opere amittit vitam sensumque priorem.
quove modo poterit pariter cum corpore quoque
confirmata cupitum aetatis tangere florem

litteris nimium recedere'. 740 *consensus* Lach. for *consensu.* 743 rightly rejected by Lach. and before him by a 'doctus quidam' ap. Lamb. as a manifest sarcastic gloss, which interrupts sense and construction: Ven. Ald. 1, not Pont. Mar. or Junt., read *cervis* for *cervos.* Lamb. *dolu' vulpibus* also. 747 *toto* B, *quoque* A and all other mss. and old eds. '*toto* praetuli, quia non possum ullam artem agnoscere in simili hoc trium versiculorum exitu, *ingenioque*, *seminioque*, *corpore quoque.* non potest autem dubitari quin utraque scriptura fuerit in archetypo' Lach. Lamb. also has *toto*: *quoque* seems a gloss from 769. 760 *sin* Pont. Mar. Ald. 1 Junt. for *sic.* *corpora* B corr. etc. for *corpore.* 763=746: of course a gloss, with no connexion with the text. Bern. includes 764 in the gloss, in my opinion not rightly. 764 *pullus* Nicc. for *paulus.* 784 *in*

vis animi, nisi erit consors in origine prima?
quidve foras sibi vult membris exire senectis?
an metuit conclusa manere in corpore putri
et domus aetatis spatio ne fessa vetusto
obruat? at non sunt immortali ulla pericla.
  Denique conubia ad Veneris partusque ferarum
esse animas praesto deridiculum esse videtur,
expectare immortalis mortalia membra
innumero numero certareque praeproperanter
inter se quae prima potissimaque insinuetur;
si non forte ita sunt animarum foedera pacta
ut quae prima volans advenerit insinuetur
prima neque inter se contendant viribus hilum.
  Denique in aethere non arbor, non aequore in alto
nubes esse queunt nec pisces vivere in arvis
nec cruor in lignis neque saxis sucus inesse.
certum ac dispositumst ubi quicquit crescat et insit.
sic animi natura nequit sine corpore oriri
sola neque a nervis et sanguine longiter esse.
quod si (posset enim multo prius) ipsa animi vis
in capite aut umeris aut imis calcibus esse
posset et innasci quavis in parte, soleret
tandem in eodem homine atque in eodem vase manere.
quod quoniam nostro quoque constat corpore certum
dispositumque videtur ubi esse et crescere possit
sorsum anima atque animus, tanto magis infitiandum
totum posse extra corpus durare genique.
quare, corpus ubi interiit, periisse necessest
confiteare animam distractam in corpore toto.
quippe etenim mortale aeterno iungere et una
consentire putare et fungi mutua posse
desiperest; quid enim diversius esse putandumst

alto. *salso* Lach. because *salso* is found in the repetition of this passage v 128: but as Lucr. so often varies in such points, I cannot bring myself to depart from the mss. 789 *longiter* Lamb. Lach. *longius* all mss. here and v 133: comp. 676. 790—793 are repeated v 134—137 without the mss. differing in a single letter. I flatter myself I have made the passage clear by a correct punctuation without the change of a word: 790 *posset enim multo prius* I enclose in brackets, and begin the apodosis at *soleret*. Lach. here and in v reads *Quid si posset enim? multo*. Mar. Ald. 1 Junt. vulg. give *Hoc si posset enim, multo*. 800 *mortale*

aut magis inter se disiunctum discrepitansque,
quam mortale quod est inmortali atque perenni
iunctum in concilio saevas tolerare procellas?
quod si forte ideo magis immortalis habendast,
quod letalibus ab rebus munita tenetur,
aut quia non veniunt omnino aliena salutis
aut quia quae veniunt aliqua ratione recedunt
pulsa prius quam quid noceant sentire queamus,
. . . .
praeter enim quam quod morbis cum corporis aegret,
advenit id quod eam de rebus saepe futuris
macerat inque metu male habet curisque fatigat
praeteritisque male admissis peccata remordent.
adde furorem animi proprium atque oblivia rerum,

Junt. for *mortalem*. 805 *saevas* Mar. Junt. for *salvas*. 806—818 = v 351—363 word for word: they here interrupt the argument, and are of course one of the many glosses with which some reader has wished either to explain or refute the poet by quoting his own verses for or against him, as the case may be. But as that which follows in the fifth book applies only to the heaven, not to the mind of which Lucr. is here speaking, he did not continue his quotation; but Ald. 1 and Junt. after Marullus followed by all editors before Lach. add v 364—373, rudely altered to suit the present subject. 'at Michahel Marullus' says Lach. justly indignant 'illo [lectore] audacior nihil veritus est ceteris transferendis immanes ineptias inferre; quos versus cum omnes libris veteribus sine exceptione omnibus abesse aut scirent aut certe deberent scire, plerique sine admonitione susceperunt, Wakefieldus, cui Forbiger adsensus est, "poetae" (id est Marulli) miratur "consideratam severitatem diligitque, per tam dilucidam ratiocinationem simpliciter mentem suam exponentis". mihi Marulli male sedula simplicitas non nimis exagitanda esse videtur: subiciam tamen eius versiculos, ut appareat quae Lambinis et Wakefieldis (ceteros nunc omitto) Lucretio dignissima visa fuerint. *At neque, uti docui, solido cum corpore* mentis *Natura est, quoniam admistum est in rebus inane, Nec tamen est ut inane, neque autem corpora desunt Ex infinito, quae possint forte coorta Corruere hanc* mentis *violento turbine* molem, *Aut aliam quamvis cladem importare pericli, Nec porro natura loci spaciumque profundi Deficit, expargi quo* possit vis animai *Aut alia quavis* possit *vi pulsa perire, Haud igitur leti praeclusa est ianua* menti'. 820 *letalibus* Lamb. for *vitalibus*. After 823 a verse is lost, which Lach. thus supplies, *Multa tamen tangunt animam mala, multa pericla*. Mar. Ald. 1 and Junt. insert after 820 the following, *Scilicet a vera longe ratione remotumst*; which Lamb. retained, but placed after 823.

824 *morbist cum corporis aegrit* AB. *morbis* Avanc. first: no 'Italus' before him. *aegret* Gif. in notes rightly for *aegrit*. Nicc., deceived by *morbist* and thinking *cum* a conjunction, wrote *cum corpus aegrotat*, which led to endless confusion in later mss. and eds.: even Lamb. was misled, and Creech and others before Lach. neglected Gifanius' hint. 826 *macerat* Flor. 31 Pont. Mar. Ald. 1 Junt. for *maceret*: yet Wak. retains the solecism.

adde quod in nigras lethargi mergitur undas.
  Nil igitur mors est ad nos neque pertinet hilum,
quandoquidem natura animi mortalis habetur,
et velut anteacto nil tempore sensimus aegri,
ad confligendum venientibus undique Poenis,
omnia cum belli trepido concussa tumultu
horrida contremuere sub altis aetheris oris,
in dubioque fuere utrorum ad regna cadendum
omnibus humanis esset terraque marique,
sic, ubi non erimus, cum corporis atque animai
discidium fuerit quibus e sumus uniter apti,
scilicet haud nobis quicquam, qui non erimus tum,
accidere omnino poterit sensumque movere,
non si terra mari miscebitur et mare caelo.
et si iam nostro sentit de corpore postquam
distractast animi natura animaeque potestas,
nil tamen est ad nos qui comptu coniugioque
corporis atque animae consistimus uniter apti.
nec, si materiem nostram collegerit aetas
post obitum rursumque redegerit ut sita nunc est
atque iterum nobis fuerint data lumina vitae,
pertineat quicquam tamen ad nos id quoque factum,
interrupta semel cum sit repetentia nostri.
et nunc nil ad nos de nobis attinet, ante
qui fuimus, *neque* iam de illis nos adficit angor.
nam cum respicias inmensi temporis omne
praeteritum spatium, tum motus materiai
multimodis quam sint, facile hoc adcredere possis,
semina saepe in eodem, ut nunc sunt, ordine posta
865 haec eadem, quibus e nunc nos sumus, ante fuisse.
858 nec memori tamen id quimus repraehendere mente;
inter enim iectast vitai pausa vageque

829 *nigras.* 'f. *pigras*' Heins. in ms. notes: Markland proposed the same, but without cause. 835 *aetheris oris* Gif. for *aetheris auris*; and so Lucr. always writes elsewhere. 844 *Distractast* Nicc. for *Distractas.* 847 *materiem* B, *materiam* A Nicc. 851 *repetentia* B rightly. *repentia* A Nicc. Flor. 31 Camb. *retinentia* Avanc. Lach. *nostri* Pius in notes, Gif. Lach. for *nostris. nobis* Pont. Avanc. *nostra* Mar. Junt. vulg. 853 *neque* added by Lach. *nec* Mar. Ald. 1 Junt. vulg. *adficit* Flor. 31 Mon. Pont. for *adfigit.* 856 *multimodis* Lach. with Wakefield's Δ for *multimodi.* 858 (865) transferred here

deerrarunt passim motus ab sensibus omnes.
debet enim, misere si forte aegreque futurumst,
ipse quoque esse in eo tum tempore, cui male possit
accidere. id quoniam mors eximit, esseque probet
864 illum cui possint incommoda conciliari,
scire licet nobis nil esse in morte timendum
nec miserum fieri qui non est posse neque hilum
differre anne ullo fuerit iam tempore natus,
mortalem vitam mors cum inmortalis ademit.

Proinde ubi se videas hominem indignarier ipsum,
post mortem fore ut aut putescat corpore posto
aut flammis interfiat malisve ferarum,
scire licet non sincerum sonere atque subesse
caecum aliquem cordi stimulum, quamvis neget ipse
credere se quemquam sibi sensum in morte futurum.
non, ut opinor, enim dat quod promittit et unde,
nec radicitus e vita se tollit et eicit,
sed facit esse sui quiddam super inscius ipse.
vivus enim sibi cum proponit quisque futurum,
corpus uti volucres lacerent in morte feraeque,
ipse sui miseret; neque enim se dividit illim,
nec removet satis a proiecto corpore et illum
se fingit sensuque suo contaminat astans.
hinc indignatur se mortalem esse creatum
nec videt in vera nullum fore morte alium se
qui possit vivus sibi se lugere peremptum
stansque iacentem *se* lacerari urive dolere.

by Lach. who is naturally surprised that it was left for him to do. 862 *misere si* Pont. Turnebus and Is. Voss. in ms. notes, before Lach., for *miserest.*

864 *mors* B corr. Flor. 31 for *mox.* *probet* Lach. *prohibet* Turnebus for *prohibe.* 868 *Differre anne ullo* Ed. for *Differre annullo anullo* A, *anullo anullo* B. *a nullo* Nicc. *isne ullo* Ed. in small ed. *Differre ante ullo* Lach.; but *differre fuerit* seems not to be Latin. *Differre an nullo* of Pont. Mar. Ald. 1 Junt. Lamb. etc. has no sense. 871 *putescat* Avanc. Wak. Lach. for *putes. putrescat* Flor. 31 Pont. Mar. Junt. Lamb. vulg. Cic. de fin. v 38 *ne putisceret* Nonius, *putresceret* mss.: de nat. deor. II 160 *ne putesceret* mss. speaking of the same thing. 873 *non sincerum* Flor. 31 Camb. Pont. Mar. for *no sincerum* A. Nicc., *nos sinc.* B. 880 *lacerent* Nicc. for *iacerent.* 881 *dividit illim* A. *vidit illum* B. *dividit illum* Nicc. *dividit hilum* Flor. 31 Camb. Mar. *vindicat hilum* Lamb. 886 *Qui* Flor. 31 Mon. Pont. Ald. 1 Junt. for *Cui.*

887 *se* added by Flor. 31 Camb. Avanc. *dolere* Mon. p. m. Lamb. for *dolore.*

nam si in morte malumst malis morsuque ferarum
tractari, non invenio qui non sit acerbum
ignibus inpositum calidis torrescere flammis
aut in melle situm suffocari atque rigere
frigore, cum summo gelidi cubat aequore saxi,
urgerive superne obtritum pondere terrae.
'Iam iam non domus accipiet te laeta, neque uxor
optima nec dulces occurrent oscula nati
praeripere et tacita pectus dulcedine tangent.
non poteris factis florentibus esse, tuisque
praesidium. misero misere' aiunt 'omnia ademit
una dies infesta tibi tot praemia vitae.'
illud in his rebus non addunt 'nec tibi earum
iam desiderium rerum super insidet una.'
quod bene si videant animo dictisque sequantur,
dissoluant animi magno se angore metuque.
'tu quidem ut es leto sopitus, sic eris aevi
quod superest cunctis privatu' doloribus aegris:
at nos horrifico cinefactum te prope busto
insatiabiliter deflevimus, aeternumque
nulla dies nobis maerorem e pectore demet.'
illud ab hoc igitur quaerendum est, quid sit amari
tanto opere, ad somnum si res redit atque quietem,
cur quisquam aeterno possit tabescere luctu.
Hoc etiam faciunt ubi discubuere tenentque
pocula saepe homines et inumbrant ora coronis,
ex animo ut dicant 'brevis hic est fructus homullis;
iam fuerit neque post umquam revocare licebit.'
tamquam in morte mali cum primis hoc sit eorum,
quod sitis exurat miseros atque arida torres,
aut aliae cuius desiderium insideat rei.
nec sibi enim quisquam tum se vitamque requirit,

893 *obtritum* Pont. Mar. Ald. 1 Junt. for *obrutum*. 894 *Iam iam* Flor. 31 4 Vat. Lach. *Amiam* A Nicc. *Vimiam* B. *At iam* Pont. Mar. Ald. 1 Junt. vulg. *At iam* is perhaps right. 897 898 Lamb. has departed widely from the mss. without any cause, reading *tibi fortibus* for *florentibus*, *miser o miser* for *misero misere*. 902 *quod* Nicc. for *Quo*. 904—908: to these verses Bern. has properly attached the mark of apostrophe. 914 *fructus* Flor. 31 Camb. for *fluctus*. 917 *torres* Lach. for *torret* A, *torrat* A corr. B Nicc. *terra* Flor. 31 Camb. Mon. Lamb. 919 *requirit* Flor. 29 corr. (Politian?) Camb. corr.

cum pariter mens et corpus sopita quiescunt;
nam licet aeternum per nos sic esse soporem,
nec desiderium nostri nos adficit ullum.
et tamen haudquaquam nostros tunc illa per artus
longe ab sensiferis primordia motibus errant,
cum correptus homo ex somno se colligit ipse.
multo igitur mortem minus ad nos esse putandumst,
si minus esse potest quam quod nil esse videmus;
maior enim turbae disiectus materiai
consequitur leto nec quisquam expergitus exstat,
frigida quem semel est vitai pausa secuta.
  Denique si vocem rerum natura repente
mittat et hoc alicui nostrum sic increpet ipsa
'quid tibi tanto operest, mortalis, quod nimis aegris
luctibus indulges? quid mortem congemis ac fles?
nam gratis anteacta fuit tibi vita priorque
et non omnia pertusum congesta quasi in vas
commoda perfluxere atque ingrata interiere:
cur non ut plenus vitae conviva recedis
aequo animoque capis securam, stulte, quietem?
sin ea quae fructus cumque es periere profusa
vitaque in offensust, cur amplius addere quaeris,
rursum quod pereat male et ingratum occidat omne,
non potius vitae finem facis atque laboris?
nam tibi praeterea quod machiner inveniamque,
quod placeat, nil est: eadem sunt omnia semper.
si tibi non annis corpus iam marcet et artus
confecti languent, eadem tamen omnia restant,
omnia si pergas vivendo vincere saecla,
atque etiam potius, si numquam sis moriturus,'

Nauger. for *requiret*. 921 *esse soporem* A Nicc. vulg. *esse praemo* B: a mere blunder, the *so* being absorbed in *esse*: yet Bern. reads *per aevum*. 922 *adficit* Lamb. ed. 1 and 2, Heins. in ms. notes for *adigit*. *attigit* Flor. 31 Camb. Mar. Avanc. Lamb. ed. 3. 935 *Nam gratis anteacta fuit tibi vita priorque* Ed. for *N. gr. fuit tibi vita anteacta priorque*. Perhaps Lucr. wrote *Nam gratis fuvit* or *fūit tibi* cet.: the *ū* is common in old writers. *N. gr. fuit haec t. v. a. pr.* Lach. *N. si grata f. t. v. a. p.* Nauger. *Nam gratis fluxit* cet. Mar. Junt. *Nam gratum f. t. v.* Nicc. *Nam gratisne fuit* Bern. 941 *offensust* Lamb. for *offensost*. 942 *male et* B Flor. 31 etc. rightly. *mali et* A Nicc. Camb. Wak. 943 *finem facis* Avanc. for *finem iacis*. 945 *placeat* Nicc. for *placet*. 948 *pergas* Lamb. ed. 3 for *perges*. 950 *nisi* Mar. Junt. for

quid respondemus, nisi iustam intendere litem
naturam et veram verbis exponere causam?
955 grandior hic vero si iam seniorque queratur
952 atque obitum lamentetur miser amplius aequo,
non merito inclamet magis et voce increpet acri?
954 'aufer abhinc lacrimas, balatro, et compesce querellas.
omnia perfunctus vitai praemia marces.
sed quia semper aves quod abest, praesentia temnis,
inperfecta tibi elapsast ingrataque vita
et nec opinanti mors ad caput adstitit ante
quam satur ac plenus possis disce*de*re rerum.
nunc aliena tua tamen aetate omnia mitte
aequo animoque agedum magnus concede: necessest.'
iure, ut opinor, agat, iure increpet inciletque;
cedit enim rerum novitate extrusa vetustas
semper, et ex aliis aliud reparare necessest;
nec quisquam in barathrum nec Tartara deditur atra:
materies opus est ut crescant postera saecla;
quae tamen omnia te vita perfuncta sequentur;
nec minus ergo ante haec quam tu cecidere, cadentque.
sic alid ex alio numquam desistet oriri
vitaque mancipio nulli datur, omnibus usu.
respice item quam nil ad nos anteacta vetustas
temporis aeterni fuerit, quam nascimur ante.
hoc igitur speculum nobis natura futuri
temporis exponit post mortem denique nostram.
numquid ibi horribile apparet, num triste videtur
quicquam, non omni somno securius exstat?

Atque ea nimirum quaecumque Acherunte profundo
prodita sunt esse, in vita sunt omnia nobis.

si. 952 (955) placed here first by Lach. 955 *balatro* certain critics in Turneb. advers. and Heins. in ms. notes for *baratre*. *barde* Ald. 1 Junt. not Mar. 958 *inperfecta* Flor. 31 Camb. for *inperfecte*. 960 *discedere* Nicc. for *discere*. 962 *agedum* Nicc. for *agendum*. *magnus* 'censor Orellii Ienenis' for *magnis*. *iam aliis* Mar. Ald. 1 Junt. vulg. *dignis* Lach. *gnatis* Bern. *humanis* and *mage sis* Ed. formerly. 966 *deditur* A Nicc. *dedit* B. *decidit* B corr. Lamb. 978 *Atque ea nimirum* AB Flor. 31 Camb. 2 Vat. Priscian rightly. Nicc. has *Atque animarum etiam*: a strange error which is repeated by 2 Vat. Brix. Ver. Ven. Mar. Ald. 1 and 2, Junt.: the last four read *Atqui*. Avanc. however at the end of his Catullus rightly recalls *Atque ea nimirum*; as do Lamb. vulg. but not

nec miser inpendens magnum timet aere saxum
Tantalus, ut famast, cassa formidine torpens;
sed magis in vita divom metus urget inanis
mortalis casumque timent quem cuique ferat fors.
nec Tityon volucres ineunt Acherunte iacentem
nec quod sub magno scrutentur pectore quicquam
perpetuam aetatem possunt reperire profecto.
quamlibet immani proiectu corporis exstet,
qui non sola novem dispessis iugera membris
optineat, sed qui terrai totius orbem,
non tamen aeternum poterit perferre dolorem
nec praebere cibum proprio de corpore semper.
sed Tityos nobis hic est, in amore iacentem
quem volucres lacerant atque exest anxius angor
aut alia quavis scindunt cuppedine curae.
Sisyphus in vita quoque nobis ante oculos est
qui petere a populo fasces saevasque secures
imbibit et semper victus tristisque recedit.
nam petere imperium quod inanest nec datur umquam,
atque in eo semper durum sufferre laborem,
hoc est adverso nixantem trudere monte
saxum quod tamen *e* summo iam vertice rusum
volvitur et plani raptim petit aequora campi.
deinde animi ingratam naturam pascere semper

Wak. 983 *cuique*. *cumque* B Lamb. etc. wrongly. 985 *quod* Camb. Junt. etc. for *quid*. 988 *dispessis* Turneb. for *dispersis*: so Ed. in II 1126: comp. Ovid. met. IV 458, and Plaut. miles 1407. *dispensis* Lamb. ed. 3. 'leg. distensis dispansis' Heins. in ms. notes. 992 *est* B corr. Flor. 31 for *es*. *et* Nicc. 994 *cuppedine* Pont. Lamb. rightly, as V 45 VI 25. *curpedine* AB. *turpedine* A corr. Nicc. Flor. 31 Camb. Junt. etc. *torpedine* Ven. Ald. 1 Gif. who says 'Ita v. nostri et aliorum fere. in q. v. *cuppedine*, quod inrepsisse puto ex aliis locis inf. lib. 5 et 6 ..contra Marull. ex hoc loco mutarat inf. lib. 5 et 6 *torpedine* pro *cupp.* supposito'. Now the Junt. reads here, as I have said, *turpedine*; V 45 and VI 25 *cupedinis*. Again Ven. not Brix. or Ver. *torpedine* here. This therefore is one of many proofs, some of which I have given elsewhere, that Gifanius had the old Venice edition with Marullus' ms. notes before him, and that this is the book belonging to Sambucus of which he speaks both in his preface to Sambucus himself and in his address to the reader: see above p. 9. [*turpedine* Mon. as I now find: and the corrector Marullus repeats the words in marg. as notable: *torpedine* must have been an earlier notion of Marullus; as in V and VI he properly corrects the ms. reading to *cuppedinis*.] 1001 *e summo iam vertice* Pont. Avanc. for *summo iam vertice*. *summo iam e vertice* Flor. 31 Camb. *a su. i. v.*

atque explere bonis rebus satiareque numquam,
quod faciunt nobis annorum tempora, circum
cum redeunt fetusque ferunt variosque lepores,
nec tamen explemur vitai fructibus umquam,
hoc, ut opinor, id est, aevo florente puellas
quod memorant laticem pertusum congerere in vas,
quod tamen expleri nulla ratione potestur.
Cerberus et furiae iam vero et lucis egestas

*

Tartarus horriferos eructans faucibus aestus,
qui neque sunt usquam nec possunt esse profecto.
sed metus in vita poenarum pro male factis
est insignibus insignis scelerisque luella,
carcer et horribilis de saxo iactu' deorsum,
verbera carnifices robur pix lammina taedae;
quae tamen etsi absunt, at mens sibi conscia factis
praemetuens adhibet stimulos terretque flagellis
nec videt interea qui terminus esse malorum
possit nec quae sit poenarum denique finis
atque eadem metuit magis haec ne in morte gravescant.
hic Acherusia fit stultorum denique vita.
  Hoc etiam tibi tute interdum dicere possis
'lumina sis oculis etiam bonus Ancu' reliquit

Mar. Junt. vulg. 1005 *circum Cum redeunt.* *victum, Cum redeunt* Lach. without cause. 1009 *congerere* B corr. etc. for *cogere.* 1010 *nulla* Nicc. for *ulla.* After 1011 I believe some verses are lost: both the words of Servius to Aen. VI 596 and his context prove to me that he is speaking of Lucretius, not of Virgil as Bernays affirms in Rhein. Mus. n. f. V p. 584, when he says 'per rotam autem ostendit negotiatores qui semper tempestatibus turbinibusque volvuntur'. I have appended the mark of a hiatus and made no change in the text. *furiae* B corr. Pont. Mar. for *funae.* For *egestas* of all mss. and of Brix. and Ver., Ven. has the remarkable reading *egenus*, adopted by Ald. 1 Junt. Lamb. vulg. Lach.; but it is of course a pure conjecture which Lach. wrongly gives to Marullus. 1013 *Qui neque.* *Quid? neque* Lach. *Haec neque* Mar. Junt. vulg. 1014 *poenarum* Nicc. for *paenarum* of AB: in ancient times there seems to have been a struggle between *paena* and the more correct *poena* which finally prevailed. *paenitet*, or later *penitet*, was alone known. 1016 *iactu' deorsum* Lamb. for *iactus eorum.* *iactu' reorum* Heins. in ms. notes. 1017 *iam mina* AB. *agmina* Nicc. Flor. 31 Brix. Ver. *lamina* Ven. vulg. *lammina* Lach.

1019 *terretque* Lach. for *torretque.* *torquetque* Heins. in ms. notes and advers. which Virg. Aen. VI 670 *sontis...flagello...quatit* might perhaps support.

1023 *Hic.* *Hinc* Pont. Mar. Junt. Lamb. vulg. without cause. 1031 *superare*

qui melior multis quam tu fuit, improbe, rebus.
inde alii multi reges rerumque potentes
occiderunt, magnis qui gentibus imperitarunt.
ille quoque ipse, viam qui quondam per mare magnum
stravit iterque dedit legionibus ire per altum
ac pedibus salsas docuit superare lucunas
et contemsit equis insultans murmura ponti,
lumine adempto animam moribundo corpore fudit.
Scipiadas, belli fulmen, Carthaginis horror,
ossa dedit terrae proinde ac famul infimus esset.
adde repertores doctrinarum atque leporum,
adde Heliconiadum comites; quorum unus Homerus
sceptra potitus eadem aliis sopitu' quietest.
denique Democritum postquam matura vetustas
admonuit memores motus languescere mentis,
sponte sua leto caput obvius optulit ipse.
ipse Epicurus obit decurso lumine vitae,
qui genus humanum ingenio superavit et omnis
restincxit, stellas exortus ut aetherius sol.
tu vero dubitabis et indignabere obire?
mortua cui vita est prope iam vivo atque videnti,
qui somno partem maiorem conteris aevi
et vigilans stertis nec somnia cernere cessas
sollicitamque geris cassa formidine mentem
nec reperire potes tibi quid sit saepe mali, cum
ebrius urgeris multis miser undique curis
atque animi incerto fluitans errore vagaris.'
  Si possent homines, proinde ac sentire videntur
pondus inesse animo quod se gravitate fatiget,

Nicc. (not Flor. 31 or Camb.) for *super ire*. Lach. encloses the v. in [ ], as wrongly retained by the first editor. 1032 *equis*. *aquis* Lamb. etc. wrongly.

1033 *fudit* Pont. Mar. Ald. 1 Junt. for *fugit*. 1034 *Scipiadas* AB Lach. *Scipiades* Nicc. vulg. 1038 *potitus* Flor. 31 Camb. Brix. Pont. Mar. for *potius*. 1040 *memores*. *memorem* Lamb. 1042 *obit* Flor. 31 Pont. Mar. for *obiit*. *iit* Lach. *iit* can scarcely be used in this unqualified way for *mortuus est*; nor is the evidence adduced by Lach. in his long and most learned note sufficient to shew that Lucr. could not have used the form *obit* before a consonant: but see notes 2. 1044 *aetherius* Lactantius Junt. *aerius* mss. 1050 *potes tibi quid sit* Lach. for *potest ibi quod sit*. *potes tibi quod sit* Mar. *potes quod sit ibi* Nicc.: hence *potes quid sit tibi* Flor. 31 Camb. Brix. Ver. Ven. Avanc. vulg. *potes quod sit tibi* Junt. Ald. 2 wrongly. 1052 *animi incerto* Lamb. for *animo*

e quibus id fiat causis quoque noscere et unde
tanta mali tamquam moles in pectore constet,
haut ita vitam agerent, ut nunc plerumque videmus
quid sibi quisque velit nescire et quaerere semper
commutare locum quasi onus deponere possit.
exit saepe foras magnis ex aedibus ille,
esse domi quem pertaesumst, subitoque *revertit*,
quippe foris nilo melius qui sentiat esse.
currit agens mannos ad villam praecipitanter,
auxilium tectis quasi ferre ardentibus instans;
oscitat extemplo, tetigit cum limina villae,
aut abit in somnum gravis atque oblivia quaerit,
aut etiam properans urbem petit atque revisit.
hoc se quisque modo fugit (at quem scilicet, ut fit,
effugere haut potis est, ingratis haeret) et odit
propterea, morbi quia causam non tenet aeger;
quam bene si videat, iam rebus quisque relictis
naturam primum studeat cognoscere rerum,
temporis aeterni quoniam, non unius horae,
ambigitur status, in quo sit mortalibus omnis
aetas, post mortem quae restat cumque manenda.
  Denique tanto opere in dubiis trepidare periclis
quae mala nos subigit vitai tanta cupido?
certa quidem finis vitae mortalibus adstat
nec devitari letum pote quin obeamus.
praeterea versamur ibidem atque insumus usque
nec nova vivendo procuditur ulla voluptas;

incerto. 1061 *revertit* added by Politian in marg. Flor. 29 Ald. 1 Junt. vulg. *reventat* Flor. 29 Flor. 31 Camb. Mar. *revertens* Pont. *revisit* Proll, de form. ant. Lucr. p. 44—48. 1063 *praecipitanter* Nicc. for *praecipiter*. 'f. *praecipiterque... instat*' Heins. in ms. notes. 1068 1069: by a better punctuation I have I think made this disputed passage quite clear: 1069 *ingratis* Lamb. rightly for *ingratius*: nothing else is to be changed; but *at quem...haeret* are to be enclosed in brackets. 1068 for *quem* Lach. *quom*: his note is most unsatisfactory and to me almost unintelligible; especially the words 'nam sese homo aut semper effugere potest aut numquam, quoniam hoc totum figurate dicitur'. Seneca de tranquill. II 14 clearly read *quem*: he explains Lucr. quite correctly. *fugit at*. *fugitat* Madvig poet. Lat. carm. sel. 1843: but Seneca, as well as our mss., clearly read *fugit at*. 1069 *haeret et angit* Mar. Junt. Lamb. vulg. For *ingratius* Ven. alone has *initus*; therefore Avanc. who founded his revision on it has *invitus adhaeret*. 1073 *Temporis aeterni* Pont. Mar. Ald. 1 Junt. first for *Aeterni temporis*. 1075 *manenda* Lamb. for *manendo*. 1078 *Certa quidem* Avanc.

sed dum abest quod avemus, id exsuperare videtur
cetera; post aliut, cum contigit illud, avemus
et sitis aequa tenet vitai semper hiantis.
posteraque in dubiost fortunam quam vehat aetas,
quidve ferat nobis casus quive exitus instet.
nec prorsum vitam ducendo demimus hilum
tempore de mortis nec delibare valemus,
quo minus esse diu possimus forte perempti.
proinde licet quot vis vivendo condere saecla;
mors aeterna tamen nilo minus illa manebit,
nec minus ille diu iam non erit ex hodierno
lumine qui finem vitai fecit, et ille,
mensibus atque annis qui multis occidit ante.

before Lamb. for *Certe equidem*: Lucr. may have written *equidem*. 1085 *fortunam* Ald. 1 Junt. first for *fortuna*. 1088 *delibare* Pont. Mar. Junt. for *deliberare*. *delibrare* Avanc. Lamb. 'f. devitare,' Heins. in ms. notes.

1089 *possimus forte* Nicc. B corr. Flor. 31 Camb. Brix. Ver. Ven. for *possumus forte*. *sorte* Ald. 1 Pius Junt. Naugerius. *morte* Lamb. first: no 'Italus' before him.

T. LUCRETI CARI

DE RERUM NATURA

LIBER QUARTUS

[Avia Pieridum peragro loca nullius ante
trita solo, iuvat integros accedere fontis
atque haurire, iuvatque novos decerpere flores
insignemque meo capiti petere inde coronam
unde prius nulli velarint tempora musae;
primum quod magnis doceo de rebus et artis
religionum animum nodis exsolvere pergo,
deinde quod obscura de re tam lucida pango
carmina, musaeo contingens cuncta lepore.
id quoque enim non ab nulla ratione videtur;
nam veluti pueris absinthia taetra medentes
cum dare conantur, prius oras pocula circum
contingunt mellis dulci flavoque liquore,
ut puerorum aetas inprovida ludificetur
labrorum tenus, interea perpotet amarum
absinthi laticem deceptaque non capiatur,
sed potius tali pacto recreata valescat,
sic ego nunc, quoniam haec ratio plerumque videtur
tristior esse quibus non est tractata, retroque
volgus abhorret ab hac, volui tibi suaviloquenti
carmine Pierio rationem exponere nostram

7 *animum.* *animos* Lactant. I 16: see I 932. 8 *pango* Flor. 31 Camb. 3 Vat. vulg. for *pando*: so I 933. 11 *Nam.* *Ac* Quintil. III 1 4 Nonius Hieronym. 13 *Contingunt.* *Inspirant* or *Aspergunt* Quintil. 17 *pacto* Lach. for *atacto*: so I 942. *a tactu* Nicc. one Vat. Ver. Ven. Ald. 1 Junt. Wak. *attactu* Flor. 31 3 Vat. *adtactu* Camb. *tactu* Lamb. ed. 3. *facto* Lamb. ed. 1 and 2,

et quasi musaeo dulci contingere melle,
si tibi forte animum tali ratione tenere
versibus in nostris possem, dum percipis omnem
naturam rerum ac persentis utilitatem.]
  Atque animi quoniam docui natura quid esset
et quibus e rebus cum corpore compta vigeret
quove modo distracta rediret in ordia prima,
nunc agere incipiam tibi, quod vementer ad has res
attinet, esse ea quae rerum simulacra vocamus:
quae, quasi membranae summo de corpore rerum
dereptae, volitant ultroque citroque per auras,
atque eadem nobis vigilantibus obvia mentes
terrificant atque in somnis, cum saepe figuras
contuimur miras simulacraque luce carentum,
quae nos horrifice languentis saepe sopore
excierunt: ne forte animas Acherunte reamur
effugere aut umbras inter vivos volitare
neve aliquid nostri post mortem posse relinqui,
cum corpus simul atque animi natura perempta
in sua discessum dederint primordia quaeque.
  Dico igitur rerum effigias tenuisque figuras
mittier ab rebus summo de corpore rerum,
51 quoi quasi membranae, vel cortex nominitandast,
quod speciem ac formam similem gerit eius imago

Gif. 32 *dereptae* B Lamb. *direptae* A Nicc. all before Lamb. 41 *quaeque. quoique* Lach. '*discessus*' he says 'non aliter dari potest quam quomodo *fugam dari* Vergilius dixit, id est concedi': but Virgil also says XII 367 *fugam dant nubila*, that is *fugiunt*: see notes 2 for many more illustrations: *discessum dederint* therefore = *discesserint*. 42 *effigias* Lamb. for *effugias* of AB. *effigies* Nicc. and all mss. and eds. between him and Lamb. 43 *summo de corpore rerum* Lach. for *summo de cortice eorum*. *summo de corpore earum* Lamb. vulg.: but comp. 31 and 64, and Lachmann's note. 44—47 (45—48) = III 31—34, except 44 *Sed quoniam* for *Et quoniam*, 47 *Quoque, possit* for *Quove, possint*, and are rightly ejected by Lach. as a gloss. In this place they are of course quite inadmissible. Mar. Junt. vulg. put them before 26; and thither, if retained, they must be transferred. To this Lach. offers the objection that while the first 24 lines are repeated word for word from the first book, in 25 we have *ac persentis utilitatem* for *qua constet compta figura*: this change he says was probably made because in 27 are the words *compta vigeret*; but had the poet really inserted 44—47 before 26, this alteration would not have been called for: see however what is said in notes 2. 48 49 (49 50) = 29 30 and seem to be repeated here without meaning because of the resemblance between what precedes and follows them there and

cuiuscumque cluet de corpore fusa vagari.
44 id licet hinc quamvis hebeti cognoscere corde.
54 principio quoniam mittunt in rebus apertis
corpora res multae, partim diffusa solute,
robora ceu fumum mittunt ignesque vaporem,
et partim contexta magis condensaque, ut olim
cum teretis ponunt tunicas aestate cicadae,
et vituli cum membranas de corpore summo
nascentes mittunt, et item cum lubrica serpens
exuit in spinis vestem; nam saepe videmus
illorum spoliis vepres volitantibus auctas:
quae quoniam fiunt, tenuis quoque debet imago
ab rebus mitti summo de corpore rerum.
nam cur illa cadant magis ab rebusque recedant
quam quae tenvia sunt, hiscendist nulla potestas;
praesertim cum sint in summis corpora rebus
multa minuta, iaci quae possint ordine eodem
quo fuerint et formai servare figuram,
et multo citius, quanto minus indupediri
pauca queunt et *quae* sunt prima fronte locata.
nam certe iacere ac largiri multa videmus,
non solum ex alto penitusque, ut diximus ante,
verum de summis ipsum quoque saepe colorem.
et volgo faciunt id lutea russaque vela
et ferrugina, cum magnis intenta theatris
per malos volgata trabesque trementia flutant;
namque ibi consessum caveai supter et omnem

what precedes and follows here. Mar. and Junt. first omitted them. 50 *Quoi* Ed. for *Qui*. *Quae* Nonius Flor. 31 Camb. vulgo and Lach. 52 *cluet* Brix. Avanc. Ald. 2 for *ciuet*. *cui et* Nicc. *tui et* Flor. 31 Camb. *eluet* Ver. Ven. *queat* Mar. Junt. 53 (44) first transferred hither by Mar. Junt. 54 *mittunt* Nicc. for *mittuntur*. 68 *eodem* Pont. Mar. Junt. for *eorum*. *rerum* Ven. Avanc. 69 *et formai* Is. Voss. in ms. notes for *et forma*. *et cum forma* B corr. *veterem et formam* Camb. *veterem et formae* Vat. 1136 and 1954 Othob. Lamb. *solitam et formae* Avanc. Nauger. *formaeque suam* Pont. Junt. *conformem* or *consimilem* conj. Lamb. *conformem* Heins. in ms. notes. 71 *et quae sunt prima* Lach. for *et sunt prima* AB. 'quadratus habet *in* ante *prima* additum antiquissima, si non prima manu' Lach.: and so Pont. Mar. Ald. 1 Junt. *et sunt prima sub* Flor. 31 Camb. 72 *iacere ac largiri* Lach. most acutely for *iacere aciergiri*. *iacere ac iaculari* Flor. 31 Camb. 2 Vat. Mar. Ald. 1 Junt. 77 *flutant* Turnebus Lamb. ed. 3 for *fluctus* B. om. A Nicc. 2 Vat. Brix. Ver.: hence *circum*, *pendent*,

scaenai speciem, patrum coetumque decorum
inficiunt coguntque suo fluitare colore.
et quanto circum mage sunt inclusa theatri
moenibu', tam magis haec intus perfusa lepore
omnia conrident correpta luce diei.
ergo lintea de summo cum corpore fucum
mittunt, effigias quoque debent mittere tenvis
res quaeque, ex summo quoniam iaculantur utraque.
sunt igitur iam formarum vestigia certa
quae volgo volitant suptili praedita filo
nec singillatim possunt secreta videri.
praeterea omnis odor fumus vapor atque aliae res
consimiles ideo diffusae *e* rebus abundant,
ex alto quia dum veniunt intrinsecus ortae,
scinduntur per iter flexum, nec recta viarum
ostia sunt qua contendant exire coortae.
at contra tenuis summi membrana coloris
cum iacitur, nil est quod eam discerpere possit,
in promptu quoniam est in prima fronte locata.
postremo speculis in aqua splendoreque in omni
quaecumque apparent nobis simulacra, necessest,
quandoquidem simili specie sunt praedita rerum
ex*tima,* imaginibus missis consistere rerum.

duras in various mss. and eds. 79 *Scaenai* Lamb. first for *Scaenal* A, *Scaenali* B. *Scaenalem* A corr. Nicc. all mss. and eds. between him and Lamb. *patrum coetumque decorum* Ed. for *patrum matrumque deorum. patrum matrumque deorumque* Nicc. all before Lach. *pulcram variumque decorem* Lach. *claram variamque deorsum* Bern. But comp. Aen. v 340, Tac. ann. xiii 54 and Camb. Journ. of phil. i 373. Lucr. often has *que* in the third place: comp. 104, and see notes 2 to ii 1050. *patrum* and *decorum* seem to me pretty certain: for *coetumque* perhaps *ornatumque* or the like. 81 *inclusa theatri Moenibu'* Ed. for *inclusa* (B, *inclaustra* A Nicc.) *theatri Moenia*: a necessary and simple correction: *Moenia* has arisen from the neighbouring *inclusa, haec, perfusa*: so ii 458 *omnia* for *omnibu'*, 919 *animalibu'* for *animalia. inclusa theatri Moenia*, the vulg. reading, has no sense. *angusta theatri Moenia* Lach. which is contrary to the truth. 91 *diffusae rebus* AB. Lamb. has rightly added *e*; and 92 he has also rightly given *intrinsecus* for *extrinsecus*: so vi 1099 *intrinsecus* A for *extrinsecus*. 94 *coorte* B, i. e. *coortae;* and so Lamb. ed. 3. *coorta* A. *qua contendant* AB most properly. *qua contendunt* Nicc. and all mss. and eds. between him and Lach.: 91 *diffusa e*, 92 *extrinsecu' torte*, 94 *coorta* Lach. whose explanation is most forced. 101 *Extima, imaginibus* Ed. for *Ex imaginibus*: the scribe neglected to repeat the *ima. Excita imaginibus* Lach. *Esse in imaginibus* Avanc. Nauger. Lamb. vulg. without meaning. *Esse et* Mar. Junt. *rerum* Lach. for *eorum*, as in 43. *earum*

sunt igitur tenues formae, rerum similesque
effigiae, singillatim quas cernere nemo
cum possit tamen, adsiduo crebroque repulsu
reiectae reddunt speculorum ex aequore visum,
nec ratione alia servari posse videntur,
tanto opere ut similes reddantur cuique figurae.
  Nunc age quam tenui natura constet imago
percipe. et in primis, quoniam primordia tantum
sunt infra nostros sensus tantoque minora
quam quae primum oculi coeptant non posse tueri,
nunc tamen id quoque uti confirmem, exordia rerum
cunctarum quam sint suptilia percipe paucis.
primum animalia sunt iam partim tantula, quorum
tertia pars nulla possit ratione videri.
horum intestinum quodvis quale esse putandumst!
quid cordis globus aut oculi? quid membra? quid artus?
quantula sunt! quid praeterea primordia quaeque
unde anima atque animi constet natura necessumst?
nonne vides quam sint subtilia quamque minuta?
praeterea quaecumque suo de corpore odorem
expirant acrem, panaces absinthia taetra

Mar. Junt. 102 103 = 65 66. 104 *formae rerum similesque* Ed. for *formarum dissimilesque*: comp. Camb. Journ. of phil. I p. 43; I have since learnt that Hugo Purmann hit upon the same correction before me: *dissimilesque* was written merely to fill up the verse. *formarum illis similesque* Lach. *formarum consimilesque* Lamb. vulg. 116 *quorum* H. Purmann Lucr. quaest. p. 27, *corum* Lach. for *eorum*. *eorum ut* Camb. Vat. 1136 Othob. Mar. Junt. *ut horum* Vat. 3276 Pont. Nauger.. *eorum...nulla ut possit* Avanc. After 126 not a few vss. must have been lost. Heins. in ms. notes says 'aliquid deest': Haverc. suspected the same. Lach. by an elaborate and acute calculation shews or endeavours to shew that one page of the archetype containing 25 lines and one heading, *Esse item maiora*, has been lost. That a page of the archetype ended with 126 is certain; that another page commenced with 127, and that this page was a left-hand or even-numbered page is no less certain, as Lach. has demonstrated. It is also perhaps more probable that 25 lines were here lost, than double that number or more, because the poet in 115 says, as Lach. points out, *percipe paucis*. But Lachmann's calculation, taken in conjunction with his general theory of the mode in which AB and the other mss. descended from the archetype, involves a great difficulty which is discussed above p. 27, 28. Lach. thus continues the sentence of 126 *duobus* [*Attingas digitis*]: Haverc. [*Contrectes digitis*]. Among the lost verses Lach. places this fragment, *qui fulmine claro Omnia per sonitus arcet, terram mare caelum*: which I believe belongs to Ennius, not to Lucr. at all, as it has nothing of his style about it; and Servius Aen. I 30 assigns it distinctly to the former, while the words of

habrotonique graves et tristia centaurea,
quorum unum quidvis leviter si forte duobus

*

quin potius noscas rerum simulacra vagari
multa modis multis nulla vi cassaque sensu?
[Sed ne forte putes ea demum sola vagari,
quaecumque ab rebus rerum simulacra recedunt,
sunt etiam quae sponte sua gignuntur et ipsa
constituuntur in hoc caelo qui dicitur aer,
135 quae multis formata modis sublime feruntur
141 nec speciem mutare suam liquentia cessant
et cuiusque modi formarum vertere in oras;
133 ut nubes facile interdum concrescere in alto
cernimus et mundi speciem violare serenam
136 aera mulcentes motu. nam saepe Gigantum
ora volare videntur et umbram ducere late,
interdum magni montes avolsaque saxa
montibus anteire et solem succedere praeter,
140 inde alios trahere atque inducere belua nimbos.]
143 Nunc ea quam facili et celeri ratione genantur
perpetuoque fluant ab rebus lapsaque cedant

. . . .

semper enim summum quicquid de rebus abundat
quod iaculentur. et hoc alias cum pervenit in res,
transit, ut in primis vitrum. sed ubi aspera saxa
aut in materiam ligni pervenit, ibi iam
scinditur ut nullum simulacrum reddere possit.
at cum splendida quae constant opposta fuerunt
densaque, ut in primis speculum est, nil accidit horum;

Probus to ecl. VI 31 are ambiguous. 129—142, strangely transposed in the mss. as may be seen by our left-hand numbering, were first brought into order by the acuteness of Lamb.: see above p. 30 for a possible explanation of this disorder. 138 *motu. nam. motum in* Nicc. the cause of great confusion in later mss. and eds. before Mar. Junt. and Lamb. 143 *genantur* Lamb. for *gerantur*: a necessary change here, though he often introduces the word without cause.

After 144 a verse has manifestly been lost: it is curious that Marullus and Lamb. should have overlooked this. 'deest *Percipe* vel *Expediam*, tum paucula a quibus illud *enim* quod subicitur pendeat' Lach. 147 and 152 *vitrum* Oppenrieder for *vestem*: a necessary correction which it is strange neither Lamb. nor Lach. should have made: Lamb. indeed sees the difficulty involved in *vestem*, Lach. does not: comp.

nam neque, uti vitrum, potis est transire, neque autem
scindi; quam meminit levor praestare salutem.
quapropter fit ut hinc nobis simulacra redundent.
et quamvis subito quovis in tempore quamque
rem contra speculum ponas, apparet imago;
perpetuo fluere ut noscas e corpore summo
texturas rerum tenuis tenuisque figuras.
ergo multa brevi spatio simulacra genuntur,
ut merito celer his rebus dicatur origo.
et quasi multa brevi spatio summittere debet
lumina sol ut perpetuo sint omnia plena,
sic ab rebus item simili ratione necessest
temporis in puncto rerum simulacra ferantur
multa modis multis in cunctas undique partis;
quandoquidem speculum quocumque obvertimus oris,
res ibi respondent simili forma atque colore.
praeterea modo cum fuerit liquidissima caeli
tempestas, perquam subito fit turbida foede,
undique uti tenebras omnis Acherunta rearis
liquisse et magnas caeli complesse cavernas.
usque adeo taetra nimborum nocte coorta
inpendent atrae formidinis ora superne;
quorum quantula pars sit imago dicere nemost
qui possit neque eam rationem reddere dictis.
  Nunc age, quam celeri motu simulacra ferantur
et quae mobilitas ollis tranantibus auras
reddita sit, longo spatio ut brevis hora teratur,
in quem quaeque locum diverso numine tendunt,
suavidicis potius quam multis versibus edam;
parvus ut est cycni melior canor, ille gruum quam
clamor in aetheriis dispersus nubibus austri.
principio persaepe levis res atque minutis
corporibus factas celeris licet esse videre.

602. 152 *potis est* Lach. for *possunt*. *autem. ante* Mon. Ven. and hence Avanc. Junt. and all eds. before Lach. 159 *genuntur* Lamb. for *geruntur*: here too a necessary correction. 167 *Res ibi* A and most mss. and eds. *Res sibi* B Camb. Ven. which Lach. thinks 'unice verum'. *Res tibi* Gif. 178 *teratur* Pont. Junt. most properly for *feratur*. 179 *tendunt* Lamb. for *tendit*. Lach. puts this verse after 175, reading *tendat*, and *momine* for *numine* with Mar. Junt., a change which I am now not inclined to acquiesce in: see II 632, and Epicurus

in quo iam genere est solis lux et vapor eius
propterea quia sunt e primis facta minutis
quae quasi cuduntur perque aeris intervallum
non dubitant transire sequenti concita plaga.
suppeditatur enim confestim lumine lumen
et quasi protelo stimulatur fulgere fulgur.
quapropter simulacra pari ratione necesse est
inmemorabile per spatium transcurrere posse
temporis in puncto, primum quod parvola causa
est procul a tergo quae provehat atque propellat,
quod superest, ubi tam volucri levitate ferantur;
deinde quod usque adeo textura praedita rara
mittuntur, facile ut quasvis penetrare queant res
et quasi permanare per aeris intervallum.
praeterea si, quae penitus corpuscula rerum
ex altoque foras mittuntur, solis uti lux
ac vapor, haec puncto cernuntur lapsa diei
per totum caeli spatium diffundere sese
perque volare mare ac terras caelumque rigare,
quid quae sunt igitur iam prima fronte parata,
cum iaciuntur et emissum res nulla moratur?
quone vides citius debere et longius ire
multiplexque loci spatium transcurrere eodem
tempore quo solis pervolgant lumina caelum?
hoc etiam in primis specimen verum esse videtur
quam celeri motu rerum simulacra ferantur,
quod simul ac primum sub diu splendor aquai
ponitur, extemplo caelo stellante serena
sidera respondent in aqua radiantia mundi.
iamne vides igitur quam puncto tempore imago
aetheris ex oris in terrarum accidat oras?
quare etiam atque etiam mira fateare necessest

cited in notes 2. 190 *fulgere* AB Nicc. Flor. 31 Camb. Mon. 3 Vat. *fulgure* 2 Vat. Brix. Ven. Mar. eds. before Lach. 195 Lach. places after 205: I wrongly followed him formerly. 199 203 in my small ed. I allowed by accident Lachmann's punctuation to stand: of course there should be a comma after *si* and after 203, the apodosis beginning at *Quid quae*. 203 *caelum*. *circum* Lach.

206 *Quone*. *Nonne* B corr. Pont. Mar. vulg. 211 *diu* AB Nicc. *divo* vulg. before Lach. 213 *mundi*. *mundo* Lach. but here, as I 1060 and IV 418, he seems not to feel that Lucr. calls the reflected image a *mundus*: a quite natural notion.

. . . .
corpora quae feriant oculos visumque lacessant.
perpetuoque fluunt certis ab rebus odores;
frigus ut a fluviis, calor ab sole, aestus ab undis
aequoris exesor moerorum litora circum.
nec variae cessant voces volitare per auras.
denique in os salsi venit umor saepe saporis,
cum mare versamur propter, dilutaque contra
cum tuimur misceri absinthia, tangit amaror.
usque adeo omnibus ab rebus res quaeque fluenter
fertur et in cunctas dimittitur undique partis
nec mora nec requies interdatur ulla fluendi,
perpetuo quoniam sentimus, et omnia semper
cernere odorari licet et sentire sonare.
  Praeterea quoniam manibus tractata figura
in tenebris quaedam cognoscitur esse eadem quae
cernitur in luce et claro candore, necessest
consimili causa tactum visumque moveri.
nunc igitur si quadratum temptamus et id nos
commovet in tenebris, in luci quae poterit res
accidere ad speciem quadrata, nisi eius imago?
esse in imaginibus quapropter causa videtur
cernundi neque posse sine his res ulla videri.
nunc ea quae dico rerum simulacra feruntur
undique et in cunctas iaciuntur didita partis;
verum nos oculis quia solis cernere quimus,
propterea fit uti, speciem quo vertimus, omnes
res ibi eam contra feriant forma atque colore.
et quantum quaeque ab nobis res absit, imago

216 *mira.* *mitti* Lach.; but Lucr. is here speaking not simply of the emission of images, but of their enormous velocity. I therefore keep *mira*, and suppose with Purmann Jahn's Jahrb. vol. 67 p. 676 and Goebel obs. Lucret. p. 25 that a verse is lost. 218 *fluunt* Lamb. rightly, as VI 924, for *fluant*. This and the ten following verses, which are repeated in the sixth book, were undoubtedly read in the fourth by Gellius and Nonius. There is no question therefore that Lucr. or his editor placed them here; there is just as little question that they are much more appropriate in VI than here. [219 *ut*. See n. to VI 925.] 229 is ejected by Lach. here and in the sixth book: it must I think be retained in both places; for to say that we always perceive all things is a simple absurdity: we always have sensation, and may at any time, *if we please*, exert the sense of sight smell hearing: again *Perpetuo...et omnia semper* would be an intolerable tautology. 240 *didita* Pont. Mar. Ald. 1 Junt.

efficit ut videamus et internoscere curat;
nam cum mittitur, extemplo protrudit agitque
aera qui inter se cumque est oculosque locatus,
isque ita per nostras acies perlabitur omnis
et quasi perterget pupillas atque ita transit.
251 propterea fit uti videamus quam procul absit
250 res quaeque. et quanto plus aeris ante agitatur
et nostros oculos perterget longior aura,
tam procul esse magis res quaeque remota videtur.
scilicet haec summe celeri ratione geruntur,
quale sit ut videamus et una quam procul absit.
illud in his rebus minime mirabile habendumst,
cur, ea quae feriant oculos simulacra videri
singula cum nequeant, res ipsae perspiciantur.
ventus enim quoque paulatim cum verberat et cum
261 acre fluit frigus, non privam quamque solemus
260 particulam venti sentire et frigoris eius,
sed magis unorsum, fierique perinde videmus
corpore tum plagas in nostro tamquam aliquae res
verberet atque sui det sensum corporis extra.
praeterea lapidem digito cum tundimus, ipsum
tangimus extremum saxi summumque colorem,
nec sentimus eum tactu, verum magis ipsam
duritiem penitus saxi sentimus in alto.
  Nunc age, cur ultra speculum videatur imago
percipe; nam certe penitus semota videtur.
quod genus illa foris quae vere transpiciuntur,
ianua cum per se transpectum praebet apertum,
multa facitque foris ex aedibus ut videantur.
is quoque enim duplici geminoque fit aere visus.

for *dedita*. 245 *curat. cogit* Lach. because, with *curat*, *internoscere* would stand he says for an accusative, and in that case Lucr. would make it govern another accusative, though he allows that Ennius does not observe such a law, as in *audere repressit*: a somewhat far-fetched distinction: see notes 2. 246 *protrudit* Lamb. for *protudit*: so 280 *procudit* Flor. 31 Camb. etc. Flor. 29 reads with Nicc. *protulit*: Politian in marg. has *pro$\overset{c}{t}$udit*; in 187 he wrote *tr.* over the *c* of *cuduntur.* 250 and 251, 260 and 261: Mar. Ald. 1 Junt. first have these verses in their right order. 260 *privam* Gif. for *primam*; 'ex v. c.' he says. 267 *ipsam* Nicc. B corr. for *ipsa.* 270 *semota* Mar. Ald. 1 Junt. for *remota*: so 288. *remmota* B, which may be right. 271 and 278 *quae vere transpiciuntur.* Lach. possessed by his theory of *quod genus* (see II 194) without any authority reads

primus enim citra postes tum cernitur aer,
inde fores ipsae dextra laevaque secuntur,
post extraria lux oculos perterget et aer
alter et illa foris quae vere transpiciuntur.
sic ubi se primum speculi proiecit imago,
dum venit ad nostras acies, protrudit agitque
aera qui inter se cumquest oculosque locatus,
et facit ut prius hunc omnem sentire queamus
quam speculum. sed ubi speculum quoque sensimus ipsum,
continuo a nobis in *id*em quae fertur imago
pervenit et nostros oculos reiecta revisit
atque alium prae se propellens aera volvit
et facit ut prius hunc quam se videamus, eoque
distare ab speculo tantum semota videtur.
quare etiam atque etiam minime mirarier est par,
illic quor reddant speculorum ex aequore visum,
aeribus binis quoniam res confit utraque.
nunc ea quae nobis membrorum dextera pars est,
in speculis fit ut in laeva videatur eo quod
planitiem ad speculi veniens cum offendit imago,
non convertitur incolumis, sed recta retrorsum
sic eliditur, ut siquis, prius arida quam sit
cretea persona, adlidat pilaeve trabive,
atque ea continuo rectam si fronte figuram
323 servet et *e*lisam retro sese exprimat ipsa.

sunt, *bene* for *vere*, and ruins the argument. 275 *tum cernitur*. *cum* Nicc. Flor. 31 Camb. etc. which has caused much confusion in the eds. before Lach.

277 *perterget* Lamb. first for *perteget*: (so *perteget* AB in 249; but there *perterget* Nicc.) *pertinget* Nicc. and so all before Lamb. 283 *ubi speculum* Mar. Junt. for *ubi in speculum*. 284 *in idem* Ed. for *in eum*: *id* was absorbed by *in*, and *em* was then changed to *eum*: *in* was lost after *id* in IV 1037. *iterum* Lach.

290 *Illic quor reddant* Ed. for *Illis quae reddunt*. Lach. puts this verse after 270, where it is quite out of place: from 107 it is manifest that the images, not the real things, 'reddunt speculorum ex aequore visum'. Lamb. and Creech think 289—291 spurious: Wak. as usual sees no difficulty in the ms. reading and boldly calls in the Pythagoreans to the rescue. 299—347 (323—347 299—322) were first placed in their proper order by Lamb. after B corr. This is one of the main passages which enabled Lach. so acutely to determine the number of lines in a page of the lost archetype of all our mss. These 49 verses + three headings amount to fifty-two or twice twenty-six; that is to say the original ms. had twenty-six lines in a page, and by some chance one leaf, the 76th, had its pages inverted; hence the transposition: see introduction p. 27. The marg. of Flor. 29 in the writing of

fiet ita, ante oculus fuerit qui dexter, ut idem
nunc sit laevus, et e laevo sit mutua dexter.
fit quoque de speculo in speculum ut tradatur imago,
quinque etiam sex*ve* ut fieri simulacra suërint.
nam quaecumque retro parte interiore latebunt,
inde tamen, quamvis torte penitusque remota,
omnia per flexos aditus educta licebit
pluribus haec speculis videantur in aedibus esse.
usque adeo speculo in speculum translucet imago,
et cum laeva data est, fit rusum ut dextera fiat,
inde retro rursum redit et convertitur eodem.
quin etiam quaecumque latuscula sunt speculorum
adsimili lateris flexura praedita nostri,
dextera ea propter nobis simulacra remittunt,
aut quia de speculo in speculum transfertur imago,
inde ad nos elisa bis advolat, aut etiam quod
circum agitur, cum venit, imago propterea quod
flexa figura docet speculi convertier ad nos.
indugredi porro pariter simulacra pedemque
ponere nobiscum credas gestumque imitari
propterea quia, de speculi qua parte recedas,
continuo nequeunt illinc simulacra reverti;
omnia quandoquidem cogit natura referri
ac resilire ab rebus ad aequos reddita flexus.
299 Splendida porro oculi fugitant vitantque tueri.
sol etiam caecat, contra si tendere pergas,
propterea quia vis magnast ipsius et alte
aera per purum graviter simulacra feruntur
et feriunt oculos turbantia compérituras.
praeterea splendor quicumque est acer adurit
saepe oculos ideo quod semina possidet ignis
multa, dolorem oculis quae gignunt insinuando.

Politian apparently, and Mar. give the same order as the Junt. viz. 298 323—325 299—322 348—352 326—341 353—363 342—347 364 of the ms. order, or that on the left of my edition. 299 *et elisam* B corr. Flor. 31 Camb. for *et lisam.* 300 *Fiet ita, ante* Lach. for *Fiet ut ante. Fiet ut...hic idem* Mar. Ald. 1 Junt. 303 *sexve* Mar. Junt. for *sex. aut sex* Lach. 304 *latebunt* Mar. Ald. 1 Junt. for *latebit.* 310 *convertitur* Lach. for *convertit*: see 295 and 317. *retrorsum* A corr. B for *retro rursum* has caused much confusion in old eds. 318 *porro pariter* A Nicc. Flor. 31 Camb. etc. *pariter porro* B. Mon. 321 *nequeunt. nequeant* A

lurida praeterea fiunt quaecumque tuentur
arquati, quia luroris de corpore eorum
semina multa fluunt simulacris obvia rerum,
multaque sunt oculis in eorum denique mixta,
quae contage sua palloribus omnia pingunt.
e tenebris autem quae sunt in luce tuemur
propterea quia, cum propior caliginis aer
ater init oculos prior et possedit apertos,
insequitur candens confestim lucidus aer
qui quasi purgat eos ac nigras discutit umbras
aeris illius; nam multis partibus hic est
mobilior multisque minutior et mage pollens.
qui simul atque vias oculorum luce replevit
atque patefecit quas ante obsederat aer
ater, continuo rerum simulacra secuntur
quae sita sunt in luce, lacessuntque ut videamus.
quod contra facere in tenebris e luce nequimus
propterea quia posterior caliginis aer
crassior insequitur qui cuncta foramina complet
obsiditque vias oculorum, ne simulacra
possint ullarum rerum coniecta movere.
quadratasque procul turris cum cernimus urbis,
propterea fit uti videantur saepe rutundae,
angulus optusus quia longe cernitur omnis
sive etiam potius non cernitur ac perit eius
plaga nec ad nostras acies perlabitur ictus,
aera per multum quia dum simulacra feruntur,
cogit hebescere eum crebris offensibus aer.
hoc ubi suffugit sensum simul angulus omnis,
fit quasi ut ad tornum saxorum structa terantur;
non tamen ut coram quae sunt vereque rutunda,

Nicc. wrongly. 342 *illius* Flor. 31 Camb. Ver. Ven. Mar. for *ullius*. 345 346 *aer Ater* Bern. for *Ater*. *ater*, *Aera* Lach. *ater Continuo r. s. adaperta s.* Flor. 31 Camb. vulg. without meaning. 351 *que vias* B corr. Flor. 31 Camb. Mar. for *quia*. 352 *coniecta* Mar. Ald. 1 Junt. for *contecta*. *movere* Bentl. rightly for *moveri*. 357 *acies* Nicc. B corr. for *ates*. *perlabitur* Lamb. ed. 3 first for *deriabitur*; from whom Gif. ed. 2 took it without acknowledgment. *derivabitur* Nicc. *delabitur* Avanc. *illabitur* Mar. Junt. *adlabitur* Lamb. ed. 1 and 2. *arlabitur* Gif. ed. 1. 361 *tornum* Flor. 31 2 Vat. Brix. Mar. for *turnum*. *tortum* Camb. *terantur* Ed. for *tuantur*. *tuamur* Lach., but *ad tornum* has no sense or construction with *tuantur* or *tuamur*, as Lamb. saw, who reads *tornata ut* for *ad*

sed quasi adumbratim paulum simulata videntur.
umbra videtur item nobis in sole moveri
et vestigia nostra sequi gestumque imitari;
aera si credis privatum lumine posse
indugredi, motus hominum gestumque sequentem;
nam nil esse potest aliut nisi lumine cassus
aer id quod nos umbram perhibere suëmus.
nimirum quia terra locis ex ordine certis
lumine privatur solis quacumque meantes
officimus, repletur item quod liquimus eius,
propterea fit uti videatur, quae fuit umbra
corporis, e regione eadem nos usque secuta.
semper enim nova se radiorum lumina fundunt
primaque dispereunt, quasi in ignem lana trahatur.
propterea facile et spoliatur lumine terra
et repletur item nigrasque sibi abluit umbras.
Nec tamen hic oculos falli concedimus hilum.
nam quocumque loco sit lux atque umbra tueri
illorum est; eadem vero sint lumina necne,
umbraque quae fuit hic eadem nunc transeat illuc,
an potius fiat paulo quod diximus ante,
hoc animi demum ratio discernere debet,
nec possunt oculi naturam noscere rerum.
proinde animi vitium hoc oculis adfingere noli.
qua vehimur navi, fertur, cum stare videtur;
quae manet in statione, ea praeter creditur ire.
et fugere ad puppim colles campique videntur
quos agimus praeter navem velisque volamus.
sidera cessare aetheriis adfixa cavernis
cuncta videntur, et adsiduo sunt omnia motu,
quandoquidem longos obitus exorta revisunt,
cum permensa suo sunt caelum corpore claro.
solque pari ratione manere et luna videntur
in statione, ea quae ferri res indicat ipsa.
exstantisque procul medio de gurgite montis
classibus inter quos liber patet exitus ingens,

tornum, a violent change. 378 *abluit* Ver. Ven. Mar. for *adluit*. 395 *videntur* Lach. for *videtur*, as plur. *ea* follows. In small ed. I thought that after 397 a verse was lost of this nature, *Fallere saepe animum simili ratione videmus*;

insula coniunctis tamen ex his una videtur.
atria versari et circumcursare columnae
usque adeo fit uti pueris videantur, ubi ipsi
desierunt verti, vix ut iam credere possint
non supra sese ruere omnia tecta minari.
iamque rubrum tremulis iubar ignibus erigere alte
cum coeptat natura supraque extollere montes,
quos tibi tum supra sol montis esse videtur
comminus ipse suo contingens fervidus igni,
vix absunt nobis missus bis mille sagittae,
vix etiam cursus quingentos saepe veruti:
inter eos solemque iacent immania ponti
aequora substrata aetheriis ingentibus oris,
interiectaque sunt terrarum milia multa
quae variae retinent gentes et saecla ferarum.
at conlectus aquae digitum non altior unum,
qui lapides inter sistit per strata viarum,
despectum praebet sub terras inpete tanto,
a terris quantum caeli patet altus hiatus;
nubila dispicere et †caelum ut videare videre
corpora mirando sub terras abdita caelo.
denique ubi in medio nobis ecus acer obhaesit

but see notes 2. Lach. reads *Exstant usque* for *Exstantisque*. 406 *tibi tum* Nauger. first for *ubi tum*. 414 *conlectus* Lamb. for *coniectus*: see III 198. 418 A has properly *ut* before *videare*: *caelum* appears to have come from *caeli* of 417 or *caelo* of 419: see notes 2: Flor. 31 has *mirando*; Nicc. Camb. etc. *miranda*. Lach. seems to have misapprehended the matter, as in 213 and I 1061: he reads *Ut prope miraclo* for *Corpora mirande*, *caeli* for *caelo*, and transposes the two verses. But I have obeyed him in reading *dispicere* for *despicere*, as ms. authority is of little weight on such a point: comp. 421 *dispeximus* AB Nicc. for *desp.* Virgil's mss. both in Aen. I 224 and georg. II 187 are nearly all in favour of *despicere*. Ph. Wagner philologus XV p. 352 quotes on the side of *despicere* Quintil. inst. VI prooem. 4 'nullam terras *despicere* providentiam', but on referring to Zumpt ed. Spald. suppl. annot. I find that the best ms. Ambros. 1, and Turic. p. m. have *nulla in terras despicere*, another *terras dispicere*: this passage therefore will not refute Lachmann's position that '*dispicere nubila* or *despicere in nubila* is 'to look upon the clouds', *despicere nubila* 'to despise the clouds': comp. for the former sense III 26 *quin omnia dispiciantur*; IV 421 *in rapidas amnis despeximus undas*; for the latter II 9 *Despicere unde queas alios*. AB on the whole support this distinction. Conington to Virgil l. l. keeps *despicere*; and Aen. I 224 he says that the reason for the distinction fails completely: but surely the fact that the personal passive *despicior* and the participle *despectus* always have the sense of being despised

flumine et in rapidas amnis despeximus undas,
stantis equi corpus transversum ferre videtur
vis et in adversum flumen contrudere raptim,
et quocumque oculos traiecimus omnia ferri
et fluere adsimili nobis ratione videntur.
porticus aequali quamvis est denique ductu
stansque in perpetuum paribus suffulta columnis,
longa tamen parte ab summa cum tota videtur,
paulatim trahit angusti fastigia coni,
tecta solo iungens atque omnia dextera laevis
donec in obscurum coni conduxit acumen.
in pelago nautis ex undis ortus in undis
sol fit uti videatur obire et condere lumen;
quippe ubi nil aliud nisi aquam caelumque tuentur;
ne leviter credas labefactari undique sensus.
at maris ignaris in portu clauda videntur
navigia aplustris fractis obnitier undae.
nam quaecumque supra rorem salis edita pars est
remorum, recta est, et recta superne guberna:
quae demersa liquorem obeunt, refracta videntur
omnia converti sursumque supina reverti
et reflexa prope in summo fluitare liquore.
raraque per caelum cum venti nubila portant
tempore nocturno, tum splendida signa videntur
labier adversum nimbos atque ire superne
longe aliam in partem ac ve*ra* ratione feruntur.
at si forte oculo manus uni subdita supter
pressit eum, quodam sensu fit uti videantur
omnia quae tuimur fieri tum bina tuendo,
bina lucernarum florentia lumina flammis
binaque per totas aedis geminare supellex
et duplicis hominum facies et corpora bina.

is some reason: to me indeed it is a conclusive one. Lamb. reads *videre et Corpora mirando s. t. a. c.* but in ed. 3 he obelises *et* and the following verse. 421 *despeximus* Flor. 31 Camb. Ver. Ven. Mar. for *dispeximus*. 436 *At maris* Nicc. B. corr. for *Amaris*. 437 *fractis* Flor. 31 Mar. for *factas*. *undae* Lach. for *undas*. *undis* vulg. 440 *liquorem* Lach. for *liquore*. 446 *ac vera ratione* Is. Voss. in ms. notes for *aque ratione*: the scribe wrote *ra* only once: 'quidam codices' says Creech: that is he had heard indirectly of Vossius' correction.

448 *fit uti* Mar. Junt. for *fit ut*. 456 *videmur* Mar. Ald. 1 Junt. for *videa-*

denique cum suavi devinxit membra sopore
somnus et in summa corpus iacet omne quiete,
tum vigilare tamen nobis et membra movere
nostra videmur, et in noctis caligine caeca
cernere censemus solem lumenque diurnum
conclusoque loco caelum mare flumina montis
mutare et campos pedibus transire videmur,
et sonitus audire, severa silentia noctis
undique cum constent, et reddere dicta tacentes.
cetera de genere hoc mir*acula* multa videmus,
quae violare fidem quasi sensibus omnia quaerunt,
nequiquam, quoniam pars horum maxima fallit
propter opinatus animi quos addimus ipsi,
pro visis ut sint quae non sunt sensibu' visa.
nam nil aegrius est quam res secernere apertas
ab dubiis, animus quas ab se protinus addit.

Denique nil sciri siquis putat, id quoque nescit
an sciri possit, quoniam nil scire fatetur.
hunc igitur contra mittam contendere causam,
qui capite ipse sua in statuit vestigia sese.
et tamen hoc quoque uti concedam scire, at id ipsum
quaeram, cum in rebus veri nil viderit ante,
unde sciat quid sit scire et nescire vicissim,
notitiam veri quae res falsique crearit
et dubium certo quae res differre probarit.
invenies primis ab sensibus esse creatam
notitiem veri neque sensus posse refelli.
nam maiore fide debet reperirier illud,
sponte sua veris quod possit vincere falsa.
quid maiore fide porro quam sensus haberi
debet? an ab sensu falso ratio orta valebit
dicere eos contra, quae tota ab sensibus orta est?

tur. 460 *noctis* B corr. Flor. 31 Camb. Pont. Mar. for *montis.* 462 *miracula* Ed. for *mirande*: *acula* was probably absorbed in *multa* and the word completed from 419. *mirando* Flor. 31 Vat. 1136 Othob. Mar. for *mirande.* *miracli* Lach. here as 419. 467 *aegrius est.* Later mss. and old. eds. also Pont. Mar. Ald. 1 Junt. Lamb. etc. *egregius*, absurdly. 468 *addit* A Nicc. Camb. 2 Vat. Junt. Creech. *abdit* B Flor. 31 3 Vat. Pont. Mar. Ald. 1 Lamb. Wak. without meaning. 471 *mittam* Mar. Ald. 1 Junt. for *mituam.* 472 *sua in statuit* Lach. for *suo in statuit.* 479 *sensus* Mar. Junt. for *sensu.* 486 *poterunt* Flor. 31 Camb. for

qui nisi sunt veri, ratio quoque falsa fit omnis.
an poterunt oculos aures reprehendere, an aures
tactus? an hunc porro tactum sapor arguet oris,
an confutabunt nares oculive revincent?
non, ut opinor, ita est. nam seorsum cuique potestas
divisast, sua vis cuiquest, ideoque necesse est
et quod molle sit et gelidum fervensve *seorsum*
et seorsum varios rerum sentire colores
et quaecumque coloribu' sint coniuncta *videre.*
seorsus item sapor oris habet vim, seorsus odores
nascuntur, sorsum sonitus. ideoque necesse est
non possint alios alii convincere sensus.
nec porro poterunt ipsi reprehendere sese,
aequa fides quoniam debebit semper haberi.
proinde quod in quoquest his visum tempore, verumst.
et si non poterit ratio dissolvere causam,
cur ea quae fuerint iuxtim quadrata, procul sint
visa rutunda, tamen praestat rationis egentem
reddere mendose causas utriusque figurae,
quam manibus manifesta suis emittere quoquam
et violare fidem primam et convellere tota
fundamenta quibus nixatur vita salusque.
non modo enim ratio ruat omnis, vita quoque ipsa
concidat extemplo, nisi credere sensibus ausis
praecipitisque locos vitare et cetera quae sint
in genere hoc fugienda, sequi contraria quae sint.
illa tibi est igitur verborum copia cassa
omnis quae contra sensus instructa paratast.
denique ut in fabrica, si pravast regula prima,
normaque si fallax rectis regionibus exit,
et libella aliqua si ex parti claudicat hilum,
omnia mendose fieri atque obstipa necesse est
prava cubantia prona supina atque absona tecta,
iam ruere ut quaedam videantur velle, ruantque

poterit. *poterint* Mar. Ver. Ven. 491 *seorsum* Bentl. for *videri*: a necessary change. Lamb. here interpolates a verse. 493 *videre* Lach. for *necessest* which has come from a neighbouring verse. 495 *Nascuntur* Ver. Ven. Mar. for *nascantur.* 496 *possint* Flor. 31 Mon. Pont. Ald. 1 Junt. for *possunt.* *possent* Camb. 498 *aequa* Flor. 31 Pont. Mar. Ald. 1 Junt. for *aeque.* 500 *poterit* Nicc. for *poteris.* 514 *si* Nicc. B corr. for *sibi.* 517 *Prava* Mar. Ald. 1

prodita iudiciis fallacibus omnia primis,
sic igitur ratio tibi rerum prava necessest
falsaque sit, falsis quaecumque ab sensibus ortast.
  Nunc alii sensus quo pacto quisque suam rem
sentiat, haudquaquam ratio scruposa relicta est.
  Principio auditur sonus et vox omnis, in auris
insinuata suo pepulere ubi corpore sensum.
corpoream *vocem* quoque enim constare fatendumst
et sonitum, quoniam possunt inpellere sensus.
praeterea radit vox fauces saepe facitque
asperiora foras gradiens arteria clamor.
quippe per angustum turba maiore coorta
ire foras ubi coeperunt primordia vocum,
scilicet expleti quoque ianua raditur oris.
haud igitur dubiumst quin voces verbaque constent
corporeis e principiis, ut laedere possint.
nec te fallit item quid corporis auferat et quid
detrahat ex hominum nervis ac viribus ipsis
perpetuus sermo nigrai noctis ad umbram
aurorae perductus ab exoriente nitore,
praesertim si cum summost clamore profusus.
ergo corpoream vocem constare necessest,
multa loquens quoniam amittit de corpore partem.
551 asperitas autem vocis fit ab asperitate
principiorum et item levor levore creatur.
542 nec simili penetrant auris primordia forma,
cum tuba depresso graviter sub murmure mugit
et reboat raucum regio cita barbara bombum,

Junt. for *parva*. 526 *vocem* om. AB Nicc.: rightly inserted by Lach. before *quoque enim*: Flor. 31 Camb. vulg. place it after. 528 *Praeterea radit* A and Gellius x 26, one Vat. Pont. Avanc. rightly. *Propterea radit* B. *Praeter radit* Nicc. one Vat. Ver. Ven. whence *Praeter radit enim* Flor. 31 Camb. 3 Vat. Brix. Mar. Nauger. vulg. *Praeter enim radit* Junt. 532 *expleti* Lach. for *expletis*, thus simply healing a desperate passage. *raditur* B Politian in marg. Flor. 29: (*creditur* in text). *reditur* A Nicc.; hence *redditur* Flor. 31 Camb. vulg. and to give a meaning to the passage, Mar. Junt. add a verse *Rauca viis, et iter laedit, qua vox it in auras*; Avanc. taking *oris* as a plur. thus *Rauca suis et iter reddit qua vox it in auras*. 542 543 (551 552) rightly placed here by Lamb. first. 543 *levo letiore* AB. *levis levore* Mar. Ald. 1 Junt. *laevor laevore* Lamb. 545 *murmure* Brix. Pont. Mar. Ald. 1 Junt. for *murmura*. 546 *Et reboat raucum regio cita barbara* Lach. for *Et revorat raucum retro cita barbara*: the older readings are

545 et validis cycni torrentibus ex Heliconis
cum liquidam tollunt lugubri voce querellam.
Hasce igitur penitus voces cum corpore nostro
exprimimus rectoque foras *e*mittimus ore,
mobilis articulat verborum daedala lingua
550 formaturaque labrorum pro parte figurat.
553 hoc ubi non longum spatiumst unde una profecta
perveniat vox quaeque, necessest verba quoque ipsa
plane exaudiri discernique articulatim;
servat enim formaturam servatque figuram.
at si interpositum spatium sit longius aequo,
aera per multum confundi verba necessest
et conturbari vocem, dum transvolat auras.
ergo fit, sonitum ut possis sentire neque illam
internoscere, verborum sententia quae sit:
usque adeo confusa venit vox inque pedita.
praeterea verbum saepe unum perciet auris
omnibus in populo, missum praeconis ab ore.
in multas igitur voces vox una repente
diffugit, in privas quoniam se dividit auris
obsignans formam verbi clarumque sonorem.
at quae pars vocum non auris incidit ipsas,
praeterlata perit frustra diffusa per auras.
pars solidis adlisa locis reiecta sonorem
reddit et interdum frustratur imagine verbi.
quae bene cum videas, rationem reddere possis
tute tibi atque aliis, quo pacto per loca sola

mostly too absurd to be mentioned. *Berecynthia barbara* Is. Voss. in ms. notes and in Catullus: *Berecynthia cornua* Bentl. 547 *Et validis cycni torrentibus ex Heliconis* Is. Voss. in ms. notes for *Et validis necti tortis ex Heliconis* of A: the middle words of this line, as of the preceding, were mutilated by some accident. *Et cycni tortis convallibus* Lach. *nete tortis* A corr. B. *nece tortis* Nicc.: hence a vast variety of strange readings, such as *Et gelidis cycni nocte oris* of Bern. 550 *emittimus* A corr. for *mittimus*. 551 *verborum* Lamb. for *nervorum*. 553 'lego *una*, unaquaeque vox perveniat. B' Bentl. for *illa*. 560 *illam*. *illa* Pont. Ald. 1 Junt. *hilum* Lamb. without cause. 563 *verbum*. *peditum* Nicc. and all later mss. and early eds.: hence *edictum* Mar. Ald. 1 Junt. vulg.: *peditum* came from the *pedita* of 562 catching the copyist's eye. 567 *verbi* Lach. for *verbis*: a necessary change. 568 *auris incidit*. '*aureis accidit*. sic reposui, a Plauto et ceteris Latini sermonis auctoribus admonitus' Lamb.; and Lach. thinks he is probably right, as Lucr. himself v 608 uses the same construction. 570 *locis*

saxa paris formas verborum ex ordine reddant,
palantis comites quom montis inter opacos
quaerimus et magna dispersos voce ciemus.
sex etiam aut septem loca vidi reddere vocis,
unam cum iaceres: ita colles collibus ipsi
verba repulsantes iterabant docta referri.
haec loca capripedes satyros nymphasque tenere
finitimi fingunt et faunos esse locuntur
quorum noctivago strepitu ludoque iocanti
adfirmant volgo taciturna silentia rumpi
chordarumque sonos fieri dulcisque querellas,
tibia quas fundit digitis pulsata canentum,
et genus agricolum late sentiscere, quom Pan
pinea semiferi capitis velamina quassans
unco saepe labro calamos percurrit hiantis,
fistula silvestrem ne cesset fundere musam.
cetera de genere hoc monstra ac portenta loquontur,
ne loca deserta ab divis quoque forte putentur
sola tenere. ideo iactant miracula dictis
aut aliqua ratione alia ducuntur, ut omne
humanum genus est avidum nimis auricularum.
  Quod superest, non est mirandúm qua ratione,
per loca quae nequeunt oculi res cernere apertas,
haec loca per voces veniant aurisque lacessant.
conloquium clausis foribus quoque saepe videmus,
nimirum quia vox per flexa foramina rerum
incolumis transire potest, simulacra renutant;
perscinduntur enim, nisi recta foramina tranant,
qualia sunt vitrei, species qua travolat omnis.

B corr. Mar. for *lopis*. *lapis* Nicc. Lach. as I now think without sufficient reason separates *solidis adlisa* from *locis*. 577 *vocis*: see n. to I 744 *frugis*. *voces* Lach. vulg. 578 *ipsi*. *ipsis* one Vat. Mon. Ver. Ven.: hence Ald. 1 Junt. vulg. before Wak. 579 *docta referri* Lach. for *dicta referri*. *dicta referre* Mar. Junt. vulg. *icta referre* Bentl. *icta* is also in Mon. 582 *iocanti* A corr. for *locanti*. 587 *velamina* Nicc. Flor. 31 Camb. Mon. vulg. for *ullamina*. *vallamina* Heins. in ms. notes, Is. Voss. in ms. notes, Wak. 590 *Cetera* Flor. 31 Camb. Mar. for *Petere*. 594 *nimis auricularum*. *nimi' miraclorum* Lach. after Bentl.: this is now the third time he has introduced into his text the form *miraclum*, which is not once found in the mss. of Lucr. 598 *videmus*. *ubi demus* Lach.: but *Conloquium clausis foribus videmus* = *C. cl. f. fieri v.* and is not the same thing at all as *Conloquium videmus*. *Cum loquimur clausis foribus, quod saepe videmus*

praeterea partis in cunctas dividitur vox,
ex aliis aliae quoniam gignuntur, ubi una
dissuluit semel in multas exorta, quasi ignis
saepe solet scintilla suos se spargere in ignis.
ergo replentur loca vocibus, abdita retro
omnia quae circum fervunt sonituque cientur.
at simulacra viis derectis omnia tendunt
ut sunt missa semel; quapropter cernere nemo
saepem ultra potis est, at voces accipere extra.
et tamen ipsa quoque haec, dum transit clausa *domorum*,
vox optunditur atque auris confusa penetrat
et sonitum potius quam verba audire videmur.
  Nec, qui sentimus sucum, lingua atque palatum
plusculum habent in se rationis plus opera*eve*.
principio sucum sentimus in ore, cibum cum
mandendo exprimimus, ceu plenam spongiam aquai
siquis forte manu premere ac siccare coëpit.
inde quod exprimimus per caulas omne palati
diditur et rarae perplexa foramina linguae.
hoc ubi levia sunt manantis corpora suci,
suaviter attingunt et suaviter omnia tractant
umida linguai circum sudantia templa.
at contra pungunt sensum lacerantque coorta,
quanto quaeque magis sunt asperitate repleta.
deinde voluptas est e suco fine palati;

Mar. Junt.: Pont. notes *videmus* as a solecism for *audimus*. 604 *ubi una* B corr. Lamb. for *ubina*. *ubi nam* Nicc. 605 *Dissuluit* B: see Plaut. miles 279 eds. Ritschl and Fleckeisen, Rhein. mus. n. f. VIII p. 451, Corssen I p. 314. *Dissiluit* A vulg. Lach. 608 *fervunt* Ed. for *fuerunt* transposing one letter: (Plaut. Pseud. 840 *fervont* A, *feerunt* Z, *fervent* vulg.): *feriunt* Lach. *fuerint* Mar. Ald. 1 Junt. vulg. *subsunt* Bern. 611 *Saepem ultra* Bern. for *Saepe supra*. *Saepem intra* Lach. *Se supra* Pont. Ald. 1 Junt. vulg. 612 *domorum* added by Lach. *viarum* Flor. 31 Camb. Mar. vulg. 615 *Nec* Mar. Junt. Bentl. Lach. for *Hoc. qui*. *quis* of Mar. Junt. as Lach. says is not necessary. *Haec quis* Avanc. Lamb. Creech without sense. 616 *plus operaeve* Lach. for *plus opere*: better than *plus operaeque* or *plus operai* or *plusque operai* of others. 619 *ac siccare coëpit*. *siccare recepit* Mar., *capessit* Pont. *exsiccareque coepit* Avanc. in Ald. 1 Lamb. etc.; but at end of his Catullus Avanc. recalls this and says '*ac siccare cöepit* per diaeresin'.

621 *perplexa*. 'in Faern. neque *perplexa* neque *per plexa*, sed *per flexa*' Lamb., and so Mon. rightly perhaps; for Lucr. elsewhere applies *perplexa* only to the entangled atoms, never to the passages of things; yet Virgil has *perplexum iter omne revolvens*. 622 *manantis* Pont. Junt. for *manantes*. 624 *sudantia*. *sidentia*

cum vero deorsum per fauces praecipitavit,
nulla voluptas est, dum diditur omnis in artus.
nec refert quicquam quo victu corpus alatur,
dummodo quod capias concoctum didere possis
artubus et stomachi umidulum servare tenorem.
  Nunc aliis alius qui sit cibu' suavis et almus
expediam, quareve, aliis quod triste et amarumst,
hoc tamen esse aliis possit perdulce videri,
tantaque *in* his rebus distantia differitasque,
ut quod ali cibus est aliis fuat acre venenum,
extetque ut serpens, hominis quae tacta salivis
disperit ac sese mandendo conficit ipsa.
praeterea nobis veratrum est acre venenum,
at capris adipes et coturnicibus auget.
ut quibus id fiat rebus cognoscere possis,
principio meminisse decet quae diximus ante,
semina multimodis in rebus mixta teneri.
porro omnes quaecumque cibum capiunt animantes,
ut sunt dissimiles extrinsecus et generatim
extima membrorum circumcaesura coercet,
proinde et seminibus constant variante figura.
semina cum porro distent, differre necessest
intervalla viasque, foramina quae perhibemus,
omnibus in membris et in ore ipsoque palato.
esse minora igitur quaedam maioraque debent,
esse triquetra aliis, aliis quadrata necessest,
multa rutunda, modis multis multangula quaedam.
namque figurarum ratio ut motusque reposcunt,
proinde foraminibus debent differre figurae,

Lach. an elegant, but not I think necessary, change. 627 *fine*. *in fine* Lamb. etc. wrongly. 631 *possis* Flor. 31 Camb. Mon. Ver. Ven. for *posses*. 632 *umidulum* Lach. for *umidum*. *humectum* Pont. Mar. Ald. 1 Junt. vulg. 633 *cibu' suavis et almus* Ed. for *cibus ut videamus*: see Camb. Journ. of phil. I p. 41: for *almus* perhaps *aptus* with Lach. *cibus unicus aptus* Lach.; but *unicus* is not at all appropriate. 636 *in* added by Nonius p. 95, and *est* at end of verse rightly om. by the same. 637 *ali* Lach. for *aliis*. 638 *Extetque ut serpens* Ed. for *Est itaque ut serpens*: VI 690 *Fert itque* mss. for *Fert itaque*. *Est aliquae ut serpens* Lach. *Est utique ut s.* Mar. Junt. Lamb. ed. 3. *Saepe etenim s.* ed. 1 and 2. 641 *coturn. cocturn.* A. *quod turn.* B. 642 *Ut quibus id* Lamb. ed. 2 and 3 for *Id quibus ut*. 648 *et*. *ex* Mon. Junt. Lamb. ed. 1 and 2, Lach. but *et* Mar. *constant variante figura* Lach. for *constant variantque figura*. *distant vari-*

et variare viae proinde ac textura coercet.
hoc ubi quod suave est aliis aliis fit amarum,
illi, cui suave est, levissima corpora debent
contractabiliter caulas intrare palati,
at contra quibus est eadem res intus acerba,
aspera nimirum penetrant hamataque fauces.
nunc facile est ex his rebus cognoscere quaeque.
quippe ubi cui febris bili superante coorta est
aut alia ratione aliquast vis excita morbi,
perturbatur ibi iam totum corpus et omnes
commutantur ibi positurae principiorum;
fit prius ad sensum *ut* quae corpora conveniebant
nunc non conveniant, et cetera sint magis apta,
quae penetrata queunt sensum progignere acerbum;
utraque enim sunt in mellis commixta sapore;
id quod iam supera tibi saepe ostendimus ante.

Nunc age quo pacto naris adiectus odoris
tangat agam. primum res multas esse necessest
unde fluens volvat varius se fluctus odorum,
et fluere et mitti volgo spargique putandumst;
verum aliis alius magis est animantibus aptus
dissimilis propter formas. ideoque per auras
mellis apes quamvis longe ducuntur odore,
volturiique cadaveribus. tum fissa ferarum
ungula quo tulerit gressum promissa canum vis
ducit, et humanum longe praesentit odorem
Romulidarum arcis servator candidus anser.
sic aliis alius nidor datus ad sua quemque
pabula ducit et a taetro resilire veneno
cogit, eoque modo servantur saecla ferarum.

Hic odor ipse igitur, naris quicumque lacessit,
est alio ut possit permitti longius alter;
sed tamen haud quisquam tam longe fertur eorum
quam sonitus, quam vox, mitto iam dicere quam res

antque figura Lamb. ed. 3. 668 *ut* added by Flor. 31 Camb. Mar. *Ut* Lach. for *Fit.* 671 672 Lach. places after 662. Bernays supposes some verses to have been lost before them; I followed him in my small ed. but now believe there is no hiatus: see notes 2. 680 *Volturiique* Pont. Ald. 1 for *Volturique*. *Vulturiique* Mar. Junt. 681 *promissa*. *permissa* Gronov. Lach. '*ꝑmissa* v. [not A or B] i.e. permissa i.e. immissa, concitata' Is. Voss. in ms. notes. 682 *Ducit.*

quae feriunt oculorum acies visumque lacessunt.
errabundus enim tarde venit ac perit ante
paulatim facilis distractus in aeris auras;
ex alto primum quia vix emittitur ex re:
nam penitus fluere atque recedere rebus odores
significat quod fracta magis redolere videntur
omnia, quod contrita, quod igni conlabefacta:
deinde videre licet maioribus esse creatum
principiis quam vox, quoniam per saxea saepta
non penetrat, qua vox volgo sonitusque feruntur.
quare etiam quod olet non tam facile esse videbis
investigare in qua sit regione locatum;
refrigescit enim cunctando plaga per auras
nec calida ad sensum decurrunt nuntia rerum.
errant saepe canes itaque et vestigia quaerunt.
[Nec tamen hoc solis in odoribus atque saporum
in generest, sed item species rerum atque colores
non ita conveniunt ad sensus omnibus omnes,
ut non sint aliis quaedam magis acria visu.
quin etiam gallum, noctem explaudentibus alis
auroram clara consuetum voce vocare,
noenu queunt rabidi contra constare leones
inque tueri: ita continuo meminere fugai,
nimirum quia sunt gallorum in corpore quaedam
semina, quae cum sunt oculis inmissa leonum,
pupillas interfodiunt acremque dolorem
praebent, ut nequeant contra durare feroces;
cum tamen haec nostras acies nil laedere possint,
aut quia non penetrant aut quod penetrantibus illis
exitus ex oculis liber datur, in remorando
laedere ne possint ex ulla lumina parte.]
Nunc age quae moveant animum res accipe, et unde
quae veniunt veniant in mentem percipe paucis.
principio hoc dico, rerum simulacra vagari
multa modis multis in cunctas undique partis
tenvia, quae facile inter se iunguntur in auris,
obvia cum veniunt, ut aranea bratteaque auri.

Dicit Lach. without cause. 698 *creatum* Mar. Junt. for *creatam*. 699 *quam vox*. *voci* Lamb. etc. perversely. 712 *rabidi* Wak. for *rapidi*. 719

quippe etenim multo magis haec sunt tenvia textu
quam quae percipiunt oculos visumque lacessunt,
corporis haec quoniam penetrant per rara cientque
tenvem animi naturam intus sensumque lacessunt.
Centauros itaque et Scyllarum membra videmus
Cerbereasque canum facies simulacraque eorum
quorum morte obita tellus amplectitur ossa;
omne genus quoniam passim simulacra feruntur,
partim sponte sua quae fiunt aere in ipso,
partim quae variis ab rebus cumque recedunt
et quae confiunt ex horum facta figuris.
nam certe ex vivo Centauri non fit imago,
nulla fuit quoniam talis natura anima*ntis*;
verum ubi equi atque hominis casu convenit imago,
haerescit facile extemplo, quod diximus ante,
propter subtilem naturam et tenvia texta.
cetera de genere hoc eadem ratione creantur.
quae cum mobiliter summa levitate feruntur,
ut prius ostendi, facile uno commovet ictu
quaelibet una animum nobis subtilis imago;
tenvis enim mens est et mire mobilis ipsa.
  Haec fieri ut memoro, facile hinc cognoscere possis.
quatenus hoc simile est illi, quod mente videmus
atque oculis, simili fieri ratione necesse est.
nunc igitur docui quoniam me forte leonem
cernere per simulacra, oculos quaecumque lacessunt,
scire licet mentem simili ratione moveri,
per simulacra leonem et cetera quae videt aeque
nec minus atque oculi, nisi quod mage tenvia cernit.
nec ratione alia, cum somnus membra profudit,

illis B corr. for *ilus*: ? *ībus*. 727 *brattea* AB, not *bractea*: so mss. of Virg. Aen. VI 209. 730 *per rara* Mar. Ald. 1 Junt. for *perara*. 735 *Omne genus* Mar. Junt. for *Omnigenus*. *Omnigenum* Nicc. 736 *fiunt* Mar. Ald. 1 Junt. for *flunt* A, *fluunt* A corr. B. 740 *anima* AB, *animai* Nicc. and all before Gif. *animalis* Lamb. ed. 3 vulg. Lach. *animantis* Gif. most properly, as Lucr. does not use the substantive *animal* in the singular, except V 823, where *omne animal* is equivalent to *omnia animalia*: see notes 2 there. 741 *ubi equi atque hominis casu*. *ubi equi casu atque hominis* Lach. who denies that the last syll. of an iambus is ever elided in Lucr. 752 *docui quoniam*. *quoniam docui* Lamb. ed. 2 and 3, etc. and Lach. *leonem* Lach. for *leonum*. *leones* Mar. Ald. 1 Junt. vulg. 755 *leonem et cetera* Lach. for *leonum cetera*: *et* was already added by Mar. Ald. 1 and

mens animi vigilat, nisi quod simulacra lacessunt
haec eadem nostros animos quae cum vigilamus,
usque adeo, certe ut videamur cernere eum quem
rellicta vita iam mors et terra potitast.
hoc ideo fieri cogit natura, quod omnes
corporis offecti sensus per membra quiescunt
nec possunt falsum veris convincere rebus.
praeterea meminisse iacet languetque sopore
nec dissentit eum mortis letique potitum
iam pridem, quem mens vivom se cernere credit.
quod superest, non est mirum simulacra moveri
bracchiaque in numerum iactare et cetera membra;
nam fit ut in somnis facere hoc videatur imago;
quippe ubi prima perit alioque est altera nata
inde statu, prior hic gestum mutasse videtur.
scilicet id fieri celeri ratione putandumst:
tanta est mobilitas et rerum copia tanta
tantaque sensibili quovis est tempore in uno
copia particularum, ut possit suppeditare.
  [Multaque in his rebus quaeruntur multaque nobis
clarandumst, plane si res exponere avemus.
quaeritur in primis quare, quod cuique libido
venerit, extemplo mens cogitet eius id ipsum.
anne voluntatem nostram simulacra tuentur
et simul ac volumus nobis occurrit imago,
si mare, si terrast cordi, si denique caelum?
conventus hominum pompam convivia pugnas,
omnia sub verbone creat natura paratque?
cum praesertim aliis eadem in regione locoque
longe dissimilis animus res cogitet omnis.
quid porro, in numerum procedere cum simulacra
cernimus in somnis et mollia membra movere,
mollia mobiliter cum alternis bracchia mittunt
et repetunt oculis gestum pede convenienti?

Junt.: Lamb. Creech Wak. all blunder sadly here. 761 *Rellicta vita* Bern. for *Reddita vita*, and before him Is. Voss. in ms. notes '*Relicta vita*, malim tamen *Reddita* media producta ut Salmasius'. *Reddita pro v.* Lach. 783 *si terrast cordi* Ed. for *si terram cordist.* [*si terra est cordi* Pont. before me, as I now find.] The frequency with which our mss. thus transpose this *st* is very remarkable: see Lach. to II 275 who cites ten instances: so 799, the repe-

scilicet arte madent simulacra et docta vagantur,
nocturno facere ut possint in tempore ludos.
an magis illud erit verum? quia tempore in uno,
cum sentimus id, et cum vox emittitur una,
tempora multa latent, ratio quae comperit esse,
propterea fit uti quovis in tempore quaeque
praesto sint simulacra locis in quisque parata.
et quia tenvia sunt, nisi quae contendit, acute 802
cernere non potis est animus; proinde omnia quae sunt
praeterea pereunt, nisi *si*quae ad se ipse paravit.
ipse parat sese porro speratque futurum
ut videat quod consequitur rem quamque; fit ergo.
nonne vides oculos etiam, cum tenvia quae sunt
cernere coeperunt, contendere se atque parare,
nec sine eo fieri posse ut cernamus acute?
et tamen in rebus quoque apertis noscere possis,
si non advertas animum, proinde esse quasi omni
tempore semotum fuerit longeque remotum.
cur igitur mirumst, animus si cetera perdit
praeterquam quibus est in rebus deditus ipse?
deinde adopinamur de signis maxima parvis
ac nos in fraudem induimus frustraminis ipsi.]

Fit quoque ut interdum non suppeditetur imago
eiusdem generis, sed femina quae fuit ante,
in manibus vir uti factus videatur adesse,
aut alia ex alia facies aetasque sequatur.
826 quod ne miremur sopor atque oblivia curant.
822 [Illud in his rebus vitium vementer avessis

tition of 774, has *Tanta mobilitast. si terra est, si cordi* Junt. 791 *repetunt. referunt* Lach. 795 *Cum sentimus id, et cum* Ed. for *Consentimus id est cum*: a slight and necessary alteration. Lamb. and Lach. in vain declare the verse to be out of place: the latter puts it, thus altered *Quod sentimus, id est?* cet., before 783, where it sadly involves the construction. 798 *sint* Flor. 31 Camb. Pont. Mar. for *sin* B, *in* A Nicc. *locis* Flor. 31 and Candidus at end of Junt. for *locos*.

799 800 801 = 774 771 772: an evident gloss here. Lamb. retains the first and rejects the two last; while he wrongly obelises the whole three in their former place, where they cannot be dispensed with. 802 *nisi quae contendit. nisi se contendit* Lamb. prompted he says by 809, and Lach.: but see notes 2. 804 *nisi si quae ad se ipse* Lach. for *nisi que ex se ipse. nisi sic sese ipse* Lamb. 805 *futurum* Pont. Junt. for *futuram*. 808 = 804. 815 *Praeterquam* Avanc. for *Praeterea quam*. 818 *non* Brix. Pont. Mar. for *nos*. 820 *vir uti* B corr. Flor. 31 Camb. Mar. for *virtuti*. *vir tunc* Nicc. *vir tum* Lamb. etc. 822

effugere, errorem vitareque praemetuenter,
lumina ne facias oculorum clara creata,
prospicere ut possemus, et ut proferre quea*mus*
proceros passus, ideo fastigia posse
surarum ac feminum pedibus fundata plicari,
bracchia tum porro validis ex apta lacertis
esse manusque datas utraque *ex* parte ministras,
ut facere ad vitam possemus quae foret usus.
cetera de genere hoc inter quaecumque pretantur,
omnia perversā praepostera sunt ratione,
nil ideo quoniam natumst in corpore ut uti
possemus, sed quod natumst id procreat usum,
nec fuit ante videre oculorum lumina nata
nec dictis orare prius quam lingua creatast,
sed potius longe linguae praecessit origo
sermonem multoque creatae sunt prius aures
quam sonus est auditus, et omnia denique membra
ante fuere, ut opinor, eorum quam foret usus;
haud igitur potuere utendi crescere causa.
at contra conferre manu certamina pugnae
et lacerare artus foedareque membra cruore
ante fuit multo quam lucida tela volarent,
et volnus vitare prius natura coegit
quam daret obiectum parmai laeva per artem.
scilicet et fessum corpus mandare quieti
multo antiquius est quam lecti mollia strata,
et sedare sitim prius est quam pocula natum.
haec igitur possunt utendi cognita causa

(826) brought here by B corr. Mar. Ald. 1 Junt. 823 *avessis* Ed. for *inesse*: p. 171 of the archetype, the terminations of the lines therefore being towards the outer margin, ended with 827: by some chance then *s* the last letter of this line, and the three last, *mus*, of 826 were lost; *avessi* was then changed to *inesse*, *quea* to *via*. *vitium vementer rebu' necessest* Lach.: a violent alteration. *inesto* Mar. Ald. 1 Junt. Gronov. *avemus Te effugere* Bern. 824 *errorem vitareque* B corr. Avanc. for *errore multareque*. *errore multas que premeditentur* Flor. 31 Camb. one Vat. corruptly for *e. v. praemetuenter* (*praemetuentur* A): this has led to further corruptions by Mar. Junt. Lamb. etc. 826 *possemus* Lach. for *possimus*, as the usage of Lucr. requires. *queamus* Lach. for *via*: see above to 823: the vulg. *viai* has no sense. 827 *fastigia*. *suffragia* Pont. 830 *ex* added by Lach. *a* Mar. Ald. 1 Junt. vulg. 836 *nata*. *natum* Lach. as in 850: but as *nata* gives a good sense, I have retained it: it seems to me more elegant than the other.

credier, ex usu quae sunt vitaque reperta.
illa quidem seorsum sunt omnia quae prius ipsa
nata dedere suae post notitiam utilitatis.
quo genere in primis sensus et membra videmus;
quare etiam atque etiam procul est ut credere possis
utilitatis ob officium potuisse creari.]
[Illud item non est mirandum, corporis ipsa
quod natura cibum quaerit cuiusque animantis.
quippe etenim fluere atque recedere corpora rebus
multa modis multis docui, sed plurima debent
ex animalibu'. *quae* quia sunt exercita motu,
multaque per sudorem ex alto pressa feruntur,
multa per os exhalantur, cum languida anhelant,
his igitur rebus rarescit corpus et omnis
subruitur natura; dolor quam consequitur rem.
propterea capitur cibus ut suffulciat artus
et recreet vires interdatus atque patentem
per membra ac venas ut amorem opturet edendi.
umor item discedit in omnia quae loca cumque
poscunt umorem; glomerataque multa vaporis
corpora, quae stomacho praebent incendia nostro,
dissupat adveniens liquor ac restinguit ut ignem,
urere ne possit calor amplius aridus artus.
sic igitur tibi anhela sitis de corpore nostro
abluitur, sic expletur ieiuna cupido.]
Nunc qui fiat uti passus proferre queamus,
cum volumus, varieque datum sit membra movere,
et quae res tantum hoc oneris protrudere nostri
corporis insuerit, dicam: tu percipe dicta.
dico animo nostro primum simulacra meandi
accidere atque animum pulsare, ut diximus ante.
inde voluntas fit; neque enim facere incipit ullam
rem quis*quam*, quam mens providit quid velit ante.
id quod providet, illius rei constat imago.

862 *quae quia* Lach. for *quia*. *et quia* Vat. 3276 Brix. Pont. *haec quia* Wak. *his, quia* Ald. 1 Junt. *his quae* Mar. *iis, quae* Lamb. 863 foll.: by a better stopping I have made the passage quite clear: the apodosis of the sentence begins with *His igitur*. Lach. inverts 863 and 864. Comp. 203. 877 *fiat* Camb. Brix. Pont. Mar. for *flat*. 878 *varieque* Ver. Ven. Mar. for *vareque*.

884 *quisquam quam* Brix. Mar. for *quis quam*. 885 *Id quod*. *At, quod*

ergo animus cum sese ita commovet ut velit ire
inque gredi, ferit extemplo quae in corpore toto
per membra atque artus animai dissita vis est.
et facilest factu, quoniam coniuncta tenetur.
inde ea proporro corpus ferit, atque ita tota
paulatim moles protruditur atque movetur.
praeterea tum rarescit quoque corpus et aer,
scilicet ut debet qui semper mobilis extat,
per patefacta venit penetratque foramina largus
et dispargitur ad partis ita quasque minutas
corporis. hic igitur rebus fit utrimque duabus,
†corporis ut ac navis velis ventoque feratur.
nec tamen illud in his rebus mirabile constat,
tantula quod tantum corpus corpuscula possunt
contorquere et onus totum convertere nostrum.
quippe etenim ventus suptili corpore tenvis
trudit agens magnam magno molimine navem
et manus una regit quantovis impete euntem
atque gubernaclum contorquet quolibet unum,
multaque per trocleas et tympana pondere magno
commovet atque levi sustollit machina nisu.

Nunc quibus ille modis somnus per membra quietem
inriget atque animi curas e pectore solvat,
suavidicis potius quam multis versibus edam;
parvus ut est cycni melior canor, ille gruum quam
clamor in aetheriis dispersus nubibus austri.
tu mihi da tenuis aures animumque sagacem,
ne fieri negites quae dicam posse retroque
vera repulsanti discedas pectore dicta,
tutimet in culpa cum sis neque cernere possis.
principio somnus fit ubi est distracta per artus
vis animae partimque foras eiecta recessit
et partim contrusa magis concessit in altum;
dissoluuntur enim tum demum membra fluuntque.

Lamb. Gif. Creech etc. wrongly. *constat* Flor. 31 Mar. for *constare.* 890 *ferit* Mar. Ald. 1 Junt. for *perit.* 897 is corrupt: see notes 2. *Corpus ut ad navis* Ed. in ed. 2. *Aeque id ut ac navis* Bern. and Ed. in ed. 1. *Corporis ut* Camb. Vat. 3276: also Lach. after Muretus. *Corpus uti, ut* Lamb. Creech. *velis ventoque. remis ventoque* Gassendi opera II p. 506 b. 905 *pondere magno.* 'immo *pondera magna*' Lach. without good reason: comp. v 556. 915 *Tutimet* Ed. with

nam dubium non est, animai quin opera sit
sensus hic in nobis, quem cum sopor inpedit esse,
tum nobis animam perturbatam esse putandumst
eiectamque foras; non omnem; namque iaceret
aeterno corpus perfusum frigore leti.
quippe ubi nulla latens animai pars remaneret
in membris, cinere ut multa latet obrutus ignis,
unde reconflari sensus per membra repente
posset, ut ex igni caeco consurgere flamma?
  Sed quibus haec rebus novitas confiat et unde
perturbari anima et corpus languescere possit,
expediam: tu fac ne ventis verba profundam.
principio externa corpus de parte necessum est,
aeriis quoniam vicinum tangitur auris,
tundier atque eius crebro pulsarier ictu,
propterea que fere res omnes aut corio sunt
aut etiam conchis aut callo aut cortice tectae.
interiorem etiam partem spirantibus aer
verberat hic idem, cum ducitur atque reflatur.
quare utrimque secus cum corpus vapulet et cum
perveniant plagae per parva foramina nobis
corporis ad primas partis elementaque prima,
fit quasi paulatim nobis per membra ruina.
conturbantur enim positurae principiorum
corporis atque animi. fit uti pars inde animai
eiciatur et introrsum pars abdita cedat,
pars etiam distracta per artus non queat esse
coniuncta inter se neque motu mutua fungi;
inter enim saepit coetus natura viasque;
ergo sensus abit mutatis motibus alte.
et quoniam non est quasi quod suffulciat artus,
debile fit corpus languescuntque omnia membra,
bracchia palpebraeque cadunt poplitesque cubanti

AB Nicc. *Tutemet* vulg. Lach. 928 *Posset* Lach. for *Possit*. 929 *confiat* Pont. Lach. for *conflat*. *confletur* Flor. 31 Lamb. vulg. 934 *eius*. *ab ibus* Lach.: but see notes 2. 944 *fit uti* AB Nicc. Flor. 31 Camb. *sicuti* Brix. *sicut* Ver. Ven. *sic, ut* Pont. Mar. vulg. wrongly. 945 *Eiciatur* Lamb. for *Eliciatur*.

952 953, though perfectly sound, are much corrupted by Lamb. Creech vulg. Is. Vossius' ms. note is worth quoting, as Haverc. and Preiger misrepresent, and consequently Wak. and Lach. misapprehend it; 'omnino legend.: *poplitesque cubanti*

saepe tamen summittuntur virisque resolvunt.
deinde cibum sequitur somnus, quia, quae facit aer,
haec eadem cibus, in venas dum diditur omnis,
efficit. et multo sopor ille gravissimus exstat
quem satur aut lassus capias, quia plurima tum se
corpora conturbant magno contusa labore.
fit ratione eadem coniectus partim animai
altior atque foras eiectus largior eius,
et divisior inter se ac distractior in test.
  Et quo quisque fere studio devinctus adhaeret
aut quibus in rebus multum sumus ante morati
atque in ea ratione fuit contenta magis mens,
in somnis eadem plerumque videmur obire;
causidici causas agere et componere leges,
induperatores pugnare ac proelia obire,
nautae contractum cum ventis degere bellum,
nos agere hoc autem et naturam quaerere rerum
semper et inventam patriis exponere chartis.
cetera sic studia atque artes plerumque videntur
in somnis animos hominum frustrata tenere.
et quicumque dies multos ex ordine ludis
adsiduas dederunt operas, plerumque videmus,
cum iam destiterunt ea sensibus usurpare,
relicuas tamen esse vias in mente patentis,
qua possint eadem rerum simulacra venire.
per multos itaque illa dies eadem obversantur
ante oculos, etiam vigilantes ut videantur
cernere saltantis et mollia membra moventis
et citharae liquidum carmen chordasque loquentis
auribus accipere et consessum cernere eundem
scenaique simul varios splendere decores.

Saepe tamae [not *tama*] *summittuntur*. Tama quid sit docet Festus, cubantem vero tamam dixit quod deorsum ad pedes tendat. sic infra *cubantia tecta*. Idem error apud Nonium in versu Lucilii in voce *differre*, ubi pro *tama* legitur *tamen*'.

959 *partim* Lach. for *parte*: comp. 918. *porro* Mar. Ald. 1 Junt. vulg. 961 *in test* Ed. for *intus*: VI 674 *qui viisus* mss. for *quivis est*: comp. 916 and 946, and *capias* in 957. *actus* Lach. 962 *quo...devinctus*. *quo...defunctus* Mon. Ven. Ald. 1 Junt. *quoi...devinctus* Lamb. without reason. 964 *in ea*. *in qua* Mar. Junt. vulg. wrongly. 968 *degere*. *cernere* Lamb. 982 *consessum* Mar. Junt. for *consensum*. 983 *Scenaique* Brix. (?), Pont. Ald. 1 Junt. for

usque adeo magni refert studium atque voluptas,
et quibus in rebus consuerint esse operati
non homines solum sed vero animalia cuncta.
quippe videbis equos fortis, cum membra iacebunt,
in somnis sudare tamen spirareque semper
et quasi de palma summas contendere viris,
aut quasi carceribus patefactis
999 venantumque canes in molli saepe quiete
991 iactant crura tamen subito vocisque repente
mittunt et crebro redducunt naribus auras,
ut vestigia si teneant inventa ferarum,
expergefactique secuntur inania saepe
995 cervorum simulacra, fugae quasi dedita cernant,
donec discussis redeant erroribus ad se.
at consueta domi catulorum blanda propago
998 discutere et corpus de terra corripere instant
proinde quasi ignotas facies atque ora tuantur.
et quo quaeque magis sunt aspera seminiorum,
tam magis in somnis eadem saevire necessust.
at variae fugiunt volucres pinnisque repente
sollicitant divom nocturno tempore lucos,
accipitres somno in leni si proelia pugnas
edere sunt persectantes visaeque volantes.
porro hominum mentes, magnis quae motibus edunt
magna, itidem saepe in somnis faciuntque geruntque,
reges expugnant, capiuntur, proelia miscent,
tollunt clamorem quasi si iugulentur ibidem.
multi depugnant gemitusque doloribus edunt

Scenatque. 984 *voluptas* Lach. for *voluntas.* 989 *de palma summas* Lamb. for *palmas. palmis* A corr. Nicc. all before Lamb. 990 *saepe quiete* which mss. add at end has of course come from 991 (999) and supplanted the words of Lucr. *colligere aestum* Lach. offers: *velle volare* might also do. 991 (999) was brought here by Ald. 1 Junt. and by Mon., but there 998 999 (997 998) precede it. 992 *vocis*: see n. to I 744 *frugis. voces* Lach. vulg. 996 *fugae* Mar. Ald. 1 Junt. first for *fuga.* 997 *redeant erroribus* Lamb. after Turnebus for *redeant terroribus.* 1000—1003 are merely 992—995 repeated because of 991 (999): see introduction p. 29. 1005 *quo. quam* Lamb. wrongly. *seminiorum. semina eorum* Lamb. 'Marull. et vulg. semina eorum' says Gif. and so Mar. changes *seminiorum* of Mon. to *semina eorum.* Junt. has rightly *seminiorum.*

1009 *que* wrongly added by Mar. Ald. 1 Junt. vulg. at end: see II 118. 1011 *motibus* Mon. Pont. Ald. 1 Junt. vulg. for *montibus. Magna* I join with what pre-

et quasi pantherae morsu saevive leonis
mandantur magnis clamoribus omnia complent.
multi de magnis per somnum rebu' loquuntur
indicioque sui facti persaepe fuere.
multi mortem obeunt. multi, de montibus altis
ut qui praecipitent ad terram corpore toto,
externantur et ex somno quasi mentibu' capti
vix ad se redeunt permoti corpŏris aestu.
flumen item sitiens aut fontem propter amoenum
adsidet et totum prope faucibus occupat amnem.
puri saepe lacum propter si ac dolia curta
somno devincti credunt se extollere vestem,
totius umorem saccatum corpori' fundunt,
cum Babylonica magnifico splendore rigantur.
tum quibus aetatis freta primitus insinuatur
semen, ubi ipsa dies membris matura creavit,
conveniunt simulacra foris e corpore quoque
nuntia praeclari voltus pulchrique coloris,
qui ciet inritans loca turgida semine multo,
ut quasi transactis saepe omnibu' rebu' profundant
fluminis ingentis fluctus vestemque cruentent.
Sollicitatur id *in* nobis, quod diximus ante,
semen, adulta aetas cum primum roborat artus.
namque alias aliud res commovet atque lacessit;
ex homine humanum semen ciet una hominis vis.
quod simul atque suis eiectum sedibus exit,
per membra atque artus decedit corpore toto
in loca conveniens nervorum certa cietque
continuo partis genitalis corporis ipsas.
inritata tument loca semine fitque voluntas
eicere id quo se contendit dira lubido,

cedes. *Magna etenim* Mar. Junt. Lamb. wrongly. *mentes*, *magnis qui mentibus e. M.* Lach. strangely. 1021 *Ut qui* A p. m. rightly. *Ut quasi* BA corr. Nicc. Flor. 31 Camb. all Vat. Mon. etc.: hence much confusion before Wak. *Se quasi* Mar. 1022 *Externantur* Lach. for *Exterruntur*. *Exterrentur* vulg. 1026 *sei* Lach. for *se*: Mar. Junt. vulg. omit *se* in 1027, and 1028 insert *ut* after (Avanc. before) *saccatum*, and read *fundant* with Brix. (?) Ver. Ven. 1032 *quoque*. *quodam* Lach. without reason I think. 1034 *Qui* Lamb. for *Quae*. 1035 *Ut* Mar. Nauger. for *Et*. 1036 *cruentent* Flor. 31 Camb. for *cruentet*.

1037 *id in nobis* Flor. 31 Camb. Pont. Avanc. at end of Catullus for *id nobis*. *id e* Lach. *idem* Brix. Ver. Ven. Avanc. in Ald. 1. 1038 *adulta* B corr.

idque petit corpus, mens unde est saucia amore.
namque omnes plerumque cadunt in vulnus et illam
emicat in partem sanguis unde icimur ictu,
et si comminus est, hostem ruber occupat umor.
sic igitur Veneris qui telis accipit ictus,
sive puer membris muliebribus hunc iaculatur
seu mulier toto iactans e corpore amorem,
unde feritur, eo tendit gestitque coire
et iacere umorem in corpus de corpore ductum;
namque voluptatem praesagit muta cupido.
Haec Venus est nobis; hinc autemst nomen amoris,
hinc illaec primum Veneris dulcedinis in cor
stillavit gutta et successit frigida cura.
nam si abest quod ames, praesto simulacra tamen sunt
illius et nomen dulce obversatur ad auris.
sed fugitare decet simulacra et pabula amoris
absterrere sibi atque alio convertere mentem
et iacere umorem conlectum in corpora quaeque
nec retinere, semel conversum unius amore,
et servare sibi curam certumque dolorem.
ulcus enim vivescit et inveterascit alendo
inque dies gliscit furor atque aerumna gravescit,
si non prima novis conturbes volnera plagis
volgivagaque vagus Venere ante recentia cures
aut alio possis animi traducere motus.
Nec Veneris fructu caret is qui vitat amorem,
sed potius quae sunt sine poena commoda sumit;
nam certe purast sanis magis inde voluptas
quam miseris. etenim potiundi tempore in ipso
fluctuat incertis erroribus ardor amantum
nec constat quid primum oculis manibusque fruantur.

Mar. Ald. 1 Junt. for *advita*. 1047 = 1034. 1057 *muta* A Nicc. Flor. 31 Camb. Mon. old eds. Junt. *multa* B Avanc. Nauger. Lamb. vulg. before Lach. 1058 *nomen*. *momen* Lach. most unpoetically; Creech more elegantly, but without necessity, *numen*: see Camb. Journ. of phil. I p. 35. Lach. also in the next verse wrongly puts a stop at *illaec*. *illaec* A corr. for *ille* A, *illa* B. *illace* Nicc. one Vat. *illa et* Flor. 31 Camb. 3 Vat. Pont. 1060 *frigida*. *fervida* Mar. Junt. (not Nauger.) Creech. 1061 *ames*. *aves* Lach. without necessity: see notes 2. 1065 *conlectum* (*collectum*) Junt. not Pont. or Mar. for *coniectum*. *congestum* Avanc. at end of Catullus.

quod petiere, premunt arte faciuntque dolorem
corporis et dentes inlidunt saepe labellis
osculaque adfligunt, quia non est pura voluptas
et stimuli subsunt qui instigant laedere id ipsum
quodcumque est, rabies unde illaec germina surgunt.
sed leviter poenas frangit Venus inter amorem
blandaque *re*frenat morsus admixta voluptas.
namque in eo spes est, unde est ardoris origo,
restingui quoque posse ab eodem corpore flammam.
quod fieri contra totum natura repugnat;
unaque res haec est, cuius quom plurima habemus,
tum magis ardescit dira cuppedine pectus.
nam cibus atque umor membris adsumitur intus;
quae quoniam certas possunt obsidere partis,
hoc facile expletur laticum frugumque cupido.
ex hominis vero facie pulchroque colore
nil datur in corpus praeter simulacra fruendum
tenvia; quae vento spes raptast saepe misella.
ut bibere in somnis sitiens quom quaerit et umor
non datur, ardorem qui membris stinguere possit,
sed laticum simulacra petit frustraque laborat
in medioque sitit torrenti flumine potans,
sic in amore Venus simulacris ludit amantis
nec satiare queunt spectando corpora coram,
nec manibus quicquam teneris abradere membris
possunt errantes incerti corpore toto.
denique cum membris conlatis flore fruuntur

1068 *Ulcus* A corr. for *Vicus*. 1081 *adfligunt* A Nicc. Flor. 31 Camb. all Vat. Mon. rightly. *adfigunt* B Pont. and in marg. Mar. Junt. Lamb. etc. 1083 *illaec germina* Lach. after a friend of Lamb. for *illae cermina* (?) A p. m. *ille germina* B. *ille haec germina* A corr. Nicc.: see 1059. 1085 *refrenat* Nicc. for *frenat*. 1089 *cuius quom, Tum* Ed. for *cuius quam, Tam*. *cuius quo mage* Lach. *cuius quo pluria* Mar. Ald. 1 Junt. *quam pluria* Lamb. etc. which is not Latin. [But comparing Ter. heaut. 997 *Nam quam maxime huic vana haec suspicio Erit, tam facillume patris pacem in leges conficiet suas;* Cato r. r. 85 9 *Quam plurimum bibit, tam maxime sitit;* and old poet (inc. fab. 160 Ribb.) ap. Quintilian IX 3 15 *Quam magis aerumna urget, tam magis ad maleficiendum urget*; and Aen. VII 787 quoted there: perhaps Lucr. mixed the two constructions and wrote as his mss. give. Compare too Plaut. aul. 229 *Quam ad probos propinquitate proxume te adiunxeris, Tam optumumst*: and see Ussing there.] 1096 *raptast* Ed. for *raptat*. *rapta est* Vat. 3276 Pont. Candidus at end of Junt. Wak. *mentem spes raptat* Lach. *mentem spe lactant* or *captant* Bentl. 1098 *membris stinguere*

aetatis, iam cum praesagit gaudia corpus
atque in eost Venus ut muliebria conserat arva,
adfigunt avide corpus iunguntque salivas
oris et inspirant pressantes dentibus ora,
nequiquam, quoniam nil inde abradere possunt
nec penetrare et abire in corpus corpore toto;
nam facere interdum velle et certare videntur:
usque adeo cupide in Veneris compagibus haerent,
membra voluptatis dum vi labefacta liquescunt.
tandem ubi se erupit nervis conlecta cupido,
parva fit ardoris violenti pausa parumper.
inde redit rabies eadem et furor ille revisit,
cum sibi quid cupiant ipsi contingere quaerunt,
nec reperire malum id possunt quae machina vincat;
usque adeo incerti tabescunt volnere caeco.
 Adde quod absumunt viris pereuntque labore,
adde quod alterius sub nutu degitur aetas.
labitur interea res et Babylonica fiunt,
languent officia atque aegrotat fama vacillans.
huic lenta et pulchra in pedibus Sicyonia rident
scilicet et grandes viridi cum luce zmaragdi
auro includuntur teriturque thalassina vestis
adsidue et Veneris sudorem exercita potat.
et bene parta patrum fiunt anademata, mitrae,
interdum in pallam atque Alidensia Ciaque vertunt.
eximia veste et victu convivia, ludi,

Avanc. for *membri stinguere* or *membris tinguere*. 1115 *conlecta* Lamb. for *coniecta*. 1118 *quid* Lach. for *quod*: a necessary change. 1121 *viris* (*vires*) Pont. Mar. Junt. for *utris*. 1123 *Babylonica* Pius in notes for *Babylonia*. *vadimonia* Mar. Junt. vulg. before Lach. 1124 *vacillans* Mar. Junt. for *vigillans*. *vacilans* Avanc. 1125 *Huic lenta* Ed. for *Unguenta*: see Camb. Journ. of phil. IV p. 287: the reading is of course quite uncertain: indeed *unguenta* may have come from *Languent* of 1124 and have expelled a totally different word: perhaps *Arguta*, if *huic* were not wanted: comp. Catull. 68 72 *Innixa arguta constituit solea*; and Tib. I 8 14. *Argentum* Lach. 1129 *fiunt* ℞ corr. Mar. Ald. 1 Junt. for *flunt*. 1130 *Alidensia* of mss. may be right: see notes 2. *alideusia* Lach. very ingeniously; but yet *alideusia* is not even a known Greek word. *ac Melitensia Ceaque* Lamb. after 'Adrianus Turnebus, seu potius Gul. Pelliserius, Episc. Montepessul.' *Ciaque* Lach. for *chia*: so Cic. de nat. deor. I 118 *Prodicus Cius* Victorius: *chiuis* or *chius* mss. 1131 *ludi* A corr. Nicc. for *luidi*. *lychni* Lach.: but see notes 2; and v 295 from which it appears that Lucr. wrote *lў̆chĭni* or *luchini* or *lichini*.

pocula crebra, unguenta coronae serta parantur,
nequiquam, quoniam medio de fonte leporum
surgit amari aliquit quod in ipsis floribus angat,
aut cum conscius ipse animus se forte remordet
desidiose agere aetatem lustrisque perire,
aut quod in ambiguo verbum iaculata reliquit
quod cupido adfixum cordi vivescit ut ignis,
aut nimium iactare oculos aliumve tueri
quod putat in voltuque videt vestigia risus.
Atque in amore mala haec proprio summeque secundo
inveniuntur; in adverso vero atque inopi sunt,
prendere quae possis oculorum lumine operto,
innumerabilia; ut melius vigilare sit ante,
qua docui ratione, cavereque ne inliciaris.
nam vitare, plagas in amoris ne iaciamur,
non ita difficile est quam captum retibus ipsis
exire et validos Veneris perrumpere nodos.
et tamen implicitus quoque possis inque peditus
effugere infestum, nisi tute tibi obvius obstes
et praetermittas animi vitia omnia primum
aut quae corpori' sunt eius, *si*quam petis ac vis.
nam faciunt homines plerumque cupidine caeci,
et tribuunt ea quae non sunt his commoda vere.
multimodis igitur pravas turpisque videmus
esse in deliciis summoque in honore vigere.
atque alios alii inrident Veneremque süadent
ut placent, quoniam foedo adflictentur amore,
nec sua respiciunt miseri mala maxima saepe.
nigra melichrus est, inmunda et fetida acosmos,
caesia Palladium, nervosa et lignea dorcas,
parvula, pumilio, chariton mia, tota merum sal,
magna atque inmanis cataplexis plenaque honoris.
balba loqui non quit, traulizi, muta pudens est;
at flagrans odiosa loquacula Lampadium fit.
ischnon eromenion tum fit, cum vivere non quit

1141 *mala haec* Flor. 31 Camb. 2 Vat. Pont. Mar. for *male haec.* 1145 *inliciaris* Ald. 1, *ill.* Mar. Junt. for *inligniaris*: so III 553 *linguntur* mss. for *licuntur.* 1152 *Aut* Lach. for *Ut. Et* Pont. Mar. *Tum* Nauger. vulg. *si quam petis* Lach. for *quam praepetis* A Nicc. Flor. 31 Camb. *quam precis* B. *quam percupis* Lamb. 1156 *deliciis* Camb. Mar. for *delictis.*

prae macie; rhadine verost iam mortua tussi.
at tumida et mammosa Ceres est ipsa ab Iaccho,
simula Silena ac saturast, labeosa philema.
cetera de genere hoc longum est si dicere coner.
sed tamen esto iam quantovis oris honore,
cui Veneris membris vis omnibus exoriatur:
nempe aliae quoque sunt; nempe hac sine viximus ante;
nempe eadem facit, et scimus facere, omnia turpi,
et miseram taetris se suffit odoribus ipsa
quam famulae longe fugitant furtimque cachinnant.
at lacrimans exclusus amator limina saepe
floribus et sertis operit postisque superbos
unguit amaracino et foribus miser oscula figit;
quem si, iam *am*missum, venientem offenderit aura
una modo, causas abeundi quaerat honestas,
et meditata diu cadat alte sumpta querella,
stultitiaque ibi se damnet, tribuisse quod illi
plus videat quam mortali concedere par est.
nec Veneres nostras hoc fallit; quo magis ipsae
omnia summo opere hos vitae poscaenia celant
quos retinere volunt adstrictosque esse in amore,
nequiquam, quoniam tu animo tamen omnia possis
protrahere in lucem atque omnis inquirere risus
et, si bello animost et non odiosa, vicissim
praetermittere *et* humanis concedere rebus.

Nec mulier semper ficto suspirat amore
quae conplexa viri corpus cum corpore iungit
et tenet adsuctis umectans oscula labris.
nam facit ex animo saepe et communia quaerens
gaudia sollicitat spatium decurrere amoris.
nec ratione alia volucres armenta feraeque

1168 *At tumida* Bern. for *At iamina*: this I had myself seen many years ago on comparing Ovid ars II 661, where he is imitating Lucr. *At Lamia* Avanc. Lach. *At gemina* Lamb. vulg. 1174 *turpi* Nauger. for *turpis.* 1176 *longe* Flor. 31 Camb. for *longi.* 1180 *iam ammissum* (*admissum*) Lamb. for *iam missum. iam ammissu* Lach. *iam iussu* Bern. *iam immissum* Mar. Ald. 1 Junt. *venientem. veniens* Ald. 1 Junt. Bentl. 1182 *cadat* Lamb. for *cadet.* 1183 *Stultitia. Stultitiae* Mar. Ald. 1 Junt. Lach. 1188 *possis* Mar. Junt. for *posses.* 1189 *inquirere risus. in usus* Pont. Junt. *lusus* Mar. Candidus at end of Junt. *anquirere nisus* Lamb. Creech etc. 1191 *et* added by Mar. Lach. *Praetermittet te* Junt.

et pecudes et equae maribus subsidere possent,
si non, ipsa quod illorum subat ardet abundans
natura et Venerem salientum laeta retractat.
nonne vides etiam quos mutua saepe voluptas
vinxit, ut in vinclis communibus excrucientur?
in triviis quam saepe canes, discedere aventis,
1210 divorsi cupide summis ex viribu' tendunt,
1204 quom interea validis Veneris compagibus haerent!
quod facerent numquam nisi mutua gaudia nossent
quae iacere in fraudem possent vinctosque tenere.
quare etiam atque etiam, ut dico, est communi' voluptas.
  Et commiscendo quom semine forte virili
1209 femina vim vicit subita vi corripuitque,
tum similes matrum materno semine fiunt,
ut patribus patrio. sed quos utriusque figurae
esse vides, iuxtim miscentes vulta parentum,
corpore de patrio et materno sanguine crescunt,
semina cum Veneris stimulis excita per artus
obvia conflixit conspirans mutuus ardor,
et neque utrum superavit eorum nec superatumst.
fit quoque ut interdum similes existere avorum
possint et referant proavorum saepe figuras
propterea quia multa modis primordia multis
mixta suo celant in corpore saepe parentis,
quae patribus patres tradunt ab stirpe profecta;
inde Venus varia producit sorte figuras

Lamb. 1198 *possent*. Lach. reads *possunt*, and refers *quod illorum subat* to the male. 1200 *salientum* Mar. Ald. 1 Junt. for *sallentum*. *retractat* Lamb. ed. 2 and 3 first for *retractant*. 1201 *etiam* om. Nicc. Flor. 31 Camb. 2 Vat. Brix. Ver. Ven. *memi* one Vat. *illos* 2 Vat. *etiam* of AB rightly added by Pont. and Avanc. 1202 *vinclis* Mar. Ald. 1 Junt. for *vinciis*. 1203 *quam* Lach. for *cum*. *quin* Mar. Junt. Lamb. ed. 1 and 2. *non saepe* Lamb. ed. 3, Creech. 1204 (1210) first brought here by Nauger. 1207 *lacere* Lamb. and above 1146 *laciamur*, without cause. 1209 *semine*. *semen* would simplify the constr. 1210 *vim vicit* Salmasius for *vi mulcit*: a certain correction, which Wak. and Lach. justly adopt: the older readings are not worth mentioning; Lamb. in vain tries to extricate himself: it appears from 500 instances that in our archetype, as in other mss. written in square capitals, *l* and *i* were often undistinguishable: 824 *errore multareque*, I 659 *ver aula* AB. 1220 *multa modis* Lamb. ed. 2 and 3 for *multimodis*; and, although Junt. has *multimodis* in the text, it would appear from his note at the end that Candidus intended to print

maiorumque refert voltus vocesque comasque.
1227 et muliebre oritur patrio de semine saeclum
maternoque mares existunt corpore creti;
1225 quandoquidem nilo magis haec *de* semine certo
fiunt quam facies et corpora membraque nobis;
semper enim partus duplici de semine constat,
atque utri similest magis id quodcumque creatur,
eius habet plus parte aequa; quod cernere possis,
sive virum suboles sivest muliebris origo.

Nec divina satum genitalem numina cuiquam
absterrent, pater a gnatis ne dulcibus umquam
appelletur et ut sterili Venere exigat aevom;
quod plerumque putant et multo sanguine maesti
conspergunt aras adolentque altaria donis,
ut gravidas reddant uxores semine largo.
nequiquam divom numen sortisque fatigant.
nam steriles nimium crasso sunt semine partim
et liquido praeter iustum tenuique vicissim.
tenve locis quia non potis est adfigere adhaesum,
liquitur extemplo et revocatum cedit abortu.
crassius his porro quoniam concretius aequo
mittitur, aut non tam prolixo provolat ictu
aut penetrare locos aeque nequit aut penetratum
aegre admiscetur muliebri semine semen.
nam multum harmoniae Veneris differre videntur.
atque alias alii complent magis ex aliisque
succipiunt aliae pondus magis inque gravescunt.
et multae steriles Hymenaeis ante fuerunt
pluribus et nactae post sunt tamen unde puellos
suscipere et partu possent ditescere dulci.
et quibus ante domi fecundae saepe nequissent
uxores parere, inventast illis quoque compar
natura, ut possent gnatis munire senectam.

multa modis. 1222 *ab* Lach. for *a*. 1225 1226 (1227 1228) I have transferred hither, the sense requiring the change. 1227 *de* added by Flor. 31 Pont. Mar. Junt. *a* Avanc. *magis*. *minus* Lamb. followed by all before Lach.
1230 *quodcunque* Flor. 31 Camb. Ver. Ven. Mar. for *quocumque*.
1234 *pater a gnatis* Brix.?, Pont. Mar. Ald. 1 Junt. for *praeter agnatis*.
1243 *cedit* Pont. Mar. Ald. 1 Junt. for *credit*. 1244 *his* Lach. for *hic*. 1252 *post sunt* Lamb. first for *possunt*; though Lucr. perhaps wrote

usque adeo magni refert, ut semina possint
seminibus commisceri genitaliter apta,
crassane conveniant liquidis et liquida crassis.
atque in eo refert quo victu vita colatur;
namque aliis rebus concrescunt semina membris
atque aliis extenvantur tabentque vicissim.
et quibus ipsa modis tractetur blanda voluptas,
id quoque permagni refert; nam more ferarum
quadrupedumque magis ritu plerumque putantur
concipere uxores, quia sic loca sumere possunt,
pectoribus positis, sublatis semina lumbis.
nec molles opu' sunt motus uxoribus hilum.
nam mulier prohibet se concipere atque repugnat,
clunibus ipsa viri Venerem si laeta retractat
atque exossato ciet omni pectore fluctus;
eicit enim sulcum recta regione viaque
vomeris atque locis avertit seminis ictum.
idque sua causa consuerunt scorta moveri,
ne complerentur crebro gravidaeque iacerent
et simul ipsa viris Venus ut concinnior esset;
coniugibus quod nil nostris opus esse videtur.
  Nec divinitus interdum Venerisque sagittis
deteriore fit ut forma muliercula ametur.
nam facit ipsa suis interdum femina factis
morigerisque modis et munde corpore culto,
ut facile insuescat *te* secum degere vitam.
quod superest, consuetudo concinnat amorem;
nam leviter quamvis quod crebro tunditur ictu,
vincitur in longo spatio tamen atque labascit.
nonne vides etiam guttas in saxa cadentis
umoris longo in spatio pertundere saxa?

pos sunt: comp. 1186 *poscaenia*. 1259 *Crassane* Ed. for *Crassaque*; as *refert conveniant* does not seem Latin any more than III 868 *differre fuerit*, and *que* is quite superfluous. *conveniant* Mar. Ald. 1 Junt. for *conveniunt*. 1262 *aliis* Ver. Ven. Mar. for *alii*. 1268 *Nec* Pont. Mar. Ald. 1 Junt. for *Ne*. *Non* Camb. 1270 *retractat* B. *retractet* A and all other mss. and eds. before Lach. 1281 *modis* Pont. Mar. Junt. for *moris*. 1282 *te secum* Bern. for *secum*. *secum nos* Lach. *vir secum* Flor. 31 Camb. vulg. 'Italice magis quam Latine' says Lach.

T. LUCRETI CARI

DE RERUM NATURA

LIBER QUINTUS

Quis potis est dignum pollenti pectore carmen
condere pro rerum maiestate hisque repertis?
quisve valet verbis tantum qui fingere laudes
pro meritis eius possit qui talia nobis
pectore parta suo quaesita*que* praemia liquit?
nemo, ut opinor, erit mortali corpore cretus.
nam si, ut ipsa petit maiestas cognita rerum,
dicendum est, deus ille fuit, deus, inclyte Memmi,
qui princeps vitae rationem invenit eam quae
nunc appellatur sapientia, quique per artem
fluctibus e tantis vitam tantisque tenebris
in tam tranquillo et tam clara luce locavit.
confer enim divina aliorum antiqua reperta.
namque Ceres fertur fruges Liberque liquoris
vitigeni laticem mortalibus instituisse;
cum tamen his posset sine rebus vita manere,
ut fama est aliquas etiam nunc vivere gentis.
at bene non poterat sine puro pectore vivi;
quo magis hic merito nobis deus esse videtur,
ex quo nunc etiam per magnas didita gentis
dulcia permulcent animos solacia vitae.
Herculis antistare autem si facta putabis,
longius a vera multo ratione ferere.
quid Nemeaeus enim nobis nunc magnus hiatus

2 *maiestate hisque repertis* Lamb. for *maiestatis atque repertis*: he proposes also *maiestate atque r.* *maiestatisque repertis* Nicc. and all before Lamb. 12 *locavit*

ille leonis obesset et horrens Arcadius sus?
denique quid Cretae taurus Lernaeaque pestis
hydra venenatis posset vallata colubris?
quidve tripectora tergemini vis Geryonai
. . . .
30 tanto opere officerent nobis Stymphala colentes
29 et Diomedis equi spirantes naribus ignem
Thracis Bistoniasque plagas atque Ismara propter?
aureaque Hesperidum servans fulgentia mala,
asper, acerba tuens, immani corpore serpens
arboris amplexus stirpem quid denique obesset
propter Atlanteum litus pelageque sonora,
quo neque noster adit quisquam nec barbarus audet?
cetera de genere hoc quae sunt portenta perempta,
sei non victa forent, quid tandem viva nocerent?
nil, ut opinor: ita ad satiatem terra ferarum
nunc etiam scatit et trepido terrore repleta est
per nemora ac montes magnos silvasque profundas;
quae loca vitandi plerumque est nostra potestas.
at nisi purgatumst pectus, quae proelia nobis
atque pericula tumst ingratis insinuandum!
quantae tum scindunt hominem cuppedinis acres
sollicitum curae quantique perinde timores!
quidve superbia spurcitia ac petulantia? quantas

Nicc. for *vocavit.* 29 foll. Mar. Ald. 1 Junt. and all succeeding eds. invert 30 and 31; I transpose 29 and 30: again Mar. Ald. 1 Junt. and all before Lach. insert between *nobis* and *Stymphala* the words *uncisque timendae Unguibus Arcadiae volucres.* Lach. weakly reads *et aves* for *nobis.* I have no doubt a verse has fallen out before 29 (30), beginning with *Quid*: such for instance as this *Quid volucres pennis aeratis invia stagna.* 31 *Thracis* Ed. for *Thracia. Thracam* Lach. *Thracen* Ald. 1 Junt.: see Camb. Journ. of phil. I p. 44. 34 *stirpem* Mon. Nauger. (*stipem* Mar. Junt.) for *stirpes.* 35 *Atlanteum* Gif. (*Atlantaeum* Lamb. and Turneb. first) for *Atianeum. Oceanum propter* Nicc. followed by many: *Oceanum* was probably written in the margin of Poggio's ms. to explain *Atlanteum. pelageque* Lamb. for *pelagique. sonora* Nicc. (not Flor. 31 or Camb.) Mon. Brix. Ver. Ven. Ald. 1 Junt. Nauger. Lach. for *severa*: it was probably in Poggio's ms.: Pont. in marg. 'alii *severa*'. 38 *Sei* Lach. *Si* Nicc. for *Sed.* 44 *tumst* Lach. for *sunt. tunc* Lamb. Gif. ed. 1. Lamb. ed. 3 remarks 'hunc locum Zoilus...secutus est tacitus et dissimulans, tamquam integrum in aliis libris repertum et non a me emendatum': Gif. then ed. 2 reads *pericula est,* and says 'sic scripsi. in o. v. *sunt.* Marull. et vulg. *tunc*': now when Lamb. had so pointedly drawn attention to it, Gif. must have been a most impudent liar, if he did not find *tunc* in Marullus' ms.

efficiunt clades! quid luxus desidiaeque?
haec igitur qui cuncta subegerit ex animoque
expulerit dictis, non armis, nonne decebit
hunc hominem numero divom dignarier esse?
cum bene praesertim multa ac divinitus ipsis
immortalibu' de divis dare dicta suërit
atque omnem rerum naturam pandere dictis.
  Cuius ego ingressus vestigia dum rationes
persequor ac doceo dictis, quo quaeque creata
foedere sint, in eo quam sit durare necessum
nec validas valeant aevi rescindere leges,
quo genere in primis animi natura reperta est
nativo primum consistere corpore creta
nec posse incolumis magnum durare per aevom,
sed simulacra solere in somnis fallere mentem,
cernere cum videamur eum quem vita reliquit,
quod superest, nunc huc rationis detulit ordo,
ut mihi mortali consistere corpore mundum
nativomque simul ratio reddunda sit esse;
et quibus ille modis congressus materiai
fundarit terram caelum mare sidera solem
lunaique globum; tum quae tellure animantes
extiterint, et quae nullo sint tempore natae;
quove modo genus humanum variante loquella
coeperit inter se vesci per nomina rerum;
et quibus ille modis divom metus insinuarit
pectora, terrarum qui in orbi sancta tuetur
fana lacus lucos aras simulacraque divom.
praeterea solis cursus lunaeque meatus
expediam qua vi flectat natura gubernans;
ne forte haec inter caelum terramque reamur
libera sponte sua cursus lustrare perennis
morigera ad fruges augendas atque animantis,
neve aliqua divom volvi ratione putemus.
nam bene qui didicere deos securum agere aevom,

notes; though Mon. has no trace of it. Junt. reads *sunt*. 51 *numero divom*. *divum numero* Lactant. 53 *Immortalibus* Flor. 31 Mar. *Inmortalibus* B Camb. *Iam mortalibus* A Nicc. etc. *de* Lamb. for *e*. 61 *incolumis* Mar. Junt. for *incolumen* A, *vinculum est* B, *incolumē* Camb. 71 *Quove*. *Quoque* Nonius, contrary to

si tamen interea mirantur qua ratione
quaeque geri possint, praesertim rebus in illis
quae supera caput aetheriis cernuntur in oris,
rursus in antiquas referuntur religiones
et dominos acris adsciscunt, omnia posse
quos miseri credunt, ignari quid queat esse,
quid nequeat, finita potestas denique cuique
quanam sit ratione atque alte terminus haerens.

Quod superest, ne te in promissis plura moremur,
principio maria ac terras caelumque tuere;
quorum naturam triplicem, tria corpora, Memmi,
tris species tam dissimilis, tria talia texta,
una dies dabit exitio, multosque per annos
sustentata ruet moles et machina mundi.
nec me animi fallit quam res nova miraque menti
accidat exitium caeli terraeque futurum,
et quam difficile id mihi sit pervincere dictis;
ut fit ubi insolitam rem adportes auribus ante
nec tamen hanc possis oculorum subdere visu
nec iacere indu manus, via qua munita fidei
proxima fert humanum in pectus templaque mentis.
sed tamen effabor. dictis dabit ipsa fidem res
forsitan et graviter terrarum motibus ortis
omnia conquassari in parvo tempore cernes.
quod procul a nobis flectat fortuna gubernans,
et ratio potius quam res persuadeat ipsa
succidere horrisono posse omnia victa fragore.

[Qua prius adgrediar quam de re fundere fata
sanctius et multo certa ratione magis quam
Pythia quae tripode a Phoebi lauroque profatur,
multa tibi expediam doctis solacia dictis;
religione refrenatus ne forte rearis
terras et solem et caelum, mare sidera lunam,
corpore divino debere aeterna manere,
propterea que putes ritu par esse Gigantum
pendere eos poenas inmani pro scelere omnis
qui ratione sua disturbent moenia mundi

the use of Lucr. 114 *Religione* Nicc. Ver. Ven. *Relligione* AB in this place only, Flor. 31 Camb. Mon. 116 *manere* Junt. for *meare*. 117 *par* Mar. Junt.

praeclarumque velint caeli restinguere solem
inmortalia mortali sermone notantes;
quae procul usque adeo divino a numine distent,
inque deum numero quae sint indigna videri,
notitiam potius praebere ut posse putentur
quid sit vitali motu sensuque remotum.
quippe etenim non est, cum quovis corpore ut esse
posse animi natura putetur consiliumque;
sicut in aethere non arbor, non aequore salso
nubes esse queunt neque pisces vivere in arvis
nec cruor in lignis neque saxis sucus inesse.
certum ac dispositumst ubi quicquit crescat et insit.
sic animi natura nequit sine corpore oriri
sola neque a nervis et sanguine longiter esse.
quod si (posset enim multo prius) ipsa animi vis
in capite aut umeris aut imis calcibus esse
posset et innasci quavis in parte, soleret
tandem in eodem homine atque in eodem vase manere.
quod quoniam nostro quoque constat corpore certum
dispositumque videtur ubi esse et crescere possit
seorsum anima atque animus, tanto magis infitiandum
totum posse extra corpus formamque animalem
putribus in glebis terrarum aut solis *in* igni
aut in aqua durare aut altis aetheris oris.
haud igitur constant divino praedita sensu,
quandoquidem nequeunt vitaliter esse animata.
  Illud item non est ut possis credere, sedes
esse deum sanctas in mundi partibus ullis.
tenvis enim natura deum longeque remota
sensibus ab nostris animi vix mente videtur;
quae quoniam manuum tactum suffugit et ictum,
tactile nil nobis quod sit contingere debet.
tangere enim non quit quod tangi non licet ipsum.
quare etiam sedes quoque nostris sedibus esse
dissimiles debent, tenues de corpore eorum;

for *pars*: comp. 881 122 *a numine distent* Flor. 31 Camb. Brix. Mar. for *animinbistent*. *animilastent* Nicc. 133 *longiter*. *longius* mss.: see III 789.
134 foll.: see III 790 foll. 152 *quod* Mar. Junt. for *quod si*. 154 *de corpore*. *pro corpore* Lamb. conj. and Ed. in ed. 1: see notes 2: *tenuest si corpu'*

quae tibi posterius largo sermone probabo.
dicere porro hominum causa voluisse parare
praeclaram mundi naturam proptereaque
adlaudabile opus divom laudare decere
aeternumque putare atque inmortale futurum
nec fas esse, deum quod sit ratione vetusta
gentibus humanis fundatum perpetuo aevo,
solicitare suis ulla vi ex sedibus umquam
nec verbis vexare et ab imo evertere summa,
cetera de genere hoc adfingere et addere, Memmi,
desiperest. quid enim inmortalibus atque beatis
gratia nostra queat largirier emolumenti,
ut nostra quicquam causa gerere adgrediantur?
quidve novi potuit tanto post ante quietos
inlicere ut cuperent vitam mutare priorem?
nam gaudere novis rebus debere videtur
cui veteres obsunt; sed cui nil accidit aegri
tempore in anteacto, cum pulchre degeret aevom,
quid potuit novitatis amorem accendere tali?
175 an, credo, in tenebris vita ac maerore iacebat,
donec diluxit rerum genitalis origo.
174 quidve mali fuerat nobis non esse creatis?
177 natus enim debet quicumque est velle manere
in vita, donec retinebit blanda voluptas.
qui numquam vero vitae gustavit amorem
nec fuit in numero, quid obest non esse creatum?
exemplum porro gignundis rebus et ipsa
notities divis hominum unde est insita primum
quid vellent facere ut scirent animoque viderent,
quove modost umquam vis cognita principiorum
quidque inter se*se* permutato ordine possent,
si non ipsa dedit specimen natura creandi?
namque ita multa modis multis primordia rerum

deorum Lach. *tenues ceu corpora eorum* Ed. in small ed. 162 *ulla vi ex. ullum de* Lamb. Creech etc. most gratuitously. 163 *summa. summam* Lamb. etc.

174 175 (175 176) rightly placed by Lamb. before 176 (174): but for *credo*, which can scarcely be right, I propose *crepera*. Lach. whom I followed formerly, puts them before 170, and reads *At* for *An* in 174. 182 *divis hominum unde est* Ed. for *hominum divis unde est*. *hominum dis unde est* Wak. Lach. *est* om. Mar. Ald. 1 Junt. Lamb. etc. *divisum deest* Nicc. Mon. Ver. Ven. 185 *sese* Brix.

ex infinito iam tempore percita plagis
ponderibusque suis consuerunt concita ferri
omnimodisque coire atque omnia pertemptare,
quaecumque inter se possent congressa creare,
ut non sit mirum si in talis dispositura
deciderunt quoque et in talis venere meatus,
qualibus haec rerum geritur nunc summa novando.

Quod *si* iam rerum ignorem primordia quae sint,
hoc tamen ex ipsis caeli rationibus ausim
confirmare aliisque ex rebus reddere multis,
nequaquam nobis divinitus esse paratam
naturam rerum; tanta stat praedita culpa.
principio quantum caeli tegit impetus ingens,
inde avidei partem montes silvaeque ferarum
possedere, tenent rupes vastaeque paludes
et mare quod late terrarum distinet oras.
inde duas porro prope partis fervidus ardor
adsiduusque geli casus mortalibus aufert.
quod superest arvi, tamen id natura sua vi
sentibus obducat, ni vis humana resistat
vitai causa valido consueta bidenti
ingemere et terram pressis proscindere aratris.
si non fecundas vertentes vomere glebas
terraique solum subigentes cimus ad ortus,
sponte sua nequeant liquidas existere in auras,
et tamen interdum magno quaesita labore
cum iam per terras frondent atque omnia florent,
aut nimiis torret fervoribus aetherius sol
aut subiti peremunt imbris gelidaeque pruinae,
flabraque ventorum violento turbine vexant.
praeterea genus horriferum natura ferarum
humanae genti infestum terraque marique
cur alit atque auget? cur anni tempora morbos
adportant? quare mors inmatura vagatur?

Pont. Mar. for *se*. 186 *specimen* Pius in notes for *speciem*. 187 *multa modis* Lamb. ed. 1 and 2 rightly for *multimodis*; but ed. 3 again *multimodis*: see 422. 191 *possent* for *possint* Lach. rightly, as 426. 193 *meatus* Flor. 31 Mar. for *maestus*. 195 *si* added by Mar. Ald. 1 Junt. 201 *avidei partem* Ed. for *avidam partem*. *avide* Bern. *aliquam* Lach. 'Marull. *aliam* pessime'

tum porro puer, ut saevis proiectus ab undis
navita, nudus humi iacet, infans, indigus omni
vitali auxilio, cum primum in luminis oras
nixibus ex alvo matris natura profudit,
vagituque locum lugubri complet, ut aecumst
cui tantum in vita restet transire malorum.
at variae crescunt pecudes armenta feraeque
nec crepitacillis opus est nec cuiquam adhibendast
almae nutricis blanda atque infracta loquella
nec varias quaerunt vestes pro tempore caeli,
denique non armis opus est, non moenibus altis,
qui sua tutentur, quando omnibus omnia large
tellus ipsa parit naturaque daedala rerum.]
  Principio quoniam terrai corpus et umor
aurarumque leves animae calidique vapores,
e quibus haec rerum consistere summa videtur,
omnia nativo ac mortali corpore constant,
debet eodem omnis mundi natura putari.
quippe etenim quorum partis et membra videmus
corpore nativo ac mortalibus esse figuris,
haec eadem ferme mortalia cernimus esse
et nativa simul. quapropter maxima mundi
cum videam membra ac partis consumpta regigni,
scire licet caeli quoque item terraeque fuisse
principiale aliquod tempus clademque futuram.
  Illud in his rebus ne corripuisse rearis
me mihi, quod terram atque ignem mortalia sumpsi
esse neque umorem dubitavi aurasque perire
atque eadem gigni rursusque augescere dixi,
principio pars terrai nonnulla, perusta
solibus adsiduis, multa pulsata pedum vi,

Gif.: Junt. as Ald. 1 has *avidam*: but in marg. of Mon. '*avidam partem*' is noted as strange. 227 *restet transire* Lactant. and Nicc. for *re et transirest*, that curiously frequent blunder of AB: see IV 783. 239 *eodem omnis* Gif. rightly for *eadem omnis*, and before him the Paris ed. of Pius. *tota eadem* Lamb. 241 *nativo ac mortalibus* Lach. for *nativom mortalibus*: not Naugerius who has *nativo mortalibus*. *nativo et mortalibus* Avanc. in notes at end of his Catullus, and vulg. *nativo in mortalibus* Mar. 245 *item* Bentl. for *idem*. 248 *Me mihi* B most rightly. *Memini* A. *Memmi* vulg.: hence Lamb. *me arripuisse* for *corripuisse* in 247. 251 *non nulla* Nicc. Camb. Ver. Ven. Mar. for *non ulla*. 257 *alid*

pulveris exhalat nebulam nubesque volantis
quas validi toto dispergunt aere venti.
pars etiam glebarum ad diluviem revocatur
imbribus et ripas radentia flumina rodunt.
praeterea pro parte sua, quodcumque alid auget,
redditur; et quoniam dubio procul esse videtur
omniparens eadem rerum commune sepulcrum,
ergo terra tibi libatur et aucta recrescit.

Quod superest, umore novo mare flumina fontes
semper abundare et latices manare perennis
nil opus est verbis: magnus decursus aquarum
undique declarat. sed primum quicquid aquai
tollitur in summaque fit ut nil umor abundet,
partim quod validi verrentes aequora venti
diminuunt radiisque retexens aetherius sol,
partim quod supter per terras diditur omnis;
percolatur enim virus retroque remanat
materies umoris et ad caput amnibus omnis
convenit, inde super terras fluit agmine dulci
qua via secta semel liquido pede detulit undas.

Aera nunc igitur dicam qui corpore toto
innumerabiliter privas mutatur in horas.
semper enim, quodcumque fluit de rebus, id omne
aeris in magnum fertur mare; qui nisi contra
corpora retribuat rebus recreetque fluentis,
omnia iam resoluta forent et in aera versa.
haut igitur cessat gigni de rebus et in res
reccidere, adsidue quoniam fluere omnia constat.

Largus item liquidi fons luminis, aetherius sol,
inrigat adsidue caelum candore recenti
suppeditatque novo confestim lumine lumen.
nam primum quicquid fulgoris disperit ei,
quocumque accidit. id licet hinc cognoscere possis,
quod simul ac primum nubes succedere soli
coepere et radios inter quasi rumpere lucis,
extemplo inferior pars horum disperit omnis

Lamb. ed. 1 and 2 for *alit* rightly; ed. 3 he restores *alit*. 258 *Redditur*. *Roditur* Mar. Junt. Lamb. vulgo before Wak. 282 *recenti* B corr. Flor. 31 Camb. Mon. for *regenti*. 288 *disperit* Nicc. B corr. for *disperis*. 291

terraque inumbratur qua nimbi cumque feruntur;
ut noscas splendore novo res semper egere
et primum iactum fulgoris quemque perire
nec ratione alia res posse in sole videri,
perpetuo ni suppeditet lucis caput ipsum.
quin etiam nocturna tibi, terrestria quae sunt,
lumina, pendentes lychini claraeque coruscis
fulguribus pingues multa caligine taedae
consimili properant ratione, ardore ministro,
suppeditare novom lumen, tremere ignibus instant,
instant, nec loca lux inter quasi rupta relinquit:
usque adeo properanter ab omnibus ignibus ei
exitium celeri celatur origine flammae.
sic igitur solem lunam stellasque putandum*st*
ex alio atque alio lucem iactare subortu
et primum quicquid flammarum perdere semper;
inviolabilia haec ne credas forte vigere.
  Denique non lapides quoque vinci cernis ab aevo,
non altas turris ruere et putrescere saxa,
non delubra deum simulacraque fessa fatisci,
nec sanctum numen fati protollere finis
posse neque adversus naturae foedera niti?
denique non monimenta virum dilapsa videmus
quaerere proporro sibi *sene* senescere credas,

Et Mar. Ald. 1 Junt. for *Ut*. 295 *lychini* Ed. for *lyclini*. *lychni* A corr. Nicc. Macrob.: Lucr. seems to have known only the trisyllabic form, whether he wrote *lychini* or *luchini* or *lichini*; or even one of the still older forms *lucini* or *licini*. Ritschl in Rhein. Mus. n. f. x p. 447—451 shews that Enn. ann. 328 wrote *lucinorum lumina bis sex*; Lucilius *lucinosque* or *luchinosque*: so *dracuma mina* (μνᾶ), *tecina* (τέχνη), *cŭcĭnus* or *cicinus* (κύκνος), and other like forms all arising from the dislike of the old Latins to certain combinations of consonants: comp. *Aesculapius Alcumena Hercules* and many such like. Lucr. or his editor may have written *y*, as it was introduced for Greek words just before his death: the aspirated *ch* was in common use some 40 years earlier, as Ritschl proves. 296 *caligine*. *fuligine* Bentl. and Wak. from a sheer misunderstanding of Lucr. 297 *properant* Mar. Ald. 1 Junt. for *proferant*. 300 *ab omnibus*. *obortis* Bruno (Harburg 1872, p. 9). 301 *celeri celatur* Mar. Madvig and Lach. for *celeri celeratur*. *toleratur* Nicc. Ver. Ven. Ald. 1 vulg. Junt. keeps the *celeratur* of Mon., Candidus not having observed that Marullus had put points of rejection under the *er*. 302 *putandumst* Lach. for *putandum*: see I 111. 312 *sene senescere* Ed. for *cumque senescere*: see Journ. of phil. n. s. IV p. 122 and notes 2. *sibi qui de se quoque dicat* Polle. *Aeraque proporro solidumque senescere ferrum* Ed. formerly: see Camb. Journ. of phil. I p. 373 and IV p. 142. *Quae fore*

non ruere avolsos silices a montibus altis
nec validas aevi vires perferre patique
finiti? neque enim caderent avolsa repente,
ex infinito quae tempore pertolerassent
omnia tormenta aetatis privata fragore.

Denique iam tuere hoc, circum supraque quod omnem
continet amplexu terram: si procreat ex se
omnia, quod quidam memorant, recipitque perempta,
totum nativum mortali corpore constat.
nam quodcumque alias ex se res auget alitque,
deminui debet, recreari, cum recipit res.

Praeterea si nulla fuit genitalis origo
terrarum et caeli semperque aeterna fuere,
cur supera bellum Thebanum et funera Troiae
non alias alii quoque res cecinere poetae?
quo tot facta virum totiens cecidere neque usquam
aeternis famae monimentis insita florent?
verum, ut opinor, habet novitatem summa recensque
naturast mundi neque pridem exordia cepit.
quare etiam quaedam nunc artes expoliuntur,
nunc etiam augescunt; nunc addita navigiis sunt
multa, modo organici melicos peperere sonores.
denique natura haec rerum ratioque repertast
nuper, et hanc primus cum primis ipse repertus
nunc ego sum in patrias qui possim vertere voces.
quod si forte fuisse antehac eadem omnia credis,
sed periisse hominum torrenti saecla vapore,
aut cecidisse urbis magno vexamine mundi,
aut ex imbribus adsiduis exisse rapaces
per terras amnes at*que* oppida cooperuisse,

proporro vetitumque senescere credas Lach. *Cedere proporro subitoque senescere casu* Mar. Junt. Lamb. ed. 1 and 2, Creech. Lamb. ed. 3 obelises this and adds the ms. verse. Is. Voss. (not Preiger) in ms. notes has *Quae ruere proporro ibi conque senescere credas.* [*Quare proporro sibi cumque senescere credas*] Bern.: Gif. and Wak. find no difficulty in the ms. reading. 318 *omnem* Mar. Junt. for *omne.* 319 *si* om. Nicc. and all later mss.: hence much confusion in eds. before Lach., Havercamp not deigning to record that AB both had *si. omne...terrai* Avanc. *terram, quod* Mar. Junt. vulg. 321 *nativum. nativo ac* Bern. 331 *Naturast mundi* Ald. 1, *Natura est* Mar. Junt. for *Natura mundist*: this common blunder of our mss. Wak. here keeps. 339 *periisse* Flor. 31 for *perisse.* 342 *atque oppida* Flor. 31 Camb. Mar. for *at oppida. ac* Nicc. 2 Vat.

tanto quique magis victus fateare necessest
exitium quoque terrarum caelique futurum.
nam cum res tantis morbis tantisque periclis
temptarentur, ibi si tristior incubuisset
causa, darent late cladem magnasque ruinas.
nec ratione alia mortales esse videmur,
inter nos nisi quod morbis aegrescimus isdem
atque illi quos a vita natura removit.
  Praeterea quaecumque manent aeterna necessust
aut, quia sunt solido cum corpore, respuere ictus
nec penetrare pati sibi quicquam quod queat artas
dissociare intus partis, ut materiai
corpora sunt quorum naturam ostendimus ante,
aut ideo durare aetatem posse per omnem,
plagarum quia sunt expertia, sicut inane est
quod manet intactum neque ab ictu fungitur hilum,
aut etiam quia nulla loci fit copia circum,
quo quasi res possint discedere dissoluique,
sicut summarum summa est aeterna neque extra
qui locus est quo dissiliant neque corpora sunt quae
possint incidere et valida dissolvere plaga.
at neque, uti docui, solido cum corpore mundi
naturast, quoniam admixtumst in rebus inane,
nec tamen est ut inane, neque autem corpora desunt,
ex infinito quae possint forte coorta
corruere hanc rerum violento turbine summam
aut aliam quamvis cladem inportare pericli,
nec porro natura loci spatiumque profundi
deficit, exspargi quo possint moenia mundi,
aut alia quavis possunt vi pulsa perire.
haut igitur leti praeclusa est ianua caelo
nec soli terraeque neque altis aequoris undis,
sed patet immani et vasto respectat hiatu.
quare etiam nativa necessumst confiteare
haec eadem; neque enim, mortali corpore quae sunt

Brix. Ver. Ven. Wak   349 *isdem* Pius in notes, Lamb. for *idem* which Lach. keeps: see II 693. Lach. was the first to join *inter nos* with what follows.   359 *fit* Lach. first for *sit*.   367 *coorta* Mar. Ald. 1 Junt. for *coperta*.   368 *Corruere*. *Proruere* Lamb. etc.   375 *immani*. *immane* Bruno l. l. p. 10: he

ex infinito iam tempore adhuc potuissent
inmensi validas aevi contemnere vires.
Denique tantopere inter se cum maxima mundi
pugnent membra, pio nequaquam concita bello,
nonne vides aliquam longi certaminis ollis
posse dari finem? vel cum sol et vapor omnis
omnibus epotis umoribus exsuperarint:
quod facere intendunt, neque adhuc conata patrantur:
tantum suppeditant amnes ultraque minantur
omnia diluviare ex alto gurgite ponti,
nequiquam, quoniam verrentes aequora venti
deminuunt radiisque retexens aetherius sol,
et siccare prius confidunt omnia posse
quam liquor incepti possit contingere finem.
tantum spirantes aequo certamine bellum
magnis *inter se* de rebus cernere certant,
cum semel interea fuerit superantior ignis
et semel, ut fama est, umor regnarit in arvis.
ignis enim superat et lambens multa perussit,
avia cum Phaethonta rapax vis solis equorum
aethere raptavit toto terrasque per omnis.
at pater omnipotens ira tum percitus acri
magnanimum Phaethonta repenti fulminis ictu
deturbavit equis in terram, solque cadenti
obvius aeternam succepit lampada mundi
disiectosque redegit equos iunxitque trementis,
inde suum per iter recreavit cuncta gubernans,
scilicet ut veteres Graium cecinere poetae.
quod procul a vera nimis est ratione repulsum.
ignis enim superare potest ubi materiai
ex infinito sunt corpora plura coorta;
inde cadunt vires aliqua ratione revictae,
aut pereunt res exustae torrentibus auris.

thinks that 369 and 372 are interpolations. 382 *certaminis ollis* Flor. 31 Camb. Mar. for *certamini solis*. 385 *patrantur*. *patrarunt* Goebel. 386 *ultraque*. *ultroque* Flor. 31 Camb. Mar. vulg. 393 *inter se* inserted by Lach. before, by Nicc. Flor. 31 Camb. Mon. vulg. after *de rebus*. 396 *superat* (perf.) *et lambens* Lach. for *superavit et ambens*. *lambens* B corr.: nor has *ambens* any existence, whether as partic. of *ambedo* or *ambio*. 399 *tum* Flor. 31 Camb. Mar. for *cum*. 405 *Graium* Flor. 31 Camb. Pont. Mar. for

umor item quondam coepit superare coortus,
ut fama est, hominum multas quando obruit urbis.
inde ubi vis aliqua ratione aversa recessit,
ex infinito fuerat quaecumque coorta,
constiterunt imbres et flumina vim minuerunt.
  Sed quibus ille modis coniectus materiai
fundarit terram et caelum pontique profunda,
solis lunai cursus, ex ordine ponam.
nam certe neque consilio primordia rerum
ordine se suo quaeque sagaci mente locarunt
nec quos quaeque darent motus pepigere profecto,
sed quia multa modis multis primordia rerum
ex infinito iam tempore percita plagis
ponderibusque suis consuerunt concita ferri
omnimodisque coire atque omnia pertemptare,
quaecumque inter se possent congressa creare,
propterea fit uti magnum volgata per aevom
omne genus coetus et motus experiundo
tandem conveniant ea quae convecta repente
magnarum rerum fiunt exordia saepe,
terrai maris et caeli generisque animantum.
  Hic neque tum solis rota cerni lumine largo
altivolans poterat nec magni sidera mundi
nec mare nec caelum nec denique terra neque aer
nec similis nostris rebus res ulla videri,
sed nova tempestas quaedam molesque coorta
omne genus de principiis, discordia quorum
intervalla vias conexus pondera plagas
concursus motus turbabat proelia miscens,

gratum. *graium* (*gratum*) Ver. Ven. 409 410 Lach. by a strange misapprehension inverts these verses and for *Aut pereunt* reads *Et pereunt*. 412 *urbis* Pont. Junt. for *undis*. Flor. 31 Camb. Ver. Ven. Mar. etc. keep *undis*, and for *hominum multas* read *hominum multos*. 428 *Omne genus* Lach. for *Omnigenus*. *Omnigenos* A corr. vulg. 429 *convecta* Lach. for *conventa*. *T. c. quae ubi convenere* Lamb. ed. 1; *T. ea c. quae ut convenere* ed. 2 and 3, followed by Creech, etc. 430 *fiunt* Flor. 31 Camb. for *fluunt*. *saepe. semper*, as II 1062 Lach. 432 *largo. claro* Macrob. 433 *Altivolans* Pont. Avanc. and Macrob. sat. VI 2 23 for *Alte volans*. *Alta volans* Mar. Junt. 437—442 (440—445) are thus arranged by Lach. after Reisacker quaest. Lucr.; and the necessity of this change is manifest, though Macrob. l. l. evidently read them in the order in which they appear in our mss. See what I say on this and similar points p. 30. 437 *Omne genus de* Lach. as

propter dissimilis formas variasque figuras
quod non omnia sic poterant coniuncta manere
445 nec motus inter sese dare convenientis.
437 diffugere inde loci partes coepere paresque
cum paribus iungi res et discludere mundum
membraque dividere et magnas disponere partes,
446 hoc est, a terris altum secernere caelum
et sorsum mare uti secreto umore pateret,
seorsus item puri secretique aetheris ignes.
  Quippe etenim primum terrai corpora quaeque,
propterea quod erant gravia et perplexa, coibant
in medio atque imas capiebant omnia sedes;
quae quanto magis inter se perplexa coibant,
tam magis expressere ea quae mare sidera solem
lunamque efficerent et magni moenia mundi.
omnia enim magis haec e levibus atque rutundis
seminibus multoque minoribu' sunt elementis
quam tellus. ideo, per rara foramina, terrae
partibus erumpens primus se sustulit aether
ignifer et multos secum levis abstulit ignis,
non alia longe ratione ac saepe videmus,
aurea cum primum gemmantis rore per herbas
matutina rubent radiati lumina solis
exhalantque lacus nebulam fluviique perennes,
ipsaque ut interdum tellus fumare videtur;
omnia quae sursum cum conciliantur, in alto
corpore concreto subtexunt nubila caelum.
sic igitur tum se levis ac diffusilis aether
corpore concreto circumdatus undique *flexit*
et late diffusus in omnis undique partis
omnia sic avido complexu cetera saepsit.
hunc exordia sunt solis lunaeque secuta,

before, for ***Omnigenus e*** B, *Omnigenis e* A Nicc. vulg. 446 *altum. **magnum*** Macr. 447 *umore* Macrob. B corr. Vat. 3276 Pont. Junt. for *umor. humorque* Nicc. Flor. 31 Camb. 4 Vat. Brix. Ver. Ven. Avanc. 458 *se* Nicc. for *et*.

459 *Ignifer*. *Signifer* Ver. Ven. Ald. 1 Junt. (not Mar.) Lamb. etc. on no ms. authority, though Lamb. falsely says all mss. have it. 460 463 *videmus... Exhalantque. videntur...Exalare* Lach.: a violent change which only impairs the beauty of the passage. 468 *flexit* Lach. for *saepsit*: *saepsit* has come from

interutrasque globi quorum vertuntur in auris;
quae neque terra sibi adscivit nec maximus aether,
quod neque tam fuerunt gravia ut depressa sederent,
nec levia ut possent per summas labier oras,
et tamen interutrasque ita sunt ut corpora viva
versent et partes ut mundi totius extent;
quod genus in nobis quaedam licet in statione
membra manere, tamen cum sint ea quae moveantur.
his igitur rebus retractis terra repente,
maxuma qua nunc se ponti plaga caerula tendit,
succidit et salso suffudit gurgite fossas.
inque dies quanto circum magis aetheris aestus
et radii solis cogebant undique terram
verberibus crebris extrema ad limina *in* artum,
in medio ut propulsa suo condensa coiret,
tam magis expressus salsus de corpore sudor
augebat mare manando camposque natantis,
et tanto magis illa foras elabsa volabant
corpora multa vaporis et aeris altaque caeli
densebant procul a terris fulgentia templa.
sidebant campi, crescebant montibus altis
ascensus; neque enim poterant subsidere saxa
nec pariter tantundem omnes succumbere partis.
  Sic igitur terrae concreto corpore pondus
constitit atque omnis mundi quasi limus in imum

470. 471 *secuta.* '*secuta, et* Y' (i.e. our A) says Havercamp. This is quite false: though he had A and B before him, he has chosen to copy out this, as well as three fourths of his worthless various readings, from the bookseller Tonson's London ed. of 1712, which gives 'collationes trium ms. codicum Vossii a Rdo Viro Rto Cannon S. T. P. factas': this collator says 'secuta, &. V. 1.' Haverc. copies even the comma and the & into his ed. This is but one of a thousand instances of his unprincipled sloth. 472 476 *Interutrasque. Interutraque* Lach. 474 *fuerunt. fuerint* Pont. Avanc. and strange to say Lamb. who made it the vulg. before Lach. 482 *salso suffudit* A corr. Lamb. for *salsos offudit. salso suffodit* Nicc. Flor. 31 Camb. Mon. etc. Wak. 485 *extrema ad limina in artum* Ed. for *extrema ad limina partem*: the scribe neglected to write *ina* twice, and to fill up the verse wrote *partem* for *rtum. extrema a limini' parte* Lach. who connects this verse with the next. *extrema ad limina apertam* Lamb. *e. a. l. raptim* Bentl. *radiis* for *radii* A Nicc. Camb. *lumina* Nicc. Flor. 31 Camb. etc. 491 *Densebant* Lamb. Lach. for *Densabant*, as our mss. in all other places make it of the 2nd conjugation: see Wagn. to Virg. geor. I 248.

confluxit gravis et subsedit funditus ut faex;
inde mare inde aer inde aether ignifer ipse
corporibus liquidis sunt omnia pura relicta,
et leviora aliis alia, et liquidissimus aether
atque levissimus aerias super influit auras,
nec liquidum corpus turbantibus aeris auris
commiscet; sinit haec violentis omnia verti
turbinibus, sinit incertis turbare procellis,
ipse suos ignis certo fert impete labens.
nam modice fluere atque uno posse aethera nisu
significat Pontos, mare certo quod fluit aestu
unum labendi conservans usque tenorem
[Motibus astrorum nunc quae sit causa canamus.
principio magnus caeli si vortitur orbis,
ex utraque polum parti premere aera nobis
dicendum est extraque tenere et claudere utrimque;
inde alium supra fluere atque intendere eodem
quo volvenda micant aeterni sidera mundi;
aut alium supter, contra qui subvehat orbem,
ut fluvios versare rotas atque haustra videmus.
est etiam quoque uti possit caelum omne manere
in statione, tamen cum lucida signa ferantur;
sive quod inclusi rapidi sunt aetheris aestus
quaerentesque viam circum versantur et ignes
passim per caeli volvunt Summania templa;
sive aliunde fluens alicunde extrinsecus aer
versat agens ignis; sive ipsi serpere possunt
quo cuiusque cibus vocat atque invitat euntis,
flammea per caelum pascentis corpora passim.
nam quid in hoc mundo sit eorum ponere certum

503 *Commiscet* Nauger. first for *Commisci.* *haec. hic* Bentl. and Lach.; but see notes 2. 507 *Pontos, mare* Lach. for *ponto mare.* *Ponti mare* Pont. Lamb. ed. 3, *tantum mare* ed. 1 and 2. 513—516 Lach. quite misapprehends and sadly mutilates this passage: 513 he reads *deorsum* for *eodem*, 515 *Hinc* for *Aut*; and places 514 after 516: not one of these changes but mars the sense.

515 *Aut.* *Ast* Nauger. vulg. wrongly. *qui* Mar. Nauger. rightly for *quis.*

518 *lucida* Flor. 31 Ver. Ven. Mar. for *lucia.* 521 *Summania*: see notes 2. *immania* Creech in notes, Lach. Pont. says '*summania* pro *immania*'. *se immania* Avanc. in notes at end of Catullus, Lamb. perversely. I once thought of *summa avia.* 524 *euntis.* *aventis* Lach. 530 *omne* B corr. Mar. Ald. 1

difficile est; sed quid possit fiatque per omne
in variis mundis varia ratione creatis,
id doceo plurisque sequor disponere causas,
motibus astrorum quae possint esse per omne;
e quibus una tamen sit in hoc quoque causa necessest
quae vegeat motum signis; sed quae sit earum
praecipere hautquaquamst pedetemtim progredientis.]
  Terraque ut in media mundi regione quiescat,
evanescere paulatim et decrescere pondus
convenit, atque aliam naturam supter habere
ex ineunte aevo coniunctam atque uniter aptam
partibus aeriis mundi quibus insita vivit.
propterea non est oneri neque deprimit auras;
ut sua cuique homini nullo sunt pondere membra
nec caput est oneri collo nec denique totum
corporis in pedibus pondus sentimus inesse;
at quaecumque foris veniunt inpostaque nobis
pondera sunt laedunt, permulto saepe minora.
usque adeo magni refert quid quaeque obeat res.
sic igitur tellus non est aliena repente
allata atque auris aliunde obiecta alienis,
sed pariter prima concepta ab origine mundi
certaque pars eius, quasi nobis membra videntur.
praeterea grandi tonitru concussa repente,
terra supra quae se sunt concutit omnia motu:
quod facere haut ulla posset ratione, nisi esset
partibus aeriis mundi caeloque revincta.
nam communibus inter se radicibus haerent
ex ineunte aevo coniuncta atque uniter apta.

Junt. for *omnem.* 531 *sit in hoc quoque causa* Ed. for *sit et haec quoque causa*. *siet haec* Lach.: but *haec* has no force and has come from the neighbouring *causa*. *siet hic* Bern. 532 *vegeat* Gif. for *vigeat*. 533 *progredientis* Lamb. for *progredientes*: *est* for *licet* is not Lucretian. 536 *supter*. *subter* Flor. 31 Mar. Junt. for *super*. 538 *vivit*. *crevit* Lach. *sidit* Lamb. ed. 2 and 3 'ex antiquae scripturae quae reperitur in codice Bertin. vestigiis', and Heins. notes that *s*, i.e. the ms. of Modius, has *sidit*, unless I mistake his meaning: but Modius made his collation with the small 2nd ed. of Lamb. so that it is probably a mere oversight; for B has *vivit*. 545 *quid quaeque obeat res* Ed. for *quit queque quaeat res*: Lach. to I 222 gives more than 40 instances in which AB change *b* to *v*: when *obeat* became *oueat*, the further corruption to *queat* was inevitable with capitals. *aveat* Lach. *vehat* Gronovius and Is. Voss. in notes. *gerat* N. P. Howard.

nonne vides etiam quam magno pondere nobis
sustineat corpus tenuissima vis animai
propterea quia tam coniuncta atque uniter apta est?
denique iam saltu pernici tollere corpus
quid potis est nisi vis animi quae membra gubernat?
iamne vides quantum tenuis natura valere
possit, ubi est coniuncta gravi cum corpore, ut aer
coniunctus terris et nobis est animi vis?
  Nec nimio solis maior rota nec minor ardor
esse potest, nostris quam sensibus esse videtur.
nam quibus e spatiis cumque ignes lumina possunt
adicere et calidum membris adflare vaporem,
nil illa his intervallis de corpore libant
flammarum, nil ad speciem est contractior ignis.
573 proinde, calor quoniam solis lumenque profusum
570 perveniunt nostros ad sensus et loca mulcent,
forma quoque hinc solis debet filumque videri,
572 nil adeo ut possis plus aut minus addere, vere.
575 lunaque sive notho fertur loca lumine lustrans
sive suam proprio iactat de corpore lucem,
quidquid id est, nilo fertur maiore figura
quam, nostris oculis qua cernimus, esse videtur.
nam prius omnia, quae longe semota tuemur
aera per multum, specie confusa videntur
quam mi*nui* filum. quapropter luna necesse est,
quandoquidem claram speciem certamque figuram

555 *uniter apta* Pont. Junt. for *uniter aucta*: 558 *uniter apta* for *uniter rapta* B corr. Flor. 31 Camb. etc. as 537. Mar. has first corrected Mon., then written *aucta* above, and then *apta* in marg.; unless the first correction is from Pontanus, the other from Marullus: it is more than probable that Pontanus had the cod. Victor. in his hands before Marullus: comp. 1152. 559 *pernici* Brix. Pont. Mar. Ald. 1 Junt. for *pernice*. *pernice attollere* Flor. 31: a mere conj. 560 *Quid* Lamb. in errata to ed. 3, Faber in his emend. for *Quis*. *animi* Lach. for *animae*; as 563. 563 *Coniunctus* Flor. 31 Camb. Pont. Mar. for *Coniuncta*.

567 *Adicere* (*Adiicere*) Lamb. for *Adlicere*: a confusion of which we have had so many examples. 568 *Nil illa his intervallis* Bern. for *Nihil nisi intervallis*. *Nil ea in his int.* Lach. *Illa ipsa intervalla nihil* Lamb. *Nilque nisi ex int.* Flor. 31 Camb. 3 Vat. Mar. *libant* Mar. Junt. for *librant*. *limant* Lamb. ed. 1 and 2, *librant* ed. 3. 570 (573) brought here by Mar. Ald. 1 Junt. 571 *loca mulcent* Lach. for *loca fulgent*. *loca tingunt* Lamb. 572 *filumque* Lamb. ed. 2 in notes and ed. 3 after Turnebus for *ilumque*. 574=571 (570). 581 *minui filum* Bentl. for *mi*

praebet, ut est oris extremis cumque notata
quantaque quantast hinc nobis videatur in alto.
postremo quoscumque vides hinc aetheris ignes;
quandoquidem quoscumque in terris cernimus *ignes,*
dum tremor *est* clarus, dum cernitur ardor eorum,
perparvom quiddam interdum mutare videtur
alteram utram in partem filum, quo longius absunt;
594 scire licet perquam pauxillo posse minores
esse vel exigua maioris parte brevique.
590 Illud item non est mirandum, qua ratione
tantulus ille queat tantum sol mittere lumen,
quod maria ac terras omnis caelumque rigando
compleat et calido perfundat cuncta vapore.
597 nam licet hinc mundi patefactum totius unum
largifluum fontem scatere atque erumpere lumen,
ex omni mundo quia sic elementa vaporis
undique conveniunt et sic coniectus eorum
confluit, ex uno capite hic ut profluat ardor.
nonne vides etiam quam late parvus aquai
prata riget fons interdum campisque redundet?
est etiam quoque uti non magno solis ab igni
aera percipiat calidis fervoribus ardor,
opportunus ita est si forte et idoneus aer,
ut queat accendi parvis ardoribus ictus;
quod genus interdum segetes stipulamque videmus
accedere ex una scintilla incendia passim.

filum. minimum filum Nicc. vulg. 584 *Quantaque quantast hinc* Eichstädt for *Quanto quoque quantast hinc*, and in the repetition 596 *Quanta quoque est tanta hinc*: 'qua emendatione' says Lach. 'effecit ut hic semel valde laudandus sit'. *Quantaque sit, nobis tanta hinc* Pont. Ald. 1 Junt. *Quanta haec cumque fuat, tanta hinc* Lamb. 586 *ignes* added by Mar. Ald. 1 Junt.: the *ignes* of 585 caused its omission. *horum* Flor. 31 Camb. *flammae* Lach. who says that *ignes* is an unmeaning repetition: but similar repetitions are very common in Lucr. 587 *est* added by Flor. 31 Camb. etc. 588 *videtur* A Nicc. Flor. 31 Camb. Mon. etc. and Lamb. ed. 1. *videntur* B Lamb. ed. 2 and 3, perhaps rightly. 589 *absunt* Lach. for *absit*: a necessary change. *cum longius absint* Lamb. 590 591 (594 595) first brought here by Mar. Ald. 1 Junt. 596=584. 598 *lumen. flumen* Avanc. Lamb. etc. without any authority. 599 *quia* AB. *qua* Nicc. Flor. 31 (Lach. is in error) Camb. Mon. all Vat. Brix. Ver. Ven. Ald. 1 Junt. *quo* Lamb. etc. *vaporis* Lamb. first for *vapore.* 605 *percipiat* Nauger. for *percipitat.* 609 *Accedere* A. *Accidere* B. *Accendere* A corr. Nicc. 2

forsitan et rosea sol alte lampade lucens
possideat multum caecis fervoribus ignem
circum se, nullo qui sit fulgore notatus,
aestifer ut tantum radiorum exaugeat ictum.
Nec ratio solis simplex *et* certa patescit,
quo pacto aestivis e partibus aegocerotis
brumalis adeat flexus atque inde revertens
cancri se ut vertat metas ad solstitialis,
lunaque mensibus id spatium videatur obire,
annua sol in quo consumit tempora cursu.
non, inquam, simplex his rebus reddita causast.
nam fieri vel cum primis id posse videtur,
Democriti quod sancta viri sententia ponit,
quanto quaeque magis sint terram sidera propter,
tanto posse minus cum caeli turbine ferri.
evanescere enim rapidas illius et acris
imminui supter viris, ideoque relinqui
paulatim solem cum posterioribu' signis,
inferior multo quod sit quam fervida signa.
et magis hoc lunam: quanto demissior eius
cursus abest procul a caelo terrisque propinquat,
tanto posse minus cum signis tendere cursum.
flaccidiore etenim quanto iam turbine fertur
inferior quam sol, tanto magis omnia signa
hanc adipiscuntur circum praeterque feruntur.
propterea fit ut haec ad signum quodque reverti
mobilius videatur, ad hanc quia signa revisunt.
fit quoque ut e mundi transversis partibus aer
alternis certo fluere alter tempore possit,
qui queat aestivis solem detrudere signis
brumalis usque ad flexus gelidumque rigorem,
et qui reiciat gelidis a frigoris umbris

Vat. Ver. Ven. *Accendi* Flor. 31 Camb. 3 Vat. Brix. Pont. Avanc. Nauger. *Accipere* Mar. Junt. Lamb.: see II 1025. 610 *et*. *e* Lach. who will never tolerate *et* for *etiam*. 613 *Aestifer ut tantum* Flor. 31 3 Vat. Mar. Junt. for *Aestiferi utantum* B, *utantur* A Nicc. *Aestiferum ut tantum* Avanc. Lamb. etc. *Aestiferum tantum* Nauger. 614 *simplex et certa* Ed. for *simplex recta*. *simplex nec certa* Lamb. *simplex aut recta* Flor. 31 Camb. 3 Vat. *ac recta* or *et recta* others. *simplex rellata* Lach. *reclusa* Bern. 617 *Cancri se* Lach. for *Canceris*. 632 *etenim* Lach.

aestiferas usque in partis et fervida signa.
et ratione pari lunam stellasque putandumst,
quae volvunt magnos in magnis orbibus annos,
aeribus posse alternis e partibus ire.
nonne vides etiam diversis nubila ventis
diversas ire in partis inferna supernis?
qui minus illa queant per magnos aetheris orbis
aestibus inter se diversis sidera ferri?
At nox obruit ingenti caligine terras,
aut ubi de longo cursu sol ultima caeli
impulit atque suos efflavit languidus ignis
concussos itere et labefactos aere multo,
aut quia sub terras cursum convortere cogit
vis eadem, supra quae terras pertulit orbem.
Tempore item certo roseam Matuta per oras
aetheris auroram differt et lumina pandit,
aut quia sol idem, sub terras ille revertens,
anticipat caelum radiis accendere temptans,
aut quia conveniunt ignes et semina multa
confluere ardoris consuerunt tempore certo,
quae faciunt solis nova semper lumina gigni;
quod genus Idaeis fama est e montibus altis
dispersos ignis orienti lumine cerni,
inde coire globum quasi in unum et conficere orbem.
nec tamen illud in his rebus mirabile debet
esse, quod haec ignis tam certo tempore possunt
semina confluere et solis reparare nitorem.
multa videmus enim, certo quae tempore fiunt
omnibus in rebus. florescunt tempore certo
arbusta et certo dimittunt tempore florem.
nec minus in certo dentes cadere imperat aetas
tempore et inpubem molli pubescere veste
et pariter mollem malis demittere barbam.
fulmina postremo nix imbres nubila venti

for *etiam*. 648 *illa* Flor. 31 Camb. Pont. Mar. for *ille*. 651 *sol ultima* Camb. Vat. 1136 and 1954 Othob. for *solvet ima caeli*. *sol extima* Flor. 31 Mar. Ald. 1 Junt. etc. Politian in marg. Flor. 29 has both *ultima* and *extima*.

656 *Matuta* Pont. Mar. Ald. 1 Junt. for *matura*. 667 *possunt* Lach. for *possit*. *possint* vulg. contrary to the unvarying usage of Lucr. 675 *Fulmina*

non nimis incertis fiunt in partibus anni.
namque ubi sic fuerunt causarum exordia prima,
atque ita res mundi cecidere ab origine prima,
consequë quoque iam redeunt ex ordine certo.
  Crescere itemque dies licet et tabescere noctes,
et minui luces, cum sumant augmina noctes,
aut quia sol idem sub terras atque superne
imparibus currens amfractibus aetheris oras
partit et in partis non aequas dividit orbem,
et quod ab alterutra detraxit parte, reponit
eius in adversa tanto plus parte relatus,
donec ad id signum caeli pervenit, ubi anni
nodus nocturnas exaequat lucibus umbras.
nam, medio cursu flatus aquilonis et austri,
distinet aequato caelum discrimine metas
propter signiferi posituram totius orbis,
annua sol in quo concludit tempora serpens,
obliquo terras et caelum lumine lustrans,
ut ratio declarat eorum qui loca caeli
omnia dispositis signis ornata notarunt.
aut quia crassior est certis in partibus aer,
sub terris ideo tremulum iubar haesitat ignis
nec penetrare potest facile atque emergere ad ortus.
propterea noctes hiberno tempore longae
cessant, dum veniat radiatum insigne diei.
aut etiam, quia sic alternis partibus anni
tardius et citius consuerunt confluere ignes
qui faciunt solem certa desurgere parte,
propterea fit uti videantur dicere verum
. . . .

Mar. Ald. 1 Junt. first for *Flumina*. 679 *Consequë quoque iam redeunt* Lach. for *Consequiae quoque iam rerum*: a brilliant emendation. *Consequae* 2 Vat. Ver. Ven. *Consequa natura est iam rerum* Flor. 31 Camb. 3 Vat. Mar. vulg. *Consequitur quoque iam series* Pont. 689—693 Lach. has quite causelessly altered this passage in many points: 690 for *metas* he reads *metans* as Pont. before him: [*caeli* Mar. for *caelum*:] 692 and 693 he inverts, 693 for *obliquo* he reads *obliqui*, joining it with *orbis*: he will not have *serpens*, *lustrans* in apposition any more than 524 *euntis*, *pascentis*; or VI 1141 *veniens*, *ortus*, and 1260 *languens*, *conveniens*; though suchlike constructions are common in Lucr. and in Cicero's Aratea which Lucr. often imitates. 692 *concludit* Lach. for *contudit*. *contundit* Mon. Brix. vulg. 700 *diei* Nicc. for *dici*. 704 it seems to me manifest that the poet

Luna potest solis radiis percussa nitere
inque dies magis *id* lumen convertere nobis
ad speciem, quantum solis secedit ab orbi,
donique eum contra pleno bene lumine fulsit
atque oriens obitus eius super edita vidit;
inde minutatim retro quasi condere lumen
debet item, quanto propius iam solis ad ignem
labitur ex alia signorum parte per orbem;
ut faciunt, lunam qui fingunt esse pilai
consimilem cursusque viam sub sole tenere.
est etiam quare proprio cum lumine possit
volvier et varias splendoris reddere formas.
corpus enim licet esse aliud quod fertur et una
labitur omnimodis occursans officiensque
nec potis est cerni, quia cassum lumine fertur.
versarique potest, globus ut, si forte, pilai
dimidia ex parti candenti lumine tinctus,
versandoque globum variantis edere formas,
donique eam partem, quaecumque est ignibus aucta,
ad speciem vertit nobis oculosque patentis;
inde minutatim retro contorquet et aufert
luciferam partem glomeraminis atque pilai;
ut Babylonica Chaldaeum doctrina refutans
astrologorum artem contra convincere tendit,
proinde quasi id fieri nequeat quod pugnat uterque
aut minus hoc illo sit cur amplectier ausis.
denique cur nequeat semper nova luna creari
ordine formarum certo certisque figuris
inque dies privos aborisci quaeque creata

refers to 660—665, and that a verse is lost such as this, *Qui faciunt solis nova semper lumina gigni*: probably its resemblance to 703 caused its omission. Lach. strangely supposes the sentence complete and joins 704 with 703, as if anybody could ever deny that the sun rose in a certain quarter: 704 which by itself has no meaning was placed after 714 by Nauger. followed by all before Lach. 705 *percussa* Flor. 31 Camb. before Lamb. for *perculsa.* 706 *magis id lumen* Lach. for *magis lumen. magis hoc* Flor. 31. *maius* Mar. Ald. 1 Junt. vulg. *magis: et lumen* Pont. Nauger. 708 723 *Donique. Donicum* Lamb. wrongly in both places. 711 *iam* Mar. Ald. 1 Junt. for *tam.* 720 *ut, si forte. ut sit forte* Lach. after J. Dousa fil. 'sine ulla causa et cum orationis sententiaeque detrimento' says Madvig emend. Liv. p. 123. 727 *Babylonica* Flor. 31 Pont. Mar. for *Babylonisa. Chaldaeum* Avanc. *Chaldeum* AB. *Chaldeam* A corr. Nicc. Flor.

atque alia illius reparari in parte locoque,
difficilest ratione docere et vincere verbis,
ordine cum *possint* tam certo multa creari.
it ver et Venus, et Veneris praenuntius ante
pennatus graditur, zephyri vestigia propter
Flora quibus mater praespargens ante viai
cuncta coloribus egregiis et odoribus opplet.
inde loci sequitur calor aridus et comes una
pulverulenta Ceres *et* etesia flabra aquilonum.
inde autumnus adit, graditur simul Euhius Euan.
inde aliae tempestates ventique secuntur,
altitonans Volturnus et auster fulmine pollens.
tandem bruma nives adfert pigrumque rigorem
reddit: hiemps sequitur crepitans hanc dentibus algu.
quo minus est mirum si certo tempore luna
gignitur et certo deletur tempore rusus,
cum fieri possint tam certo tempore multa.
  Solis item quoque defectus lunaeque latebras
pluribus e causis fieri tibi posse putandumst.
nam cur luna queat terram secludere solis
lumine et a terris altum caput obstruere ei,
obiciens caecum radiis ardentibus orbem;
tempore eodem aliud facere id non posse putetur
corpus quod cassum labatur lumine semper?
solque suos etiam dimittere languidus ignis
tempore cur certo nequeat recreareque lumen,
cum loca praeteriit flammis infesta per auras,
quae faciunt ignis interstingui atque perire?

31 Camb. etc. 733 *aborisci*. *abolisci* AB. *abolesci* Mar. Junt. *aboriri* Brix. Pont. Avanc. *abolescere* Lamb. 736 *possint* added by Lach.: see 750: *videas* by Flor. 31 Camb. Mar. vulg. 737 *Veneris*. *veris* Pont. Bentl. Wak. Lach. 738 *zephyri*. *zephyrus* Pont. Mar. Ald. 1 Junt. vulgo Lach.: but see notes 2. 742 *Pulverulenta Ceres* Pont. Mar. Ald. 1 Junt. for *Pulverunta Ceres*. *et* added by Mar. Ald. 1 Junt. 747 *Reddit* Flor. 31 Camb. for *Redit*. *Prodit hiemps*, Lach. *crepitans* Flor. 31 Vat. Mon. Brix. for *creditans*. *hanc* B rightly. *ac* A. *accentibus algi* Nicc. Flor. 31 Camb. Mon. Vat. Junt. *algu* Bergk for *algi*. *algus* Lamb. *algor* Lach. 750 *fieri* Mar. Ald. 1 Junt. for *fleri*. *florere queant* one Vat.

753 *solis* Lamb. first for *possis*. *posces* Mar. Ald. 1 Junt. 761 *perire* Mar. Ald. 1 Junt. for *periri*. Fleckeisen krit. miscellen p. 55 defends *periri* on the analogy of *fieri*, for which Ennius ann. 15 has *fiere*, and of *vēniri* sometimes used for *vēnire*: but the scribe was unconsciously misled by the other infinitive.

et cur terra queat lunam spoliare vicissim
lumine et oppressum solem super ipsa tenere,
menstrua dum rigidas coni perlabitur umbras;
tempore eodem aliut nequeat succurrere lunae
corpus vel supra solis perlabier orbem,
quod radios interrumpat lumenque profusum?
et tamen ipsa suo si fulget luna nitore,
cur nequeat certa mundi languescere parte,
dum loca luminibus propriis inimica per exit?
  Quod superest, quoniam magni per caerula mundi
qua fieri quicquid posset ratione resolvi,
solis uti varios cursus lunaeque meatus
noscere possemus quae vis et causa cieret,
quove modo *possent* offecto lumine obire
et neque opinantis tenebris obducere terras,
cum quasi conivent et aperto lumine rursum
omnia convisunt clara loca candida luce,
nunc redeo ad mundi novitatem et mollia terrae
arva, novo fetu quid primum in luminis oras
tollere et incertis crerint committere ventis.
  Principio genus herbarum viridemque nitorem
terra dedit circum collis camposque per omnis,
florida fulserunt viridanti prata colore,
arboribusque datumst variis exinde per auras
crescendi magnum inmissis certamen habenis.
ut pluma atque pili primum saetaeque creantur
quadripedum membris et corpore pennipotentum,
sic nova tum tellus herbas virgultaque primum
sustulit, inde loci mortalia saecla creavit
multa modis multis varia ratione coorta.
nam neque de caelo cecidisse animalia possunt
nec terrestria de salsis exisse lacunis.
linquitur ut merito maternum nomen adepta
terra sit, e terra quoniam sunt cuncta creata.
multaque nunc etiam existunt animalia terris

768 *fulget*. *fulgit* Lamb. Lach. 771=764. 776 *possent* added by Brix. *soleant* (not *valeant*) Flor. 31 Camb. Mar. Ald. 1 Junt. Nauger. Lamb. Gif. Creech Wak. 782 *Tollere et* Pont. Mar. Ald. 1 Junt. for *Tolleret*. *crerint committere* Orelli ecl. poet. Lat., Madvig in Henrichsen de frag. Gott. p. 36, Lach. all

imbribus et calido solis concreta vapore;
quo minus est mirum si tum sunt plura coorta
et maiora, nova tellure atque aethere adulta.
principio genus alituum variaeque volucres
ova relinquebant exclusae tempore verno,
folliculos ut nunc teretis aestate cicadae
lincunt sponte sua victum vitamque petentes.
tum tibi terra dedit primum mortalia saecla.
multus enim calor atque umor superabat in arvis.
hoc ubi quaeque loci regio opportuna dabatur,
crescebant uteri terram radicibus apti;
quos ubi tempore maturo patefecerat aestus
infantum fugiens umorem aurasque petessens,
convertebat ibi natura foramina terrae
et sucum venis cogebat fundere apertis
consimilem lactis, sicut nunc femina quaeque
cum peperit, dulci repletur lacte, quod omnis
impetus in mammas convertitur ille alimenti.
terra cibum pueris, vestem vapor, herba cubile
praebebat multa et molli lanugine abundans.
at novitas mundi nec frigora dura ciebat
nec nimios aestus nec magnis viribus auras.
omnia enim pariter crescunt et robora sumunt.
  Quare etiam atque etiam maternum nomen adepta
terra tenet merito, quoniam genus ipsa creavit
humanum atque animal prope certo tempore fudit
omne quod in magnis bacchatur montibu passim,
aeriasque simul volucres variantibu' formis.
sed quia finem aliquam pariendi debet habere,
destitit, ut mulier spatio defessa vetusto.
mutat enim mundi naturam totius aetas
ex alioque alius status excipere omnia debet,

three independently for *credunt committere*. *tentaret credere* Lamb. 800 *maiora* Pont. Mar. Avanc. in notes at end of Catullus, Junt. for *maiore*. 805 *primum*. *passim* Lach. without any necessity. 808 *terram* AB Nicc. rightly. *terrae* vulg. before Lach. 809 *aestus* Lach. for *aestas*. *aetas* Mar. Ald. 1 Junt. vulg. 812 *Et* Flor. 31 Camb. for *Ut*. 823 *animal* Mar. Ald. 1 Junt. for *anima*. *animas* A corr. Nicc. all later mss. *animans* Wak.: but *animans* is feminine in Lucr. 824 *magnis* Flor. 31 Camb. Mon. Pont. for *magni*. 825

nec manet ulla sui similis res: omnia migrant,
omnia commutat natura et vertere cogit.
namque aliut putrescit et aevo debile languet,
porro aliut clarescit et *e* contemptibus exit.
sic igitur mundi naturam totius aetas
mutat et ex alio terram status excipit alter:
quod potuit nequit, ut possit quod non tulit ante.
Multaque tum tellus etiam portenta creare
conatast mira facie membrisque coorta,
androgynum, interutrasque nec utrum, utrimque remotum,
orba pedum partim, manuum viduata vicissim,
muta sine ore etiam, sine voltu caeca reperta,
vinctaque membrorum per totum corpus adhaesu,
nec facere ut possent quicquam nec cedere quoquam
nec vitare malum nec sumere quod foret usus.
cetera de genere hoc monstra ac portenta creabat,
nequiquam, quoniam natura absterruit auctum
nec potuere cupitum aetatis tangere florem
nec reperire cibum nec iungi per Veneris res.
multa videmus enim rebus concurrere debere,
ut propagando possint procudere saecla;
pabula primum ut sint, genitalia deinde per artus
semina qua possint membris manare remissis;
feminaque ut maribus coniungi possit, habere
mutua qui mutent inter se gaudia uterque.
Multaque tum interiisse animantum saecla necessest
nec potuisse propagando procudere prolem.
nam quaecumque vides vesci vitalibus auris,
aut dolus aut virtus aut denique mobilitas est

Aeriasque Mar. Ald. 1 Junt. for *Aeriaeque.* 833 *clarescit* Lach. for *crescit*: he also suggests *succrescit*, which may be right: or *tum crescit*. *concrescit* Ald. 1 Junt. not Pont. or Mar. *e* added by Mar. Ald. 1 Junt. 836 *Quod potuit nequit, ut* Ed. for *Quod potuit nequeat*. *pote uti nequeat* Lach. *tulit ut* Bentl. 838 *facie* Flor. 31 Brix. for *facit*. 839 *interutrasque*. *interutraque* Lach. *Androgynum, interutraque nec utrum, utrimque remotum* Lach. most acutely for *Androgynem inter utras nec utramque utrumque remotum*. *Androgynem interutra neutrumque utrinque remotam* Mar.: *utrinque* is in Brix. 841 *Muta* Nauger. for *Multa*.

844 *foret usus* Lamb. for *volet usus*, as IV 831. 852 *remissis*. *remissa* Lach. 853 *coniungi possit, habere*. *coniungi possit avere* Lach.: a most awkward phrase: the wish of the female is not important. 854 *Mutua qui*

ex ineunte aevo genus id tuta*ta* reservans.
multaque sunt, nobis ex utilitate sua quae
commendata manent, tutelae tradita nostrae.
principio genus acre leonum saevaque saecla
tutatast virtus, volpes dolus et fuga cervos.
at levisomna canum fido cum pectore corda
et genus omne quod est veterino semine partum
lanigeraeque simul pecudes et bucera saecla
omnia sunt hominum tutelae tradita, Memmi.
nam cupide fugere feras pacemque secuta
sunt et larga suo sine pabula parta labore,
quae damus utilitatis eorum praemia causa.
at quis nil horum tribuit natura, nec ipsa
sponte sua possent ut vivere nec dare nobis
utilitatem aliquam quare pateremur eorum
praesidio nostro pasci genus esseque tutum,
scilicet haec aliis praedae lucroque iacebant
indupedita suis fatalibus omnia vinclis,
donec ad interitum genus id natura redegit.
  Sed neque Centauri fuerunt, nec tempore in ullo
esse queunt duplici natura et corpore bino
ex alienigenis membris compacta, potestas
hinc illinc vis*que* ut non sat par esse potissit.
id licet hinc quamvis hebeti cognoscere corde.
principio circum tribus actis impiger annis
floret ecus, puer hautquaquam; nam saepe etiam nunc
ubera mammarum in somnis lactantia quaeret.

mutent Bern. for *Mutua qui metuent. Mutua quis nectent* Mar. Ald. 1 Junt. *nectant* Nauger. Lamb. *Mutuaque insinuent* Lach. 859 *tutata* Brix. Pont. Mar. Ald. 1 Junt. for *tuta.* 863 *et fuga* B Avanc. *ut fuga* A Nicc. Mon. Junt. 865 *veterino* Nonius Pont. Mar. Avanc. Junt. *veteri non* mss. 868 *secuta* Lamb. in errata to ed. 3 first for *secutae.* 871 *nil* Pont. Mar. Ald. 1 Junt. for *ni* A, *in* B. 880 *potestas Hinc illinc visq. ut non sat par esse potissit* Ed. for *potestas Hinc illinc par vis ut non sat* (B, *sit* A) *pars esse potissit*: *par* I assume was written in the margin to take the place of the unmeaning *pars*, and thus got into the text: so above 117 *pars esse* mss. for *par esse*; and II 1017 *par* for *pars. p. H. i. partis ut si par e. p.* Lach. which I hardly understand. Lamb. reads *queat* for *queunt* after Mar. Ald. 1 and Junt. joining *potestas* with what precedes, and ed. 3 has *Hinc illinc par vis ut non sic esse potissit. p. H. i. parilis quis non superesse potissit* Bern. 884 *hautquaquam* Nicc. for *hautquamquam. nam* om. A Nicc. and later mss.: hence *quia* Avanc. *quin* Mar. Junt. Lamb. etc. *haut ita quamquam*

post ubi ecum validae vires aetate senecta
membraque deficiunt fugienti languida vita,
tum demum puero illi aevo florente iuventas
occipit et molli vestit lanugine malas.
ne forte ex homine et veterino semine equorum
confieri credas Centauros posse neque esse,
aut rabidis canibus succinctas semimarinis
corporibus Scyllas et cetera de genere horum,
inter se quorum discordia membra videmus;
quae neque florescunt pariter nec robora sumunt
corporibus neque proiciunt aetate senecta
nec simili Venere ardescunt nec moribus unis
conveniunt, neque sunt eadem iucunda per artus.
quippe videre licet pinguescere saepe cicuta
barbigeras pecudes, homini quae est acre venenum.
flamma quidem *vero* cum corpora fulva leonum
tam soleat torrere atque urere quam genus omne
visceris in terris quodcumque et sanguinis extet,
qui fieri potuit, triplici cum corpore ut una,
prima leo, postrema draco, media ipsa, Chimaera
ore foras acrem flaret de corpore flammam?
quare etiam tellure nova caeloque recenti
talia qui fingit potuisse animalia gigni,
nixus in hoc uno novitatis nomine inani,
multa licet simili ratione effutiat ore,
aurea tum dicat per terras flumina vulgo
fluxisse et gemmis florere arbusta suësse
aut hominem tanto membrorum esse impete natum,
trans maria alta pedum nisus ut ponere posset
et manibus totum circum se vertere caelum.
nam quod multa fuere in terris semina rerum

Flor. 31 Camb. 885 *lactantia* Flor. 31 Mon. Ver. Ven. for *laetantia*. *quaeret*. *quaerit* Mon. Pont. Ald. 1 Junt. Lamb. 888 *puero illi* Ed. for *puerili*. *pueris* Avanc. Lamb. Lach.; perhaps Lucr. wrote *puero li*. 889 *Occipit* Mar. Ald. 1 Junt. for *Officit*. 892 *rabidis* Heins. in ms. notes, and Bentl. for *rapidis*: see IV 712. 896 *proiciunt* Lamb. in notes to ed. 2 and in ed. 3, after Turnebus, for *proficiunt*. 901 *vero* added by Ald. 1 Junt. (not Pont. or Mar.) vulg. *Denique f. q.* Lach. *Ardua*, *Ignea* others. 904 *ut una* Brix. Pont. Avanc. for *ut unam*. *iuncta* Mar. Junt. 906 *foras* Nauger. for *feras*. *ferox* Pont. Junt. *ferens* Mar. 914 *ponere* B corr. Mar. Junt. for *pondere*. *pandere* Avanc. 923

tempore quo primum tellus animalia fudit,
nil tamen est signi mixtas potuisse creari
inter se pecudes compactaque membra animantum,
propterea quia quae de terris nunc quoque abundant
herbarum genera ac fruges arbustaque laeta
non tamen inter se possunt complexa creari,
sed res quaeque suo ritu procedit et omnes
foedere naturae certo discrimina servant.
At genus humanum multo fuit illud in arvis
durius, ut decuit, tellus quod dura creasset,
et maioribus et solidis magis ossibus intus
fundatum, validis aptum per viscera nervis,
nec facile ex aestu nec frigore quod caperetur
nec novitate cibi nec labi corporis ulla.
multaque per caelum solis volventia lustra
volgivago vitam tractabant more ferarum.
nec robustus erat curvi moderator aratri
quisquam, nec scibat ferro molirier arva
nec nova defodere in terram virgulta neque altis
arboribus veteres decidere falcibu' ramos.
quod sol atque imbres dederant, quod terra crearat
sponte sua, satis id placabat pectora donum.
glandiferas inter curabant corpora quercus
plerumque; et quae nunc hiberno tempore cernis
arbita puniceo fieri matura colore,
plurima tum tellus etiam maiora ferebat.
multaque praeterea novitas tum florida mundi
pabula dura tulit, miseris mortalibus ampla.
at sedare sitim fluvii fontesque vocabant,
ut nunc montibus e magnis decursus aquai
claru' citat late sitientia saecla ferarum.
denique nota vagi silvestria templa tenebant

Sed res quaeque Ed. for *Sed si quaeque. Sed sic quodque* Mar. (*sic* Pont.). *Res sic* Lamb. *Sed vis* Lach. 925 *At* Lach. for *Et*; and the change seems necessary. 934 *molirier* Brix. Junt. for *mollerier. mollirier* Pont. Mar. as A corr. 944 *dura* Vat. 3276 Nauger. for *dira*: a certain correction. *dia* Avanc. 947 *Claru' citat late* Forbiger for *Claricitati a te. Clarior accitat* Flor. 31 2 Vat. Mar. Ald. 1 Junt. Lamb. ed. 1 and 2. *Claricitat late* Lamb. ed. 3 after Sim. Bosius. *Clarior invitat* Politian in marg. Flor. 29. *Clarigitat late* Lach. who sneers at Forbiger: but see notes 2. 948 *nota vagi silvestria* Lach.

nympharum, quibus e scibant umori' fluenta
lubrica proluvie larga lavere umida saxa,
umida saxa, super viridi stillantia musco,
et partim plano scatere atque erumpere campo.
nĕcdum res igni scibant tractare neque uti
pellibus et spoliis corpus vestire ferarum,
sed nemora atque cavos montis silvasque colebant
et frutices inter condebant squalida membra
verbera ventorum vitare imbrisque coacti.
nec commune bonum poterant spectare neque ullis
moribus inter se scibant nec legibus uti.
quod cuique obtulerat praedae fortuna, ferebat
sponte sua sibi quisque valere et vivere doctus.
et Venus in silvis iungebat corpora amantum;
conciliabat enim vel mutua quamque cupido
vel violenta viri vis atque inpensa libido
vel pretium, glandes atque arbita vel pira lecta.
et manuum mira freti virtute pedumque
consectabantur silvestria saecla ferarum
975 missilibus saxis et magno pondere clavae;
968 multaque vincebant, vitabant pauca latebris;
saetigerisque pares subu' *sic* silvestria membra
nuda *da*bant terrae nocturno tempore capti,
circum se foliis ac frondibus involventes.
nec plangore diem magno solemque per agros
quaerebant pavidi palantes noctis in umbris,

for *n. vagis s.* *noctivagi* Nauger. (not Junt.) vulg. *nocte vagi* Bentl. 949 *quibus escibant* AB Vat. 1706 Reg. ('Nic. Heinsii'). *quibus e scibant* Lach. first after them. *aestibant* Nicc. *excibant* Camb. Pont. *exibant* Flor. 31. *umori'* Bentl. Lach. for *umore*. 962 *iungebat* Nicc. for *lugebat*. *lugebat* (*iungebat*) Ver. Ven. 968 (975) first brought to this place by Nauger. not Avanc. who like Mar. and Junt. places it after 961. 970 *subu' sic silvestria* Ed. for *subus silvestria*: *sic* could easily fall out in this position. *suibus* Camb. Ver. Ven. vulg.; but Lucr. uses *sŭbus* in VI 974 977: Luc. Mueller de re metr. p. 350 defends *sūbus*, from Varro Eumen. 22 *An colubrae an volvae de Albuci subus Athenis*. Lach. deals with this passage in a most arbitrary way: he splits 970 (969) into two verses, supposes the end of one and the beginning of the other to be lost and inserts 968 (975) between them: thus *S. p. s.* [*ardorique leonum*] *M. s. e. m. p. c.* [*Inde cavis temere abiecti*] *s. m.*: a more unconvincing note than his I never read, or more sophistical objections to the present text. 971 *Nuda dabant* Lamb. ed. 3 first for *Nudabant* which Wak. indignantly restores, making these simple sons of earth unclothe their naked limbs and rival the

974 sed taciti respectabant somnoque sepulti,
976 dum rosea face sol inferret lumina caelo.
a parvis quod enim consuerant cernere semper
alterno tenebras et lucem tempore gigni,
non erat ut fieri posset mirarier umquam
nec diffidere ne terras aeterna teneret
nox in perpetuum detracto lumine solis.
sed magis illud erat curae, quod saecla ferarum
infestam miseris faciebant saepe quietem.
eiectique domo fugiebant saxea tecta
spumigeri suis adventu validique leonis
atque intempesta cedebant nocte paventes
hospitibus saevis instrata cubilia fronde.
  Nec nimio tum plus quam nunc mortalia saecla
dulcia linquebant labentis lumina vitae.
unus enim tum quisque magis deprensus eorum
pabula viva feris praebebat, dentibus haustus,
et nemora ac montis gemitu silvasque replebat
viva videns vivo sepeliri viscera busto.
at quos effugium servarat corpore adeso,
posterius tremulas super ulcera taetra tenentes
palmas horriferis accibant vocibus Orcum,
donique eos vita privarant vermina saeva
expertis opis, ignaros quid volnera vellent.
at non multa virum sub signis milia ducta
una dies dabat exitio nec turbida ponti
aequora fligebant navis ad saxa virosque.
hic temere incassum frustra mare saepe coortum
saevibat leviterque minas ponebat inanis,

famed exploit of Prince Vortigern's grandsire. 976 *rosea* Flor. 31 Brix. Pont. Mar. for *rotea*. 984 *Eiectique* Flor. 31 Camb. etc. for *Electique* B, *Et lectique* A Nicc. 985 *validique*. *validive* Lach.; but comp. 987 *Hospitibus saevis* in plur. 989 *labentis* Muretus Lamb. Lach. for *lamentis*. 993 *vivo* Flor. 31 Camb. Mon. etc. for *vino*. 995 *ulcera* Flor. 31 Camb. Mar. for *vicerat*. *viscera* A corr. Nicc. Ver. Ven. 997 *Donique* Is. Voss. in ms. notes, Lach. for *Denique*. *Doniquom* Heins. in ms. notes. *Donec* Mar. Junt. *Donicum* Lamb. 1001 *fligebant* Lach. for *lidebant*. *ledebant* A corr. Camb. Mon. Ver. Ven. *laedebant* vulg. *lidebant* may be from Lucr.: see notes 2. 1002 *Hic* Lach. for *Nec*. *Sed* Lamb. The rest of this verse is quite causelessly altered by Mar. Junt. Lamb.
1003 *ponebat* Mar. Ald. 1 Junt. for *potebas*. *poscebat* Flor. 31 Camb. 1006

nec poterat quemquam placidi pellacia ponti
subdola pellicere in fraudem ridentibus undis,
improba naucleri ratio cum caeca iacebat.
tum penuria deinde cibi languentia leto
membra dabat, contra nunc rerum copia mersat.
illi *in*prudentes ipsi sibi saepe venenum
vergebant, nu*rui nunc* dant sollertius ipsi.
  Inde casas postquam ac pellis ignemque pararunt,
et mulier coniuncta viro concessit in unum
. . . .
cognita sunt, prolemque ex se videre creatam,
tum genus humanum primum mollescere coepit.
ignis enim curavit ut alsia corpora frigus
non ita iam possent caeli sub tegmine ferre,
et Venus inminuit viris puerique parentum
blanditiis facile ingenium fregere superbum.
tunc et amicitiem coeperunt iungere aventes
finitimi inter se nec laedere nec violari,
et pueros commendarunt muliebreque saeclum,
vocibus et gestu cum balbe significarent
imbecillorum esse aecum misererier omnis.
nec tamen omnimodis poterat concordia gigni,

naucleri ratio cum Ed. for *navigii ratio tum.* The v. is ejected by Lach. as spurious: the *ri* of *naucleri* was absorbed in *ratio*; and then the corruption was easy.

1008 *dabat* Flor. 31 Camb. for *daeant* B, *deant* A. *dedant* Nicc. Ver. Ven. 1009 *Illi imprudentes* Mar. Ald. 1 Junt. for *Illi prudentes.* 1010 *nurui nunc dant sollertius ipsi* Ed. for *nudant sollertius ipsi*, the scribe having omitted the similar letters: *ipsi* is dat.; see notes 2. *nuptis nunc dant sollertiu' sponsi* Ed. in small ed. *nunc se nudant s. ipsi* Lach. which can hardly be right. *nunc dant letum sol. ipso* Mar. *nunc dant aliis sol. ipsi* Junt. vulg. and Ed. in ed. 1; but *ipsi* is then solecistic.

1011 *casas* Flor. 31 Camb. Mon. Brix. Pont. for *cassas. pellis* (*pelles*) Mon. Brix. Ver. Ven. for *pellus. pelvis* Flor. 31 Camb. 1012 a verse is lost here of this nature *Hospitium, ac lecti socialia iura duobus*: see notes 2. Mar. Ald. 1 Junt. vulg. give *Castaque privatae Veneris connubia laeta.* 1013 *Cognita sunt. Conubium* Lach. *Coniugium* Bern. 1016 *ferre* Flor. 31 Camb. Pont. Mar. for *ferri.*

1019 *amicitiem* A Nicc. Flor. 31 Camb. Gif. *amicitiam* B Mon. Avanc. at end of Catullus, Junt. Lamb. *aventes Finitimi inter se. habentes* A corr. Nicc. Flor. 31 Camb. etc. *Finitim* A Nicc. Ver. Ven.: hence though Mar. Junt. rightly read *aventes*, yet Nauger. Lamb. Creech Wak. vulg. before Lach. keep the absurd *habentes. Finitima* Brix. Pont. Ald. 1 Nauger. Lamb. vulg. but *Finitimi* B Camb. Mar. rightly. *violari* Lach. for *violare.* 1023 *omnis* (*omneis*) Mar. Junt. for *omni*: a certain correction, yet strange to say Nauger. Lamb. etc. have adopted the

sed bona magnaque pars servabat foedera caste;
aut genus humanum iam tum foret omne peremptum
nec potuisset adhuc perducere saecla propago.
  At varios linguae sonitus natura subegit
mittere et utilitas expressit nomina rerum,
non alia longe ratione atque ipsa videtur
protrahere ad gestum pueros infantia linguae,
cum facit ut digito quae sint praesentia monstrent.
sentit enim vim quisque suam quoad possit abuti.
cornua nata prius vitulo quam frontibus extent,
illis iratus petit atque infestus inurget.
at catuli pantherarum scymnique leonum
unguibus ac pedibus iam tum morsuque repugnant,
vix etiam cum sunt dentes unguesque creati.
alituum porro genus alis omne videmus
fidere et a pinnis tremulum petere auxiliatum.
proinde putare aliquem tum nomina distribuisse
rebus et inde homines didicisse vocabula prima,
desiperest. nam cur hic posset cuncta notare
vocibus et varios sonitus emittere linguae,
tempore eodem alii facere id non quisse putentur?
praeterea si non alii quoque vocibus usi
inter se fuerant, unde insita notities est
utilitatis et unde data est huic prima potestas,
quid vellet facere ut sciret animoque videret?

omnium of one Vat. and Ald. 1 1025 *caste* Flor. 31 for *casti*. *servabant casti* Mar. Junt. Lamb. vulg. contrary to usage of Lucr. 1032 *monstrent* Mar. or Mon. and Junt. for *monstret*. Flor. 30 has the mark of *n* over the *e*, but whether from the hand of Nicc. I could not tell. 1033 *vim* Brix. (?) Ver. Ven. Avanc. for *vis*. *vi...sua* Flor. 31 Mar. Junt. *vis...suas* Luc. Mueller de re metr. p. 382, perhaps rightly: comp. II 586 III 265. *quod* i.e. *quoad* AB. *quam* Avanc. Lamb. in all 3 eds. Creech etc.: Lamb. says in his notes that he had once thought of *quoad*, but much preferred *quam*. 1035 *infestus* Flor. 31 Mar. Junt. Nauger. Wak. Lach. for *infessus*. *infensus* Mon. Pont. Avanc. Lamb.: but *infestus* is a Lucretian word, *infensus* not 1038 *Vix etiam cum* Mar. Junt. for *Vix tiam cum* B, *Vix iam cum* A Nicc. etc. *Vix quoque iam cum* Flor. 31. *Vix iam etiam cum* Avanc. *Vix iam cum ipsis* Pont. Nauger. Lamb. ed. 1 and 2; *Vix dum etiam cum* ed. 3.

1039 *porro* Ald. 1 Junt. for *proporro*. 1040 *pinnis* B, *pennis* A Nonius Nicc. (VI 834 *pinnarum* A, *pennarum* B). 1048 *Utilitatis et* Mar. Avanc. Junt. for *Utilitas et*. Ald. 1 has the misprint *Utilitatis etiam*, but Avanc. corrects it at end of his Catullus. Lach. takes no notice of this and similar corrections, though his

cogere item pluris unus victosque domare
non poterat, rerum ut perdiscere nomina vellent.
nec ratione docere ulla suadereque surdis,
quid sit opus facto, facilest; neque enim paterentur
nec ratione ulla sibi ferrent amplius auris
vocis inauditos sonitus obtundere frustra.
postremo quid in hac mirabile tantoperest re,
si genus humanum, cui vox et lingua vigeret,
pro vario sensu varia res voce notaret?
cum pecudes mutae, cum denique saecla ferarum
dissimilis soleant voces variasque ciere,
cum metus aut dolor est et cum iam gaudia gliscunt.
quippe etenim licet id rebus cognoscere apertis.
inritata canum cum primum magna Molossum
mollia ricta fremunt duros nudantia dentes,
longe alio sonitu rabie *re*stricta minantur,
et cum iam latrant et vocibus omnia complent.
et catulos blande cum lingua lambere temptant
aut ubi eos iactant pedibus morsuque petentes
suspensis teneros imitantur dentibus haustus,
longe alio pacto gannitu vocis adulant,
et cum deserti baubantur in aedibus aut cum

own Catullus shews that he knew the edition of Avanc. 1049 Avanc. followed by Lamb. Lach. etc. but not by Junt. or Nauger. has corrupted the sense by reading *Quid vellet, facere ut scirent animoque viderent*: on comparing what precedes and follows, it is manifest that the construction must be the same as 183 *Quid vellent facere ut scirent*: *first* he, like the gods there, had to know what he wanted himself; then *item* 1050 to make others to know. *scirēt* is like *fulgēt* in II 27. 1053 *Quid sit opus facto facilest* Lach. for *facile si*. *faciles neque enim* Flor. 31 Camb. Mar. Ald. 1 Junt. Lamb. ed. 1 and 2; but ed. 3 *Quid facto esset opus; neque enim faciles*: a violent change; but his knowledge of Latin taught him that in the old reading *sit* and the position of *neque enim* were quite indefensible. 1058 *varia res* Bentl. for *varias res*: the attraction of *res* has caused the error: 1090 *alia re* mss. for *alia res*. 1062 *licet id rebus* Lach. after Gif. in note for *licet in rebus*. *id licet e rebus* Lamb. 1063 *magna*. *inmane* Lach. without cause. 1064 *fremunt* Mar. Ald. 1 Junt. for *premunt*. *tremunt* Nonius. 1065 *alio* Flor. 31 Camb. Mar. etc. for *alia*. *rabie restricta* Lach. for *rabie stricta*. *rabies districta* Flor. 31 Camb. 2 Vat. Mar. *rabie districta* Pont. Lamb. *rabie distracta* 2 Vat. Nauger. *minantur* Pont. Nauger. for *minatur*. 1067 *Et* Lach. for *At* which even Lamb. retains. 1068 *iactant* Nauger. for *lactant*. *petentes* Flor. 31 Mon. Ver. Ven. etc. for *potentes*. *patente* Is. Voss. in ms. notes. 1069 *teneros imitantur*. *veros imitantur* Faber in notes. *teneros minitantur* Lach.: but they refine

plorantis fugiunt summisso corpore plagas.
denique non hinnitus item differre videtur,
inter equas ubi equus florenti aetate iuvencus
pinnigeri saevit calcaribus ictus amoris,
et fremitum patulis ubi naribus edit ad arma,
et cum sic alias concussis artibus hinnit?
postremo genus alituum variaeque volucres,
accipitres atque ossifragae mergique marinis
fluctibus in salso victum vitamque petentes,
longe alias alio iaciunt in tempore voces,
et quom de victu certant praedaeque repugnant.
et partim mutant cum tempestatibus una
raucisonos cantus, cornicum ut saecla vetusta
corvorumque greges ubi aquam dicuntur et imbris
poscere et interdum ventos aurasque vocare.
ergo si varii sensus animalia cogunt,
muta tamen cum sint, varias emittere voces,
quanto mortalis magis aecumst tum potuisse
dissimilis alia atque alia res voce notare!
[Illud in his rebus tacitus ne forte requiras,
fulmen detulit in terram mortalibus ignem
primitus, inde omnis flammarum diditur ardor.
multa videmus enim caelestibus inlita flammis
fulgere, cum caeli donavit plaga vapore.
et ramosa tamen cum ventis pulsa vacillans
aestuat in ramos incumbens arboris arbor,
exprimitur validis extritus viribus ignis

too much I think, nor do I see any real difference in sense between *imitantur* and *minitantur*. 1071 *deserti baubantur* Nonius Nicc. for *desertibus aubantur*, i.e. *deserti b. aubantur*, AB: so vi 1241 *Poenibus at*: Aen. xi 572 *Nutribus at* P. 1076 *patulis ubi naribus* Lach. for *patulis sub naribus*: this slight change I adopt, but with hesitation for other reasons and also on account of the apparent imitation of Virgil georg. iii 85 *Collectumque fremens volvit sub naribus ignem*: 'turpe et obscenum loquendi genus' really comes to nothing: Aen. xi 736 *At non in Venerem segnes nocturnaque bella*; georg. iii 98 *siquando ad proelia ventum est*, and the like are quite as coarse. 1080 *salso. salsis* Lamb. tacitly. 1082 *praedaeque* Avanc. rightly for *praedataque. praedaque* A corr. Nicc. vulg. 1084 *ut* Nauger. for *et*. Ald. 1 Junt. omit the word; and also Mar., but he changes *ubi* of next v. to *uti*. 1088 *Muta* Flor. 31 Mar. Ald. 1 Junt. for *Multa*. 1090 *res* Nicc. for *re*: comp. n. to 1058. 1094 *inlita* Lach. for *insita. incita* Mar. Junt. vulg. 1095 *vapore* Lach. for *vaporis. vapores* vulg. *vare* Nonius. 1096 *Et* Mar.

et micat interdum flammai fervidus ardor,
mutua dum inter se rami stirpesque teruntur.
quorum utrumque dedisse potest mortalibus ignem.
inde cibum coquere ac flammae mollire vapore
sol docuit, quoniam mitescere multa videbant
verberibus radiorum atque aestu victa per agros.
  Inque dies magis hi victum vitamque priorem
commutare novis monstrabant rebu' *be*nigni,
ingenio qui praestabant et corde vigebant.
condere coeperunt urbis arcemque locare
praesidium reges ipsi sibi perfugiumque,
et pecus atque agros divisere atque dedere
pro facie cuiusque et viribus ingenioque;
nam facies multum valuit viresque vigentes.
posterius res inventast aurumque repertum,
quod facile et validis et pulchris dempsit honorem;
divitioris enim sectam plerumque secuntur
quamlubet et fortes et pulchro corpore creti.
quod siquis vera vitam ratione gubernet,
divitiae grandes homini sunt vivere parce
aequo animo; neque enim est umquam penuria parvi.
at claros homines voluerunt se atque potentes,
ut fundamento stabili fortuna maneret
et placidam possent opulenti degere vitam,
nequiquam, quoniam ad summum succedere honorem
certantes iter infestum fecere viai,
et tamen e summo, quasi fulmen, deicit ictos
invidia interdum contemptim in Tartara taetra;

Junt. for *Ut*. 1099 *Et micat* Mar. Ald. 1 Junt. for *Emicat* which Lamb. in errata to ed. 3 wrongly restores. 1102 *coquere. quoq*; *uere* A, *coq. uere* B, *quoquere* Nicc. and Lach. 1105 *hi victum* Nauger. for *invictum. et victum* Mar. Ald. 1 Junt. 1106 *rebu' benigni* Lach. for *rebus et igni.* 1110 *Et pecus atque agros* Lach. for *Et pecudes atque agros*: comp. 1291 where for *pecus* B has *pecudes. Et pecudes et agros* Flor. 31 Camb. Pont. Mar. vulg. *divisere atque dedere* Pont. Mar. Ald. 1 Junt. for *diviseratque debere. divisim ut quisquis haberet* Camb. 1112 *viresque vigentes* Faber in notes for *viresque vigebant. viresque vigorque* Lach.: *vigebant* he says has come from 1107: clearly *vires vigebant* could only mean 'their strength was then in its vigour': a meaning here quite out of place. 1116 *creti* Flor. 31 Camb. Brix. Ver. Ven. Mar. for *certi.* 1120 is much corrupted by Lamb. 1124 *Certantes iter* Mar. Ald. 1 Junt. for *Certan-*

1131 invidia quoniam, ceu fulmine, summa vaporant
plerumque et quae sunt aliis magis edita cumque;
1127 ut satius multo iam sit parere quietum
quam regere imperio res velle et regna tenere.
proinde sine incassum defessi sanguine sudent,
angustum per iter luctantes ambitionis;
1133 quandoquidem sapiunt alieno ex ore petuntque
res ex auditis potius quam sensibus ipsis,
nec magis id nunc est neque erit mox quam fuit ante.

Ergo regibus occisis subversa iacebat
pristina maiestas soliorum et sceptra superba,
et capitis summi praeclarum insigne cruentum
sub pedibus vulgi magnum lugebat honorem;
nam cupide conculcatur nimis ante metutum.
res itaque ad summam faecem turbasque redibat,
imperium sibi cum ac summatum quisque petebat.
inde magistratum partim docuere creare
iuraque constituere, ut vellent legibus uti.
nam genus humanum, defessum vi colere aevom,
ex inimicitiis languebat; quo magis ipsum
sponte sua cecidit sub leges artaque iura.
acrius ex ira quod enim se quisque parabat
ulcisci quam nunc concessumst legibus aequis,
hanc ob rem est homines pertaesum vi colere aevom.
inde metus maculat poenarum praemia vitae.
circumretit enim vis atque iniuria quemque
atque, unde exortast, ad eum plerumque revertit,
nec facilest placidam ac pacatam degere vitam
qui violat factis communia foedera pacis.
etsi fallit enim divom genus humanumque,
perpetuo tamen id fore clam diffidere debet;

tesque inter: *iter* Flor. 31 Brix. Pont. before them. 1127 1128 (1131 1132) I have brought to this place: Lach. puts them after 1135. 1128 *aliis* Lamb. for *altis*. 1131 *sine* Flor. 31 Camb. 3 Vat. Mar. for *side*. 1141 *redibat* Flor. 31 Mar. Ald. 1 Junt. for *recidat*. 1145 *vi colere* Flor. 31 Camb. Mar. for *vicere* A, *vigere* B, *vincere* Nicc.: comp. 1150. 1151 *Inde*. *Unde* Mar. Junt. Lamb. etc. Gif. attributes *inde* to Marullus, from a confusion prob. between the *Inde* which Ven. rightly has, and Marullus' change to *Unde*.

1152 *vis* Camb. Brix. Mar. for *ius*. *circumretitae nimis* Pont. and so in dark ink on an erasure in Mon.; but *enim vis* is written over in a paler ink, like that most

quippe ubi se multi per somnia saepe loquentes
aut morbo delirantes protraxe ferantur
et celata *mala* in medium et peccata dedisse.]
  Nunc quae causa deum per magnas numina gentis
pervulgarit et ararum compleverit urbis
suscipiendaque curarit sollemnia sacra,
quae nunc in magnis florent sacra rebu' locisque,
unde etiam nunc est mortalibus insitus horror
qui delubra deum nova toto suscitat orbi
terrarum et festis cogit celebrare diebus,
non ita difficilest rationem reddere verbis.
quippe etenim iam tum divom mortalia saecla
egregias animo facies vigilante videbant
et magis in somnis mirando corporis auctu.
his igitur sensum tribuebant propterea quod
membra movere videbantur vocesque superbas
mittere pro facie praeclara et viribus amplis.
aeternamque dabant vitam, quia semper eorum
subpeditabatur facies et forma manebat,
et tamen omnino quod tantis viribus auctos
non temere ulla vi convinci posse putabant.
fortunisque ideo longe praestare putabant,
quod mortis timor haut quemquam vexaret eorum,
et simul in somnis quia multa et mira videbant
efficere et nullum capere ipsos inde laborem.
praeterea caeli rationes ordine certo
et varia annorum cernebant tempora verti
nec poterant quibus id fieret cognoscere causis.
ergo perfugium sibi habebant omnia divis
tradere et illorum nutu facere omnia flecti.
in caeloque deum sedes et templa locarunt,
per caelum volvi quia nox et luna videtur,
luna dies et nox et noctis signa severa

used: another indication that Pontanus may have had possession of the ms. before Marullus. 1160 *mala* added by Lach. *diu* Mar. Ald. 1 Junt. vulg. 1177 *Et tamen omnino. Et manet omnino* Lamb. most perversely. 1178 *ulla vi* Brix. Mar. Ald. 1 Junt. for *illa vi. illa* (*ulla*) Ver. Ven. 1189 *nox. lux* Lach. *sol* Lamb. 1190 *severa. serena* Candidus at end of Junt. Lach. which Lamb. also prefers: the change of course is very slight; but *severa* is to my taste the more

noctivagaeque faces caeli flammaeque volantes,
nubila sol imbres nix venti fulmina grando
et rapidi fremitus et murmura magna minarum.
O genus infelix humanum, talia divis
cum tribuit facta atque iras adiunxit acerbas!
quantos tum gemitus ipsi sibi, quantaque nobis
volnera, quas lacrimas peperere minoribu' nostris!
nec pietas ullast velatum saepe videri
vertier ad lapidem atque omnis accedere ad aras
nec procumbere humi prostratum et pandere palmas
ante deum delubra nec aras sanguine multo
spargere quadrupedum nec votis nectere vota,
sed mage pacata posse omnia mente tueri.
nam cum suspicimus magni caelestia mundi
templa, super stellisque micantibus aethera fixum,
et venit in mentem solis lunaeque viarum,
tunc aliis oppressa malis in pectora cura
illa quoque expergefactum caput erigere infit,
nequae forte deum nobis inmensa potestas
sit, vario motu quae candida sidera verset.
temptat enim dubiam mentem rationis egestas,
ecquaenam fuerit mundi genitalis origo,
et simul ecquae sit finis quoad moenia mundi
solliciti motus hunc possint ferre laborem,
an divinitus aeterna donata salute
perpetuo possint aevi labentia tractu
inmensi validas aevi contemnere viris.
praeterea cui non animus formidine divum
contrahitur, cui non correpunt membra pavore,
fulminis horribili cum plaga torrida tellus
contremit et magnum percurrunt murmura caelum?
non populi gentesque tremunt, regesque superbi
corripiunt divum percussi membra timore,

poetical. 1192 *sol.* *ros* Lamb. 1198 *ullast velatum.* *ulla velatumst* mss. and eds. before Mar. and Ald. 1. 1203 *pacata* Junt. (not Pont. or Mar.) for *placata*: a necessary correction which Nauger. rejects, but Lamb. ed. 2 and 3 properly adopts. 1207 *in pectora.* *in pectore* Ald. 1 Junt. followed by Nauger. Lamb. Creech etc. most absurdly. 1214 *Sollicĭti* Bentl. for *Et taciti*: he refers to I 343 and VI 1038. *Et tanti* one Vat. Ald. 1 Lamb. 1220 *Fulminis* Mar.

nequid ob admissum foede dictumve superbe
poenarum grave sit solvendi tempus adultum?
summa etiam cum vis violenti per mare venti
induperatorem classis super aequora verrit
cum validis pariter legionibus atque elephantis,
non divom pacem votis adit ac prece quaesit
ventorum pavidus paces animasque secundas,
nequiquam, quoniam violento turbine saepe
correptus nilo fertur minus ad vada leti?
usque adeo res humanas vis abdita quaedam
opterit et pulchros fascis saevasque secures
proculcare ac ludibrio sibi habere videtur.
denique sub pedibus tellus cum tota vacillat
concussaeque cadunt urbes dubiaeque minantur,
quid mirum si se temnunt mortalia saecla
atque potestatis magnas mirasque relinqunt
in rebus viris divum, quae cuncta gubernent?
  Quod superest, aes *at*que aurum ferrumque repertumst
et simul argenti pondus plumbique potestas,
ignis ubi ingentis silvas ardore cremarat
montibus in magnis, seu caeli fulmine misso,
sive quod inter se bellum silvestre gerentes
hostibus intulerant ignem formidinis ergo,
sive quod inducti terrae bonitate volebant
pandere agros pinguis et pascua reddere rura,
sive feras interficere et ditescere praeda.
nam fovea atque igni prius est venarier ortum
quam saepire plagis saltum canibusque ciere.
quidquid id est, quacumque e causa flammeus ardor

Ald. 1 Junt. first for *Fulmini*. *Fulmine* Nicc. *Fulmine terribili* Flor. 31. 1224 *Nequid* Lach. for *Nequod*: a necessary change, if it is joined with *admissum*.

1225 *adultum* Lach. for *adauctum*. *adactum* Pont. Mar. Ald. 1 Junt. Lamb. etc. 1226 *Summa* F or. 31 Mar. Ald. 1 Junt. for *Summe*. 1229 *adit ac prece* Flor. 31 Camb. Mar. for *adita prece*. 1230 enclosed by Lach. in [ ].

1237 *dubiaeque*. *dubiaeve* Bentl.: but see notes 2. 1241 *superest aes atque aurum* Mar. Ald. 1 Junt. for *superest aeque aurum*. 1244 *caeli fulmine misso* BA corr. Nicc. all later mss. and eds.: *caelo* A p. m. alone. *caeli* is quite right: see I 489. *caelo* Lach. who says 'neque dixit alibi Lucretius *fulmen caeli*, sed *plagam caeli* supra 1095': but why his once using *plaga caeli*, should prevent him from twice using *fulmen caeli*, my mind cannot comprehend. 1252 *Quidquid*. *Quicquid* AB; and so the lex Rubria 26 and the ancient and sole ms. of Livy XLV

horribili sonitu silvas exederat altis
ab radicibus et terram percoxerat igni,
manabat venis ferventibus in loca terrae
concava conveniens argenti rivus et auri,
aeris item et plumbi. quae cum concreta videbant
posterius claro in terra splendere colore,
tollebant nitido capti levique lepore
et simili formata videbant esse figura
atque lacunarum fuerant vestigia cuique.
tum penetrabat eos posse haec liquefacta calore
quamlibet in formam et faciem decurrere rerum
et prorsum quamvis in acuta ac tenvia posse
mucronum duci fastigia procudendo,
ut sibi tela darent, silvasque ut caedere possent
materiemque dolare et levia radere tigna
et terebrare etiam ac pertundere perque forare.
nec minus argento facere haec auroque parabant
quam validi primum violentis viribus aeris,
nequiquam, quoniam cedebat victa potestas
nec poterat pariter durum sufferre laborem.
tum fuit in pretio magis *aes* aurumque iacebat
propter inutilitatem hebeti mucrone retusum.
nunc iacet aes, aurum in summum successit honorem.
sic volvenda aetas commutat tempora rerum.
quod fuit in pretio, fit nullo denique honore;
porro aliut succedit et *e* contemptibus exit
inque dies magis adpetitur floretque repertum

32 9: Lucr. may therefore have written *quicquid* here, though elsewhere his mss. have *quidquid* for the relative; *quicquid* in the sense of *quicque*, rightly according to the rule explained in notes 2 to 1 22 *quicquam*. 1253 *altis* A Nicc. Flor. 31 Camb. Mon. Brix. Ver. Ven. Junt. *altas* BA corr. Avanc. Lamb. 1254 *Ab* Junt. first for *A*, rightly: not Pont. or Mar.

1258 *in terra splendere* Lach. first for *in terras*. *in terris* Lamb. 1259 *capti* Flor. 31 Ver. Ven. Mar. for *capiti*. 1266 *darent, silvasque ut caedere possent* Lach. for *parent silvasque et cedere possint*. [But perhaps the mss. are right: compare Plaut. Amph. 192 *praemisit ut nuntiem*; and see Ussing there.] 1267 *dolare et levia radere* Mar. Junt. (Ald. 1 has *ac* for *et*) for *dolaret levare ac radere*: which seems the simplest change. *domo, levare ac radere* Lach. *laevare dolare et radere* Lamb. Lach. also suggests *dolare secare ac* or *dolare aequare ac*. 1272 *poterat* Lamb. and Lach. for *poterant*: this I have received with some hesitation.

1273 *Tum* Lach. for *Nam*. *aes* added by Flor. 31 Camb. Pont. Mar. 1278 *e*

laudibus et miro est mortalis inter honore.
Nunc tibi quo pacto ferri natura reperta
sit facilest ipsi per te cognoscere, Memmi.
arma antiqua manus ungues dentesque fuerunt
et lapides et item silvarum fragmina rami,
et flamma atque ignes, postquam sunt cognita primum.
posterius ferri vis est aerisque reperta.
et prior aeris erat quam ferri cognitus usus,
quo facilis magis est natura et copia maior.
aere solum terrae tractabant, aereque belli
miscebant fluctus et vulnera vasta serebant
et pecus atque agros adimebant; nam facile ollis
omnia cedebant armatis nuda et inerma.
inde minutatim processit ferreus ensis
versaque in obprobrium species *est* falcis ahenae,
et ferro coepere solum proscindere terrae
exaequataque sunt creperi certamina belli.
et prius est armatum in equi conscendere costas
et moderarier hunc frenis dextraque vigere
quam biiugo curru belli temptare pericla.
et biiugos prius est quam bis coniungere binos
et quam falciferos armatum escendere currus.
inde boves *lu*cas turrito corpore, taetras,
anguimanus, belli docuerunt volnera Poeni
sufferre et magnas Martis turbare catervas.
sic alid ex alio peperit discordia tristis,
horribile humanis quod gentibus esset in armis,
inque dies belli terroribus addidit augmen.
Temptarunt etiam tauros in moenere belli
expertique sues saevos sunt mittere in hostis.
et validos partim prae se misere leones

added by Brix. Pont. Mar. 1285 *flamma atque* B corr. Flor. 31 Camb. 4 Vat. for *flammatque ignes*. *flammae atque* Mar. Nauger. Lamb. etc. 1294 *obprobrium*. *obscenum* all the mss. of Macrob. sat. VI 1 63, collated by Ianus: a curious variation. Lach. who depended on an old edition of Macrobius, is mistaken in supposing that *obscenum* is not the ms. reading. 1297 *armatum*. *reppertum* Lamb. etc. and 1301 *inventum* Mar. Junt. Lamb. etc. for *armatum*: both needless changes.

1300 *biiugos* Faber for *biiugo*: *biiugo* makes the construction extremely harsh, and, as Faber says, has come from 1299. 1302 *taetras* (*tetras*) Lach. for *tetros*: rightly, see 1339. 1310 *partim*. *Parthi* Camb. 2 Vat.: a reading adopted by

cum doctoribus armatis saevisque magistris
qui moderarier his possent vinclisque tenere,
nequiquam, quoniam permixta caede calentes
turbabant saevi nullo discrimine turmas,
terrificas capitum quatientes undique cristas,
nec poterant equites fremitu perterrita equorum
pectora mulcere et frenis convertere in hostis.
inritata leae iaciebant corpora saltu
undique et adversum venientibus ora petebant
et nec opinantis a tergo deripiebant
deplexaeque dabant in terram volnere victos,
morsibus adfixae validis atque unguibus uncis.
iactabantque suos tauri pedibusque terebant
et latera ac ventres hauribant supter equorum
cornibus et terram minitanti fronte ruebant.
et validis socios caedebant dentibus apri
tela infracta suo tinguentes sanguine saevi,
in se fracta suo tinguentes sanguine tela,
permixtasque dabant equitum peditumque ruinas.
nam transversa feros exibant dentis adactus
iumenta aut pedibus ventos erecta petebant,
nequiquam, quoniam ab nervis succisa videres
concidere atque gravi terram consternere casu.
siquos ante domi domitos satis esse putabant,
effervescere cernebant in rebus agundis
volneribus clamore fuga terrore tumultu,
nec poterant ullam partem redducere eorum;
diffugiebat enim varium genus omne ferarum;
ut nunc saepe boves lucae ferro male mactae
diffugiunt, fera facta suis cum multa dedere.

Lamb. Creech Wak. vulg. before Lach. 1311 *doctoribus. ductoribus* Ver. Ven. Mar. Ald. 1 Junt. Nauger. Lamb. etc. 1315 Lach. rejects as spurious; and Ed. in ed. 1. 1319 *petebant* Vat. 640 Urbin. Mon. Junt. for *patebant.*

1320 *deripiebant* A Lach. *diripiebant* B Nicc. Flor. 31 Camb. Mon. all before Lach. 1323 *suos. sues* Ver. Ven. Avanc. Lamb. etc. 1325 *fronte* Lach. for *mente* which has no meaning. *ad terramque minanti mente* Mar. Lamb. Gif. Creech etc. and this Candidus doubtless meant to read. 1327 1328 Mon. Junt. Lach. and Ed. in small ed. omit the second; Lamb. ed. 1 obelises the first, ed. 2 and 3 both: but see notes 2. 1330 *dentis adactus* Mar. Junt. for *dentis adauctus* B, *dentibus adauctus* A Nicc. Camb. *dentibus ictus* Politian in marg. Flor.

SI FUIT UT FACERENT SED VIX ADDUCOR UT ANTE
NON QUIERINT ANIMO PRAESENTIRE ATQUE VIDERE
QUAM COMMUNE MALUM FIERET FOEDUMQUE FUTURUM
ET MAGIS ID POSSIS FACTUM CONTENDERE IN OMNI
IN VARIIS MUNDIS VARIA RATIONE CREATIS
QUAM CERTO ATQUE UNO TERRARUM QUOLIBET ORBI
sed facere id non tam vincendi spe voluerunt,
quam dare quod gemerent hostes, ipsique perire,
qui numero diffidebant armisque vacabant.
Nexilis ante fuit vestis quam textile tegmen.
textile post ferrumst, quia ferro tela paratur,
nec ratione alia possunt tam levia gigni
insilia ac fusi radii scapique sonantes.
et facere ante viros lanam natura coegit
quam muliebre genus; nam longe praestat in arte
et sollertius est multo genus omne virile;
agricolae donec vitio vertere severi,
ut muliebribus id manibus concedere vellent
atque ipsi pariter durum sufferre laborem
atque opere in duro durarent membra manusque.
At specimen sationis et insitionis origo
ipsa fuit rerum primum natura creatrix,
arboribus quoniam bacae glandesque caducae
tempestiva dabant pullorum examina supter;
unde etiam libitumst stirpis committere ramis
et nova defodere in terram virgulta per agros.
inde aliam atque aliam culturam dulcis agelli
temptabant fructusque feros mansuescere terra*m*
cernebant indulgendo blandeque colendo.
inque dies magis in montem succedere silvas
cogebant infraque locum concedere cultis,
prata lacus rivos segetes vinetaque laeta

29. 1340 *facta.* *fata* B corr. Lach.: but see notes 2. 1341—1346 Lach. justly ejects the last three of these verses as the work of an interpolator; but it is no less certain that the first three are likewise spurious; *Si fuit ut facerent* is obviously a comment on *Sed facere id non tam* cet. Lach. to make sense and grammar is compelled to read *Sic fuit* with Mar. Ald. 1 Junt. Lamb. for *Si fuit*, and to transpose 1342 and 1343: see Camb. Journ. of phil. IV p. 288: 1345 = 528.

1351 *tela paratur.* *tela parantur* Lamb. perversely. 1368 *terram* Lach. for

collibus et campis ut haberent, atque olearum
caerula distinguens inter plaga currere posset
per tumulos et convallis camposque profusa;
ut nunc esse vides vario distincta lepore
omnia, quae pomis intersita dulcibus ornant
arbustisque tenent felicibus opsita circum.
At liquidas avium voces imitarier ore
ante fuit multo quam levia carmina cantu
concelebrare homines possent aurisque iuvare.
et zephyri, cava per calamorum, sibila primum
agrestis docuere cavas inflare cicutas.
inde minutatim dulcis didicere querellas,
tibia quas fundit digitis pulsata canentum,
avia per nemora ac silvas saltusque reperta,
per loca pastorum deserta atque otia dia.
haec animos ollis mulcebant atque iuvabant
cum satiate cibi; nam tum *haec* sunt omnia cordi.
saepe itaque inter se prostrati in gramine molli
propter aquae rivom sub ramis arboris altae
non magnis opibus iucunde corpora habebant,
praesertim cum tempestas ridebat et anni
tempora pingebant viridantis floribus herbas.
tum ioca, tum sermo, tum dulces esse cachinni
consuerant. agrestis enim tum musa vigebat;
tum caput atque umeros plexis redimire coronis
floribus et foliis lascivia laeta monebat,
atque extra numerum procedere membra moventes
duriter et duro terram pede pellere matrem;
unde oriebantur risus dulcesque cachinni,
omnia quod nova tum magis haec et mira vigebant.
et vigilantibus hinc aderant solacia somni,
ducere multimodis voces et flectere cantus
et supera calamos unco percurrere labro;

terra. 1388 1389=1454 1455, and are here quite out of place. 1391 *tum haec sunt omnia* 'ut quidam legunt' says Lamb. for *tum sunt omnia*: comp. 1404. *tum sunt carmina* Lach. *otia* Faber. 1397 *ioca* Flor. 31 Mar. Ald. 1 Junt. for *loca*. 1400 *monebat* Flor. 31 Mar. Junt. for *movebat*. 1405 *solacia somni* Lamb. Lach. for *solacia somno*. 'secutus sum codicem Vaticanum' says Lamb. All the mss. at present in the Vatican have, I believe, *somno*: but again and again

unde etiam vigiles nunc haec accepta tuentur
et numerum servare *re*cens didicere, neque hilo
maiorem interea capiunt dulcedini' fructum
quam silvestre genus capiebat terrigenarum.
nam quod adest praesto, nisi quid cognovimus ante
suavius, in primis placet et pollere videtur,
posteriorque fere melior res illa reperta
perdit et immutat sensus ad pristina quaeque.
sic odium coepit glandis, sic illa relicta
strata cubilia sunt herbis et frondibus aucta.
pellis item cecidit vestis contempta ferinae;
quam reor invidia tali tunc esse repertam,
ut letum insidiis qui gessit primus obiret,
et tamen inter eos distractam sanguine multo
disperiisse neque in fructum convertere quisse.
tunc igitur pelles, nunc aurum et purpura curis
exercent hominum vitam belloque fatigant;
quo magis in nobis, ut opinor, culpa resedit.
frigus enim nudos sine pellibus excruciabat
terrigenas; at nos nil laedit veste carere
purpurea atque auro signisque ingentibus apta,
dum plebeia tamen sit quae defendere possit.
ergo hominum genus incassum frustraque laborat
semper et *in* curis consumit inanibus aevom,
nimirum quia non cognovit quae sit habendi
finis et omnino quoad crescat vera voluptas.
idque minutatim vitam provexit in altum
et belli magnos commovit funditus aestus.

At vigiles mundi magnum versatile templum
sol et luna suo lustrantes lumine circum
perdocuere homines annorum tempora verti

Lamb. speaks in the same vague way of Vatican and other mss. 1409 *servare recens* Ed. for *servare genus*: *servare* first absorbed the *re*, then *cens* became *genus*. *sonis* Lach. Certainly *genus* is quite unmeaning. *numeris* Nicc. as well as Flor. 31 Ver. Ven. Avanc. in Ald. 1; but at end of his Catullus he bids us read *numerum*.

1410 *Maiorem* Flor. 31 Camb. for *Maiore*. *dulcedini'* Lamb. rightly for *dulcedine*. 1418 *ferinae* Junt. (not Pont. or Mar.) for *ferina*. *vestis contemta ferinast* Lamb. ed. 2 and 3. 1419 *tunc* Brix. Pont. Mar. Ald. 1 Junt. for *nunc*. 1431 *in* added by Flor. 31 Camb. Mon. Pont. Ald. 1 Junt. 1436 *magnum versatile*. *magnum ac versatile* Ed. in small ed.; and *ac* may have fallen

et certa ratione geri rem atque ordine certo.
Iam validis saepti degebant turribus aevom
et divisa colebatur discretaque tellus,
iam mare velivolis florebat puppibus; urbes
auxilia ac socios iam pacto foedere habebant,
carminibus cum res gestas coepere poetae
tradere; nec multo priu' sunt elementa reperta.
propterea quid sit prius actum respicere aetas
nostra nequit, nisi qua ratio vestigia monstrat.
Navigia atque agri culturas moenia leges
arma vias vestes *et* cetera de genere horum,
praemia, delicias quoque vitae funditus omnis,
carmina picturas, et daedala signa polire,
usus et impigrae simul experientia mentis
paulatim docuit pedetemtim progredientis.
sic unumquicquid paulatim protrahit aetas
in medium ratioque in luminis erigit oras.
namque alid ex alio clarescere et ordine debet
artibus, ad summum donec venere cacumen.

out after *m*: *et* is added by Mar. Ald. 1 Junt. Lamb. vulg. *versatili'* Lach. 1442 *Iam* Lach. for *Tum*. *propter odores* all mss. which Wak. absurdly defends. *puppibus* (*puppib.*) *et res* Lach. *puppibus* is unquestionably right; but *res* appears strange without any epithet; I have written therefore *puppibus; urbes*. *Tum mare velivolum florebat navibu' pandis* Junt. (not Pont. or Mar.) Lamb. etc. probably after Servius. 1449 *et* added by Flor. 31 Camb. 1451 *polire* Flor. 31 Vat. 640 Urbin. and 1954 Othob. Mar. Ald. 1 Junt. Lamb. Lach. for *polito*. 1455 *erigit*. *eruit* Junt. (not Pont. or Mar.) Lamb. etc. wrongly. 1456 *clarescere et ordine debet* Ed. for *clarescere corde videbant*: one *e* was absorbed by the other; then *tordine debet* passed into *corde videbant*. *clarescere conveniebat* Lach. who joins *Artibus* with *venere*.

T. LUCRETI CARI

DE RERUM NATURA

LIBER SEXTUS

Primae frugiparos fetus mortalibus aegris
dididerunt quondam praeclaro nomine Athenae
et recreaverunt vitam legesque rogarunt,
et primae dederunt solacia dulcia vitae,
cum genuere virum tali cum corde repertum,
omnia veridico qui quondam ex ore profudit;
cuius et extincti propter divina reperta
divolgata vetus iam ad caelum gloria fertur.
nam cum vidit hic ad victum quae flagitat usus
omnia iam ferme mortalibus esse parata
et, proquam posset, vitam consistere tutam,
divitiis homines et honore et laude potentis
affluere atque bona gnatorum excellere fama,
nec minus esse domi cuiquam tamen anxia corda,
atque animi ingratis vitam vexare *sine ulla*
pausa atque infestis cogei saevire querellis,

1 *frugiparos* AB. *frugiferos* A corr. Nicc. and later mss. and eds. before Wak. 4 *solacia* Nicc. for *solaci*. 7 *extincti* Mar. Ald. 1 Junt. for *extincta*. 10 *mortalibus* Nicc. for *acortalibus*. 11 *proquam posset* Lach. for *proquam possent*: a simple and certain correction of a much-vexed passage. *per quae possent* Mar. Avanc. Madvig, deceived by this, conjectured in Henrichsen de frag. Gott. *per quae possent vita c. tuta*. Lamb. and Creech obelise the verse. 13 *excellere* Mar. Ald. 1 Junt. for *excolere* A Nicc., *excollere* B. *extollere* Flor. 31 Camb. Pont. 14 *corda* Mar. Ald. 1 Junt. for *cordi*. 15 *querellis* of mss. has of course come from 16 and has supplanted the words of Lucr. who wrote *sine ulla Pausa atque*. Lach. retains *querellis* here and in 16 reads *Passimque...periclis*. *cogei* Lach., *cogi* Lamb., rightly for *coget*: a common corruption in our mss. Mar. Avanc. Junt. corrupt the passage greatly. Lamb. followed by Gif. Creech, etc.

intellegit ibi vitium vas efficere ipsum
omniaque illius vitio corrumpier intus
quae conlata foris et commoda cumque venirent;
partim quod fluxum pertusumque esse videbat,
ut nulla posset ratione explerier umquam;
partim quod taetro quasi conspurcare sapore
omnia cernebat, quaecumque receperat, intus.
veridicis igitur purgavit pectora dictis
et finem statuit cuppedinis atque timoris
exposuitque bonum summum quo tendimus omnes
quid foret, atque viam monstravit, tramite parvo
qua possemus ad id recto contendere cursu,
quidve mali foret in rebus mortalibu' passim,
quod fieret naturali varieque volaret
seu casu seu vi, quod sic natura parasset,
et quibus e portis occurri cuique deceret,
et genus humanum frustra plerumque probavit
volvere curarum tristis in pectore fluctus.
nam veluti pueri trepidant atque omnia caecis
in tenebris metuunt, sic nos in luce timemus
interdum, nilo quae sunt metuenda magis quam
quae pueri in tenebris pavitant finguntque futura.
hunc igitur terrorem animi tenebrasque necessest
non radii solis nec lucida tela diei
discutiant, sed naturae species ratioque.
quo magis inceptum pergam pertexere dictis.

Et quoniam docui mundi mortalia templa
esse *et* nativo consistere corpore caelum,

contracts the two verses into one, thus *Atque animum infestis cogi servire querelis*: *servire* also Ver. Ven. Mar. Ald. 1 Junt. *Causam quae* Avanc. Nauger. for *Pausa atque*. 17 *vas* Mar. Ald. 1 Junt. for *fas*. 25 *cuppedinis* A rightly, as v 45; and so Marullus in marg. of cod. Victor. properly corrects: Lactantius inst. VII 27 has *torpedinis*, from whom Mar. probably got his first notion mentioned by Gifanius: see n. to III 994: unless he rather when young derived it from his master Pontanus who expressly notes '*torpedinis* est apud Lactantium'. 27 *tramite parvo*. *tramite prono* Lamb. *limite prono* Junt. apparently after Lactantius inst. VII 27. Lach. rightly joins *tramite parvo* with what follows. 28 *recto* A corr. Nicc. Flor. 31 Camb. Mon. Lactant. for *recta*. 30 *fieret* Iac. Susius in Tonson, Lach. for *fuerit*. *flueret* Mar. Ald. 1 Junt. vulg. *naturali*. *naturae vi* Lamb. *naturali viro atque* Mar. Ald. 1 Junt. 31 *casu*. *causa* Lach. 32 *Et quibus* Flor. 31 Camb. Pont. Mar. for *E quibus*. 34 *Volvere* Ver. Ven. Mar. for *Volnere*. 44 *et*

et quaecumque in eo fiunt fierique necessest,
pleraque ressolui, quae restant percipe porro,
quandoquidem semel insignem conscendere currum

*

ventorum, ex ira ut placentur, *ut* omina rursum
quae fuerint sint placato conversa furore:
cetera quae fieri in terris caeloque tuentur
mortales, pavidis cum pendent mentibu' saepe,
et faciunt animos humilis formidine divom
depressosque premunt ad terram propterea quod
ignorantia causarum conferre deorum
cogit ad imperium res et concedere regnum.
nam bene qui didicere deos securum agere aevom,
si tamen interea mirantur qua ratione
quaeque geri possint, praesertim rebus in illis
quae supera caput aetheriis cernuntur in oris,
rursus in antiquas referuntur religionis
et dominos acris adsciscunt, omnia posse

added by Flor. 31 Camb. Brix. Mar. 46 *ressolui* Goebel obs. Lucr. p. 18 for *dissolui*: comp. v 773 *Qua fieri quicquid posset ratione resolvi*: a friend suggests that iv 500 *dissolvere causam* may support *dissolui* here: but see notes 2. *fiunt, fateare necessest Pleraque dissolui* Lach. most unsuitably, as if only *pleraque*, not *omnia*, were to be dissolved. *fiunt possuntque, n. P. dissolui* Bern. to which the same objection applies. Lamb. seeing this difficulty, in ed. 2 and 3 gives *fiunt fientque, necesse Esse ea dissolui.* 47—49 an exceedingly corrupt passage; yet I fancy that I have amended it without much violence: in 47 I have changed nothing; after it there is manifestly a hiatus of several verses, the general sense of which I have attempted to give in my translation. The ms. reading of 48 and 49 is as follows, *Ventorum exirtant placentur omnia rursum Que fuerint sint placato conversa favore*: with *exirtant* for *ex ira ut*, comp. iv 820 *virtuti* for *vir uti*. *omnia* for *omina* is an almost unfailing blunder of mss. *furore* is from Lamb. ed. 2 and 3, and Auratus for *favore*. So Sen. Octav. 800 and 806 mss. have *furore* and *furor* for *favore* and *favor*. The older emendations in Ald. 1 Junt. Lamb. etc. are so devoid of all probability that I will not cite them: Lamb. indeed believes the lines not to be Lucretius'; nor is Lachmann's text much happier: *institui conscendere currum Ventosum et certant plangentia flamina rursum, Quae fuerint, sine, placato conversa furore*: then at 50 he begins a new paragraph, and 52 for *Et faciunt* gives *Haec faciunt*, though Lactantius twice over has the ms. reading. Bern. supposes a lacuna both before and after 48 which he thus leaves, *Ventorum existant, placentur omnia rursum*: 52 Mar. Junt. Lamb. etc. for *Et faciunt* have *Efficiunt.* 56 57=90 91=i 153 154: here in the 6th book Lach. rejects them in the first, retains them in the second place: to me it is manifest that in both places they come from the annotator who thought they were in point and consequently jotted them down in

quos miseri credunt, ignari quid queat esse,
quid nequeat, finita potestas denique cuique
quanam sit rationi atque alte terminus haerens;
quo magis errantes caeca ratione feruntur.
quae nisi respuis ex animo longeque remittis
dis indigna putare alienaque pacis eorum,
delibata deum per te tibi numina sancta
saepe oberunt; non quo violari summa deum vis
possit, ut ex ira poenas petere inbibat acris,
sed quia tute tibi placida cum pace quietos
constitues magnos irarum volvere fluctus,
nec delubra deum placido cum pectore adibis,
nec de corpore quae sancto simulacra feruntur
in mentes hominum divinae nuntia formae,
suscipere haec animi tranquilla pace valebis.
inde videre licet qualis iam vita sequatur.
quam quidem ut a nobis ratio verissima longe
reiciat, quamquam sunt a me multa profecta,
multa tamen restant et sunt ornanda politis
versibus; est ratio caeli *specie*sque tenenda,
sunt tempestates et fulmina clara canenda,
quid faciant et qua de causa cumque ferantur;
ne trepides caeli divisis partibus amens,
unde volans ignis pervenerit aut in utram se
verterit hinc partim, quo pacto per loca saepta
insinuarit, et hinc dominatus ut extulerit se.
tu mihi supremae praescribta ad candida calcis
currenti spatium praemonstra, callida musa
Calliope, requies hominum divomque voluptas,

the margin in his usual fashion. 68 *longeque* Nicc. for *longique*. *remittis* Flor. 31 Camb. Brix. for *remitti*. 71 *oberunt* Wak. for *oderunt*. *aderunt* Mar. Ald. 1 Junt. Lamb. etc. 72 *ex ira* Mar. Ald. 1 Junt. for *exire*. 73 *quietos* Mar. Junt. for *quietus*. 74 *fluctus* Flor. 31 Mar. Ald. 1 Junt. for *fletus*.

76 *feruntur* Brix. Ald. 1 Junt. (not Pont. or Mar.) for *fuerunt*. *ferunt* Ver. Ven.

82 *sunt ornanda*. *sunt tornanda* Flor. 31 Politian in marg. Flor. 29.

83 *est ratio caeli* (*caelis* Brix.) *speciesque tenenda* Brix. Avanc. Lamb. ed. 1 and 2 for *est ratio caelisque tenenda*: the scribe omitted *specie* because of the following *squete*. *est ratio fulgendi visque tonandi* Lach. which seems to me most improbable. *est ratio superum caelique* Flor. 31 Camb. 2 Vat. Lamb. ed. 3. 85—89 Lach. encloses in [ ]. 90 91=56 57=I 153 154: see above. Lach. admits them here. 92 *ad candida calcis* Lamb. and Turnebus for *ac candida callis*: a certain

te duce ut insigni capiam cum laude coronam.
Principio tonitru quatiuntur caerula caeli
propterea quia concurrunt sublime volantes
aetheriae nubes contra pugnantibu' ventis.
nec fit enim sonitus caeli de parte serena,
verum ubicumque magis denso sunt agmine nubes,
tam magis hinc magno fremitus fit murmure saepe.
praeterea neque tam condenso corpore nubes
esse queunt quam sunt lapides ac tigna, neque autem
tam tenues quam sunt nebulae fumique volantes;
nam cadere aut bruto deberent pondere pressae
ut lapides, aut ut fumus constare nequirent
nec cohibere nives gelidas et grandinis imbris.
dant etiam sonitum patuli super aequora mundi,
carbasus ut quondam magnis intenta theatris
dat crepitum malos inter iactata trabesque;
interdum perscissa furit petulantibus auris
et fragilis *sonitus* chartarum commeditatur:
id quoque enim genus in tonitru cognoscere possis:
aut ubi suspensam vestem chartasque volantis
verberibus venti versant planguntque per auras.
fit quoque enim interdum *ut* non tam concurrere nubes
frontibus adversis possint quam de latere ire
diverso motu radentes corpora tractim,
aridus unde auris terget sonus ille diuque
ducitur, exierunt donec regionibus artis.

emendation. 102 *nubes* Flor. 31 Pont. Mar. Ald. 1 Junt. for *nure. mire* Nicc. Brix. Ver. Ven. 103 *lapides* Flor. 31 Ver. Ven. for *pepides. tigna* Flor. 31 Camb. Mar. Junt. for *iigna. ugna* Nicc. *ligna* Ver. Ven. Avanc. 105 *Nam cadere aut bruto* Flor. 31 Camb. all Vat. Brix. Ver. Ven. Mar. Junt. for *Nam cadere avi* B, *Nam candere aut* A corr. (says Lach. but ? p. m. also) Nicc. *aut* is unquestionably right: comp. 1198 *avi* mss. for *aut. Nam cadere abrupto* Avanc. *Nam aut cadere abrupto* Lamb. *ab bruto* Lach. 110 *malos* Flor. 31 Mar. Junt. for *matos. muros* Brix. Avanc. *matos* (*muros*) Ver. Ven. 112 *sonitus* added by Flor. 31 Camb. etc. 114 *que. ve* Mar. Junt. Lach. 115 *planguntque* Pont. Mar. Junt. for *planguentque.* 116 *ut* added by Flor. 31 Vat. 640 Urbin. and 1136 Othob. Pius. 118 *corpora tractim* Gronov. Faber for *corpore tractim.* '*f. corpora tactu*' Heins. in ms. notes. *corpore tractum* Nicc. Flor. 31 Camb. all Vat. etc. *corpori' tractum* Mar. Junt. 120 *exierunt* Vat. 1706 Reg. for *exierum*: also Heins. in ms. notes has '*exierunt* s' i.e. the ms. of Modius who must therefore have read in it *exierunt*, as the ed. Paris. 1565 has *exierit*, as well as Lamb. ed. 1

Hoc etiam pacto tonitru concussa videntur
omnia saepe gravi tremere et divolsa repente
maxima dissiluisse capacis moenia mundi,
cum subito validi venti conlecta procella
nubibus intorsit sese conclusaque ibidem
turbine versanti magis ac magis undique nubem
cogit uti fiat spisso cava corpore circum,
post ubi conminuit vis eius et impetus acer,
tum perterricrepo sonitu dat scissa fragorem.
nec mirum, cum plena animae vensicula parva
saepe ita dat torvum sonitum displosa repente.
Est etiam ratio, cum venti nubila perflant,
ut sonitus faciant. etenim ramosa videmus
nubila saepe modis multis atque aspera ferri;
scilicet ut, crebram silvam cum flamina cauri
perflant, dant sonitum frondes ramique fragorem.
fit quoque ut interdum validi vis incita venti
perscindat nubem perfringens impete recto.
nam quid possit ibi flatus manifesta docet res,
hic, ubi lenior est, in terra cum tamen alta
arbusta evolvens radicibus haurit ab imis.
sunt etiam fluctus per nubila, qui quasi murmur
dant in frangendo graviter; quod item fit in altis
fluminibus magnoque mari, cum frangitur aest*us*.
fit quoque, ubi e nubi in nubem vis incidit ardens
fulminis, haec multo si forte umore recepit
ignem, continuo *ut* magno clamore trucidet;
ut calidis candens ferrum e fornacibus olim

and 3. Is. Voss. too and Creech prefer *exierunt*. *exierit* Flor. 31 Camb. 3 Vat. Ald. 1 Junt. Lamb. *exierint* Brix. Ver. Ven. Mar.; but *exierit* Mar. ap. Victor. in ed. Ven. 124 *concollecta* AB. *conlecta* Nicc. Brix. *collecta* A corr. Camb.

128 *conminuit*. *commovit* A corr. Flor. 31 Camb. Mon. Brix. Ver. Ven. vulg. before Lach. 129 *scissa* Bern. for *missa*. *fissa* Lach.: it is clearly the *nubes*, not the *procella*, which is here spoken of; though all editors before Lach. retain *missa*, which Isidore too orig. XIII 8 must have read: the corruption therefore must be old. 131 *torvum* Ed. for *parvum*. *magnum* Is. Voss. in ms. notes and Wak. *pariter* Mar. Junt. Lamb. etc. *Saepe det haut parvum* Lach. *Noenu ita det p.* Bern.: but see notes 2. 132 and 136 *perflant* A corr. Nicc. for *perfiant*.

133 *Ut*. *Cur* Lamb. wrongly. 141 *Arbusta evolvens* A corr. Flor. 31 Pont. Mar. for *Arbusta volvens*. *Arbuste volvens* Nicc. Camb. 144 *aestus* Flor. 31 Camb. etc. for *aest.* *aestu* A corr. Nicc. Mon. Ver. Ven. vulg. 147 *ut* added

stridit, ubi in gelidum propere demersimus imbrem.
aridior porro si nubes accipit ignem,
uritur ingenti sonitu succensa repente;
lauricomos ut si per montis flamma vagetur
turbine ventorum comburens impete magno;
nec res ulla magis quam Phoebi Delphica laurus
terribili sonitu flamma crepitante crematur.
denique saepe geli multus fragor atque ruina
grandinis in magnis sonitum dat nubibus alte.
ventus enim cum confercit, franguntur, in artum,
concreti montes nimborum et grandine mixti.
  Fulgit item, nubes ignis cum semina multa
excussere suo concursu; ceu lapidem si
percutiat lapis aut ferrum; nam tum quoque lumen
exilit et claras scintillas dissipat ignis.
sed tonitrum fit uti post auribus accipiamus,
fulgere quam cernant oculi, quia semper ad auris
tardius adveniunt quam visum quae moveant res.
id licet hinc etiam cognoscere: caedere si quem
ancipiti videas ferro procul arboris auctum,
ante fit ut cernas ictum quam plaga per auris
det sonitum; sic fulgorem quoque cernimus ante
quam tonitrum accipimus, pariter qui mittitur igni
e simili causa, concursu natus eodem.
  Hoc etiam pacto volucri loca lumine tingunt
nubes et tremulo tempestas impete fulgit.
ventus ubi invasit nubem et versatus ibidem
fecit ut ante cavam docui spissescere nubem,
mobilitate sua fervescit; ut omnia motu
percalefacta vides ardescere, plumbea vero
glans etiam longo cursu volvenda liquescit.

by Lamb. *trucidet* Junt. not Pont. or Mar. for *trucidat.* Lach. on the contrary in 145 for *Fit* reads *Id.* 149 *propere* Mar. Ald. 1 Junt. for *propter.* 151 *repente* Flor. 31 Brix. Pont. for *recente.* 154 *res ulla* Macrob. sat. VI 4 5 for *res uita. res ulla uita* Ver. Ven. *resina* Flor. 31 Camb. 158 *in artum. in arto* Lach.: but somewhat involved constructions are by no means avoided by Lucr.: comp. 176 and III 843. 165 *Fulgere* Nicc. B corr. for *Fugere.* 168 *Ancipiti* Flor. 31 Mon. Brix. for *Ungipiti. videas* Mar. Junt. for *videat.* 172 *E simili* A Nicc. Flor. 31 (Lach. wrongly assigns to it *Et*) 2 Vat. Brix. Mar. Junt. Lamb. *Et simili* B Camb. Mon. 3 Vat. Ver. Ven. Avanc. 179 *liquescit* Pont. Mar.

ergo fervidus hic nubem cum perscidit atram,
dissipat ardoris quasi per vim expressa repente
semina quae faciunt nictantia fulgura flammae;
inde sonus sequitur qui tardius adficit auris
quam quae perveniunt oculorum ad lumina nostra.
scilicet hoc densis fit nubibus et simul alte
extructis aliis alias super impete miro;
ne tibi sit frudi quod nos inferne videmus
quam sint lata magis quam sursum extructa quid extent.
contemplator enim, cum montibus adsimulata
nubila portabunt venti transversa per auras,
aut ubi per magnos montis cu*mu*lata videbis
insuper esse aliis alia atque urguere superne
in statione locata sepultis undique ventis:
tum poteris magnas moles cognoscere eorum
speluncasque velut saxis pendentibu' structas
cernere, quas venti cum tempestate coorta
conplerunt, magno indignantur murmure clausi
nubibus in caveisque ferarum more minantur;
nunc hinc nunc illinc fremitus per nubila mittunt
quaerentesque viam circum versantur et ignis
semina convolvunt *e* nubibus atque ita cogunt
multa rotantque cavis flammam fornacibus intus,
donec divolsa fulserunt nube corusci.
  Hac etiam fit uti de causa mobilis ille
devolet in terram liquidi color aureus ignis,
semina quod nubes ipsas permulta necessust
ignis habere; etenim cum sunt umore sine ullo,
flammeus est plerumque colos et splendidus ollis.

Ald. 1 Junt. for *quiescit*: a certain correction. *calescit* Lach. utterly destroying the force of the passage. 180 *perscidit* Flor. 31 Camb. Mon. Brix. for *perscindit*.

183 *adficit* Bentl. for *adlicit*. *adtigit* Lamb. conj. *adcidit* Heins. in ms. notes. 184 *lumina* B. *limina* A Nicc. Flor. 31 three Vat. 185 *alte* Mar. Ald. 1 Junt. for *alti*. 187 188 wrongly placed by Lach. after 193 on account of the neuters: see 759 I 352 IV 934. 187 *Ne*. *Nec* Mon. Lach. 188 *sint* Mar. Junt. for *sit*. *extructa* Ald. 1 Junt. for *extricta*. 191 *cumulata* B corr. Brix. Ver. Ven. Mar. for *culata*. *procul alta* Flor. 31 Camb. 192 *urguere* A Nicc. *urgere* B. *superne* Bentl. for *superna*. 201 *e* added by Nicc. 205 *color* Serv. ad ecl. VI 33, Mar. Avanc. Nauger. *calor* AB Nicc. Flor. 31 Camb. Junt. mss. of Macrob. sat. VI 5 4: yet *color* must be right: the mss. of Macrobius sometimes agree strangely with those of Lucr. in corruptions. 208 *Flammeus est*

quin etiam solis de lumine multa necessest
concipere, ut merito rubeant ignesque profundant.
hasce igitur cum ventus agens contrusit in unum
compressitque locum cogens, expressa profundunt
semina quae faciunt flammae fulgere colores.
fulgit item, cum rarescunt quoque nubila caeli.
nam cum ventus eas leviter diducit euntis
dissoluitque, cadant ingratis illa necessest
semina quae faciunt fulgorem. tum sine taetro
terrore et sonitu fulgit nulloque tumultu.
  Quod superest, *quali* natura praedita constent
fulmina, declarant ictus et inusta vaporis
signa notaeque gravis halantis sulpuris auras.
ignis enim sunt haec non venti signa neque imbris.
praeterea sae*pe* accendunt quoque tecta domorum
et celeri flamma dominantur in aedibus ipsis.
hunc tibi subtilem cum primis ignibus ignem
constituit natura minutis mobilibusque
corporibus, cui nil omnino obsistere possit.
transit enim validum fulmen per saepta domorum,
clamor ut ac voces, transit per saxa, per aera,
et liquidum puncto facit aes in tempore et aurum,
curat item vasis integris vina repente
diffugiant, quia nimirum facile omnia circum
conlaxat rareque facit lateramina vasis
adveniens calor eius et insinuatus in ipsum
mobiliter soluens differt primordia vini.

Flor. 31 Camb. Mar. for *Flammeusq.* *splendidus ollis* Flor. 31 Mar. Camb. corr. but p. m., Mar. for *splendidusolis.* 209 *Quin etiam* Lach. for *Quippe enim. Quippe etenim* vulg. 210 *rubeant* Flor. 31 Camb. Brix. Pont. Mar. for *iubeant.* 213 *fulgere. fulgore* Avanc. Lach. in defiance of Epicurus and Lucretius assigning colour to atoms. 216 *ingratis* Pius in notes for *ingratius.* 218 *sonitu* Vat. 1954 Othob. Mar. Ald. 1 Junt. for *sonis. sonitis* Flor. 31 Camb. one Vat. *atque sonis* Pont. 219 *quali* added by Lamb. *quod sic* Flor. 31 Camb. 220 *ictus et* Flor. 31 Pont. Mar. Ald. 1 Junt. vulg. for *ictu et. ictu loca* Lach. 221 *auras* Mon. (or Mar.) Junt. for *auris.*

223 *saepe* Is. Voss. in ms. notes for *se. per se* Flor. 31 vulg. 226 *mobilibusque* Ald. 1 Junt. (not Pont. or Mar.) for *montibusque.* 228 229 Lach. makes one verse out of these two by omitting *per s. d. C. ut ac v. tr.* 229 *saxa* B corr. for *sasca.*

231 *Curat item. Curat utei* Lach. *Curat item ut* Lamb.: but surely there is sufficient authority for omitting *ut* after *curat.* 234 *et insinuatus* Lach. for *ut insinuatus.*

quod solis vapor aetatem non posse videtur
efficere usque adeo pellens fervore corusco:
tanto mobilior vis et dominantior haec est.
  Nunc ea quo pacto gignantur et impete tanto
fiant ut possint ictu discludere turris,
disturbare domos, avellere tigna trabesque,
et monimenta virum demoliri atque cremare,
exanimare homines, pecudes prosternere passim,
cetera de genere hoc qua vi facere omnia possint,
expediam, neque *te* in promissis plura morabor.
  Fulmina gign*ier* e crassis alteque putandumst
nubibus extructis; nam caelo nulla sereno
nec leviter densis mittuntur nubibus umquam.
nam dubio procul hoc fieri manifesta docet res;
quod tum per totum concrescunt aera nubes,
undique uti tenebras omnis Acherunta reamur
liquisse et magnas caeli complesse cavernas:
usque adeo taetra nimborum nocte coorta
inpendent atrae formidinis ora superne:
cum commoliri tempestas fulmina coeptat.
praeterea persaepe niger quoque per mare nimbus,
ut picis e caelo demissum flumen, in undas
sic cadit effertus tenebris procul et trahit atram
fulminibus gravidam tempestatem atque procellis,
ignibus ac ventis cum primis ipse repletus,
in terra quoque ut horrescant ac tecta requirant.
sic igitur supera nostrum caput esse putandumst
tempestatem altam. neque enim caligine tanta
obruerent terras, nisi inaedificata superne

ut insinuatur Nicc. Flor. 31 Camb. vulg.: but *ut* for *ubi* is not Lucretian. 237 *pellens* Ed. for *tellens*. *tollens* A corr. Nicc. *pollens* Lamb. vulg. Lach. *cellens* Wak. 241 *tigna* Lamb. first (not Flor. 31) for *igna*. *ligna* Nicc. later mss. and eds. before Lamb. 242 *demoliri* Mar. Ald. 1 Junt. for *commoliri*: prepositions seem often to be confounded in our mss. *cremare* Ed. for *ciere* which has no meaning: the last letters, which were on the outside margin of this the 259th page of the archetype, were lost. *lamenta* Lach. for *monimenta*: a violent change which destroys the whole force of the passage. 245 *te* added by Flor. 31 Camb. Pont. Mar. 246 *gignier* Mar. Ald. 1 Junt. for *gigni*. *nunc gigni* Flor. 31 Camb. *crassis* Nicc. for *classis*. 250 *tum* Lach. for *tunc*. 257 *demissum flumen* Junt. for *dimissum fulmen*. *demissum fulmen* Mar. Avanc. which is repeated as a correction at the end of his Catullus and must be a misprint for

multa forent multis exempto nubila sole;
nec tanto possent venientes opprimere imbri,
flumina abundare ut facerent camposque natare,
si non extructis foret alte nubibus aether.
hic igitur ventis atque ignibus omnia plena
sunt; ideo passim fremitus et fulgura fiunt.
quippe etenim supra docui permulta vaporis
semina habere cavas nubes et multa necessest
concipere ex solis radiis ardoreque eorum.
hoc ubi ventus eas idem qui cogit in unum
forte locum quemvis, expressit multa vaporis
semina seque simul cum eo commiscuit igni,
insinuatus ibi vortex versatur in arto
et calidis acuit fulmen fornacibus intus.
nam duplici ratione accenditur, ipse sua cum
mobilitate calescit et e contagibus ignis.
inde ubi percaluit venti vis *et* gravis ignis
impetus incessit, maturum tum quasi fulmen
perscindit subito nubem, ferturque coruscis
omnia luminibus lustrans loca percitus ardor.
quem gravis insequitur sonitus, displosa repente
opprimere ut caeli videatur templa superne.
inde tremor terras graviter pertemptat et altum
murmura percurrunt caelum; nam tota fere tum
tempestas concussa tremit fremitusque moventur.
quo de concussu sequitur gravis imber et uber,
omnis uti videatur in imbrem vertier aether
atque ita praecipitans ad diluviem revocari:
tantus discidio nubis ventique procella
mittitur, ardenti sonitus cum provolat ictu.
est etiam cum vis extrinsecus incita venti

flumen. 258 *effertus* Lach. for *et fertus.* *et fertur* vulg. 269 *plena* Flor. 31 Camb. Mon. etc. for *plana.* 272 *habere* Pont. Mar. Ald. 1 Junt. for *haecdere.* *hac de re* Nicc. 277 *arto* Lach. for *alto.* 281 *venti vis et gravis ignis* Bentl. for *gravis venti vis igni.* *gravida, aut vis ignis et acer* Lach. *vis venti vel gravis ignis* Mar. Junt. Lamb. etc. 286 *videatur* Ed. for *videantur*: the scribe has adapted the verb to *templa*: see I 1108: in 467 *videatur* mss. for *videantur.* Lach. reads *Exprimere* for *Opprimere,* Bern. *Occidere.* 290 *concussu* B corr. Pont. Mar. Ald. 1 Junt. for *concussus.* 291 *uti* Pont. Mar. Ald. 1 Junt. for *ut.* *ita ut* Flor. 31 Camb. 292 *revocari* Lach. for *revocare.* 296 *calidam*

incidit in calidam maturo fulmine nubem;
quam cum perscidit, extemplo cadit igneus ille
vertex quem patrio vocitamus nomine fulmen.
hoc fit idem in partis alias, quocumque tulit vis.
fit quoque ut interdum venti vis missa sine igni
igniscat tamen in spatio longoque meatu,
dum venit, amittens in cursu corpora quaedam
grandia quae nequeunt pariter penetrare per auras;
atque alia ex ipso conradens aere portat
parvola quae faciunt ignem commixta volando;
non alia longe ratione ac plumbea saepe
fervida fit glans in cursu, cum multa rigoris
corpora dimittens ignem concepit in auris.
fit quoque ut ipsius plagae vis excitet ignem,
frigida cum venti pepulit vis missa sine igni,
nimirum quia, cum vementi perculit ictu,
confluere ex ipso possunt elementa vaporis
et simul ex illa quae tum res excipit ictum;
ut, lapidem ferro cum caedimus, evolat ignis,
nec, quod frigida vis ferrist, hoc setius illi
semina concurrunt calidi fulgoris ad ictum.
sic igitur quoque res accendi fulmine debet,
opportuna fuit si forte et idonea flammis.
nec temere omnino plane vis frigida venti
esse potest, ea quae tanta vi missa supernest,
quin, prius in cursu si non accenditur igni,
at tepefacta tamen veniat commixta calore.
  Mobilitas autem fit fulminis et gravis ictus,
et celeri ferme percu*rru*nt fulmina lapsu,
nubibus ipsa quod omnino prius incita se vis

Bern. rightly for *valida*. *gravidam* Bentl. Lach. *fulmine* Mar. Ald. 1 Junt. for *culmine*. 298 *patrio* Flor. 31 Camb. 3 Vat. etc. for *spatio*. *quam spatio* (*quem patrio*) Ver. Ven. *Latio* B corr., perhaps rightly. *quem*. *quod* Camb. 2 Vat. Mar. Junt. Lamb. 302 *Dum venit, amittens*. 'Immo *Cum venit amittens*: alioquin oratio non constat' Lach. 308 *concepit* Flor. 31 Camb. Mon. Ver. Ven. for *concipit*. 309 *ipsius* Mar. Ald. 1 Junt. for *ipsis*. 315 *illi* Lach. for *ille*. *illa* Flor. 31 vulg. 320 *ea quae* Lach. first for *ex quae*. *ex quo* vulg. without sense. *tanta vi missa* Flor. 31 Camb. 2 Vat. Pont. for *tantaumissa*. *tanta immissa* Nicc. Ver. *tanta vi immissa* Mar. Ald. 1 Junt. 321 *cursu si* Flor. 31 Camb. for *cursus*. 323 *Mobilitas* A corr. Camb. etc. for *Nobilitas*. 324 *Et* Mar. Nauger. for *At*. *Ac* Junt. Wak. *percurrunt* Lach. for *percunt*. *pergunt* A corr. Nicc. *iam per-*

colligit et magnum conamen sumit eundi,
inde ubi non potuit nubes capere inpetis auctum,
exprimitur vis atque ideo volat impete miro,
ut validis quae de tormentis missa feruntur.
adde quod e parvis et levibus est elementis,
nec facilest tali naturae opsistere quicquam;
inter enim fugit ac penetrat per rara viarum,
non igitur multis offensibus in remorando
haesitat, hanc ob rem celeri volat impete labens.
deinde, quod omnino natura pondera deorsum
omnia nituntur, cum plagast addita vero,
mobilitas duplicatur et impetus ille gravescit,
ut vementius et citius quaecumque morantur
obvia discutiat plagis itinerque sequatur.
denique quod longo venit impete, sumere debet
mobilitatem etiam atque etiam, quae crescit eundo
et validas auget viris et roborat ictum.
nam facit ut quae sint illius semina cumque
e regione locum quasi in unum cuncta ferantur,
omnia coniciens in eum volventia cursum.
forsitan ex ipso veniens trahat aere quaedam
corpora quae plagis incendunt mobilitatem.
incolumisque venit per res atque integra transit
multa, foraminibus liquidus quia transvolat ignis.
multaque perfringit, cum corpora fulminis ipsa
corporibus rerum inciderunt, qua texta tenentur.
dissoluit porro facile aes aurumque repente
confervefacit, e parvis quia facta minute
corporibus vis est et levibus ex elementis,
quae facile insinuantur et insinuata repente
dissoluont nodos omnis et vincla relaxant.
autumnoque magis stellis fulgentibus apta

gunt Flor. 31 Camb. 2 Vat. *pergunt sic* Mar. Junt. Lamb. 335 *Deinde, quod. Adde quod* Lach. which seems to me much weaker than the ms. reading. 336 *plagast* Lach. for *plaga si. plaga sit* Flor. 31 Camb. all before Lach. 347 *incendunt* B rightly. *incedunt* A Nicc. *intendunt* Mar. Ald. 1 Junt. Lamb. etc. 349 *transvolat* Nauger. vulg. for *transviat. trameat* Gif. 350 *perfringit* Mar. Ald. 1 Junt. vulg. for *perfrigit* B, *perfigit* A, *perfregit* A corr. all later mss. Ver. Ven.: comp. 138 *perfringens* A corr. vulg. *perfingens* A, *perfrigens* B. Lach. keeps *perfigit*, which can hardly be right. 357 *apta* Turnebus Bentl. Wak. Lach. for

concutitur caeli domus undique totaque tellus,
et cum tempora se *veris* florentia pandunt.
frigore enim desunt ignes ventique calore
deficiunt neque sunt tam denso corpore nubes.
interutrasque igitur cum caeli tempora constant,
tum variae causae concurrunt fulminis omnes.
nam fretus ipse anni permiscet frigus *et* aestum,
quorum utrumque opus est fabricanda ad fulmina nubi,
ut discordia *sit* rerum magnoque tumultu
ignibus et ventis furibundus fluctuet aer.
prima caloris enim pars et postrema rigoris,
tempus id est vernum; quare pugnare necessest
dissimilis *res* inter se turbareque mixtas.
et calor extremus primo cum frigore mixtus
volvitur, autumni quod fertur nomine tempus,
hic quoque confligunt hiemes aestatibus acres.
propterea *freta* sunt haec anni nominitanda,
nec mirumst, in eo si tempore plurima fiunt
fulmina tempestasque cie*tur* turbida caelo,
ancipiti quoniam bello turbatur utrimque,
hinc flammis illinc ventis umoreque mixto.
  Hoc est igniferi naturam fulminis ipsam
perspicere et qua vi faciat rem quamque videre,
non Tyrrhena retro volventem carmina frustra
indicia occultae divum perquirere mentis,
unde volans ignis pervenerit aut in utram se
verterit hinc partim, quo pacto per loca saepta
insinuarit, et hinc dominatus ut extulerit se,
quidve nocere queat de caelo fulminis ictus.

alta. 359 *se veris* Flor. 31 Camb. Mar. etc. for *seris*. *seris* (*veris*) Ver. Ven.

360 *calore* Mar. ap. Victor. in ed. Ven. Ald. 1 Junt. for *calores*. 362 *Interutrasque*. *Interutraque* Lach. 364 *et* added by Mar. Junt. *frigidus aestum* Nicc. to Avanc. *ad aestum* Nonius. 365 *nubi* Lach. for *nobis* which has no sense. 366 *sit* added by Mar. Ald. 1 Junt. *sic* Flor. 31 Camb. 368 *et*, *rigoris* Mar. Junt. vulg. for *est*, *ligoris*. Lach. keeps *est*, and for *id* reads *ut*.

370 *res inter se* Flor. 31 Camb. 3 Vat. for *inter se*. *inter se res* Ver. Ven. Mar. vulg. Lach. wrongly, as *inter se* is metrically one word. 374 *freta* added by Lach. most acutely. Flor. 31 Camb. Mar. vulg. add *bella* after *haec*. 375 *eo si* B corr. Lamb. for *eos*. *si in eo sic* Camb. Mar. *si in eo tum* Avanc. *si in eo iam* Pont. Junt. 376 *cietur turbida* B corr. Flor. 31 Camb. Brix. for *cie turbida*.

382 *mentis* Flor. 31 Camb. 2 Vat. Mar. for *menti*. 384 *hinc* Mar. Lach. for *hic*,

quod si Iuppiter atque alii fulgentia divi
terrifico quatiunt sonitu caelestia templa
et iaciunt ignem quo *quo*iquest cumque voluptas,
cur quibus incautum scelus aversabile cumquest
non faciunt icti flammas ut fulguris halent
pectore perfixo, documen mortalibus acre,
et potius nulla sibi turpi conscius in re
volvitur in flammis innoxius inque peditur
turbine caelesti subito correptus et igni?
cur etiam loca sola petunt frustraque laborant?
an tum bracchia consuescunt firmantque lacertos?
in terraque patris cur telum perpetiuntur
optundi? cur ipse sinit neque parcit in hostis?
denique cur numquam caelo iacit undique puro
Iuppiter *in ter*ras fulmen sonitusque profundit?
an simul ac nubes successere, ipse in eas tum
descendit, prope ut hinc teli determinet ictus?
in mare qua porro mittit ratione? quid undas
arguit et liquidam molem camposque natantis?
praeterea si vult caveamus fulminis ictum,
cur dubitat facere ut possimus cernere missum?
si nec opinantis autem volt opprimere igni,
cur tonat ex illa parte, ut vitare queamus,
cur tenebras ante et fremitus et murmura concit?
et simul in multas partis qui credere possis
mittere? an hoc ausis numquam contendere factum,
ut fierent ictus uno sub tempore plures?
at saepest numero factum fierique necessest,
ut pluere in multis regionibus et cadere imbris,
fulmina sic uno fieri sub tempore multa.
postremo cur sancta deum delubra suasque
discutit infesto praeclaras fulmine sedes
et bene facta deum frangit simulacra suisque
demit imaginibus violento volnere honorem?

as in 88. 389 *quo quoiquest. quo cuique est* Flor. 31 Camb. Mar. etc. for *quo inquest. voluptas* Junt. first (not Flor. 31 or Mar.) for *voluntas.* 401 *Iuppiter in terras* Nicc. B corr. for *Iuppiterras*: but both B and Nicc. spell *Iupiter.* 402 *ipse in eas tum* Lamb. first for *ipse in aestum. ipsus in aestum* Flor. 31 Camb. 3 Vat. Mar. Wak. 406 *Praeterea. Propterea* A Nicc. *si vult* Avanc. Candidus at end of Junt. Nauger. for *si vivit* B, *si iuvit* A, *senuit* Nicc. *sevi ut* Flor. 31 Camb.

altaque cur plerumque petit loca plurimaque eius
montibus in summis vestigia cernimus ignis?
  Quod superest, facilest ex his cognoscere rebus,
presteras Grai quos ab re nominitarunt,
in mare qua missi veniant ratione superne.
nam fit ut interdum tamquam demissa columna
in mare de caelo descendat, quam freta circum
fervescunt graviter spirantibus incita flabris,
et quaecumque in eo tum sint deprensa tumultu
navigia in summum veniant vexata periclum.
hoc fit ubi interdum non quit vis incita venti
rumpere quam coepit nubem, sed deprimit, ut sit
in mare de caelo tamquam demissa columna,
paulatim, quasi quid pugno bracchique superne
coniectu trudatur et extendatur in undas;
quam cum discidit, hinc prorumpitur in mare venti
vis et fervorem mirum concinnat in undis;
versabundus enim turbo descendit et illam
deducit pariter lento cum corpore nubem;
quam simul ac gravidam detrusit ad aequora ponti,
ille in aquam subito totum se inmittit et omne
excitat ingenti sonitu mare fervere cogens.
fit quoque ut involvat venti se nubibus ipse
vertex conradens ex aere semina nubis
et quasi demissum caelo prestera imitetur.
hic ubi se in terras demisit dissoluitque,
turbinis inmanem vim provomit atque procellae.
sed quia fit raro omnino montisque necessest
officere in terris, apparet crebrius idem
prospectu maris in magno caeloque patenti.
  Nubila concrescunt, ubi corpora multa volando

saevi ut Mar. Junt. 421 *loca* B corr. Flor. 31 Camb. Mon. Ver. Ven. for *ioca. que eius* Lach. for *que plus. que huius* Lamb. 424 *Grai* Flor. 31 Camb. Brix. for *Grali. Graii* B corr. Mar. *Graiei* Lach.: Lucretius wrote either *Graiei* or *Grai*, not *Graii.* 426 *tamquam* Flor. 31 Camb. Ver. Ven. Mar. for *tam cum.*

428 *incita* Flor. 31 Camb. Mar. etc. for *lacita.* 430 *veniant* Lach. for *veniunt*: Flor. 31 Mar. Junt. Lamb. vulg. keep *veniunt*, and 429 read *sunt.* 440 *detrusit* Lamb. first for *detruit. detrudit* A corr. Nicc. 447 *procellae* Flor. 31 Vat. 640 Urbin. Vat. 1136 Othob. Mar. for *procellat* which Wak. absurdly retains. 449 *Officere* Flor. 31 Camb. Mon. for *Officeret.* 452 *supero* Lach. for *super. supera*

hoc supero in caeli spatio coiere repente
asperiora, moris quae possint indupedita
exiguis tamen inter se comprensa teneri.
haec faciunt primum parvas consistere nubes;
inde haec comprendunt inter se conque gregantur
et coniungendo crescunt ventisque feruntur
usque adeo donec tempestas saeva coortast.
fit quoque uti montis vicina cacumina caelo
quam sint quoque magis, tanto magis edita fument
adsidue furvae nubis caligine crassa
propterea quia, cum consistunt nubila primum,
ante videre oculi quam possint, tenvia, venti
portantes cogunt ad summa cacumina montis.
hic demum fit uti turba maiore coorta
et condensa queant apparere et simul ipso
vertice de montis videantur surgere in aethram.
nam loca declarat sursum ventosa patere
res ipsa et sensus, montis cum ascendimus altos.
praeterea permulta mari quoque tollere toto
corpora naturam declarant litore vestes
suspensae, cum concipiunt umoris adhaesum.
quo magis ad nubis augendas multa videntur
posse quoque e salso consurgere momine ponti;
nam ratio consanguineast umoribus ollis.
praeterea fluviis ex omnibus et simul ipsa

Lamb. conj. *coiere* Flor. 31 Camb. Brix. Mar. for *coire.* 453 *moris* Lach. for *modis*: a certain correction. 454 *comprensa* Mar. Lamb. for *compressa.* 456 *haec* Lach. for *ea*: *ea* might possibly be defended by 188, and 215 *eas*: see notes 2 there: but the harshness would be very great. 460 *quoque. quaeque* Camb. 2 Vat. Ald. 1 Mar. Junt. Lamb. etc. wrongly. 461 *furvae* Bentl. Lach. for *fulvae. nubis* Mar. Ald. 1 Junt. for *nubes.* 465 *turba maiore* Pont. Mar. Ald. 1 Junt. for *turbammor. turba minore* Flor. 31 Camb. 466 *Et condensa queant apparere* Lach. most acutely for *Et condensatque arta parere. Et condensa atque arta* Flor. 31, 3 Vat. Pont. Mar. Avanc. at end of Catullus. 467 *videantur* Flor. 31 Camb. Vat. 640 Urbin. 1136 Othob. Lamb. for *videatur.* 468 *loca* Flor. 31 Camb. Mar. Junt. for *lo. so* Nicc. *se* Brix. Ver. Ven. Ald. 1. 469 *et sensus* Avanc. for *et sensum*: Mar. Junt. Nauger. have *ad sensum.* 473 *Quo magis* Mon. Ald. 1 Junt. for *Quod magis.* 474 *consurgere momine* Flor. 31 Camb. Vat. 1136 and 1954 Othob. Mar. for *consurgerem homine.* 475 *consanguineast* Is. Voss. in ms. notes for *consanguinea se. cum sanguine ob eumoribus* Nicc. *cum sanguine abest* Flor. 31 Camb. 4 Vat. Lamb. *ollis* Lach. for *omnis.* Avanc. at end of Catullus says ‘ non percipio illum mancum versum *Nam ratio cum*

surgere de terra nebulas aestumque videmus,
quae velut halitus hinc ita sursum expressa feruntur
suffunduntque sua caelum caligine et altas
sufficiunt nubis paulatim conveniundo;
urget enim quoque signiferi super aetheris aestus
et quasi densendo subtexit caerula nimbis.
fit quoque ut huc veniant in caelum extrinsecus illa
corpora quae faciunt nubis nimbosque volantis;
innumerabilem enim numerum summamque profundi
esse infinitam docui, quantaque volarent
corpora mobilitate ostendi quamque repente
inmemorabile *per* spatium transire solerent.
haut igitur mirumst si parvo tempore saepe
montibu' tam magnis tempestas atque tenebrae
coperiunt maria ac terras inpensa superne,
undique quandoquidem per caulas aetheris omnis
et quasi per magni circum spiracula mundi
exitus introitusque elementis redditus extat.
Nunc age, quo pacto pluvius concrescat in altis
nubibus umor et in terras demissus ut imber
decidat, expediam. primum iam semina aquai
multa simul vincam consurgere nubibus ipsis
omnibus ex rebus pariterque ita crescere utrumque
et nubis et aquam quaecumque in nubibus extat,
ut pariter nobis corpus cum sanguine crescit,
sudor item atque umor quicumque est denique membris.
concipiunt etiam multum quoque saepe marinum
umorem, veluti pendentia vellera lanae,
cum supera magnum mare venti nubila portant.

sanguine ab humoribus omnis': which he found in Ven. 483 *huc* Vat. 3276 Avanc. for *hunc*. *hinc* Flor. 31 Camb. 2 Vat. Mon. *hunc coetum* Mar. Junt. Lamb. vulg. *illa* Flor. 31 Camb. Vat. 640 Urbin. Mar. for *illi* A, *ille* B. 488 *per* added by Pont. Mar. Junt. 490 *Montibu' tam magnis* Ed. for *Tam magnis montis*: *Tam magnis montib.* was the first corruption: see 189 and IV 140. *Tam magnis nimbis* Lach. *Tam magnae molis* Bern. *Tam magnos montis* Pont. Mar. Ald. 1 Junt. vulg. 491 *Coperiunt* Lach. rightly for *Coperiant*. [I now think it probable that Lucr. wrote *coperiant* as given by the mss: compare Cic. Laelius 29 *quid mirum est si animi hominum moveantur?* see Mueller ap. Seyffert p. 206: so here Lucr. seems to realise a special case before his eyes.] 492 *caulas* Mar. Ald. 1 Junt. for *cavias*. 496 *demissus* Flor. 31 Mon. Lamb. for *dimissus*.

498 *vincam* Flor. 31 Camb. Mon. Ver. Ven. for *vineam*. 503 *Concipiunt*

consimili ratione ex omnibus amnibus umor
tollitur in nubis. quo cum bene semina aquarum
multa modis multis convenere undique adaucta,
confertae nubes *umorem* mittere certant
dupliciter; nam vis venti contrudit et ipsa
copia nimborum turba maiore coacta
urget, de supero premit ac facit effluere imbris.
praeterea cum rarescunt quoque nubila ventis
aut dissolvuntur, solis super icta calore,
mittunt umorem pluvium stillantque, quasi igni
cera super calido tabescens multa liquescat.
sed vemens imber fit, ubi vementer utraque
nubila vi cumulata premuntur et impete venti.
atque tenere diu pluviae longumque morari
consuerunt, ubi multa cientur semina aquarum
atque aliis aliae nubes nimbique rigantes
insuper atque omni vulgo de parte feruntur,
terraque cum fumans umorem tota redhalat.
hic ubi sol radiis tempestatem inter opacam
adversa fulsit nimborum aspargine contra,
tum color in nigris existit nubibus arqui.

Cetera quae sorsum crescunt sorsumque creantur,
et quae concrescunt in nubibus, omnia, prorsum
omnia, nix venti grando gelidaeque pruinae
et vis magna geli, magnum duramen aquarum,
et mora quae fluvios passim refrenat euntis,

Brix. Pont. Mar. for *Concidiunt*. 509 *umorem* Ed. for *vi venti* which as Creech has seen comes from the *vis venti* of 510: he proposes *imbres tum*: what Lucr. wrote must be quite uncertain. *umentia* Lach. after a conj. of Wak. 511 *turba maiore* Mar. Ald. 1 Junt. for *turbam more*: the same error as in 465. *minore* Flor. 31 Camb. 3 Vat. 512 *Urget de supero* Lach. for *Urgete supero*. *Urget et e supero* A corr. Nicc. vulg. 515 *stillantque* B corr. Lamb. for *stillante*.

516 *Cera* Flor. 31 Pont. Mar. Ald. 1 Junt. for *Tela*. *Teda* B corr. 518 *vi. aquis* Lach. thereby ruining the sense. 519 *Atque tenere* Lach. for *At retineret*. *At remanere* Bern. 520 *cientur* Lach. from a conj. of Wak., for *fientur*. *fluentur* Flor. 31 Camb. Wak. *fuerunt* Mar. Ald. 1 Junt. 523 *umorem*. *humorem* AB: often as this and cognate words occur, this is the only instance where B has the aspirate: A has it in three other places: II 1114 *Umor ad humorem* A. *redhalat* Is. Voss. in ms. notes for *redralat*: he also proposes *relatrat* 'i.e. reposcit'. *rehalat* A corr. vulg. 524 *inter* Nicc. for *inte* B, *ime* A.

527 *sorsum...sorsumque* Koch in Rhein. mus. n. f. VIII p. 640 for *sursum...sursumque*. *cursu...cursuque* Lach. 531 *euntis* B corr. Pont. Avanc. for *avintis*. *aventis*

perfacilest tamen haec reperire animoque videre
omnia quo pacto fiant quareve creentur,
cum bene cognoris elementis reddita quae sint.
  Nunc age quae ratio terrai motibus extet
percipe. et in primis terram fac ut esse rearis
supter item ut supera ventosis undique plenam
speluncis multosque lacus multasque lucunas
in gremio gerere et rupes deruptaque saxa;
multaque sub tergo terrai flumina tecta
volvere vi fluctus summersaque saxa putandumst;
undique enim similem esse sui res postulat ipsa.
his igitur rebus subiunctis suppositisque
terra superne tremit magnis concussa ruinis,
subter ubi ingentis speluncas subruit aetas;
quippe cadunt toti montes magnoque repente
concussu late disserpunt inde tremores.
et merito, quoniam plaustri concussa tremescunt
tecta viam propter non magno pondere tota,
nec minus exultant, ut scrupus cumque viai
ferratos utrimque rotarum succutit orbes.
fit quoque, ubi in magnas aqüae vastasque lucunas
gleba vetustate e terra provolvitur ingens,
ut iactetur aquae fluctu quoque terra vacillans;

A corr. *aquantis* Flor. 31 Mar. Junt. 533 *fiant* Mar. Ald. 1 Junt. for *fluant.* 536 *terram* Flor. 31 Camb. etc. for *terras.* 537 *supera* Avanc. for *super. supra est* Mar. Junt. *supera'st* Lamb. etc. *ventosis* Wak. for *ventis*, 'egregie' says Lach. justly. 541 *summersaque saxa* Flor. 31 Camb. 3 Vat. Mar. vulg. for *summersosca.* '*summerso capte* i.e. capite. sic Enn. *Capitibus nutantes pinus*' Is. Voss. in ms. notes. 542 *similem* Junt. first for *simile. esse sui* Ald. 1 Junt. for *esse vi. simile esse et par* Mar. 548 *plaustri* Lach. for *plaustris.* 550 *exultant, ut scrupus cumque viai* Ed. for *exultantes dupuis cumque vim*: see notes 2: Lach. rightly saw that *vim* meant *viai*: so 465 and 511 the mss. have *mmore* for *maiore*; but the rest of his reading *et ubi lapi' cumque* seems to me to pervert the meaning, as Lucr. is giving two distinct instances of great results from small causes; and it would be a really monstrous exaggeration to say that houses shake in the way a carriage does, when the wheels are struck up by a stone on the road. *ubi currus cumque equum vi* Flor. 31 Camb. and 3 Vat.: but Camb. in text and Vat. 1136 Othob. in marg. have also the ms. reading. *ubi currus cunque equitum vi* Mar. Junt. Lamb. ed. 1. *ubi currus fortis equum vis* ed. 2 and 3, the *fortis equum vis* being from Avanc. *aedes, ubi cumque equitum vis* Wak. *sola Pisaeumque flumen* Is. Voss. in ms. notes: he adds *cum* after *Ferratos.* 552 *in magnas aqüae. magnas in aquae* Lamb. vulg. before Lach. 554 *vacillans* B corr. Avanc. for *vacillas.*

ut vas inter*dum* non quit constare, nisi umor
destitit in dubio fluctu iactarier intus.
  Praeterea ventus cum per loca subcava terrae
collectus parte ex una procumbit et urget
obnixus magnis speluncas viribus altas,
incumbit tellus quo venti prona premit vis.
tum supera terram quae sunt extructa domorum
ad caelumque magis quanto sunt edita quaeque,
inclinata *tu*ment in eandem prodita partem
protractaeque trabes inpendent ire paratae.
et metuunt magni naturam credere mundi
exitiale aliquod tempus clademque manere,
cum videant tantam terrarum incumbere molem!
quod nisi respirent venti, vis nulla refrenet
res neque ab exitio possit reprehendere euntis.
nunc quia respirant alternis inque gravescunt
et quasi collecti redeunt ceduntque repulsi,
saepius hanc ob rem minitatur terra ruinas
quam facit; inclinatur enim retroque recellit
et recipit prolapsa suas in pondere sedes.
hac igitur ratione vacillant omnia tecta,
summa magis mediis, media imis, ima perhilum.
  Est haec eiusdem quoque magni causa tremoris,
ventus ubi atque animae subito vis maxima quaedam
aut extrinsecus aut ipsa tellure coorta
in loca se cava terrai coniecit ibique
speluncas inter magnas fremit ante tumultu
versabunda*que* portatur, post incita cum vis

555 *inter dum* Lach. for *inter*. *in terra* Mar. Ald. 1 Junt. vulg. perhaps rightly. 563 *Inclinata tument* Ed. with Vat. 3276 for *Inclinata minent*: the *tu* was absorbed by the preceding *ta* and then *ment* passed into *minent*: the Verona palimpsest of Lucan v 160 has *consultamultu* for *consulta tumultu*: comp. 1195 *tenta mebat* of mss. for *tenta tumebat*, and v 1409 *servare genus* for *servare recens*. *Inclinata meant* Lach. *abeunt* Bern. *minant* Flor. 31 Camb. Mar. Ald. 1 Junt.: see Prisc. inst. VIII 29: I wrongly read *minantur* in small ed. *micant* Pius in text. Lamb. retains *minent*. At the end of this verse A and Nicc. have a. a. q. q. B has *aqueq*. which Bern. praef. p. III thinks a mere repetition of the end of 562, A introducing a further corruption: but Nicc. proves that the archetype agreed with A, not B. 568 *venti, vis nulla* Mar. Wak. for *ventis nulla*. 574 *in pondere* A Nicc. vulg. rightly. *in pondera* B Turneb. Lach. The passages I quote in notes 2 will prove that Turneb. and Lach. are quite mistaken in supposing that the sing.

exagitata foras erumpitur et simul altam
diffindens terram magnum concinnat hiatum.
in Syria Sidone quod accidit et fuit Aegi
in Peloponneso, quas exitus hic animai
disturbat urbes et terrae motus obortus.
multaque praeterea ceciderunt moenia magnis
motibus in terris et multae per mare pessum
subsedere suis pariter cum civibus urbes.
quod nisi prorumpit, tamen impetus ipse animai
et fera vis venti per crebra foramina terrae
dispertitur ut horror et incutit inde tremorem;
frigus uti nostros penitus cum venit in artus,
concutit invitos cogens tremere atque movere.
ancipiti trepidant igitur terrore per urbis,
tecta superne timent, metuunt inferne cavernas
terrai ne dissoluat natura repente,
neu distracta suum late dispandat hiatum
adque suis confusa velit comple*re* ruinis.
proinde licet quamvis caelum terramque reantur
incorrupta fore aeternae mandata saluti;
et tamen interdum praesens vis ipsa pericli
subdit et hunc stimulum quadam de parte timoris,
ne pedibus raptim tellus subtracta feratur
in barathrum rerumque sequatur prodita summa
funditus et fiat mundi confusa ruina.
 [Principio mare mirantur non reddere maius
naturam, quo sit tantus decursus aquarum,
omnia quo veniant ex omni flumina parte.
adde vagos imbris tempestatesque volantes,
omnia quae maria ac terras sparguntque rigantque;
adde suos fontis; tamen ad maris omnia summam

cannot be used in the same sense as the plur. 582 *que* added by Flor. 31 Camb. Pont. etc. 585 *Syria. Tyria* Lamb. etc. without cause. 586 *quas* Avanc. for *qua.* 588 *ceciderunt* Mon. Ver. Ven. for *cecideret. cecidere et* Flor. 31 Camb. 589 *pessum* Nicc. B corr. for *possum.* 600 *Adque* Lach. for *Idque. Imque* Lamb. in the additions to ed. 3. 604 *Subdit et hunc* A Flor. 31 Camb. etc. *Subdita et hunc* BA corr. Nicc. *Subdit athuc* Lach. *Subditat hunc* Mar. Junt. Lamb. etc. 605 *subtracta* Nicc. for *substructa.* 608—638 are proved by Lach. to be quite unconnected with what precedes or follows. Mar. Junt. vulg. prefix this verse *Nunc ratio reddenda augmen cur nesciat aequor.* 609

guttai vix instar erunt unius adaugmen;
quo minus est mirum mare non augescere magnum.
praeterea magnam sol partem detrahit aestu.
quippe videmus enim vestis umore madentis
exsiccare suis radiis ardentibu' solem:
at pelage multa et late substrata videmus.
proinde licet quamvis ex uno quoque loco sol
umoris parvam delibet ab aequore partem;
largiter in tanto spatio tamen auferet undis.
tum porro vènti quoque magnam tollere partem
umoris possunt verrentes aequora, ventis
una nocte vias quoniam persaepe videmus
siccari mollisque luti concrescere crustas.
praeterea docui multum quoque tollere nubes
umorem magno conceptum ex aequore ponti
et passim toto terrarum spargere in orbi,
cum pluit in terris et venti nubila portant.
postremo quoniam raro cum corpore tellus
est, et coniunctast, oras maris undique cingens,
debet, ut in mare de terris venit umor aquai,
in terras itidem manare ex aequore salso;
percolatur enim virus retroque remanat
materies umoris et ad caput amnibus omnis
confluit, inde super terras redit agmine dulci
qua via secta semel liquido pede *de*tulit undas.]
Nunc ratio quae sit, per fauces montis ut Aetnae
expirent ignes interdum turbine tanto,
expediam. neque enim mediocri clade coorta
flammea tempestas Siculum dominata per agros
finitimis ad se convertit gentibus ora,

Naturam Pont. Mar. Ald. 1 Junt. first for *Natura.* 614 *adaugmen. ad augmen* Nicc. followed by all mss. and eds. before Lach. 616 *magnam sol* Pont. Junt. for *sol magnam. magnam partem sol* Mar. 624 *aequora, ventis* Lach. for *aequora venti. aequora ponti* Nicc. vulg. perhaps rightly, as the words are often confused: comp. I 276: and *ventis* is somewhat awkward. 629 *orbi* Mar. Junt. for *orbis. orbe* Flor. 31 Camb. Avanc. 632 *maris* B corr. Pont. Mar. Junt. (not Flor. 31) for *magis.* 638 *pede detulit* A corr. for *pede tulit.* 641 *mediocri clade coorta* Is. Voss. in ms. notes for *media grecia de coorta*: a fine and certain correction. *media de glade* Vat. 1954 Othob. *media de clade* two Vat. Pius in notes, Nauger. Lamb. *media quae clade* Avanc. *dia de clade* Fab. *Enceladi de clade* Bentl. before he knew Vossius' emendation. 642 *Flammea* Heins. in

fumida cum caeli scintillare omnia templa
cernentes pavida complebant pectora cura,
quid moliretur rerum natura novarum.
  Hisce tibi in rebus latest alteque videndum
et longe cunctas in partis dispiciendum,
ut reminiscaris summam rerum esse profundam
et videas caelum summai totius unum
quam sit parvula pars et quam multesima constet,
nec tota pars, homo terrai quota totius unus.
quod bene propositum si plane contueare
ac videas plane, mirari multa relinquas.
numquis enim nostrum miratur siquis in artus
accepit calido febrim fervore coortam
aut alium quemvis morbi per membra dolorem?
opturgescit enim subito pes, arripit acer
saepe dolor dentes, oculos invadit in ipsos,
existit sacer ignis et urit corpore serpens
quamcumque arripuit partim, repitque per artus,
nimirum quia sunt multarum semina rerum,
et satis haec tellus nobis caelumque mali fert,
unde queat vis immensi procrescere morbi.
sic igitur toti caelo terraeque putandumst
ex infinito satis omnia suppeditare,
unde repente queat tellus concussa moveri
perque mare ac terras rapidus percurrere turbo,
ignis abundare Aetnaeus, flammescere caelum;
id quoque enim fit et ardescunt caelestia templa,
et tempestates pluviae graviore coortu
sunt, ubi forte ita se tetulerunt semina aquarum.
'at nimis est ingens incendi turbidus ardor.'
scilicet et fluvius quivis est maximus ei
qui non ante aliquem maiorem vidit, et ingens
arbor homoque videtur, et omnia de genere omni

ms. notes for *Flammae*. 648 *dispiciendum* Nicc. for *despiciendum*. 652 corrupted by Mar. Junt. Lamb. etc. 653 *propositum* B corr. Ver. Ven. Mar. for *propositus*. *propositum est* Flor. 31 Camb. *plane* B corr. Flor. 31 Camb. Mon. for *plani*. 663 *nobis* Mar. Junt. Lamb. etc. for *morbi* which has come from 664. *orbi* Lach. 674 *quivis est* Bentl. for *qui visus*. *quivis ut* Heins. in ms. notes, and Is. Voss. in ms. notes. *qui non est* Lamb. *est* is added after *ei* by Flor.

maxima quae vidit quisque, haec ingentia fingit,
cum tamen omnia cum caelo terraque marique
nil sint ad summam summai totius omnem.
 Nunc tamen illa modis quibus inritata repente
flamma foras vastis Aetnae fornacibus efflet,
expediam. primum totius subcava montis
est natura, fere silicum suffulta cavernis.
omnibus est porro in speluncis ventus et aer;
ventus enim fit, ubi est agitando percitus aer.
hic ubi percaluit calefecitque omnia circum
saxa furens, qua contingit, terramque, et ab ollis
excussit calidum flammis velocibus ignem,
tollit se ac rectis ita faucibus eicit alte.
fert itaque ardorem longe longeque favillam
differt et crassa volvit caligine fumum
extruditque simul mirando pondere saxa;
ne dubites quin haec animai turbida sit vis.
praeterea magna ex parti mare montis ad eius
radices frangit fluctus aestumque resorbet.
ex hoc usque mari speluncae montis ad altas
perveniunt subter fauces. hac ire fatendumst
. . . .
et penetrare mari penitus res cogit aperto
atque efflare foras ideoque extollere flammam
saxaque subiectare et arenae tollere nimbos.
in summo sunt vertice enim crateres, ut ipsi
nominitant; nos quod fauces perhibemus et ora.
 Sunt aliquot quoque res quarum unam dicere causam
non satis est, verum pluris, unde una tamen sit;

31 Camb. one Vat. Lamb. 683 *fere silicum* A corr. Flor. 31 Camb. for *feres illi cum.* 687 *contingit* Flor. 31 Brix. Mar. for *contigit.* 690 *Fert itaque* Heins. in ms. notes and Lach. for *Fert itque. Fecitque* Nicc. *Vertitque* Is. Voss. in ms. notes. 695 *resorbet* Flor. 31 Camb. 3 Vat. Mar. for *resolvet*: a fine correction. 697 see Camb. Journ. of phil. i p. 40, where I said that at least one verse is here lost: in the smaller ed. I proposed a verse such as this, *Fluctibus admixtam vim venti; intrareque ab isto*: which will serve to shew the general meaning. Lach. violently reads *penitus percocta in apertum* for *penitus res cogit aperto.* 701 *vertice enim* Turneb. advers. xxii 19, Is. Voss. in ms. notes, Bentl. for *verticeni.* Turneb. also proposes and seems to prefer *vertigeni* which Lamb. ed. 3 adopts from him. *vertice item* Mar. Ald. 1 Junt. 702 *quod. quas* Pont.

corpus ut exanimum siquod procul ipse iacere
conspicias hominis, fit ut omnis dicere causas
conveniat leti, dicatur ut illius una.
nam neque eum ferro nec frigore vincere possis
interiisse neque a morbo neque forte veneno,
verum aliquid genere esse ex hoc quod contigit ei
scimus. item in multis hoc rebus dicere habemus.
  Nilus in aestatem crescit campisque redundat,
unicus in terris Aegypti totius amnis.
is rigat Aegyptum medium per saepe calorem,
aut quia sunt aestate aquilones ostia contra,
anni tempore eo qui etesiae esse feruntur,
et contra fluvium flantes remorantur et undas
cogentes sursus replent coguntque manere.
nam dubio procul haec adverso flabra feruntur
flumine, quae gelidis ab stellis axis aguntur.
ille ex aestifera parti venit amnis ab austro,
inter nigra virum percocto saecla colore
exoriens penitus media ab regione diei.
est quoque uti possit magnus congestus harenae
fluctibus adversis oppilare ostia contra,
cum mare permotum ventis ruit intus harenam;
quo fit uti pacto liber minus exitus amni
et proclivis item fiat minus impetus undis.
fit quoque uti pluviae forsan magis ad caput ei
tempore eo fiant, quod etesia flabra aquilonum
nubila coniciunt in eas tunc omnia partis.
scilicet ad mediam regionem eiecta diei
cum convenerunt, ibi ad altos denique montis
contrusae nubes coguntur vique premuntur.
forsitan Aethiopum penitus de montibus altis

Mar. Junt. Lamb. etc. wrongly: see Lach. III 94. 705 *iacere* Flor. 31 Camb. Brix. Mar. for *iaceret*. 708 *nam neque* Flor. 31 Camb. Mar. for *namque*.

710 *Verum* Mar. Ald. 1 Junt. for *Utrum*. *contigit ei* (*eii*) Is. Voss. in ms. notes for *contioitel* A, *contioite* B, *contioites* Nicc. two Vat.: a certain correction. *concio dicat* Flor. 31 two Vat. Ald. 1 Lamb. ed. 1 and 3. *concio credat* Camb. one Vat. Mon. Junt. Lamb. ed. 2. 719 *flabra* Flor. 31 Camb. Ver. Ven. for *flabro*.

727 *amni* Mar. Junt. for *amnis*. 729 *ei* AB Nicc. all Vat. Brix. Ver. Ven. *eius* Flor. 31 Camb. Pont. Mar. Ald. 1 Junt. vulg. before Lach. 730 *quod* Mar. Junt. rightly for *quo*, as *tunc* follows; but as Junt. writes it compendiously, no one before

crescat, ubi in campos albas descendere ningues
tabificis subigit radiis sol omnia lustrans.
Nunc age, Averna tibi quae sint loca cumque lacusque
expediam, quali natura praedita constent.
principio quod Averna vocantur nomine, id ab re
inpositumst, quia sunt avibus contraria cunctis,
e regione ea quod loca cum venere volantes,
remigi oblitae pennarum vela remittunt
praecipitesque cadunt molli cervice profusae
in terram, si forte ita fert natura locorum,
aut in aquam, si forte lacus substratus Avern*ist.*
is locus est Cumas aput, acri sulpure montes
oppleti calidis ubi fumant fontibus aucti.
est et Athenaeis in moenibus, arcis in ipso
vertice, Palladis ad templum Tritonidis almae,
quo numquam pennis appellunt corpora raucae
cornices, non cum fumant altaria donis:
usque adeo fugitant non iras Palladis acris
pervigili causa, Graium ut cecinere poetae,
sed natura loci ope sufficit ipsa suapte.
in Syria quoque fertur item locus esse videri,
quadripedes quoque quo simul ac vestigia primum
intulerint, graviter vis cogat concidere ipsa,
manibus ut si sint divis mactata repente.
omnia quae naturali ratione geruntur,

Lach. adopted it. 736 *descendere* Lamb. for *decedere.* 740 *quod. quo* Lach.: I now think him wrong. *quod..., nomen id* Flor. 31 Mar. Ald. 1 Junt. vulg. before Wak. *nomen aornis* Gervas. Tilleberiensis: see Lach. 743 *Remigii* Mar. Junt., *Remigi oblitae* Lach. for *Remigio oblitae.* 746 *substratus* Brix. Avanc. Nauger., *subiratus* (*substratus*) Ver. Ven. for *subiratus. Avernist* Ed., *Averno'st* Lamb., for *Averni.* Lach. inserts *est* before *si forte*; but the passage he quotes in support is not more in point than the one he cites in favour of *aut sex* in IV 303 (327), the metre there ruling the order of the words. 747 *Is* B. *His* A Nicc. *acri sulpure* Salmas. Heins. in ms. notes, Is. Voss. in ms. notes, Bentl. for *ecri suiper*: the readings of older editors are too absurd to mention. *montes* B, *montis* A Nicc. which is probably what Lucr. wrote. For *montes...aucti* Heins. suggests *olentes...agri.* 749 *Est et. Est ut* Lach. intolerant of *et* for *etiam.* 755 *ope sufficit* Ed. for *opus efficit*: a transposition of only two letters: comp. III 374. *vi ibus officit* Lach.: a harsh and inadmissible elision: see L. Mueller de re metr. p. 284. *loci hoc opus* Avanc. Lamb. *suapte. sua vi* Lamb. 759 *si sint divis mactata. si fit divis mactatu'* Lach.: an awkward and uncalled-for change: see IV 934. *fit* seems hardly Latin, the

et quibus effiant causis apparet origo;
ianua ne forte his Orci regionibus esse
credatur, post hinc animas Acheruntis in oras
ducere forte deos manis inferne reamur,
naribus alipedes ut cervi saepe putantur
ducere de latebris serpentia saecla ferarum.
quod procul a vera quam sit ratione repulsum
percipe; nam de re nunc ipsa dicere conor.
  Principio hoc dico, quod dixi saepe quoque ante,
in terra cuiusque modi rerum esse figuras;
multa, cibo quae sunt, vitalia, multaque, morbos
incutere et mortem quae possint adcelerare.
et magis esse aliis alias animantibus aptas
res ad vitai rationem ostendimus ante
propter dissimilem naturam dissimilisque
texturas inter sese primasque figuras.
multa meant inimica per auris, multa per ipsas
insinuant naris infesta atque aspera iactu,
nec sunt multa parum tactu vitanda neque autem
aspectu fugienda saporeque tristia quae sint.
  Deinde videre licet quam multae sint homini res
acriter infesto sensu spurcaeque gravesque;
arboribus primum certis gravis umbra tributa
usque adeo, capitis faciant ut saepe dolores,
siquis eas supter iacuit prostratus in herbis.
est etiam magnis Heliconis montibus arbos

structure of the sentence calling for a subjunctive. 761 *effiant causis* Lach. for *e fiant causis*: perhaps *ecfiant*. *e causis fiant* Flor. 31 Camb. 3 Vat. Mar. vulg. rightly perhaps. 762 *ne forte his* Ed. for *ne poteis*. *ne potis* A corr. Nicc.: perhaps *is* should be retained. *puteis* Turneb. *Puteis* Lach. i.e. Puteolanis: a quite unexampled form, and not I think suited to the context. *ne potius* Flor. 31 Camb. 2 Vat. Mar. etc.: hence Lamb. *ne his Orci potius*. *ne posita hiis* Wak.

763 *post hinc*. *posta, hinc* Mar. Junt. Lamb. etc. 764 *inferne* Lamb. for *inferna*. 768 *nam de re nunc ipsa* B. *de re* om. A: hence omitted or transposed in later mss. *namque ipsa de re* vulg. 771 *cibo quae sunt* Wak. first for *cibo eque sunt*. *homini quae sunt* Lamb. etc. 777 *auris* Mar. (acc. to Victor. but not in ms.) Ald. 1 Junt. for *auras*. 778 *aspera iactu* Ed. for *aspera tactu*: *iacere, adiectus* are specially said of smell, as II 846 IV 673: comp. also II 1047. Bentl. defends *tactu*, perhaps rightly. *aspera adactu* Lach.: but *adactu* implies a violent thrust or effort, as of a weapon, a tooth. *odore* Lamb. ed. 2 and 3.

780 *tristia* Flor. 31 Camb. Mon. Ver. Ven. for *tristitia*. 788 *ideo terris* Mar.

floris odore hominem taetro consueta necare.
scilicet haec ideo terris ex omnia surgunt,
multa modis multis multarum semina rerum
quod permixta gerit tellus discretaque tradit.
nocturnumque recens extinctum lumen ubi acri
nidore offendit nares, consopit ibidem,
concidere et spumas qui morbo mittere suevit.
castoreoque gravi mulier sopita recumbit
et manibus nitidum teneris opus effluit ei,
tempore eo si odoratast quo menstrua solvit.
multaque praeterea languentia membra per artus
solvunt atque animam labefactant sedibus intus.
denique si calidis etiam cunctare lavabris
plenior et laveris, solio ferventis aquai
quam facile in medio fit uti des saepe ruinas!
carbonumque gravis vis atque odor insinuatur
quam facile in cerebrum, nisi aquam praecepimus ante!
at cum membra domus percepit fervidu', nervis
tum fit odor viri plagae mactabilis instar.
nonne vides etiam terra quoque sulpur in ipsa
gignier et taetro concrescere odore bitumen;
denique ubi argenti venas aurique secuntur,
terrai penitus scrutantes abdita ferro,
qualis expiret Scaptensula subter odores?
quidve mali fit ut exhalent aurata metalla!
quas hominum reddunt facies qualisque colores!

Ald. 1 Junt. for *indeo tris*. 789 is rightly joined by Camb. Lamb. Gif. Wak. with 790. Creech Lach. etc. connect it with 788. 791 *acri* Lamb. ed. 2 first for *acris*. 793 *et spumas* Madvig in Henrichsen de fragm. Gottorp. p. 37 for *et pumos*: *spumas* Lamb. found in marg. of cod. Memmian. Lach. puts this verse after 801 and reads *et spumam ut* perversely: older corrections are unworthy of notice. 798 *labefactant* Flor. 31 Camb. Mar. Ver. Ven. for *labefaciant*.

799 *cunctare* Lach. for *cunctere*. 800 *et laveris, solio* Lach. for *efflueris solio*. *et frueris solio* Madv. l. l.: the passage is very doubtful. 803 *aquam* Flor. 31 Camb. Pont. Mar. Junt. for *aqua*. 804 *membra domus* Vat. 3276 Brix. Pius in notes, Gronov. Lach. for *membra domnus*. *domin'* Nicc. *dominus* Ver. Ven. Nauger. *donus* Flor. 31 Camb. two Vat. *membra domans* Mar. Junt. Is. Voss. in ms. notes, Madv. l. l. *membra hominis* Lamb. *fervidu', nervis* Ed. (*fervida, nervis* Wak.): the *n* of *nervis* was written over the line and wrongly attached to *domus*: hence *domnus*. *fervidior vis* Lach. for *fervida servis* A Nicc. *fervida fervis* B: *fervida febris* Lamb. Is. Voss. in ms. notes, Madv. 805 *viri* Pius in notes, Lach. for *vini*.

806 *ipsa* Flor. 31 Camb. Pont. for *ipso*. 808 *argenti* Flor. 31 Camb. Mon.

nonne vides audisve perire in tempore parvo
quam soleant et quam vitai copia desit,
quos opere in tali cohibet vis magna necessis?
hos igitur tellus omnis exaestuat aestus
expiratque foras in apertum promptaque caeli.
  Sic et Averna loca alitibus summittere debent
mortiferam vim, de terra quae surgit in auras,
ut spatium caeli quadam de parte venenet;
quo simul ac primum pennis delata sit ales,
impediatur ibi caeco correpta veneno,
ut cadat e regione loci, qua derigit aestus.
quo cum conruit, hic eadem vis illius aestus
reliquias vitae membris ex omnibus aufert.
quippe etenim primo quasi quendam conciet aestum;
posterius fit uti, cum iam cecidere veneni
in fontis ipsos, ibi sit quoque vita vomenda
propterea quod magna mali fit copia circum.
  Fit quoque ut interdum vis haec atque aestus Averni
aera, qui inter avis cumquest terramque locatus,
discutiat, prope uti locus hic linquatur inanis.
cuius ubi e regione loci venere volantes,
claudicat extemplo pinnarum nisus inanis
et conamen utrimque alarum proditur omne.
hic ubi nixari nequeunt insistereque alis,
scilicet in terram delabi pondere cogit
natura, et vacuum prope iam per inane iacentes
dispergunt animas per caulas corporis omnis.

*

frigidior porro in puteis aestate fit umor,

Pont. for *argento*. 813 *audisve* Flor. 31 Camb. Mar. for *audire*. 815 *necessis* Lach. for *necessest*. 817 *apertum* B. *aperta* A Nicc. vulg. before Lach. *apertaque* Flor. 31. 818 *et*. *ea* Lach. ever intolerant of *et* for *etiam*. *alitibus* Flor. 31 Camb. Mar. for *malitbus*. 829 *fit*. *sit* Junt. Lamb. vulg.: a solecism. 832 *hic* Mon. p. m. Lach. for *hinc*. *linquatur* Flor. 31 Camb. Ver. Ven. Mar. for *linquitur*. 840 clearly something is wanting to connect this verse with what precedes. Lach. has proved that a new leaf, the 142nd, of the archetype began here: in all probability then one leaf had dropped out in this place. Lach. inserts four fragments, *Non mihi si linguae centum sint oraque centum, Aerea vox. Mensibu' frigus. Cameraeque caminis. Ne oblimet.* The first certainly appears Lucretian: where it came in the poem, cannot be said; the rest are very doubtful. 840 *Que* is prefixed to *Frigidior* in A, *uae* (i.e. *quae*) in B, *Cur* by

rarescit quia terra calore et semi*na* siquae
forte vaporis habet, propere dimittit in auras.
quo magis est igitur tellus effeta calore,
fit quoque frigidior qui in terrast abditus umor.
frigore cum premitur porro omnis terra coitque
et quasi concrescit, fit scilicet ut coeundo
exprimat in puteos siquem gerit ipsa calorem.
  Esse apud Hammonis fanum fons lūce diurna
frigidus et calidus nocturno tempore fertur.
hunc homines fontem nimis admirantur et acri
sole putant supter terras fervescere raptim,
nox ubi terribili terras caligine texit.
quod nimis a verast longe ratione remotum.
quippe ubi sol nudum contractans corpus aquai
non quierit calidum supera de reddere parte,
cum superum lumen tanto fervore fruatur,
qui queat hic supter tam crasso corpore terram
percoquere umorem et calido satiare vapore?
praesertim cum vix possit per saepta domorum
insinuare suum radiis ardentibus aestum.
quae ratiost igitur? nimirum terra magis quod
rara tepet circum fontem quam cetera tellus
multaque sunt ignis prope semina corpus aquai.
hoc ubi roriferis terram nox obruit umbris,
extemplo penitus frigescit terra coitque.
hac ratione fit ut, tamquam compressa manu sit,
exprimat in fontem quae semina cumque habet ignis,
quae calidum faciunt aqüae tactum atque saporem.
inde ubi sol radiis terram dimovit obortus

Nicc. 841 *Rarescit* Lamb. for *Arescit*. *semina* Flor. 31 Camb. for *semi*. *si quae* Avanc. at end of Catullus for *siqua* which he kept in Ald. 1 as did all editors before Lach. 842 *habet, propere* Nicc. Camb. Mon. Ver. Ven. vulg. for *habet proprie* B Flor. 31, *propriae* A. *proprii* Bern. whom I followed in small ed. forgetting that Nicc., i. e. Poggio's ms. in all likelihood, had *propere*. 846 *ut coeundo* Lamb. for *in coeundo*. *in quo eundo* Nicc. 851 *raptim* Lamb. for *partim*. 857 *supter* Pont., *subter* Mar. Ald. 1 Junt. for *super*. 858 *satiare* Vat. 1954 Othob. Pius in notes, Turneb. advers. xxvi 13 for *soclare*. *sotiare* Camb. Avanc. *sol dare* Nicc. *sociare* Flor. 31 Mar. Junt. *donare* Bern. 862 *Rara* Lamb. Turneb. adv. xxvi 13 for *Para*. *tepet* Lach. for *tenet*. 864 *umbris* Mar. (ap. Victor., not in ms.), Avanc. at end of Catull., Junt. for *undis*. 865 *penitus* Lach. for *sonitus*. *subtus* Ald. 1 Junt. vulg. *solito* Mar. 868 *aqüae* Lach.

et rarefecit calido gliscente vapore,
rursus in antiquas redeunt primordia sedes
ignis et in terram cedit calor omnis aquai.
frigidus hanc ob rem fit fons in luce diurna.
praeterea solis radiis iactatur aquai
umor et in lucem tremulo rarescit ab aestu;
propterea fit uti quae semina cumque habet ignis
dimittat; quasi saepe gelum, quod continet in se,
mittit et exolvit glaciem nodosque relaxat.
  Frig*id*us est etiam fons, supra quem sita saepe
stuppa iacit flammam concepto protinus igni,
taedaque consimili ratione accensa per undas
conlucet, quocumque natans impellitur auris.
nimirum quia sunt in aqua permulta vaporis
semina de terraque necessest funditus ipsa
ignis corpora per totum consurgere fontem
et simul exspirare foras exireque in auras,
non ita multa tamen, calidus queat ut fieri fons,
propterea dispersa foras erumpere cogit
vis per aquam subito sursumque ea conciliari.
quod genus endo marist Aradi fons, dulcis aquai
qui scatit et salsas circum se dimovet undas;
et multis aliis praebet regionibus aequor
utilitatem opportunam sitientibu' nautis,
quod dulcis inter salsas intervomit undas.
sic igitur per eum possunt erumpere fontem
et scatere illa foras, in stuppam semina quae cum

after Bede for *laticis*: Lamb. too notices it in notes. *saporem* Lamb. for *vaporem*: a necessary change, though Bede also has *vaporem*. 870 *gliscente* Wak. for *miscente*, 'eleganter et vere' says Lach. 877 *Dimittat* Camb. for *Demittat*.

878 *nodosque* Vat. 3276 Mon. (not Flor. 31) Pont. Ald. 1 Candidus at end of Junt. for *nobosque*. *novosque* A corr. *venasque* Flor. 31 Camb. 3 Vat. Mar. Junt.

879 *Frigidus* Flor. 31 Camb. Mon. Ver. Ven. for *frigus*. 887 *Non ita multa* Is. Voss. in ms. notes for *Non ita muita*: though Haverc. knew of this, neither he nor any editor before Lach. adopted it. *Non tam vita* Nicc. *Non tam multa* Pont. *Non tam viva* vulg. 888 *Propterea* Lach. for *Praeterea*. 890 *marist Aradi fons* Bern. Lach. for *maris parat fons*: a certain correction, as A and B have each this heading 'de fonte aradi in mare'. *mari Aradio fons* Is. Voss. in ms. notes. *mari spirat fons* Flor. 31 Camb. Mar. etc. 889 *conciliari* Lamb. for *conciliare*.

892 *praebet* Flor. 31 Camb. Mar. Junt. for *praeter*. 894 *dulcis* Flor. 31 Camb. Ver. Ven. for *dulcit*. 896 *quae* Ven. (*que* mss. Brix. Ver.) rightly retained by N. P. Howard who corrects old punctuation. *quo* Lamb. vulgo Lach.

conveniunt aut in taedai corpore adhaerent,
ardescunt facile extemplo, quia multa quoque in se
semina habent ignis stuppae taedaeque latentis.
nonne vides etiam, nocturna ad lumina linum
nuper ubi extinctum admoveas, accendier ante
quam tetigit flammam, taedamque pari ratione?
multaque praeterea prius ipso tacta vapore
eminus ardescunt quam comminus imbuat ignis.
hoc igitur fieri quoque in illo fonte putandumst.
  Quod superest, agere incipiam quo foedere fiat
naturae, lapis hic ut ferrum ducere possit,
quem Magneta vocant patrio de nomine Grai,
Magnetum quia fit patriis in finibus ortus.
hunc homines lapidem mirantur; quippe catenam
saepe ex anellis reddit pendentibus ex se.
quinque etenim licet interdum pluresque videre
ordine demissos levibus iactarier auris,
unus ubi ex uno dependet supter adhaerens
ex alioque alius lapidis vim vinclaque noscit:
usque adeo permananter vis pervolat eius.
  Hoc genus in rebus firmandumst multa prius quam
ipsius rei rationem reddere possis,
et nimium longis ambagibus est adeundum;
quo magis attentas auris animumque reposco.
  Principio omnibus ab rebus, quascumque videmus,
perpetuo fluere ac mitti spargique necessest
corpora quae feriant oculos visumque lacessant.
perpetuoque fluunt certis ab rebus odores;
frigus ut *a* fluviis, calor ab sole, aestus ab undis
aequoris exesor moerorum litora propter.
nec varii cessant sonitus manare per auras.

897 *aut in tedai corpore* Is. Voss. in ms. notes for *aut indeda corpora*: *in tedai* Pont. also. *in teda cum corpora* Mar. s. m. Ald. 1 Junt. 898 *quia* Flor. 31 Camb. Mar. for *qui*. 899 *latentis* Bern. for *tenentes*. *tepentis* Lach. 907 *lapis* B corr. Flor. 31 Camb. Pont. Mar. for *lapsi*. 908 *Quem* B corr. Flor. 31 Camb. Mar. for *Quam*. 909 *fit*. *sit* Nicc. Flor. 31 Mon. vulg. 'parum Latine' says Lach.: but it is I think defensible, as giving their motive, not the poet's inference: comp. III 100 *Harmoniam Grai quam dicunt, quod faciat nos*. *ortus*. *ortu* Lach. as II 387. 912 *Quinque* B corr. Flor. 31 Mar. for *Qui neque*. 913 *demissos* Lamb. first for *demisso*. 916 *permananter* Flor. 31 Camb. Mar. for *permanater*. *pervolat* Turneb. adv. XXVI 13, Bentl. for *pervalet*. [925 *ut*. *it* Kannen-

denique in os salsi venit umor saepe saporis,
cum mare versamur propter, dilutaque contra
934 cum tuimur misceri absinthia, tangit amaror.
usque adeo omnibus ab rebus res quaeque fluenter
930 fertur et in cunctas dimittitur undique partis
nec mora nec requies interdatur ulla fluendi,
perpetuo quoniam sentimus, et omnia semper
cernere odorari licet et sentire sonare.

936 Nunc omnis repetam quam raro corpore sint res
commemorare; quod in primo quoque carmine claret.
quippe etenim, quamquam multas hoc pertinet ad res
noscere, cum primis hanc ad rem protinus ipsam,
qua de disserere adgredior, firmare necessest
nil esse in promptu nisi mixtum corpus inani.
principio fit ut in speluncis saxa superne
sudent umore et guttis manantibu' stillent.
manat item nobis e toto corpore sudor,
crescit barba pilique per omnia membra, per artus.
diditur in venas cibus omnis, auget alitque
corporis extremas quoque partis unguiculosque.
frigus item transire per aes calidumque vaporem
sentimus, sentimus item transire per aurum
atque per argentum, cum pocula plena tenemus.
denique per dissaepta domorum saxea voces
pervolitant, permanat odor frigusque vaposque
ignis, qui ferri quoque vim penetrare suëvit
denique qua circum Galli lorica coercet.
956 et, tempestate in terra caeloque coorta,
955 morbida visque simul cum extrinsecus insinuatur,
in caelum terrasque remotae iura facessunt,

giesser in Philologus IV supplem. B p. 510.] 935 again om. by Lach.: see IV 229. 937 *claret* Flor. 31 Camb. Mar. for *clare.* 941 *mixtum corpus* Brix. (not Flor. 31) Pont. Mar. for *corpus mixtum.* 942 *superne* Lach. for *superna.* 954 *Galli* Lach. for *caeli.* *coli* Nicc. *colli* Brix. Ver. Ven. Mar. Avanc. Nauger. Wak. *corpus* Mar. al. em. Junt. Lamb. ed. 1 and 2. *corii* Flor. 31 Camb. 3 Vat. Lamb. ed. 3. 955 956 I have transposed: comp. 1098 foll.: Lach. awkwardly puts it after 947: Bern. keeps it in its place and reads *E tempestate in... coortast...remotas iure*; but *remotae* clearly belongs to *tempestate.* 955 *tempestate in* Lach. for *tempestatem.* *tempestates...coortae* Avanc. followed by Nauger. Lamb. etc. 957 *iure* B Vienna frag. A corr. Flor. 31 Camb. all Vat. Pont. *in re* Nicc.

quandoquidem nil est nisi raro corpori' nexu.
Huc accedit uti non omnia, quae iaciuntur
corpora cumque ab rebus, eodem praedita sensu
atque eodem pacto rebus sint omnibus apta.
principio terram sol excoquit et facit are,
at glaciem dissolvit et altis montibus altas
extructas*que* nives radiis tabescere cogit.
denique cera liquefit in eius posta vapore.
ignis item liquidum facit aes aurumque resolvit,
at coria et carnem trahit et conducit in unum.
umor aquae porro ferrum condurat ab igni,
at coria et carnem mollit durata calore.
barbigeras oleaster eo iuvat usque capellas,
effluat ambrosius quasi vero, et nectare tinctus;
qua nil est homini quod amariu' frondeat esca.
denique amaracinum fugitat sus et timet omne
ungentum; nam saetigeris subus acre venenumst,
quod nos interdum tamquam recreare videtur.
at contra nobis caenum taeterrima cum sit
spurcities, eadem subus haec iucunda videtur,
insatiabiliter toti ut volvantur ibidem.
Hoc etiam superest, ipsa quam dicere de re
adgredior quod dicendum prius esse videtur.
multa foramina cum variis sint reddita rebus,
dissimili inter se natura praedita debent
esse et habere suam naturam quaeque viasque.
quippe etenim varii sensus animantibus insunt,
quorum quisque suam proprie rem percipit in se;
nam penetrare alio sonitus alioque saporem

which is the same thing. *iurae* A p. m. caused by *remotae*, or as Lach. says because the archetype had both *iure* and *iura* which he reads and I now read: see notes 2.

958 *raro corpori' nexu* Lach. for *raro corpore nexum.* 962 *sol* Flor. 31 Camb. Mar. etc. for *quo.* 964 *que* added by Flor. 31 Pont. Mar. Ald. 1 Junt. *extructas ningueis* Avanc. at end of Catull. *alte Extructas ningues* Nauger.

965 *liquefit. liquescit* Vat. 640 Urbin. Ver. Ven. Ald. 1 Junt. (not Mar.) Lamb. 'liquescit. s' Heins. in ms. notes: but on this cod. Modii see introduction p. 24.

971 *ambrosius* Ed. for *ambrosias. ambrosiae quasi vere et nectari' linctus* Lach. elegantly, perhaps rightly. 972 *Qua...amariu' frondeat esca* Lach. for *Qua... marius fronde ac exscet* A, *extet* B Vienn. fragm. Nicc.: *amarius* Flor. 31 Camb. two Vat. Mar. 973 *amaracinum* Mar. Junt. for *maracinum.* 977 *iucunda* Camb. Mar. Ald. 1 Junt. Gif. for *ciunda* A, *inunda* B. *iocunda* Flor. 31

cernimus e sucis, alio nidoris odores.
991 praeterea manare aliud per saxa videtur,
atque aliud lignis, aliud transire per aurum,
argentoque foras aliud vitroque meare.
nam fluere hac species, illac calor ire videtur,
995 atque aliis aliut citius transmittere eadem.
scilicet id fieri cogit natura viarum
multimodis varians, ut paulo ostendimus ante,
990 propter dissimilem naturam textaque rerum.
998 Quapropter, bene ubi haec confirmata atque locata
omnia constiterint nobis praeposta parata,
quod superest, facile hinc ratio reddetur et omnis
causa patefiet quae ferri pelliciat vim.
principio fluere e lapide hoc permulta necessest
semina sive aestum qui discutit aera plagis,
inter qui lapidem ferrumque est cumque locatus.
hoc ubi inanitur spatium multusque vacefit
in medio locus, extemplo primordia ferri
in vacuum prolapsa cadunt coniuncta, fit utque
anulus ipse sequatur eatque ita corpore toto.
nec res ulla magis primoribus *ex* elementis
indupedita suis arte conexa cohaeret
quam validi ferri natura et frigidus horror.
quo minus est mirum, quod dico, ibus ex elementis
corpora si nequeunt e ferro plura coorta
in vacuum ferri, quin anulus ipse sequatur;
quod facit, et sequitur, donec pervenit ad ipsum
iam lapidem caecisque in eo compagibus haesit.
hoc fit idem cunctas in partis, unde vacefit
cumque locus, sive e transverso sive superne

two Vat. *munda* Nicc. *res munda* Lamb. 986 987 *alio, alioque, alio. alia, aliaque, alia* Lamb. 988 989=995 996 (996 997). 991 *lignis* Wak. Lach. for *ignis. tignis* Flor. 31 Camb. Mar. Ald. 1 Junt. *per ligna* Lamb. 997 (990) first placed here by Lamb. not Wak. 1001 *pelliciat vim* Flor. 31 Camb. Mar. for *peliciatum* B, *perliceatum* A. 1006 *ferri* Flor. 31 Camb. Pont. Mar. for *ferre.* 1007 *fit utque* Mar. Nauger. for *fit ut qui.* 1009 *ex* added by B corr. Flor. 31 Pont. Mar. *tunc* Camb. 1011 *natura et* Wak. for *naturae.* 1012 *quod dico, ibus ex elementis* Ed. for *quod dicitur ex elementis. quo ducitur* Lach. which I do not understand. *quod paulo diximus ante* Lamb. wildly. *quod ducitur,* [*ex elementis*] Bern. 1013 *e ferro* B Camb. Avanc.

corpora continuo in vacuum vicina feruntur;
quippe agitantur enim plagis aliunde nec ipsa
sponte sua sursum possunt consurgere in auras.
huc accedit item (quare queat id magis esse,
haec quoque res adiumento motuque iuvatur)
quod, simul a fronte est anelli rarior aer
factus inanitusque locus magis ac vacuatus,
1033 continuo fit uti qui post est cumque locatus
1026 aer a tergo quasi provehat atque propellat.
semper enim circumpositus res verberat aer;
sed tali fit uti propellat tempore ferrum,
parte quod ex una spatium vacat et capit in se.
1030 hic, tibi quem memoro, per crebra foramina ferri
parvas ad partis subtiliter insinuatus
trudit et inpellit, quasi navem velaque ventus.
1034 denique res omnes debent in corpore habere
aera, quandoquidem raro sunt corpore et aer
omnibus est rebus circumdatus adpositusque.
hic igitur, penitus qui in ferrost abditus aer,
sollicito motu semper iactatur eoque
verberat anellum dubio procul et ciet intus
scilicet: ille eodem fertur quo praecipitavit
iam semel et partem in vacuam conamina sumpsit.
  Fit quoque ut a lapide hoc ferri natura recedat
interdum, fugere atque sequi consueta vicissim.
exultare etiam Samothracia ferrea vidi
et ramenta simul ferri furere intus ahenis
in scaphiis, lapis hic Magnes cum subditus esset:
usque adeo fugere ab saxo gestire videtur.

te ferro A. *te ferre* Nicc. whence *referre* Brix. Ver. Ven. *de ferro* Flor. 31 Mar. Junt. vulg. before Lach. 1018 *e* Flor. 31 Camb. for *et*. *ex* Mon. Ver. Ven.
1020 *plagis* Flor. 31 Camb. Pont. Mar. for *plagit*. 1022 1023 not a letter is to be changed: only the stopping is to be mended. *item*. *utei* Lach. *iuvatur*. *iuvetur* Lach.; Wak. has been misled by a blunder of Haverc. 1025 *magis* Camb. Ver. Ven. Mar. for *magnis*. *magis locus* Flor. 31. 1026 (1033) first placed here in Ald. 1 and Junt. not by Pont. or Mar. 1027 *Aer a tergo* Mar. Ald. 1 Junt. for *Erat ergo*. 1032 *Parvas*. *Privas* Gif. *Primas* Lamb. ed. 3. 1033 *ventus* Pius for *ventis*. 1040 *ille* Lach. for *illo* B Vienn. frag.: om. A Nicc. Camb. etc. *atque* Flor. 31 Mar. Junt. vulg. *isque* Wak. conj. 1047 *ab saxo* Lach. for *a saxo*. 1059 *Et* Lach. for *At* BA corr.

aere interposito discordia tanta creatur
propterea quia nimirum prius aestus ubi aeris
praecepit ferrique vias possedit apertas,
posterior lapidis venit aestus et omnia plena
invenit in ferro neque habet qua tranet ut ante.
cogitur offensare igitur pulsareque fluctu
ferrea texta suo; quo pacto respuit ab se
atque per aes agitat, sine eo quod saepe resorbet.
illud in his rebus mirari mitte, quod aestus
non valet e lapide hoc alias impellere item res.
pondere enim fretae partim stant: quod genus aurum;
et partim raro quia sunt cum corpore, ut aestus
pervolet intactus, nequeunt inpellier usquam;
lignea materies in quo genere esse videtur.
interutrasque igitur ferri natura locata
aeris ubi accepit quaedam corpuscula, tum fit,
inpellant ut eam Magnesia flumine saxa.
  Nec tamen haec ita sunt aliarum rerum aliena,
ut mihi multa parum genere ex hoc suppeditentur
quae memorare queam inter se singlariter apta.
saxa vides primum sola colescere calce.
glutine materies taurino iungitur uno,
ut vitio venae tabularum saepius hiscant
quam laxare queant compages taurea vincla.
vitigeni latices aqüai fontibus audent
misceri, cum pix nequeat gravis et leve olivom.
purpureusque colos conchyli iungitur uno
corpore cum lanae, dirimi qui non queat usquam,
non si Neptuni fluctu renovare operam des,
non, mare si totum velit eluere omnibus undis.

Ad A p. m. *Ac* Nicc. Flor. 31 Camb. Mon. vulg. 1062 *Interutrasque. Interutraque* Lach. 1064 *eam* Mar. Ald. 1 Junt. for *eum*. *flumine* Nicc. Flor. 31 all Vat. Brix. Ver. Ven. for *flumina*. *flumina saxi* Wak. 1067 *singlariter* Flor. 31 Pont. Avanc. Nauger. vulg. for *singulariter*: comp. 1088 *coplata* AB p. m. *copulata* corr. *inter singillariter* Lach.: a most unrhythmical verse. *apta* Flor. 31 Camb. etc. for *aptam*. 1068 *vides* Pont. Mar. Ald. 1 Junt. for *vide*. *colescere* Lach. for *coolescere*. *coalescere* Nicc. Flor. 31 3 Vat. Mon. 1069 *uno* Lach. for *una*, as in 1074: but Mar. Junt. Lamb. etc. there read *una*: *uno* is not certain.

1072 *aqüai*. *in aquai* Mar. Ald. 1 Junt. vulg. wrongly: comp. 552 and 868.

1077 *eluere* B corr. Vienn. frag. Mar. for *eiuere* B, *eiuvere* A Nicc. 1078 *non*

denique non auro res aurum copulat una
aerique *aes* plumbo fit uti iungatur ab albo?
cetera iam quam multa licet reperire! quid ergo?
nec tibi tam longis opus est ambagibus usquam,
nec me tam multam hic operam consumere par est,
sed breviter paucis praestat comprendere multa.
quorum ita texturae ceciderunt mutua contra,
ut cava conveniant plenis haec illius illa
huiusque inter se, iunctura haec optima constat.
est etiam, quasi ut anellis hamisque plicata
inter se quaedam possint coplata teneri;
quod magis in lapide hoc fieri ferroque videtur.
  Nunc ratio quae sit morbis aut unde repente
mortiferam possit cladem conflare coorta
morbida vis hominum generi pecudumque catervis,
expediam. primum multarum semina rerum
esse supra docui quae sint vitalia nobis,
et contra quae sint morbo mortique necessest
multa volare. ea cum casu sunt forte coorta
et perturbarunt caelum, fit morbidus aer.
atque ea vis omnis morborum pestilitasque
aut extrinsecus ut nubes nebulaeque superne
per caelum veniunt, aut ipsa saepe coortae
de terra surgunt, ubi putorem umida nactast
intempestivis pluviisque et solibus icta.
nonne vides etiam caeli novitate et aquarum
temptari procul a patria quicumque domoque
adveniunt ideo quia longe discrepitant res?
nam quid Brittanni caelum differre putamus,
et quod in Aegypto est qua mundi claudicat axis,
quidve quod in Ponto est differre, et Gadibus atque

auro res Faber em. for *non res auro* B, *res auro* A Nicc. 1079 *Aerique aes* Lamb. excellently for *Aeraque*. 1083 *praestat* B Avanc. Bentl. *restat* A Nicc. vulg.
1089 *fieri* Flor. 31 Camb. Mar. etc. for *ferri*. 1090 to 1191, i.e. two leaves, are wanting in cod. Victor. or Mon.: the readings of 'Marul.' given to these vss. I have taken from Victorius' copy of Ven. spoken of in the introduction. 1091 *cladem* B. corr. Ald. 1 Junt. for *cradem*. 1099 *extrinsecus* B Ald. 1 Junt. *intrinsecus* A Nicc. 1100 *coortae* Lach. for *coorta*: but I am not sure it is necessary. 1101 *putorem*. *putrorem* Nauger. Lamb. etc.
1106 *Brittanni* Ed. for *Brittannis*. *Britannum* Lamb. 1109 *colore* Flor. 31

usque ad nigra virum percocto saecla colore?
quae cum quattuor inter se diversa videmus
quattuor a ventis et caeli partibus esse,
tum color et facies hominum distare videntur
largiter et morbi generatim saecla tenere.
est elephas morbus qui propter flumina Nili
gignitur Aegypto in media neque praeterea usquam.
Atthide temptantur gressus oculique in Achaeis
finibus. inde aliis alius locus est inimicus
partibus ac membris: varius concinnat id aer.
proinde ubi se caelum quod nobis forte alienum
commovet atque aer inimicus serpere coepit,
ut nebula ac nubes paulatim repit et omne
qua graditur conturbat et immutare coactat;
fit quoque ut, in nostrum cum venit denique caelum,
corrumpat reddatque sui simile atque alienum.
haec igitur subito clades nova pestilitasque
aut in aquas cadit aut fruges persidit in ipsas
aut alios hominum pastus pecudumque cibatus,
aut etiam suspensa manet vis aere in ipso
et, cum spirantes mixtas hinc ducimus auras,
illa quoque in corpus pariter sorbere necessest.
consimili ratione venit bubus quoque saepe
pestilitas et iam pigris balantibus aegror.
nec refert utrum nos in loca deveniamus
nobis adversa et caeli mutemus amictum,
an caelum nobis ultro natura coruptum
deferat aut aliquid quo non consuevimus uti,
quod nos adventu possit temptare recenti.
  Haec ratio quondam morborum et mortifer aestus

Vat. 640 Urbin. Ald. 1 Junt. for *calore*: so 722. *percoctaque saecla calore* Vat. 3276 Brix. Nauger. Lamb. 1115 *Aegypto* Flor. 31 Pont. Junt. for *Aegypta*. *Aegypti* Nicc. Ver. Ven.: hence *Aegypti in medio* Avanc. 1121 *Ut* Pont. Ald. 1 Junt. for *Ve*. 1122 *graditur conturbat* Flor. 31 Camb. Brix. Pont. for *graditus conturbas*. *Quadragitas graditus conturbas* Nicc. Ver. Ven. 1124 *reddatque* Flor. 31 Camb. Marul. for *reddetque*. 1132 *balantibus* Flor. 31 Marul. for *calantibus*. *talaribus* Nicc. old eds. 1135 *ultro* Avanc. for *vitro*. *intro* Nicc. *vitio* Flor. 31 Camb. *coruptum* Flor. 31 Lamb. ed. 1, Wak. *corumptum* AB: *corruptum* Nicc. *alienum* Bentl. *coortum* Lach. *inimicum* Io. Colombinus ap. Lamb. *cruentum* joint emend. of Lamb. Turneb. and Auratus. 1138 *mortifer*

finibus in Cecropis funestos reddidit agros
vastavitque vias, exhausit civibus urbem.
nam penitus veniens Aegypti finibus ortus,
aera permensus multum camposque natantis,
incubuit tandem populo Pandionis omnei,
inde catervatim morbo mortique dabantur.
principio caput incensum fervore gerebant
et duplicis oculos suffusa luce rubentes.
sudabant etiam fauces intrinsecus atrae
sanguine et ulceribus vocis via saepta coibat
atque animi interpres manabat lingua cruore
debilitata malis, motu gravis, aspera tactu.
inde ubi per fauces pectus complerat et ipsum
morbida vis in cor maestum confluxerat aegris,
omnia tum vero vitai claustra lababant.
spiritus ore foras taetrum volvebat odorem,
rancida quo perolent proiecta cadavera ritu.
atque animi prorsum *tum* vires totius, omne
languebat corpus leti iam limine in ipso.
intolerabilibusque malis erat anxius angor
adsidue comes et gemitu commixta querella.
singultusque frequens noctem per saepe diemque
corripere adsidue nervos et membra coactans
dissoluebat eos, defessos ante, fatigans.
nec nimio cuiquam posses ardore tueri
corporis in summo summam fervescere partem,
sed potius tepidum manibus proponere tactum
et simul ulceribus quasi inustis omne rubere
corpus, ut est per membra sacer dum diditur ignis.
intima pars hominum vero flagrabat ad ossa,

aestus Macrob. sat. vi 2 7, Pont. Ald. 1 Junt. Lamb. for *mortifer ae*: the last letters having dropped out. *mortifer aer* Lamb. in notes. *mortiferai* Camb. *morti' ferai* Lach. who is then driven to read in 1141 *morbus* for *ortus*: *orcus* Avanc.

1139 *in Cecropis* Macrob. l. l. Flor. 31 Camb. Pont. Junt. for *in Cecropit*. *in Cecropiis* A corr. Nicc. *Finibu' Cecropiis* Lamb. 1143 *omnei* Lach. *omni* Marul. Avanc. for *omnem* A Nicc. *omne* B. *omnes Unde* Junt., *omnes Inde* Brix. Nauger. Lamb. etc. 1147 *atrae*. *atro* Vat. 640 Urbin. Ald. 1 Junt. Lamb. *artae* mss. of Macrob. vi 2 9. 1156 *tum* added by Wak. after *prorsum*. Flor. 31 Ver. Ven. vulg. add *et* before *omne*, perhaps rightly. 1165 *potius* Marul. Ald. 1 Junt. for *totius*. 1167 *dum*. *cum* A corr. Nicc. vulg. before Lach.

flagrabat stomacho flamma ut fornacibus intus.
nil adeo posses cuiquam leve tenveque membris
vertere in utilitatem, at ventum et frigora semper.
in fluvios partim gelidos ardentia morbo
membra dabant nudum iacientes corpus in undas.
1178 multi praecipites lymphis putealibus alte
1174 inciderunt ipso venientes ore patente:
insedabiliter sitis arida, corpora mersans,
aequabat multum parvis umoribus imbrem.
nec requies erat ulla mali: defessa iacebant
1179 corpora. mussabat tacito medicina timore,
quippe patentia cum totiens ardentia morbis
lumina versarent oculorum expertia somno.
multaque praeterea mortis tum signa dabantur,
perturbata animi mens in maerore metuque,
triste supercilium, furiosus voltus et acer,
sollicitae porro plenaeque sonoribus aures,
creber spiritus aut ingens raroque coortus,
sudorisque madens per collum splendidus umor,
tenvia sputa minuta, croci contacta colore
salsaque, per fauces raucas vix edita tussi.
in manibus vero nervi trahere et tremere artus
a pedibusque minutatim succedere frigus
non dubitabat. item ad supremum denique tempus
conpressae nares, nasi primoris acumen
tenve, cavati oculi, cava tempora, frigida pellis
duraque, in ore trucei rictum, frons tenta *tu*mebat.

1171 *Vertere in utilitatem* Lamb. for *verteret utilitatem*: but he reads also *posset* and suggests *quicquam* in 1170 without cause. *at ventum* Lach. for *ad ventum* which the older editors keep and connect with what follows: Lucr. prob. wrote *ad* for *at*. *frigora* Flor. 31 Camb. Marul. for *frigore*. 1174 (1178) brought here first by Nauger.: placed after 1171 by Marul. Junt. *lymphis* Flor. 31 Camb. Marul. for *nymphis*. 1176 *mersans* A Nicc. *inerrans* B. *messans* Vienn. frag. acc. to Rhein. mus. n. f. xv p. 409. *inurens* Bern.: but clearly B's reading is a mere clerical error. 1178 *mali* mss. of Macrob. VI 2 13, Brix. for *mari*. 1180 *ardentia morbis*. *ac nuntia mortis* Lach.: a fine, but not I think necessary emendation. 1186 *spiritus* Macrob. Flor. 31 Camb. Pont. for *spiritum*. 1187 *umor*. *humor* mss. of Macrob. VI 2 11 for *umum*. 1189 *raucas* mss. of Macr. Pont. Avanc. for *rauca*. *tussi* Marul. Junt. for *tusse*. *tussis* mss. of Macr. 1195 *in ore trucei* Ed. for *inoretiacet* B Vienn. frag. *inhoretiacet* A. *inhorret iacet* Nicc.: the *-et* is the common corruption of the old termination *-ei*; comp. 16 *coget* for

nec nimio rigidi post artus morte iacebant.
octavoque fere candenti lumine solis
aut etiam nona reddebant lampade vitam.
quorum siquis ibei vitarat funera leti,
ulceribus taetris et nigra proluvie alvi
posterius tamen hunc tabes letumque manebat,
aut etiam multus capitis cum saepe dolore
corruptus sanguis expletis naribus ibat:
huc hominis totae vires corpusque fluebat.
profluvium porro qui taetri sanguinis acre
exierat, tamen in nervos huic morbus et artus
ibat et in partis genitalis corporis ipsas.
et graviter partim metuentes limina leti
vivebant ferro privati parte virili,
et manibus sine nonnulli pedibusque manebant
in vita tamen, et perdebant lumina partim:
usque adeo mortis metus his incesserat acer.
atque etiam quosdam cepere oblivia rerum
cunctarum, neque se possent cognoscere ut ipsi.
multaque humi cum inhumata iacerent corpora supra
corporibus, tamen alituum genus atque ferarum
aut procul apsiliebat, ut acrem exeiret odorem,
aut, ubi gustarat, languebat morte propinqua.
nec tamen omnino temere illis solibus ulla
comparebat avis, nec *tris*tia saecla ferarum

cogei and 1199; so I 84 mss. *Triviat*, II 636 *Armat et*. *rictum* Lamb. for *rectum*. *Duratusque horret rictus* Vat. 3276. *inhorrescens rictum* Lach. after Rutgersius. *inhorrebat rictum* Lamb. *in ore iacens rictu* Nonius. *tenta tumebat* Heins. in ms. notes and Lach. for *tenta mebat*. *tecta meabat* Nicc. *tenta meabat* Flor. 31 Camb. 2 Vat. Mon. *tenta manebat* Nonius B corr. Vat. 3276. 1196 *rigidi* Lach. for *rigida*. *post artus*. *post strati* Lamb. *prostrati* Pont.' Junt. 1199 *ibei* Ed. for *ut est*: *ibei* became first *iuet*, then *ut est*: see n. to 1195. *vix* Lach. without force. 1200 *Ulceribus* Lamb. after Thucydides for *Viceribus*: *i* and *l* confused as in 500 other places: so 1271 *Viceribus*, *Visceribus* A corr. Nicc. vulg. here as there. Wak. in both places argues for *visceribus*; but A and B 1166 had *Et simul viceribus*; 1148 *Sanguine et viceribus*; V 995 *super vicerat tetra*, *viscera* A corr.; IV 1068 *Vicus enim*, *Ulcus* A corr.: thus in every place where the word occurs in Lucr. our sole original authority substituted *i* for *l*: this may serve to shew on what sandy foundations Wak. builds, when he maintains *iacere coniectum umorem* against *conlectum*, and fifty suchlike cases. 1205 *qui* Lamb. for *cul*.

1212 *his* Mon. Brix. Junt. for *iis*. *is* Flor. 31 Camb. *incesserat* Lamb. for *incusserat*. 1217 *exeiret* Lach., *exiret* Brix. for *exciret*. 1219 *solibus*.

exeibant silvis. languebant pleraque morbo
et moriebantur. cum primis fida canum vis
strata viis animam ponebat in omnibus aegre;
extorquebat enim vitam vis morbida membris.
[incomitata rapi certabant funera vasta.]
nec ratio remedi communis certa dabatur;
nam quod ali dederat vitalis aeris auras
volvere in ore licere et caeli templa tueri,
hoc aliis erat exitio letumque parabat.
illud in his rebus miserandum magnopere unum
aerumnabile erat, quod ubi se quisque videbat
implicitum morbo, morti damnatus ut esset,
deficiens animo maesto cum corde iacebat,
funera respectans animam amittebat ibidem.
quippe etenim nullo cessabant tempore apisci
ex aliis alios avidi contagia morbi,
1245 lanigeras tamquam pecudes et bucera saecla.
1237 idque vel in primis cumulabat funere funus
nam quicumque suos fugitabant visere ad aegros,
vitai nimium cupidos mortisque timentis
1240 poenibat paulo post turpi morte malaque,
desertos, opis expertis, incuria mactans.
qui fuerant autem praesto, contagibus ibant
atque labore, pudor quem tum cogebat obire
blandaque lassorum vox mixta voce querellae.
1246 optimus hoc leti genus ergo quisque subibat.

. . . .

sedibus Macrob. vi 2 14, Brix. Pont. Junt. 1220 *nec tristia* Macrob. l. l., Brix. Pont. Avanc. for *nectia*. *nec fortia* Flor. 31 Camb. 2 Vat. Mar. Junt. *nec noctibu'* Lamb. Pont. proposes also *agrestia*; and Mar. in marg. Ven. *inertia*. *nec noxia* Is. Voss. in ms. notes, Heins. in ms. notes, who also proposes *nec inertia*. 1221 *Exeibant* Lach. for *Exicbant* A, *Exibant* B, *Exiebant* Nicc. 1225 in my small ed. I placed before 1235: I still think that the poet's words would thereby be rendered more consecutive; but I now see that 1235 should not be severed from 1234, Lucr. having misapprehended a sentence of Thucydides: I have therefore now left 1225 in its place, as an imperfect fragment: see notes 2. 1234 *amittebat* B rightly. *imittebat* A. *mittebat* Nicc. whence much error. 1235 *apisci* Flor. 31 Camb. Brix. Pont. Mar. for *apiscit*. 1237 (1245) placed here by Bentl. after Thucyd.: Mar. Junt. Lamb. etc. put it after 1242 (1241). 1239 *visere* Flor. 31 Camb. for *utsere*. 1241 *Poenibat* Turneb. ap. Lamb. for *Poenibus at* (i.e. *Poenib. at*) B, *Poenibus et* A Nicc. etc.: comp. v 1071. 1242 *incuria* Flor. 31, *in curia*

inque aliis alium, populum sepelire suorum
certantes: lacrimis lassi luctuque redibant;
inde bonam partem in lectum maerore dabantur.
nec poterat quisquam reperiri, quem neque morbus
nec mors nec luctus temptaret tempore tali.
  Praeterea iam pastor et armentarius omnis
et robustus item curvi moderator aratri
languebat, penitusque casa contrusa iacebant
corpora paupertate et morbo dedita morti.
exanimis pueris super exanimata parentum
corpora nonnumquam posses retroque videre
matribus et patribus natos super edere vitam.
nec minimam partem ex agris *is* maeror in urbem
confluxit, languens quem contulit agricolarum
copia conveniens ex omni morbida parte.
omnia conplebant loca tectaque; quo magis aestus
. . . .
confertos ita acervatim mors accumulabat.
multa siti protracta viam per proque voluta
corpora silanos ad aquarum strata iacebant
interclusa anima nimia ab dulcedine aquarum,
multaque per populi passim loca prompta viasque
languida semanimo cum corpore membra videres
horrida paedore et pannis cooperta perire
corporis inluvie, pelli super ossibus una,
ulceribus taetris prope iam sordique sepulta.
omnia denique sancta deum delubra replerat

Brix. Ver. Ven. for *incura.* 1247 one or more verses are evidently lost here, or the passage was left in an unfinished state. 1249 *in lectum* Mar. Junt. for *iniectum*: *in letum* Mar. p. m. in Mon. and Victorii Ven. 1250 *morbus* Flor. 31 Camb. Mon. for *morbo.* 1259 *ex agris is maeror* Ed. for *ex agris maeroris. is* was absorbed by *agris*; then *maeroris* was written to fill up the verse. 1260 *Confluxit, languens. Confluxit labes* Lach.: a violent alteration. 1262 *conplebant. complebat* Junt. not Pont. or Mar., *complebant* Lamb. for *condiebant. condebant* A corr. Nicc. *aestus. astu* Lach. *aestus* however agrees so entirely with the words of Thucydides, that I think a verse has fallen out such as *quo magis aestus Conficiebat eos* cet. *aestu* Mar. Junt. Bern. 1264 *protracta* Lach. for *prostrata*: Wak. reads *structa* for *strata* in 1265. 1265 *iacebant* Ver. Ven. for *tacebant. tacebant* Nicc. with *i* written over *t*: hence, while Flor. 31 Camb. etc. keep *tacebant,* Ver. Ven. which usually adhere to the older text of Nicc., have the corrected reading. 1271 *Ulceribus* Lamb. first for *Viceribus. Visceribus* A corr. Nicc. Flor.

corporibus mors exanimis onerataque passim
cuncta cadaveribus caelestum templa manebant,
hospitibus loca quae complerant aedituentes.
nec iam religio divom nec numina magni
pendebantur enim: praesens dolor exsuperâbat.
nec mos ille sepulturae remanebat in urbe,
quo pius hic populus semper consuerat humari;
perturbatus enim totus trepidabat, et unus
quisque suum pro re *praesenti* maestus humabat.
multaque *res* subita et paupertas horrida suasit;
namque suos consanguineos aliena rogorum
insuper extructa ingenti clamore locabant
subdebantque faces, multo cum sanguine saepe
rixantes potius quam corpora desererentur.

31 Camb. all Vat.: Lach. separates 1270 from the context by [ ]. 1274 *manebant* Camb. Brix. vulg. for *manebat* A, *manebit* B. *tenebat* Lach. 1279 *Quo pius* Is. Voss. in ms. notes, Wak. Lach. *Huc pius* A Nicc. Camb. 2 Vat. Brix. Ver. Ven. *Quo prius* B Vienn. frag. Lamb. *Ut prius* Flor. 31 two Vat. Avanc. at end of Catull. Creech. *Ut pius* one Vat. Mar. Ald. 1 Junt. 'Lucretii ingenium parum cognoverunt qui praeoptant *prius*' says Lach.: yet the *οἷς πρότερον ἐχρῶντο* of Thuc. II 52 speaks strongly in favour of B and Lamb.: comp. Aen. IV 464 *piorum* Med., *priorum* Vat. Pal. etc. *humari. humare* N. P. Howard, perhaps rightly. 1280 *trepidabat* B. *repedabat* A Nicc. Flor. 31 Camb. two Vat. Mon. etc. 1281 *praesenti* added by Ed. *conpostum* Lach. *consortem* Flor. 31 Camb. Mar. before, Junt. Lamb. etc. after *pro re*. *cognatum* Avanc. 1282 *res subita et* Camb. Vat. 1136 and 1954 Othob. for *subita et* A, *subita fit* B. *res subitae et* Lach. *vis subita et* Flor. 31 Vat. 640 Urbin. Mar. Ald. 1 Junt. Lamb. *mors subita et* Bern.

1285 *faces* Flor. 31 Camb. Mar. for *fauces*.

END OF VOL. I.

CAMBRIDGE: PRINTED BY JOHN CLAY, M.A. AT THE UNIVERSITY PRESS.